The Man Behind The Men

The Honorable Elijah Muhammad

THE MAN BEHIND THE MEN

By Michael "Mikal" Saahir

Words Make People Publishing, Inc.
Indianapolis, IN

The Honorable Elijah Muhammad: The Man Behind The Men
Copyright 2011 Michael Saahir
All rights reserved. Published 2011
Printed in the United States of America

No part of this book may be reproduced or utilized in any form or by any means, electronic or mechanical, including photocopying, recording or by any information storage and retrieval system without permission in writing. Inquiries should be addressed to:
Words Make People Publishing, Inc.

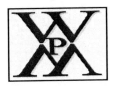

P.O. Box 18533
Indianapolis, IN 46218, USA
Email: wordsmakepeople@gmx.com
www.wordsmakepeople.com

FIRST EDITION
First Printing January 2011

Saahir, Michael
The Honorable Elijah Muhammad: The Man Behind The Men
p. cm.

1. Elijah Muhammad—History. 2. American History—Islam.
3. Muhammad Ali. 4. Louis Farrakhan. 5. Wallace Deen Mohammed.
6. Malcolm X. 7. Nation of Islam.

Michael Saahir. The Honorable Elijah Muhammad: The Man Behind The Men
ISBN 978-0-9842989-0-7 Pbk

Cover illustration by: 4castmagazine.com
Photos from: Kwantu Spears, Ali Adib Hassan (Edsel Ford)

Editor: C.B. Hanif is an award-winning writer, editor, multimedia journalist, blogger, media commentator, speaker and media & interfaith consultant. He has served as editor of the Atlanta Voice newspaper, on the editorial board of The Palm Beach Post newspaper and is a member of the international Organization of News Ombudsmen. His website is www.cbhanif.com.

Printed in the United States of America
at First Quality Printing in Indianapolis, Indiana

Second Printing

LCCN 2010942165

This book is printed on acid-free paper

Dedication

I dedicate this humble effort to the life and legacy of Mr. Elijah Muhammad, his family and the unsung men and women, who followed him. Many of these individuals sacrificed what little comfort they may have had, including family ties and careers in order to make a better day for Al-Islam in America.

Special thanks to my best friend and loving wife Carolyn, and to my sons and daughter (Mikal, Hamidullah, Muhammed and Aline "Kita"), for their patience and support, not only with this project that required I spend time and effort giving steadfast attention to the task at hand, but with the many other obligations as well, and thanks to my father Oliver Flanagan for always being there. To my mother, Gloria Ann, I pray that God grant you peace and paradise.

§§§

"For a good tree bringeth not forth corrupt fruit; neither doth a corrupt tree bring forth good fruit. For every tree is known by his own fruit.
— *Bible Luke 6:43-44**

"Do not you see how God makes a parable of a good word that is as a good tree. Its roots are firmly established. Its branches reach up toward the heaven giving its fruits at all times with permission from its Lord. And God set forth parables for people in order that they may be thoughtful. And the parable of a corrupt word is as a corrupt tree. Its roots are shallow in the earth, and there is not for it any stability. God will establish in strength those who believe by the Word that is firm, in this world and in the Hereafter. And God leaves to stray those who are wrongdoers; and God does whatsoever He Wills."
— *Holy Qur'an 14:24-27***

§§§

*All Bible quotes throughout this book taken from the King James Version.

**All Qur'an quotes throughout this book taken from the Yusuf Ali translation.

Contents

Dedication .... *iv*
Foreword .... *viii*
About the Author .... *xi*
A Note from the Author .... *xiii*
A Special Note to My Friends .... *xv*
Acknowledgements .... *xvii*

Chapters

1. Introduction 18
2. The Challenges 25
3. Elijah Muhammad Through the Eyes of Others 31
4. Mr. Elijah Muhammad 54
5. El-Hajj Malik El-Shabazz (Malcolm X) 67
6. On Calling White Man the Devil 91
7. Muhammad Ali 103
8. Not Bearing Their Names - "Do For Self" 119
9. Minister Louis Farrakhan 140
10. Was God with Elijah Muhammad? 158
11. Imam W. Deen Mohammed 167
12. Students Achieved Their Individuality 203
13. Elijah Muhammad's Mental and Spiritual Genealogy 214
14. Non-African Americans Influenced by E. Muhammad 222
15. The Importance of Last Sermons 242
16. An Exodus: From Slavery to Freedom, Justice and Equality 246
17. Elijah Muhammad on Salat (Islamic prayer) 261
18. Elijah Muhammad – A man of Non-Violence 264
19. The Possibility of Forgiving Elijah Muhammad 276
20. Epilogue 297

100 Quotes of the Hon. Elijah Muhammad *311*
Glossary *317*
Bibliography *318*
Index *326*

Foreword

Few American leaders have been more misunderstood than Elijah Muhammad. During his life, he was denounced as a cult leader, a race supremacist and a teacher of hate. Even today misconceptions about Muhammad abound, spanning generational, gender, and philosophical boundaries, although Black residents of larger urban areas tend to be more knowledgeable about the man and his achievements than their rural counterparts.

Despite Muhammad's and the Nation of Islam's importance to 20th century African American history, little has been written about the man. Except for Claude Andrew Clegg's *An Original Man*, and Karl Evanzz's *The Messenger*, much of Muhammad's life and work has been mired in simplistic, popular images and distorted all-too-brief snapshots. To be sure, a host of books, beginning in the 1960s, were written about the Nation of Islam, which portrayed it, almost without exception, as a separatist organization or in relation to what is arguably its most important member — Malcolm X. Consequently, Elijah Muhammad and his historical importance have suffered from an inability of the American public, the media and scholars to move beyond caricatures of the man and vitiated his role in shaping Islam in the United States as well as African American racial and political consciousness.

Michael Saahir's *The Man Behind the Men* represents a heartfelt effort to understand Elijah Muhammad and his legacy. This book represents a labor of love. Saahir's effort, though presented in a scholarly format, is a deeply personal perspective of Elijah Muhammad by one individual who was inspired by him. In this role, he authenticates the significant role that Muhammad played in shaping the religious and philosophical thinking of many young African Americans politically, socially and economically during the 1960s as well as introducing Black Americans to Islam and popularizing it as an alternative to Christianity in the United States.

On the surface, at least, Saahir appears well-qualified for this task. Imam or Islamic Minister of the Nur-Allah Islamic Center in Indianapolis, IN since 1992, Saahir writes a monthly column for *The Indianapolis Recorder* which discusses questions and concerns that Muslims especially and Americans in general have about Islam. He is also a contributor to *Muslim Journal*, a national Islamic newspaper.

Saahir's goal is ambitious. Like Clegg, Saahir seeks to capture the life and meaning of Elijah Muhammad — both as a man and as a leader — and to understand him within his historical context. He wants to provide the reader with an account of Elijah Muhammad's life that goes beyond the popular, though distorted, perception of the man as a demagogue that is so prevalent in American popular culture and highlight the many positive contributions of the leader of the Nation of Islam. In particular, he attempts to demonstrate how Elijah Muhammad's teachings to members of the Nation resonated in the lives of four of its best-known followers — Malcolm X, Muhammad Ali, Louis Farrakhan, and Elijah's son Warith Ud-Deen Mohammed.

FOREWORD

The world in which Elijah Muhammad was born and grew to adulthood was a world which most contemporary Americans have little, if any familiarity. Indeed, the entire United States at that time was a country awash in racial prejudice and discrimination. Elevators in southern cities, such as Birmingham, Alabama displayed signs reserving them for "Niggers and Freight," while nooses were not mere symbols of black oppression, but an all-too-real horrific enforcer of American apartheid. Legal segregation was the rule in the South, while de-facto segregation was the norm in northern states. A 1969 *Foreign Affairs* article, worth reading even today, reminds us that as late as the 1940s the world was still by and large a Western white-dominated world. Long established patterns of white power and the exploitation of non-whites were still the generally accepted order of things. All the accompanying assumptions and mythologies about race and color were still mostly taken for granted. White supremacy "was a generally assumed and accepted state of affairs in the United States as well as in Europe's empires." And understanding the depth, breadth and intensity of the racial violence, terror and oppression that manifested itself in the lives of African Americans is key to understanding Elijah Muhammad and the attractiveness of the Nation of Islam's black separatist, racial solidarity, self-help message to growing numbers of African Americans in the post-WWII United States.

Economic factors also played a critical role on both Muhammad's leadership and the maturation of the Nation of Islam. Circumstances and conditions, such as Muhammad's experiences of poverty in the agrarian South as a child and in the urban North as a young adult were directly related to his later attraction to the NOI as a vehicle of financial uplift as well as spiritual and racial empowerment. This emphasis on economics was not necessarily a contradictory element in Elijah's Muhammad's message to his followers and can be traced to the founding of the organization during the Great Depression. In fact, thousands of African Americans were attracted to Elijah Muhammad and his movement because of their willingness to address earthly concerns. While Saahir's book does not maintain that Elijah Muhammad was motivated solely by materialism, his leadership, and the Nation of Islam were increasingly shaped by both an emphasis on material concerns and the larger patterns of American society.

Towards these ends, Saahir's discussion and analysis advances two major themes in explaining Elijah Muhammad's life, views and leadership. The first of these is lengthy discussion of the importance of historical circumstances and conditions, such as Muhammad's southern rural and northern urban background during the 1920s and 1930s in shaping Muhammad's theological, philosophical and socio-economic perspectives. Second, is his significance as a prominent icon of the quasi-Islamic and racial separatist movements, which emerged among African Americans in the post-World War II United States; and that he personally was the primary guiding force behind the beliefs, rituals, and

THE MAN BEHIND THE MEN

operation of the Nation of Islam for more than forty years. From his feelings of personal persecution to the organizational triumphs and crises of the 1960s and 1970s, the experiences and philosophy of Elijah Muhammad were essential to the fashioning of the Nation of Islam as a significant religious movement in the United States. In short, to understand the nature and appeal of varieties of Islam and black nationalism in the 20th century African American community, one must examine the life and work of Elijah Muhammad. His leadership illuminates the importance of leaders before him, such as Martin Delaney, Marcus Garvey and Noble Drew Ali as well as those who came after him.

To be sure, Saahir offers a perspective that is at odds with many traditional interpretations of Elijah Muhammad and his work. He is convinced that far from being anti-white and opposed to the 1960s civil rights movement Muhammad's position on both was much more complex than this. In fact, Saahir argues that Muhammad's portrayal of whites as devils was never a steadfast doctrine in the Nation of Islam — as exemplified by examples of whites who were members of the Nation of Islam that Saahir identifies and briefly presents their experiences in his book. Moreover, he was sympathetic to the struggle of civil rights activists and, on occasion, subsidized their work. Saahir believes strongly that despite Muhammad's human shortcomings and theological departures from traditional Islam in the formative and growth years of the Nation, his essentially good intentions for the spiritual and secular rehabilitation of his people bore fruit, when viewed through the prism of the lives and accomplishments of men such as Malcolm X., Louis Farrakhan, Muhammad Ali, and Warith Ud-Deen Muhammad.

The reader may not agree with all that Saahir says about Elijah Muhammad and his legacy. One may object, for example, to Saahir's proclivity to minimize Muhammad's seeming departure from orthodox Islam and the teachings of the Prophet during the early years of the Nation of Islam's development. One may take issue with his claim that privately Elijah Muhammad was more sympathetic to the goals of the civil rights movement and racial integration than many of his public pronouncements or official NOI policy indicated. That said, the author hopes that his book will inspire additional research on Elijah Muhammad as well as the Muslim movement in the United States. Much still remains to be said and written about Muhammad and his important role in 20th century United States history; and Saahir's book is an important contribution to that effort.

Monroe H. Little, Jr.
Program Director and Associate Professor of History
Indiana University – Purdue University Indianapolis (IUPUI)

About the Author

Michael "Mikal" Saahir
(4castmagazine.com)

Michael was born in 1956 and reared as Michael Flanagan, the son of Oliver and Gloria (Brown) Flanagan. Michael is the third of six children and was educated in the Indianapolis Public School system — with the exception of attending the third grade at Barbour Elementary in Rockford, IL.

Very much a child-product of the 1960s and the 1970s, Michael experienced and was very much influenced by both the turbulence and the soul searching of both decades. His journey through this era delivered him to the threshold of Elijah Muhammad's Nation of Islam. "I'm gonna be a Black Muslim when I get grown," Michael determined. "As soon as I turn 18, I'm gonna join," he declared.

The vast majority of Michael's Protestant religious upbringing was nurtured at the loving and caring Kingsley Terrace Church of Christ. But as a teenager it was the message of Elijah Muhammad that most strongly resonated in his life. For Michael, at that stage of life, it was Elijah Muhammad's Nation of Islam that provided a base and framework in which to try and make sense of the convoluted era.

Although never a member of the Nation of Islam, Michael did try to join in late 1974. Being a self-analyzer Michael could not get pass the first step of correctly writing a standardized letter to Mr. W.F. Muhammad (W.D. Fard). Any error in writing this letter invalidated the whole letter thus requiring the writer to begin the process again. Elijah Muhammad died before Michael could complete an error-free letter; therefore, he did not join the Muslim community until May of 1976, 15 months after the passing of the Muslim leader. At this time Michael became a student of Elijah Muhammad's son, Imam W. Deen Mohammed.

THE MAN BEHIND THE MEN

Michael's religious development evolved within the experience of the African American Islamic community in Indianapolis at the mosque that later became known as the Nur-Allah (Light of God) Islamic Center. In 1980 he legally changed his name to Michael Ibn *(son of)* Oliver Saahir. It was during this time that many people began calling him "Mikal," the Arabic form of Michael.

Shortly after completing the Islamic pilgrimage, called *Hajj* to Mecca, Saudi Arabia in 1991, Mikal was chosen to be the Resident Imam of the Nur-Allah Islamic Center. Again in 2003 Mikal, along with his wife Carolyn completed the rites of Hajj.

Currently Mikal is very active in many interfaith efforts, namely with the Catholic-based Focolare Movement. He also is active with Protestant Christians, Jews, Buddhists and believers of other faiths. Twice he has met and greeted His Holiness, the 14th Dalai Lama of Tibet, Tenzin Gyatso.

Mikal's interest in writing *The Honorable Elijah Muhammad: The Man Behind the Men* came as a result of seeing a regular diet being fed to the public of mostly negative images, portrayals and reports on Elijah Muhammad. This writing effort, which began as Mikal's final project for graduation from Martin University in Indianapolis, is not an attempt to rewrite the history on Elijah Muhammad. Instead it is an effort at fulfilling an obligation to share some aspects of this great man that to date have gone unreported.

Mikal is a follower of Muhammed* Ibn Abdullah, the Messenger of God who lived in the 7th century; the leader of all Muslims, better known as the seal of the prophets. Today Mikal appreciates the Honorable Elijah Muhammad as one of the world's greatest reformers; a man whom God chose to use as a masterful worker and helper in healing the damaged African American soul and mind.

Mikal's other achievements and activities include serving his city as an Indianapolis firefighter since January 1979. Since 1992 he has written a column called *Al-Islam in America* in *The Indianapolis Recorder*. He is a regular contributor to *Muslim Journal*, a national Islamic publication. Mikal is the father of four children and the grandfather of many.

---

*To distinguish Muhammed the Prophet from Mr. Elijah Muhammad, throughout this book I will always spell the Prophet's name with an "e."

A Note from the Author

In preparation for writing this book, in the fall of 2004 while at my doctor's office, I was re-reading *An Original Man: the Life and Times of Elijah Muhammad* by Claude Andrew Clegg. When the nurse came in with a welcoming smile to begin her routine of checking my pulse and blood pressure, I laid the book on the countertop. I briefly thought, "I'd better place the book face down." I didn't ant the nurse, who happened to be Caucasian, to be offended by the picture of Elijah Muhammad or his name, both of which stood out vividly on the book's cover. However, I rethought that action and concluded, "Well, it will be okay to place the book with the cover revealed. After all, it's only a book and I'm doing research."

Well, I was wrong! After she had checked my pulse and blood pressure, she turned to the countertop to write down the results, and her pleasurable countenance disappeared as she stared at the book, studying the name and picture of Elijah Muhammad — the whole cover. Obviously disturbed by the book's cover, she almost was not able to properly record my vitals.

I was embarrassed. It was not my intent to offend her but now it was too late. I wanted to explain that Elijah Muhammad was not the man as portrayed in history, but I sensed from the altered ambience in the room and the look on her face that something about either Elijah Muhammad's name or his picture had stunned her to silence. Her smile never returned.

After seeing my doctor my next stop was to a local pharmacy to fill my prescription. Again I carried Clegg's book to read while I waited for my prescription to be filled. As I prepared to pay the cashier, who also happened to be a female Caucasian, I was sure this time to place the book face down. One uneasy moment a day was enough. While in the process of retrieving money from my pocket the cashier leaned back away from the counter in order to read the book's spine. As she picked up the book she exclaimed, "Oh, a biography. I love biographies." I thought, "Oh boy, here we go again."

As she began focusing in on the cover asking who was the subject of the book, I immediately went on the defense in order to diffuse another potentially embarrassing moment. I explained, "That is the biography of Elijah Muhammad." I quickly added, "He is probably best known for calling white folks devils, but towards the end of his life he began to change." Her response shocked me. Without hesitation she replied, "They were devils."

I looked at her thinking; "Doesn't she realize what she is saying? Doesn't she realize that she is a white woman and that by Elijah Muhammad's definition she would be classified as a devil?" With a sincere and unwavering voice she quickly made a distinction. "Some of them were devils at that time."

THE MAN BEHIND THE MEN

Both the nurse and the cashier appeared to be at least in their late 50s, no older than in their early 70s. Both women were seemingly from the same generation. But in less than a two-hour span of time I received two contrasting responses from these women who saw the cover of the same book. The disparity between these reactions probably captures the two extremes — between which lay variant degrees of responses — which the name and face of Elijah Muhammad, even to this day, can evoke.

These diametric reactions expressed by these two women underscore the need for this book, *The Honorable Elijah Muhammad: The Man Behind the Men*. The nurse's whole demeanor changed from friendly to somber when she prejudged Clegg's book — and possibly prejudged me accordingly — from its cover; whereas, the cashier's attitude changed me from attempting a humble apologetic approach to a silent conclusion of, "Yeah, she's right!"

Mr. Elijah Muhammad cannot be fully described or defined in either of the ladies' reactions. His life was too multifaceted. Hopefully this book, *The Honorable Elijah: The Man Behind the Men*, will allow its readers opportunities to review Elijah Muhammad from other perspectives that delves deeper into under reported aspects of his life. Also the readers may get a fuller picture of Elijah Muhammad as they discover aspects of the lives and legacies of the four important men discussed in this book: Minister Malcolm X Shabazz, former heavyweight boxing champion Muhammad Ali, Minister Louis Farrakhan, and Imam W. Deen Mohammed — "Four Stars" who Elijah influenced and made possible their international successes.

The complete works of Elijah Muhammad have to be quantified and qualified in light of the realities that he faced and lived during the America of old. The good that he achieved must be supported by people of all races and cultures in the new America we enjoy today. We should study his challenges and shortcomings recognizing the context and era in which he lived. Regarding his sins we pray for him as we should for any human being; that Allah (God) forgive him and grant him paradise.

To My Special Friends

My Special Friends are those individuals – both Muslims and non-Muslims — I have enjoyed working and meeting with over lunch as we planned our next adventure together as people of faith, believers who believe as I do, in the oneness of God and the oneness of humanity.

I feel the need to add this special note because I cherish our relationships, and I strongly believe that our future is much brighter than our past successes. Nonetheless, I KNOW well the importance of writing this book on Elijah Muhammad. An honorable man who is greatly misunderstood by the average person even though he — in his many unorthodox ways — contributed much that has benefited our society.

When I have mentioned to some that I was writing a book on Elijah Muhammad, often I could see their countenance change from a warm smile to a confused but friendly grin. Once, while at a public lunch, I shared my desire to write on Elijah Muhammad with a group that I had met post-9/11. To my dismay, one of my friends in the group replied, "Wasn't he a kook!?" I wasn't disturbed by the "kook" analogy because I understood that this reaction, which by and large reflected the common misconceptions of Elijah Muhammad, only reaffirmed for me the necessity of this work. I truly pray that writing this book will underscore the serious need for other books that show a fuller picture of the Honorable Elijah Muhammad.

Writing this message to my Special Friends reminds me of the story of the wife of Lot (called Lut in the Qur'an). The Qur'an states in sura (chapter) 26, ayat (verse) 171 that Lot led all of his people to safety except for his wife, "an old woman who lingered behind." The Bible states in Genesis 19:26, "But his wife looked back..." Lot's wife unnecessarily looked back on a part of her past for which she still had an unnatural yearning. Her desire was to go back to a bitter past for the sake of her personal satisfaction.

The Honorable Elijah Muhammad: the Man Behind the Men, is not a repeat of the tendency and desire that is personified in the wife of Lot. The intent of this book is not to merely revisit an unpleasant racial era of America. Instead it is designed to correct improper images of Elijah Muhammad and other incomplete and inaccurate images surrounding his life.

In surveying, if benchmarks are not properly established, then projected readings are tainted. Elijah Muhammad is one of many benchmarks in America's overall history, particularly African American history. It is important that the benchmarks established by Elijah Muhammad be reviewed without bias and properly recalibrated as needed.

THE MAN BEHIND THE MEN

When we remember the great Thomas Jefferson, we first think of him as the original author of the Declaration of Independence and the Statute of Virginia for Religious Freedom. He is thought of as the third president of the United States and one of the architects of the United States of America. We don't think of him, and properly so, mainly as a slave owner or as father to six children by his African American slave-mistress Sally Hemmings. It would be unfair to the greater contributions of Jefferson to emphasize his personal and business life over the greater good he produced for our nation. The same applies to Elijah Muhammad; his greater good has yet to be recognized and duly rewarded. A similar renewed look was given to the ex-Klansman turned senator, the late Robert Bird from West Virginia. He too was forgiven inspite of his former polarizing racial views.

To my dear and Special Friends of all faith persuasions, it is necessary and crucial that I write this book. This note is not an apology from me, but a declaration that I am committed more than ever to our future progress as friends. However, the Honorable Elijah Muhammad is one person in history who has been misrepresented; therefore, an important part of me has been misrepresented. As with any friendship, true friends want to be transparent with all their close friends.

If you can, and I believe that you can, please support me in my effort to share a more accurate picture of Mr. Elijah Muhammad. Hopefully, after you have read The Honorable Elijah Muhammad: The Man Behind the Men, we can sit down for lunch and a wonderful conversation.

Thank you
Michael "Mikal" Saahir

Acknowledgements

My first acknowledgement is to our Creator, Allah (Glory and praises to Him, the Exalted). At this time it is important that I acknowledge the *Kalimah Shahadah*, the Islamic creed that testifies the following: I, Michael "Mikal" Saahir openly bear witness that there is but One G_d*, Allah — and there is absolutely nothing in His creation, whatsoever, that is comparable with Him. And I openly bear witness that Muhammed Ibn Abdullah, to whom the Qur'an was revealed in the 7th century, is the Messenger of Allah and the final Prophet for humanity.

The adage "No man is an island unto himself" was proven true over and again throughout this project. As with any occasion for making acknowledgements someone important may unintentionally be forgotten; nonetheless, I treasure the contributions of each and every contributor, whether big or small.

Alphabetically I acknowledge the following:

4Castmagazine.com of Indianapolis, IN; Imam Ayman Abdul-Mujeeb of Los Angeles, CA; Musa Abdullah of Cincinnati, OH; Imam Abdur-Rahim and Saabirah Ahmad of Indianapolis, IN; Aminah Ali of Chicago, IL; Matthew Ali of Los Angeles, CA; Marvis Aleem of Washington, D.C.; Osman Almanza of Detroit, MI; Imam Samuel Ansari of St. Louis, MO; Murjan A. Bahar of Frankfort, KY; Imam Hameed El-Amin of Huntsville, AL; Omar Farooq of Terre Haute, IN; Imam C.B. Hanif of West Palm Beach, FL; Tom Hartmann of Brooklyn, NY; Ali Adib Hasan of Fort Worth, TX; Islamic History Project (IHP); Muhammad Jihad of Indianapolis, IN; Mr. Robert Kolentus of Martin University in Indianapolis, IN; Elijah Mohammed III of Chicago, IL; Imam Bilal N. Muhammad of Kansas City, MO; Imam Ilyas Muhammad of Nashville, TN; Mukhtar Muhammad of Jacksonville, FL; William (3X) Muhammad of Indianapolis, IN; Julie Mundell of Indianapolis, IN; Muslim Journal; Ayesha K. Mustafaa of Chicago, IL; Imam Ilyas Nashid of Cincinnati, OH; Zakiyyah Nu'Man of Jersey City, NJ; Imam Ibrahim Pasha of Atlanta, GA; Aaron "Harun" Pinner of Indianapolis, IN; Amatullah Sharif of Chicago, IL; Malik A. Sharif of Brooklyn, NY; Imam Faheem Shuaibe of Oakland, CA; Imam Muhammad Siddeeq of Indianapolis, IN; Kwantu Spears of Lake Mary, Fl; Amatullah Umrani of Milwaukee, WI.

---

*The spelling of G_d for "god" is used for when referencing or mentioning our Creator to avoid the spelling "God", which in reverse spells "Dog". It is disrespectful to have a spelling for our Creator that reminds the reader of a dog.

-§- CHAPTER -§-
ONE

Introduction

(Photographer and Date Unknown)

Note the spelling of Elijah's last name: Mohammed

I want to teach you who you are. So many people have been made blind, deaf and dumb to the knowledge of God. Why are they made deaf and dumb to the knowledge of God? Because they are blind, deaf and dumb to the knowledge of self.

— Elijah Muhammad
Our Saviour Has Arrived (2)

INTRODUCTION

The well known adage, "Behind every good man is a good woman," remains a true statement; however, within the Nation of Islam that saying could be rivaled by the phrase "Behind four internationally renowned good African American men is a good man — Mr. Elijah Muhammad."

This altered statement is based upon the reality that Elijah Muhammad must be properly placed in the pages of history as a controversial, but a great American figure. Many facts about the commendable accomplishments of Mr. Muhammad have been obscured and denied, leaving most Americans with a seemingly inviolable and prepackaged, but imbalanced description of him.

To date most of the books on the life of Elijah Muhammad have either marginalized him as one who is extremely militant, or dismissed him as one who is unimportant in the African American struggle for freedom and justice. This book, *The Honorable Elijah Muhammad: The Man Behind the Men*, offers America and the world another perspective on the life of Elijah Muhammad, with information to help the reader better appreciate some of his achievements and better understand the environmental circumstances that shaped and gave birth to Elijah Muhammad.

To revisit the life of Elijah Muhammad, even through the successes and challenges of four of his most renowned students, requires that both the writer and the reader are willing to retrace some of America's ugly past. Any effort to effectively understand another individual requires mental and maybe even spiritual flexibility in order to appreciate the conditions and social mores in which the individual actually lived, even if those conditions are shameful, embarrassing or disagreeable by today's social standards of diversity.

The various forms of racism as witnessed in slavery and Jim Crow have been major factors in the shaping of America. Class distinctions based primarily on race are the very factors that helped to produce the Nation of Islam and men like Elijah Muhammad. Subsequently, racism indirectly is the germ responsible for giving birth to the four men highlighted in this book; Malcolm X, Muhammad Ali, Louis Farrakhan, and W. Deen Mohammed.

The Biblical words, "For every tree is known by *his* (italics are mine) own fruit" is appropriate for describing one of Elijah Muhammad's underreported accomplishments. The "fruit," as the Nation of Islam taught, "...is the best part of the tree," a manifestation of the tree's potential and ultimate purpose. Today many people want to applaud and praise the fruit that the leadership of Elijah Muhammad produced while repudiating the progenitor. The fruit and its tree are eternally inseparable, the same as Elijah Muhammad is with the four men mentioned above. *The Honorable Elijah Muhammad: The Man Behind the Men* is an attempt to balance the unfair image that the world has been given of Mr. Muhammad by offering a fresh perspective through four of his protégés.

THE MAN BEHIND THE MEN

Notwithstanding his highly published tirades against white people, particularly white Americans — even to the point of not only labeling white people as a "devil," but as "the Devil," — there is an Elijah Muhammad that America has yet to learn about. For example, few people knew of the handful of white Americans who, with Elijah Muhammad's approval, were registered and active members of the Nation of Islam.

The Man Behind the Men will venture further and state that in addition to discovering a fuller picture of Elijah Muhammad, this book will attempt to show how America also owes a debt to Elijah Muhammad. What is the proper compensation for the many contributions he has made to the progress of America as shown in his work of recreating many African American men and women who had given up on America; many who in fact had given up on life?

Whereas in 1886 the Statue of Liberty was erected to welcome the surging crowds of predominantly European immigrants by proclaiming "give us your tired, your poor, your huddled masses yearning to breathe free," Elijah Muhammad, from 1933 to 1975, was busy striving to fulfill those same human aspirations in black men and women whose cry for freedom had yet to be answered for more than 300 years. The Nation of Islam under his leadership actually was a continuation, albeit from a different psychology, of previous African American leaders such as Booker T. Washington, W.E.B. DuBois, Frederick Douglass and others who wanted to improve the dismal lives of African Americans.

The debt owed to Elijah Muhammad can be paid by giving him his long overdue and proper place in history. He helped to relieve America's burden by reducing crime as he rehabilitated thousands, if not millions of criminals and other wayward people.

He revived and built up many inner-city neighborhoods with community and economic development. His Whiting H&G fish program during the 1970s helped to secure employment for many American dock workers when he imported millions of pounds of fish from Peru that his male soldiers — the Fruit of Islam — sold in the ghettos of America.

In education of African American youth, Elijah Muhammad's achievements have not been matched. He established a national independent private school system that provided a quality education to thousands of youth while employing hundreds of teachers and many principals and administrators.

One major debt that white America owes to Elijah Muhammad is his giving them a mirror-reflection of the ugly white racist tendencies that were so prevalent during his lifetime. The open cruelties that were regularly meted out by many Caucasians upon African Americans and other non-white populations; even against white non-Protestant groups, were very

INTRODUCTION

inhumane. Not only did Elijah Muhammad's life and mission come on the heels of chattel slavery, his heralding came in the midst of worldwide European imperialism and a strong belief in the power of Anglo-Saxonism, a belief that the white man's brain and civilization was the apex of all human achievements. Elijah Muhammad's constant reverberations of "the white man is the Devil" allowed America an opportunity to reflect, review and reassess herself, and change. This harsh charge calling America "a devil nation" helped the United States of America change her moral character and correct legislation that in the past had favored segregation. His actions led to legal and moral upgrades in America that ultimately resulted in all Americans of every race enjoying a better life.

Though many may not agree, Elijah Muhammad is very much one of America's myriad great leaders, present and past. He was an independent thinker — bold, courageous and industrious — all of which are life goals and qualities that every American can relate to and claim as their own.

Mr. Muhammad's radical method and approach to addressing racial disparities, religious shortcomings and economic deficiencies in the lives of African Americans were often discomforting especially for white Americans. Nonetheless, Elijah Muhammad is as much American as apple pie; a pie that many African Americans either overtly or covertly tasted, and often-times delightfully savored.

The tendency in the collective conscience of America — indeed, the human conscience - is to forget or eliminate any efforts or ideologies that do not allow us to look and feel good about ourselves. In order for America to fully realize and achieve her potential this tendency must cease. For America to maintain her role as a leading nation, all who have contributed to her greatness must be acknowledged. We can't continue to conveniently forget or sanitize, marginalize, categorize, mislabel or overlook the groups or events that are not pleasing to our memory. Individuals and groups such as Elijah Muhammad and his Nation of Islam must be given their proper place in American society and history.

This is especially true with any history that reminds America of her past immaturity towards her disenfranchised citizens such as Native Americans, Asian Americans, African Americans and many non-affluent Caucasian Americans. Regardless of the discomforting reminders of America's unpleasant past, that often accompany most discussions about Elijah Muhammad, still it is crucially important to incorporate into America's history the great works that Elijah Muhammad achieved as a social reformer that benefited all Americans to variant degrees.

Many historians, tainted by acquiescing to the status quo, have reported only a confrontational and racist picture of Elijah Muhammad and his Nation of Islam. It was Elijah Muhammad's willingness to publicly address America's racial problem, albeit upon his own terms, that makes him unpopular in the collective memory of many circles in America. The time has come to reintroduce Elijah Muhammad and his honorable achievements to the public consciousness of America and the world. More will be said later regarding the important role of historians in recording his history.

We must remember that Elijah Muhammad was a very sincere man who truly believed that he was teaching 100 percent truth. He was not against adjusting his emphasis in order to achieve the aims and objectives of uplifting and liberating black folks; a leader who never exhibited disingenuousness towards the soul of his work of improving the lives of African Americans.

As one reviews his life they should remember that it was a racially disproportionate America that gave birth to Elijah Muhammad, not Mecca, Africa, or England nor some other foreign society. Journalist Mike Wallace noted this reality on his nightly television show *Newsbeat*. For five consecutive days in 1959, beginning July 13th, Wallace introduced Elijah's community to the American public in a report dubbed "The Hate that Hate Produced." While recognizing a failure on the part of some whites in Christianity, as well as delivering a wakeup call to America, Wallace said during his exposé on the Nation of Islam, "Unless the story is told; a small, but growing segment of the American Negro population has learned to hate before the Christian white man could learn to love."

In his 2005 book *Between You and Me: A Memoir*, Wallace speaks about the creation and publication of his "The Hate that Hate Produced."

> (Louis Lomax) proposed that we collaborate on a documentary about the Black Muslims, and it led to one of the most explosive pieces I've ever been involved in. Lomax did most of the reporting, and I anchored the Channel 13 broadcast, which we called "The Hate That Hate Produced." The title sounds like tabloid hype, but the story more than lived up to its billing. Our report included film coverage of a Muslim rally steeped in an atmosphere of pure venom. One speaker after another condemned Caucasians as "white devils" who, down through the centuries, had committed every crime imaginable against black men and women. There also were interviews with the leader of the movement, Elijah Muhammad, and its New York minister, Malcolm X, who told Lomax that "the white man was the serpent in the Garden of Eden. By nature he is evil." Moreover, in his interview with Lomax, Muhammad predicted that within a decade a "general insurrection" of Black Americans would erupt and inflict "plenty of bloodshed."
>
> Nothing quite like it had ever been broadcast or published (at least not in the mainstream press), and when we aired,

INTRODUCTION

> "The Hate That Hate Produced," we struck more than a few nerves. Moderate Negro Leaders, like my friend Roy Wilkins of the NAACP, charged that we had grossly exaggerated the size and significance of the Black Muslims. Even more censorious were most of the reviewers, who accused us of sensationalism and fearmongering. Our response to these criticisms from the power centers of the white media was a defiant challenge: "All right, don't take our word for it. Go see for yourselves." And they did. Over the next few months, The New York Times, Newsweek magazine, and other influential voices in American journalism published reports on the Black Muslims that verified the essence of what we had aired.
>
> (86-87)

It is important to note that Elijah Muhammad's community did not harvest violent people filled with hate that Wallace and Lomax spoke of. He forbade his followers to carry weapons of any kind, "not even a pen-knife." Elijah taught, "When a man puts weapons in his pockets, or a gun, I will make it clear, it takes his mind off God's protection and puts it on the gun to protect him." Even while African Americans were suffering from open racism and class discrimination, Elijah Muhammad still obligated his followers to obey the laws of America and to always give their employers a full day's work for their pay. He enjoined them to demonstrate the best character: clean, just, polite.

The importance of the reader to recall the context in which Elijah Muhammad lived cannot be reiterated enough. Try to imagine what it must have been like to see the world through the eyes of a young Colored boy in the Deep South who had seen his friend who had been lynched still hanging from a tree. Attempt to see in your mind's eye how Elijah felt as a young family man in Detroit, MI, trying to feed his household on a meager income during the Depression of 1929, that resulted in him becoming a drunkard and his family relying upon public assistance.

With this backdrop of difficulties think of how Elijah Poole felt when he encountered W.D. Fard, a Caucasian-looking man with a new and strange message called "Islam." Mr. Fard taught Elijah Muhammad and other Negroes of Detroit slums: "I'm your Saviour." Mr. Fard told them, "You have been robbed of the true knowledge of self," and he challenged his listeners to "rise up and claim your own." Elijah Muhammad became very endeared to W.D. Fard, sincerely following Fard's effort to uplift every African American out of the "muck and the mire" of degradation.

It was quite easy for Elijah to conclude that Fard was divine, but in time it appears that Elijah realized that Fard's divinity was not omniscient and omnipotent. Elijah's own description of Fard is a man who spent 20 years traveling in and out of America attending a number of universities to "study every education system of the civilized world." Also Fard could only "speak 16 languages and write 10 of them, but speak 16 fluently." Elijah Muhammad stated that one school Fard attended was in California where, "he lived with a white family out there, he says, while he was going to the University of California." Did Fard intentionally show his finiteness? All Muslims believe that no one is capable of teaching the Supreme Creator.

Nonetheless, Elijah Muhammad remained loyal to Fard's program for 40-plus years. Along the way he groomed men and women towards excellence. Studying the successes of four of his top lieutenant's national and international acclaims, hopefully will challenge the readers to seek more knowledge about the success stories of Elijah Muhammad, and gain a better appreciation of the little man from Deepstep, GA.

This introduction is a glimpse of Elijah's journey from a public sot to a commander with a cause. From him being a total social reject to becoming a catalyst for a mental and moral reformation that enhanced both racial pride and financial growth for his followers. This is a book that follows a man from being a lost Negro named Elijah Poole to becoming *The Honorable Elijah Muhammad: The Man Behind the Men*.

-§- CHAPTER -§-
TWO

The Challenges

Accepting, or even merely considering that Elijah Muhammad is worthy of being titled the "man behind the men" can present a series of challenges that may vary according to the individual's perceptions of Elijah Muhammad and according to the principles they uphold. Race also may be a factor influencing the depth of the challenge one could face when revisiting their opinions of the man who led a group commonly misnamed the "Black Muslims."

Elijah Muhammad was born in and shaped by America, the country in which he lived, died and was eulogized and buried. For many people these undeniable facts, alone, represent a serious challenge as we try to reconcile our nation's life and history with such controversial figures as Mr. Elijah Muhammad. This is one of many challenges discussed in this chapter. If we deny that these challenges exist, we cheat ourselves. If we ignore these challenges we belittle ourselves. However, if we engage these challenges we enrich ourselves.

We must review the life of Elijah Muhammad with the broadmindedness promoted by Nicholas Rowe (1674-1718) the English dramatist, writer and poet who said, "The brave do never shun the light; Just are their thoughts, and open are their tempers; Truly without disguise they love and hate; Still are they found in the fair face of day, And heav'n and men are judges of their actions."

This book may cause some Caucasian Americans to repel as they read the pro-black racial overtones that were prevalent in the teachings of Elijah Muhammad. Can white America — in the midst of reading text that promotes black superiority — permit their minds to quietly listen, discern, and glean from Elijah Muhammad's message what he was actually importing to his people and to America as a nation?

Can white Americans accept that maybe there is another context in which they could view the contributions and life of a man who for more than 40 years called them a race of devils? And who for the majority of his adult life accused white Americans of committing the worse form of slavery ever known to humankind.

Getting acquainted with Elijah Muhammad as he is presented in this book is a task that will challenge, yet benefit all Americans. The challenge for non-Muslim African Americans is somewhat similar to the challenge mentioned above, but with the added obligation of seeing Elijah Muhammad through their own mind's eye, even as he scrutinizes — if not ridicules — some of their post-slavery traditions and institutions. Many African Americans may find portions of this book on Elijah Muhammad discomforting, particularly those who want to quickly and quietly move forward from a hideous past of injustice, bigotry and inferiority, without investigating the root causes of those sins.

There are special burdens that must be shouldered by African American intellectuals to review, rectify and correlate Elijah Muhammad's thinking and progress with that of the overall African American history and struggle. This research on the part of lettered African Americans is essential if a true understanding and appreciation of the evolution of African American life is to be attained. This book offers a challenge to African Americans to reinvestigate the life of Elijah Muhammad, the Nation of Islam and the contributions he made to the African American community, so that he can take his appropriate place among other African American giants.

This book may offer a special challenge for some preservers of history, whether archived in textbooks, print or voice media, Hollywood movies or documentaries. Later we'll discuss how Hollywood has taken undue liberties in their cinematic presentation of Elijah Muhammad.

To date most historians seem to have intentionally overlooked the great social, economic, and spiritual contributions that Elijah Muhammad made to a large number of deprived black men and women in America, and the positive effect that continues to benefit a nationwide audience. Subsequent chapters of *The Honorable Elijah: The Man Behind the Men* addresses the need for historians to rise up to the journalistic standards for recording history; standards that seem to have been neglected when it came to preserving the history of Elijah Muhammad.

Educators are obligated to read this book in order to offer their students another perspective on this multifaceted human being. The FBI's *File:105-24822* reports Elijah Muhammad asking, "Where are our degreed scholars' and scientists' works in the way of trying to help themselves and their people to self independence?" There already exists a serious void when it comes to America's students being taught African American history. There is more to African American history than our beloved Dr. Martin Luther King and the noble struggles of the Civil Rights Movement. Additionally, the 28 days of Black History Month that February provides is not enough time to educate anyone on the many African Americans and Caucasian Americans who are a part of the African American experience. This book presents a challenge to our educators to add to their curricula and increase their information base on such greats as Elijah Muhammad, Paul Robeson, Marcus Garvey and the many other under-recognized African Americans who have fulfilled a vital part of America's overall growth. America's educators, on all levels of education, owe their students the opportunity for their minds to encounter the legacy of the Honorable Elijah Muhammad.

THE CHALLENGES

Our political landscape must accept the challenges that may accompany reading this book. Elijah Muhammad did not endorse any political party, candidates or even allow Nation of Islam members to participate in the electoral process; nonetheless, he was an effective contributor to the political fiber of America, especially in the African American community. His words resonated with such political figures as the Rev. Jesse Jackson and former Chicago Mayor Richard Joseph Daley. Elijah Muhammad's four *star-students* highlighted in this book also had an impact on American politics that has resulted in imams today offering benedictions for many legislative bodies on every level of government. Today there are hundreds of Muslims, men and women, who are seeking and winning elections in largely Caucasian non-Muslim locales. Muslim politicians, who today are working for the betterment of all Americans, have to varying degrees been influenced by and are benefitting from the good contributions of Elijah Muhammad.

FBI's *File:105-24822* also reports Elijah Muhammad stating, "If we love freedom for self, remember that we must assume our own responsibility, so we are free to exercise the freedom of actions as well as freedom of thinking. Both the clergy and political classes of our people should remember this and preach it."

The Honorable Elijah Muhammad: The Man Behind the Men also presents a challenge for the overall Islamic communities of America. Considering his non-traditional practice of Islam, the challenge of how to best record the life of Elijah Muhammad in the Muslim American mosaic must be addressed. Most Muslims in America — indigenous or immigrant — in one way or another are standing on the shoulders of his work.

The challenges that imams must accept are numerous because they too are indebted to and obligated to know about Elijah Muhammad. Regardless of whether an imam agrees with the methodology of Elijah Muhammad, not a single one of them can dismiss the fact that to this day Elijah Muhammad remains the one individual who introduced the name Muhammad to more Americans than any person in history. He is probably responsible, more than any other imam in the world, for Americans learning and sharing the Islamic greetings of "As-Salaam Alaikum." And even to this day no Muslim individually or collectively has achieved the success enjoyed by Elijah Muhammad in providing Muslim community development. This book will challenge the imams in America and the world to revisit the unique style that Elijah used to present his version of Islam to unlettered African Americans. These imams should commit to further study the eschatology that Elijah inherited from Mr. Fard.

Muslims who still identify Elijah Muhammad's teachings as the whole truth often will find themselves challenged by modernity. With the continuing maturity of America's social and religious life, on the part of both Caucasians and African Americans, the Muslims who choose to adhere to Elijah Muhammad's every word as unalterable are challenged by Elijah Muhammad's change of emphasis during his lifetime. These Muslims must address the appropriateness of adhering literally to a race-based message that Elijah himself was moving away from at the end of his life. Was his version of Islam meant to remain understood as he received it from W.D. Fard? On the surface Elijah Muhammad's Nation of Islam, which he called a "baby nation," seems to address the needs only of African Americans. But as the "baby nation" grows and develops should not Elijah Muhammad's message and the application of that message grow exponentially? The challenge for those who still identify as followers of Elijah Muhammad and claim that the intent of his message was not to evolve with modernity, is the challenge of applying his older race-laden message in an ever diversifying world.

Religious leaders of faith traditions other than Islam may find this book challenging on two points. It may serve well for all religious leaders to investigate the potency of Elijah Muhammad's work that led so many African Americans to migrate to Islam. Also, what do the Muslims who extend from Elijah Muhammad's mission possess that will aid the reconciliation of America's splintered religious communities? Elijah Muhammad challenged the core thinking of America's religious institutions of his day as he made a niche for his Nation of Islam in the ghettos of America. Every religious leader must read this book in search of some issues that divided religion in America as well as for that which can unite religion in America.

Whatever our mindset may be today, hopefully our intelligence will rise and surmount the horizons of our prejudices and biases. We pray that this book will help us all. For the writer too is challenged because one cannot honestly write unless there is a willingness to search and discover the unknown, even if the end results prove all premises of the writer to be wrong.

Writing a book on Elijah Muhammad also challenges the writer to undertake a calculated and oftentimes complicated risk that accompanies writing about a racially charged epoch such as the one in which Elijah Muhammad struggled and flourished. The writer must capture the bittersweet era of American history that Elijah Muhammad lived in, and then effectively relay the spirit of that era to a modern-day, post-Civil Rights Movement, generation. This is a challenging task because the Elijah Muhammad of yesterday must be recorded in a proper manner that connects him with humanity's future progress. However, it's a necessary task because Elijah's contributions to humanity are still being manifested daily by the thousands of individuals who have emanated from the "baby nation" he once nurtured.

THE CHALLENGES

O you who believe! Stand out firmly for justice, as witnesses to Allah (God), even as against yourselves, or your parents, or your kin, and whether it be (against) rich or poor: for Allah can best protect both. Follow not the lusts (of your hearts), lest you swerve, and if you distort (justice) or decline to do justice, verily Allah is well acquainted with all that you do.
Qur'an sura 4: Ayat 135

The Qur'an, the book that Elijah Muhammad lifted up as a holy text, reads "Stand out firmly for justice...lest you swerve...or decline to do justice." This is one of the many challenges that must be met when writing about a controversial figure who lived in an isolated and segregated society that intentionally reported only one aspect of that individual in order to show them as negative.

The Canadian Thomas C. Haliburton (1796-1865), a jurist, homespun philosopher and author, said "Hear one side and you will be in the dark. Hear both and all will be clear." If we can meet the challenge of hearing more than one perspective on Elijah Muhammad then the clarity of his life and purpose will benefit all.

This writer further acknowledges the diligent progress made in building diverse relationships that transcend racial, religious, and ethnic barriers; progress that may not correspond with or complement the image that the world has of Elijah Muhammad. Therefore, is writing on Elijah Muhammad important enough to risk relationships that have taken years to establish? Many may question the wisdom of writing a book that may bewilder close associates and maybe even provoke them to question this writer's commitment to understanding and improving upon race relations and interfaith exchanges?

Yes, these advancements in humane exchange are extremely important. Yet, with sincere humility another question must be asked: Is not there a higher obligation this writer owes to present a significant aspect of African American development that heretofore has been grossly misrepresented? There remains an unfulfilled debt this writer owes to society to present the Honorable Elijah Muhammad in a proper light and context that the decorum of history necessitates. He had a fundamental impact upon America. We must recognize that we would be remiss to allow Elijah Muhammad to be misreported to future generations.

Currently for one to dare verbalize Elijah Muhammad's name in a positive light in certain settings is taboo. It is even more extraordinary to write a book with many arguments in favor of Mr. Muhammad. Therefore, the challenge faced by the writer extends to many sectors of our society. Can the person who reads this book begin to look at Elijah Muhammad with fresh eyes and with the intent of taking away something new that may benefit them as a reader, as a student of history, or as a human being who truly loves freedom?

THE MAN BEHIND THE MEN

Lastly, it seems that most Americans want a clear conscience even at the expense of conveniently eliminating from our collective memories facts of history that may be discomforting. Due to most people having limited access to better information about this man, Elijah Muhammad is a very discomforting figure, and therefore deemed easily marginalized or even dispensable.

As a country, Americans have to develop the ability to honestly speak on aspects of our history that may cause us uneasiness or possible embarrassment. We have to study disregarded but important aspects of our total American heritage without opting for the easy way out — the pathway dressed with half truths and lies – or ignoring certain truths along that path.

This is a challenge that we all have to meet as we read *The Honorable Elijah: The Man Behind the Men*, that is if we truly want to understand and demystify the undue shroud that conceals his great legacy. No, he did not teach Islam as ordained by the Qur'an or as exemplified by Muhammed the 7th-century prophet of Islam. But he did teach with sincere dedication according to the best understanding available to him, W.D. Fard's version of "Islam."

The Honorable Elijah Muhammad's legacy continues to struggle through a type of character assassination. This is very similar to the image problems, whether accurate or exaggerated, that most minorities and other marginalized people had to endure and overcome. The former followers and students of Elijah Muhammad who benefited from his leadership are obligated to speak up and clarify, and when necessary defend his character.

Our country is full of successful African Americans, in every field of life who owe their success to the Honorable Elijah Muhammad. A challenge too exists for these individuals whether they will publicly acknowledge this truth?

As indicated in the *Introduction*, many Americans have been marginalized resulting in many races and ethnicities suffering character assassination. Probably the group most emblematic of this torment is the African American and the Native American Indians. But many others, for example most new immigrants, have endured some type of negative character alteration process. Malcolm X, due to sources within and external to the Nation of Islam, lost his life as a result of a character assassination initiative left unchecked. Even today we see Muslims and Arabs being mislabeled as "towel heads," "jihadist" and other names resulting in them being abused by those who feel themselves to be the "real Americans."

Whenever a person or a group's character is allowed to be denigrated or assassinated in the minds of the public, then as history has witnessed, such people soon become the target of degradation and abuse that oftentimes has led to death.

May we all accept our respective challenges as we read about *The Honorable Elijah Muhammad, the Man Behind the Men*, the little uneducated man from Georgia, who in one way or another, challenged us all to think, reflect and adjust our lives.

-§- CHAPTER -§-
THREE

The Honorable Elijah Muhammad Through the Eyes of Others

"The evil that men do lives after them; The good is oft interred with their bones"
— William Shakespeare

Elijah Muhammad's image as illustrated by Hollywood, the FBI, and through many social commentaries has been skewed at best. He has yet to be presented to the public through the eyes of his followers. One consequence of many writers overlooking or omitting the positive contributions of Elijah Muhammad has helped to create an aura of mystique. This mystique, coalesced with his racially based version of Islam, often led many to either revere him or despise him.

The sacred texts of both Muslims and Christians acknowledge that every individual is due recognition for the good fruits they produce. The Qur'an states, "That man can have nothing but what he strives for; That (the fruit of) his striving will soon come in sight: Then will he be rewarded with a reward complete; That to thy Lord is the final Goal." (Sura 53: verses 39-42, Yusuf Ali translation).

The Bible quotes Christ Jesus: "For a good tree bringeth not forth corrupt fruit; neither doth a corrupt tree bring forth good fruit. For every tree is known by his own fruit." (Luke 6:43-44, King James Version).

These scriptural verses are not religion or denomination specific; therefore applicable to believers of many faiths. These Biblical and Qur'anic verses promotes that any man or woman who brings forth produce will be remunerated accordingly.

A serious biography of Mr. Muhammad is sorely needed, notes Robert C. Smith, professor of political science at San Francisco State University. Quoting the great Christian theologian Dr. C. Eric Lincoln, Smith points out in his book, *We Have No Leaders: African Americans in the Post-Civil Rights Era*, that Mr. Muhammad was one of the most remarkable men of the 20th century. "Largely unlettered, he made an enormous contribution to the dignity and self-esteem of blacks in the United States, in addition to making Islam a respectable force in the Black community" (page 315; note 42).

Many African American historians, and movie producers, have failed to show Elijah Muhammad in a balanced and just way. The question that begs to be answered is why history — whether preserved on film, in books or otherwise — has yet to report a more complete picture of Elijah Muhammad?

Post-civil rights African American historians should be free of the pressures to be politically correct when giving an account of the works of

Elijah Muhammad. Their reports should include both his challenges and successes. But oddly many African Americans historians have followed suit by continuing to write only disparagingly about Mr. Elijah Muhammad.

The same disciplines of preserving history must be applied to Elijah Muhammad as to every historical figure and event. Are these recorders of history, among African American historians, hindered by some allegiance to political correctness? Are they still under the pressures of the civil rights days where Elijah Muhammad was only shown as a narrow-minded racist? To show Elijah Muhammad only as an acrimoniously bitter, conniving, jealous leader, or as a mysterious, austere recluse distant from the day-to-day African American community is unjust, unethical and fails to meet the disciplines of reporting history.

Too often history has been politicized or written to appease a certain hegemony or societal trend while spitefully promoting misrepresentations of that society's disenfranchised. Many African American achievements have been written *out* of history through intentional omissions by racist historians who did not want to report on African American excellence. Still this disdainful overlooking of greatness by many white historians didn't deter dedicated African American teachers, who over the generations often risked their jobs by quietly interjecting African American achievements into their otherwise lily-white class lessons. Yet it is a sad fact that even in the first decade of the 21st century, many students of all races graduate from high school without knowing that African Americans invented the lawn mower, gas mask, refrigerator, air conditioner, stoplight and many other daily conveniences.

Worse than that, many of our high school graduates know little if anything about Elijah Muhammad, Marcus Garvey, Timothy Drew Ali, Paul Robeson and others simply because they by and large have been written out of mainstream history.

Almost 20 years before the advent of Elijah Muhammad's teacher, W.D. Fard, Dr. Carter G. Woodson recognized the need for African Americans to learn more of their own history. On the opening page of his book the *Mis-Education of the Negro*, Dr. Woodson argues that African Americans' lack of education about their history is "the seat of the problem." Dr. Woodson explained:

> The "educated Negroes" have the attitude of contempt toward their own people because in their own as well as in their mixed schools Negroes are taught to admire the Hebrew, the Greek, the Latin and the Teuton and to despise the African. Of the hundreds of Negro high schools recently examined by an expert in the United States Bureau of Education only eighteen offered a course taking up the history of the Negro, and in most of the Negro colleges and universities where the Negro is thought of, the race is studied only as a problem or dismissed as of little consequence.

ELIJAH MUHAMMAD
THROUGH THE EYES OF OTHERS

Not much has changed to improve the mis-education of African Americans in the field of teaching history. The little progress that has been made regarding teachers having access to — and the dissemination of — African American history since Dr. Carter's 1933 *The Mis-Education of the Negro* is inconsequential and minuscule compared to the overall advancement in other fields of education.

Accessibility to credible information on Elijah Muhammad easily can be obtained and documented by talking with many of his former followers. Despite the availability of this valuable information, the history of Elijah Muhammad continues to be reported in ways that do not show him completely, nor his accomplishments in proper context.

Only the historians who have written on Elijah Muhammad can best answer why they opted to partially depict him. But in this day and age we cannot let fear, political correctness or substandard journalism — not even the creative rights and theatrical licensing afforded Hollywood movie makers — be accepted as reasons for improperly showing Elijah Muhammad or any other important historical figure.

Professor Edward E. Curtis, the Millennium Scholar of the Liberal Arts and Associate Professor of Religious Studies at Indiana University-Purdue University Indianapolis (IUPUI) — who has written extensively on the Nation of Islam — suggests that the difficulty in researching the Nation of Islam is due to the fact that "the scholars' only sources originate either with movement members themselves or with the surveillance and counterintelligence operations of the FBI."

Of the two research sources recommended by Curtis, the contributions from Nation of Islam members — whose lives were totally consumed by Nation of Islam tenets and teachings — provides historians the best primary information source. The only possible taint to the information offered from pre-1975 Nation of Islam members that may demote their contributions to a secondary source could occur if researchers deem these members information inferior because it was learned by rote. But these Muslims loved Elijah Muhammad and the Nation of Islam and they are eager and proud to share their black-oriented Islamic experiences. Their Nation of Islam catechism styled lessons may have been learned by rote, but their commitment to Elijah Muhammad was genuine and is worthy of note.

Information on Elijah Muhammad and the Nation of Islam acquired from FBI sources mainly are secondary, even tertiary. Information contaminated by the FBI's stated intentions to contain the Nation of Islam and to smear the Muslims' image.

Other sources of information on the history of the Nation of Islam include the *Pittsburgh Courier*, the numerous interviews given by Elijah Muhammad and his top officials, *The Autobiography of Malcolm X*, and the research conducted by Dr. E. U. Essien-Udom, Dr. C. Eric Lincoln, and more recently by Claude Andrew Clegg, to name a few.

THE MAN BEHIND THE MEN

Another important quality of Elijah Muhammad that must be reviewed by students of history is the branches of leadership that extended from his leadership. The four most renowned men of Elijah's former Nation of Islam still are popular in society today: the son and successor of Elijah Muhammad, Imam W. Deen Mohammed; Minister Louis Farrakhan, the leader of a renewed version of the Nation of Islam; Malcolm X (Malik Shabazz), the former National Spokesman of Mr. Elijah Muhammad; and three-time Heavyweight Boxing Champion, Muhammad Ali. These four men, whether alive or deceased, are still influencing the life of millions of people around the world. No other student or follower of any other past or present African American leader is being quoted and having as much an impact and influence upon society today as these four students of Elijah Muhammad.

The students of the great Dr. Martin Luther King, even with their mainstream acceptance, have not had nearly the impact upon America and the world as the students of Elijah Muhammad. Very few youth, adults, or world leaders quote the students of Dr. King. Seldom, if ever, do you hear of a group of young African American males gathering on their own prerogative, to review and discuss a lecture by Jesse Jackson, Andy Young, or Dr. Ralph Abernathy. However from amongst young rap artists, particularly in the 1990s, to world leaders, you'll hear the religious, political or social views of the former students of Elijah Muhammad quoted or acknowledged by both youth and elders.

Marvin X El Muhajir of Oakland, CA, a member of the original Nation of Islam identified Elijah Muhammad as the greatest teacher ever for African Americans and his students as the best proof of Elijah Muhammad's greatness. In his *Teacher and Spirituality* paper, Marvin X said, "The Honorable Elijah Muhammad was our greatest teacher. We need only list a few of his students such as Malcolm X, Warithdeen Muhammad, Muhammad Ali, Minister Farrakhan and myself among thousands of others here and around the world. Name another teacher with such outstanding students!"

Every human being has positive and weak attributes. To overly praise their strong points while ignoring their shortcomings will yield an untrue picture of the whole person. A myopic approach that focuses only on the negative or only on the positive cheats the student of history of an accurate education. More importantly, such biased accounts rob the historian of the opportunity to honor the standards of historical scholarship, or historiography; a discipline that Dr. Conrad W. Worrill defined as "the science of how history is written."

The American Historical Association strongly promotes fair and accurate reporting to society and educational institutions. A few of the values their *Statement on Standards of Professional Conduct* encourages historians to abide include:

ELIJAH MUHAMMAD
THROUGH THE EYES OF OTHERS

The Scholarship, the uncovering and exchange of new information and the shaping of interpretations, is basic to the activities of the historical profession. The profession communicates with students in textbooks and classrooms; to other scholars and the general public in books, articles, exhibits, films, and historic sites and structures; and to decision makers in memoranda and testimony... Integrity is one of these issues. It requires an awareness of one's own bias and a readiness to follow sound method and analysis wherever they may lead... Historians must not misrepresent evidence or the sources of evidence, must be free of the offense of plagiarism, and must not be indifferent to error or efforts to ignore or conceal it.

The dismissal of the contributions of Elijah Muhammad seems to be a conscious effort even amongst many African American historians. He was a contemporary of Dr. Martin Luther King, but when African American history writers compare the Civil Rights Movement with the Nation of Islam, Malcolm X is juxtaposed with Dr. King in place of Elijah Muhammad. The minimizing of Elijah Muhammad's role in black history and the lifting up of Malcolm X above him is thievery. How much longer will his positive contributions be overlooked? When will Elijah Muhammad be properly rewarded in history for his labors with the poor and rejected black man and woman of America?

Elijah Muhammad and Martin Luther King — MARCH 1968.
(Photographer and Date Unknown)

Every novice historian knows that Malcolm X was never the leader of the Nation of Islam. Malcolm was the National Spokesman for the message of Mr. Muhammad. But he was never the leader. As the National Spokesman every conversation and comment of Malcolm was prefaced with the phrase, "The Honorable Elijah Muhammad teaches us..."

THE MAN BEHIND THE MEN

Malcolm acknowledged this fact in his autobiography. "In every radio or television appearance, in every newspaper interview, I always made it crystal clear that I was Mr. Muhammad's *representative*. Anyone who ever heard me make a public speech during this time knows that at least once a minute I said, "The Honorable Elijah Muhammad teaches—" I would refuse to talk with any person who ever tried any so-called "joke" about my constant reference to Mr. Muhammad." (297)

Despite this fact of Malcolm's willful submission to Elijah Muhammad as his leader and teacher, many writers reporting on the Nation of Islam have a bias that favors Malcolm over highlighting the leadership of Elijah Muhammad. Maybe this tendency on the part of the media to prefer Malcolm came from the fact Elijah Muhammad's syntax and hesitancy in his speech did not meet the glitz-and-glamour expectations of some in the public and the media.

Mike Wallace of CBS television was one such writer who preferred Malcolm X over Elijah Muhammad. In his book *Between You and Me*, Wallace described Elijah Muhammad as "a remote and rather shy man who, in his rare public appearances, did not come across as all that articulate and forceful." Comparatively Wallace states, "The man who did possess those qualities in great abundance was the movement's most visible and vocal spokesman, Malcolm X, an ex-convict who had converted to the Nation of Islam while serving time for burglaries."

Even with Wallace's acknowledgement that the Nation of Islam had delivered Malcolm from a life of crime, Wallace's only follow up references to Elijah Muhammad are negative and critical. But journalists such as Wallace who preferred to highlight the negative aspects associated with Elijah Muhammad only weaken their credibility in terms of journalism standards.

Throughout history many well known articulate public individuals who possess power and influence will remind their admirers that they owe much of their success to an uneducated or inarticulate individual who is the main source directly responsible for them being who they are today. Many leaders in society even to this day have life stories of being reared by poorly educated parents or grandparents who spoke broken English. For many Nation of Islam members, who today are living successful lives, Elijah Muhammad was their uneducated and inarticulate parent; the little man from Georgia with a third grade education acquired in the first decade of the 20th century.

Another determining factor that has strong sway on how Elijah Muhammad is viewed is Malcolm X's assassination. Dr. Razi Hassan, a chemist at Alabama A&M University was a member at Elijah Muhammad's Temple No. 7 in New York City from 1970 to 1975. As a member of the Nation of Islam, Hassan's name was Robert C29X ("C" for the Roman

ELIJAH MUHAMMAD
THROUGH THE EYES OF OTHERS

numeral 100, thus Robert 129X). Today Dr. Hassan serves as an imam in Huntsville, AL. He is one of many who believe that the assassination of Malcolm X is one factor in why Elijah Muhammad has repeatedly been misrepresented in America.

Dr. Hassan noted, "The first real image that we get of the Honorable Elijah Muhammad is that of the assassinator of Malcolm X. We fall in love with a person after they are dead. After they die they become a saint, and the person responsible becomes the devil."

One of Dr. Hassan's duties in the Nation of Islam during the early 1970s was selling the *Muhammad Speaks* newspaper. "People on the streets of New York used to say that to me all the time, 'I'm not going to buy that damned paper because y'all killed Malcolm.' Hassan believes that with the assassination of Malcolm, "the establishment killed two birds with one stone; Malcolm and the image of the Honorable Elijah Muhammad."

Dr. Hassan adds that following Malcolm's death "words were put into his mouth" by those who wish to use Malcolm's image for their own agendas, when in fact Malcolm was adjusting to the rigors of a transition from being a minister for Elijah Muhammad to being a Muslim seeking orientation in the universal world of Islam. Speaking on the vacuum this rapid transition imposed on Malcolm, Dr. Hassan stated, "Malcolm left the Nation of Islam on November 22, 1963. He was assassinated February 25, 1965. In other words, he only had about 15 months to study Islam. Even the most zealous spirit could not evolve to the level of a Muslim imam in such a short time."

Dr. Hassan contends that "Malcolm did not have time to evolve to anything of philosophic importance after he left the Nation of Islam. There simply wasn't enough time. Most of the speeches that we hear today by Malcolm are between November 23, 1963 and February 25, 1965, which were basically political commentary and anti-Elijah Muhammad and Nation of Islam rhetoric."

Dr. Amiri YaSin Al-Hadid, the former professor and chair of the Department of Africana Studies at Tennessee State University, shared that Malcolm, in the short span of time between leaving the Nation of Islam and his death, had memorized in Arabic half of the *juz'* titled Amma, an equivalent of 1/60th of Islam's holy book. In his book *Between Cross and Crescent: Christian and Muslim Perspectives on Malcolm and Martin*, co-authored with Lewis V. Baldwin, Al-Hadid seems to confirm that Malcolm realized his shortcomings in classical Islam. Dr. Al-Hadid noted:

> Imam Warith Deen Mohammed said Malcolm invited him to assist in the development of the Muslim Mosque, Inc. Because Imam Muhammad's [sic] understanding of Sunni Islam and

religion were more advanced than Malcolm's at that time, Malcolm wanted him to provide the religious leadership while he himself focused on the cultural and political leadership. (76)

Even Bruce Perry, in the biography he wrote titled *Malcolm: The Life of a Man Who Changed Black America*, limits Malcolm's contributions to the African American struggle as that of an influential spokesman. Perry notes in his concluding paragraph:

> Malcolm X fathered no legislation. He engineered no stunning Supreme Court victories or political campaigns. He scored no major electoral triumphs. Yet, because of the way he articulated his followers' grievances and anger, the impact he had on the body politic was enormous. (380)

Dr. Martin Luther King in his autobiography misplaced the credit due to Elijah Muhammad when he credited Malcolm with having "the great ability to put his finger on the existence and root of the problem" (pg 265). Dr. King overlooked acknowledging that Malcolm acquired this "great ability" from none other than Elijah Muhammad. A dutiful study of the pre-1975 Nation of Islam unequivocally will reveal without doubt the reality that Elijah Muhammad was well established as the sole leader of the Nation of Islam and that Malcolm and all other members worked, studied, and spoke under Elijah's authority.

The Federal Bureau of Investigation's COINTELPRO (COunterINTELligence PROgram) offers another view on Elijah Muhammad. But the agency's avowed object being to destroy Elijah Muhammad renders it, at best, a skewed source of information. Even with the FBI acknowledging that the COINTELPRO was established in 1956 for domestic spying in order to disrupt, discredit, and/or neutralize those deemed to be "un-American," some historians still rely upon the FBI's COINTELPRO files as a dependable source when writing about Mr. Elijah Muhammad.

Karl Evanzz's biography, *The Messenger: The Rise and Fall of Elijah Muhammad*, is written largely from the FBI's COINTELPRO files. Notwithstanding that many tactics of COINTELPRO were less than noble; at times it also seems as if Mr. Evanzz himself — in addition to rehashing the COINTELPRO files — has a preconceived bias against Elijah Muhammad that may disallow him to write impartially on his subject. Evanzz quotes the FBI COINTELPRO files on Elijah Muhammad hundreds of times as if Evanzz, like former FBI Director J. Edgar Hoover, mainly is focused on seeing Elijah Muhammad fall from grace.

The efforts of the FBI, under Hoover, knew few if any limits when it came to surveillance of Elijah Muhammad and the Nation of Islam. Baba Zak A.

ELIJAH MUHAMMAD
THROUGH THE EYES OF OTHERS

Kondo in his book *ConspiracyS: Unravelling the Assassination of Malcolm X* [sic] details some of the tactics the FBI used to disrupt the Nation of Islam.

> They placed the most active members on the Security Index and directed FBI agents to internally disrupt the NOI, using informant-agents who circulated false rumors about Muslim leaders, and placed phone and microphone bugs in the NOI headquarters and in the homes of Elijah Muhammad...The FBI's strategy was actually a simple one: use the Malcolm-Muhammad Family conflict not only to internally disrupt the NOI, but more significantly to divide Malcolm and his mentor. (120)

Carl T. Rowan, an award-winning syndicated columnist, forthrightly questioned the creditability of FBI reports on Elijah Muhammad and other renowned African Americans. Unlike Evanzz, instead of heavily relying upon COINTELPRO files as a primary source, Rowan highlighted the plausibility of FBI agents having ulterior motives in their reporting on Elijah Muhammad. Rowan, in his book *Breaking Barriers: A Memoir* supports his suspicion of possible FBI culpability in the assassination of Dr. Martin Luther King, Jr. by citing the extreme measures taken by the FBI in their surveillance on Elijah Muhammad.

> My suspicions intensified in the summer of 1969 when I read about boxer Muhammad Ali's attempt, in federal court in Houston, to overturn his five-year sentence for refusing to be drafted. That case forced the FBI to reveal that it had been engaged in massive eavesdropping on Ali, Ling, and other black Americans. Agent C. Barry Pickett of the FBI testified that for eight hours a day, five days a week, for four years, he had used a telephone tap and a microphone planted in the home of Elijah Muhammad to listen in on conversations of the late leader of the black Muslims. This was 8,300 hours of eavesdropping by one FBI agent on a single black American. Common sense suggested that whereas Pickett worked eight hours a day, at least two other agents were eavesdropping for a minimum of 16,000 hours — with someone covering weekends. (293)

Not every one in America's government believed that Elijah Muhammad was un-American. Men such as Attorney General Robert Kennedy, the brother of former U.S. President John F. Kennedy, to the disgruntlement of Hoover, held different views toward Elijah Muhammad. Kondo, highlighting an article from the *Chicago Daily News*, points out that Kennedy stated that the Nation of Islam was not "subversive" but was simply an organization that was fighting for black rights.

Kondo argues, "The Bureau's worst fear was that (Robert) Kennedy's comments would 'legitimize' the NOI and thus force the FBI to abandon its campaign to disrupt and destroy the organization." But Hoover had little reason to fear Robert Kennedy interfering. According to Claude Andrew Clegg III in his book, *An Original Man*, President John F. Kennedy while acknowledging that the "Justice Department has not received any reliable information that the 'Black Muslims' are violating any federal law," nonetheless, he allowed the FBI to conduct open-ended surveillance and counterintelligence. Clegg notes that Hoover even after the Kennedy's had acknowledged that Elijah Muhammad and the Nation of Islam were acting legally, still Hoover "personally prosecuted the war against Elijah Muhammad and his followers, often using illegal tactics." (173)

For fifteen years innocent American citizens such as Elijah Muhammad and Dr. King endured violations of their civil rights due to inexcusable and repugnant Cointelpro activities. In 1976 the 94th U.S. Congress convened a congressional Select Committee whose purpose was to "study governmental operations with respect to intelligence activities." In April of 1976 — eight years after the assassination of Dr. King — Congress wrote, in part: "The Committee finds that covert action programs have been used to disrupt the lawful political activities of individual Americans and groups and to discredit them, using dangerous and degrading tactics which are abhorrent in a free and decent society." The committee concluded, "The actions taken against Dr. King are indefensible. They represent a sad episode in the dark history of covert actions directed against law abiding citizens by a law enforcement agency."

Cinematic portrayals of Elijah Muhammad have followed similar degrading presentations as that given in the COINTELPRO reports and the biased reports of some historians. The movies *Malcolm X* (1992) directed by Spike Lee and *Ali* (2001) directed by Michael Mann also opted to show Elijah Muhammad in a negative light, while overlooking the positive contributions he made to Malcolm X and Muhammad Ali. Maybe these historians and movie directors individually could be innocent of overlooking the many positive contributions of Elijah Muhammad, but collectively there is a strong case for intentional disregard.

Keith A. Owens, the senior editor for the *Michigan Chronicle*, confirms in his February 22-28, 2006 issue that most historians have not given the proper attention that is due to Elijah Muhammad. In his commentary titled "The Nation of Islam: Made in Detroit", Owens, while stating that the Nation of Islam "made a lasting national impact," further acknowledges that the Nation of Islam historically and contemporarily has been glossed over.

ELIJAH MUHAMMAD
THROUGH THE EYES OF OTHERS

The rise of the Nation of Islam (NOI) is without question one of the most significant developments in modern American Black history. Unfortunately, due to the perpetual controversy and, some might say, mystery that has surrounded the organization since its inception more than 70 years ago, most mainstream history texts either dismiss the movement altogether or gloss over it. More to the point, it's hard for an all-Black organization that has referred to White people as "devils" to receive mainstream acceptance – not that the NOI has ever cared anything about that sort of acceptance. Consequently, the Nation has often been viewed as more of a fringe element than anything else; ragingly militant and pro-Black at its best, out-of-date and out-of-touch at its worst. Although most are familiar with the story of the late Malcolm X, and today's Minister Louis Farrakhan continues to draw huge crowds wherever he speaks — with or without press coverage — a dwindling number are aware of the late Elijah Muhammad, who served as mentor to both Malcolm X and Farrakhan. Even fewer have heard of Wallace D. Fard, later known as Master Wallace Fard Muhammad, who established the NOI in Detroit during the 1930s.

To better understand and appreciate the works of Elijah Muhammad it is imperative that further examination is done in order to appreciate the environment that gave birth to his mind and soul. It is important to have some insights into his pre-adulthood circumstances and events that may have sparked in Elijah Muhammad a yearning that led him to emerge from being merely a product of his environment to become a leader who produced men and women.

Elijah Muhammad was born only 32 years after the end of the horrendous institution of chattel slavery. The South changed very slowly while retaining a slave-like culture with the evil effects of slavery still pulsating heavily during his childhood and young adult years. The right to vote and equal access to Georgia's public schools were not available to Elijah Poole due to the legalized systems that allowed disfranchisement and supported segregation. Decades would pass before these basic human and civil rights would be granted to Georgia's African American citizens.

The era that Elijah Muhammad was born into was also a time when lynching African Americans, particularly males was very common. The value of a black man's life was far less than that of a white man's life. It was custom for Caucasians to abuse African Americans in every way humanly possible.

No arena of African American life was inviolable, not even religion, which often depicted God, the angels, and the prophets as Caucasians.

THE MAN BEHIND THE MEN

Though Elijah was the son of a Baptist preacher, in Elijah's mind the church too had fallen short when it came to adequately addressing why African Americans were treated so unjustly. Religiously, politically and socially the African American community was ill equipped to provide young Elijah with a sense or value of himself that was fulfilling.

Elijah Muhammad's closeness to chattel slavery provided him with many firsthand accounts from ex-slaves whose stories would have had great impact upon him, ingraining in him strong sensitivities to the subpar state and condition of his people.

As a young man living daily in oppression that stifled his human potential, Elijah's unjust Georgia childhood setting would later provide him with a testimonial and a reminder of the cruelties African Americans had suffered from white racists in America. This same childhood background would be a factor that influenced Elijah Muhammad as he interpreted the many lessons he would receive from his teacher, Mr. W.D. Fard. His open wounds produced by racism and unjust class distinctions would be slow to heal. Even after the healing process the subsequent mental and social scars would serve as vivid reminders of his years of pain and suffering.

As the leader of the Nation of Islam, Elijah Muhammad strongly criticized the material and moral state of African Americans. For many years, without hesitation he publicly pointed an accusative finger at white America for the sad state of affairs in the African American community.

Another dynamic of Elijah's generation being reared so close to American slavery was their witnessing of the abject social conditions of the majority of African Americans; a disorder that created in many of them humiliation and silent resentments that were often masked by an artificial grin, accommodating smile or humble "Yes-suh!"

Elijah Poole suffered under such societal illnesses, and like the other men and women of his era, he too internalized the burdens and damage that develop when a human being is treated as less than human. Living involuntarily in post-slavery servitude resulted in many African American men despising their unjust treatment and resenting those who committed wrongs against African Americans.

R&B entertainer James Brown acknowledged that his father, Joe Brown, displayed this type of artificial survival temperance. James Brown spoke well of his father except for his father's privately exhibited resentment of white people. In his autobiography, *James Brown the Godfather of Soul* co-written with Bruce Tucker, James Brown wrote about his father's two-faced approach towards white people:

ELIJAH MUHAMMAD
THROUGH THE EYES OF OTHERS

> He had a temper about white people, too, but he never showed it to *them*. Where white people were concerned, I would say my father threw a rock and hit his hand. He'd call white people "crackers," curse' em and everything when they weren't around, but when he was in front of them, he'd say, Yessir, nawsir." (6)

In 1999 comedian and social critic Chris Rock, while addressing a majority young adult audience during his *Bigger and Blacker* stand-up comedy show at the Apollo Theater in Harlem, NY, began to address the sensitive issue of race. In his brash comical style Rock dared to address the strong residual racism that resides in many older black men such as Joe Brown.

Chris Rock's comedy act, which was cablecast on *Home Box Office (HBO)* was sharply criticized for implying that racial tensions still exist between whites and blacks. Rock rhetorically asked his audience who they thought the most racist people are. He answered his own question, "Old black men." He surmised, "I know you white folks know an old black man down at the job and (you all) say, 'Oh, Willie is so nice'." After reminding his audience that senior black men have endured extreme forms of white racism that younger black men have not experienced, Chris Rock interjects, "Willie hates your guts... The old black man always kisses the white man's ass...As soon as the white man leaves," Rock states, Willie will begin saying, "Cracker-ass Cracker... I hate you Cracker-ass Crackers."

Chris Rock noted that Willie will never openly show his hate or dislike for the white man, whereas many African Americans, such as Elijah Muhammad, boldly spoke out and challenged the unjust status quo of oppressive Jim Crow. Unlike Joe Brown or Chris Rock's Willie character, Elijah Muhammad was not two-faced. The Willie and the Joe Brown type possessed a public face that smiles and grins while hiding festering resentment towards white people, and also a private face that was a mixture of spite, disgust, and distrust towards white people. Elijah Muhammad's Nation of Islam presented only one face to white America; a consistent yet honest presentation that gave his black-oriented Muslim community a type of relief system designed for diffusing any pent-up antipathy they may have internalized toward white Americans.

Another means provided by Elijah Muhammad's Nation of Islam for diffusing black men's resentment towards whites was his emboldening them to believe they were, by nature, above the white man socially, morally, and mentally. This is an important aspect of Elijah Muhammad's life, and one of the proper historical contexts in which he must be studied. As instructed by Fard, Elijah Muhammad administered to African Americans an over-inflated self-worth. A successful reverse-psychology, if for no other reason than that it lessened resentment towards white people.

Nor did Elijah Muhammad hide his discontent behind euphemisms. His public rejections of white America's 20th century mistreatment of African

Americans was blatant and void of the ambiguity used by others who veiled their distrust and disapproval of white people under the phrase, "the evils of the West," or "the western man." Although stinging and offensive, he simply called, at that time, all white people "the devil."

The unjust negative conditions that shaped Elijah as a child and as a young man may have also fueled his drive to better his life. Two centuries of slavery, compounded by over 100 years of open racism to which African Americans had to submit, were negatives that shaped his thinking and feelings. This negativity produced a general spite and resentment towards white people in him and in the vast majority of African Americans, not to mention the shame and inferiority complex regarding their race.

Elijah Muhammad's fervent accusations toward all white people for the misdeeds of white hegemony have led many to charge him with being a man who taught hatred of Caucasians. Again we reference Mike Wallace's opting to describe Elijah's Muslim community as "The Hate that Hate Produced", a title that clearly indicates that Wallace sensed a degree of innocence in Elijah Muhammad and the Nation of Islam's aversion to white people. Wallace's title explains that if the Nation of Islam is to be classified as a hate group then there needs to be an exposé on the larger group or larger cause that brought about an African American "hate-based" group.

It is important to note that as Elijah's 42 years of leadership over the Nation of Islam evolved, so did his views on race relations. While creating a sub-nation within a nation — the Nation of Islam within the United States of America — Elijah Muhammad was always conscious of the interactions of these two connected, yet ideologically opposed "nations." The changing state of affairs of America and the world always factored into his decision making as he developed and groomed his Nation of Islam.

Still his main objective was to fulfill the mission given to him by Mr. Fard: uplifting the total life of African Americans. No matter how these two "nations" interrelated or how much the political or cultural seasons in America changed, all concerns were secondary to his mission of resurrecting the black man and woman of America. The social and spiritual ills Elijah experienced as a child and young adult reinforced his resolve to relieve African Americans of any remnants of those miserable years.

Regardless of one's take on Mr. Elijah Muhammad, when his life is studied from the perspective of the internationally recognized African American leaders and figures he produced, which no other person including the beloved Rev. Dr. Martin Luther King has been able to replicate, one must agree that Elijah Muhammad is a man who made men. What other leader, of any race, gender, or nationality has produced more world renowned African Americans as Elijah Muhammad? If we review Elijah Muhammad through the "fruit" that he has produced then we will begin to see him as he properly should be seen.

ELIJAH MUHAMMAD
THROUGH THE EYES OF OTHERS

In his book *Our Saviour Has Arrived* Elijah Muhammad stated, "I want to teach you who you are. So many people have been made blind, deaf and dumb to the knowledge of God. Why are they made deaf and dumb to the knowledge of God? Because they are blind, deaf and dumb to the knowledge of self." (27)

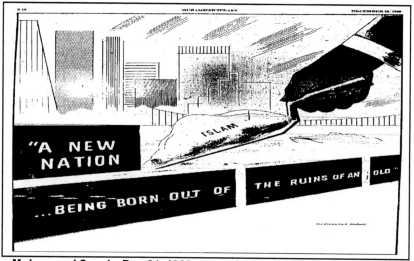

Muhammad Speaks Dec 24, 1969 promoting building "A new nation..."
(Muslim Journal file)

Another important aspect of Elijah Muhammad's Nation of Islam is its ability to distinguish itself from the general society. The charge that Elijah Muhammad's Nation of Islam was a black only separatist group that excluded whites is misleading. There were a few exceptions that allowed a handful of white membership — an issue that we will discuss later in detail.

The full exclusion imposed by the Nation of Islam extended far beyond only excluding membership of white people. The rule was that only indigenous African Americans who were direct descendants of American slaves qualified for membership. And even then often educated African Americans were not readily welcomed in the Nation of Islam because it was believed that their education, therefore their thinking, was a product of white America. Another challenge an educated person presented was a higher probability of their unwillingness to accept, without asking difficult questions, some of the mythological and religious interpretations offered by Elijah and Mr. Fard. In order for Elijah to cultivate the following he wanted he had to ensure that the Nation of Islam, as with any womb, was insulated from as many outside influences as possible.

THE MAN BEHIND THE MEN

The complete name of the Nation of Islam given in 1929 was *The Lost-Found Nation of Islam in the Wilderness of North America*. Elijah Muhammad's arduous task of seeking to reshape the lives of African Americans required him to maintain an autocratic leadership. In his mind he was taking back, or "stealing" back from the white man the stolen, "lost-found" black man and woman of America. Elijah, after hearing the message of Mr. W.D. Fard felt that he had the greater right to black Americans than the white man. So he quietly began to retrieve them under a metaphorical "cover of darkness" as indicated in I Thessalonians 5:2: "...the Lord cometh as a thief in the night."

In Elijah Muhammad's mind if the white man justified stealing Africans for the purpose of chattel slavery then surely Elijah was justified to reclaim the descendants of those slaves even if it meant stealing them as a thief working under the cover of darkness. In order to effectively remove the "slave mind" from his converts Elijah Muhammad's autocratic rule firmly restricted outsiders from the inner operations of the Nation of Islam. That is another reason why new members were sought from poorer African American neighborhoods while more affluent African Americans were shunned.

This closed-door policy of the Nation of Islam added to the aura of mystique surrounding the leadership of Elijah Muhammad, but also served two additional roles, one that was detrimental and the other beneficial. While the Nation of Islam was able to isolate itself from the influences of other social and religious organizations, this led to a negative outcome in that it gave efforts such as the FBI's COINTELPRO operations leverage to use against Elijah Muhammad to further alienate him from other civil rights groups. On the other hand the air of secrecy that was produced by this closed-door environment gave the Nation of Islam a distinction of self-governance — a quality that was marketed as a sign of Elijah's independence from the "white man." An image that also gave a new sense of self-reliance that proudly resonated with Nation of Islam members as well as outside admirers of the Nation of Islam.

The negative image increased when the public by-and-large accepted the perception that Elijah's leadership as the "Messenger of Allah" was mystical or distant — a perception that was punctuated with charges of hatred, murder, and avarice. This combination made Elijah an easy target for government officials to portray as unfit to be followed. Sadly, this distorted image of Elijah Muhammad lingers until this day.

Not to be deterred, Elijah made good use of both features; the mystical appeal that gave him a special divine distinction as the "Messenger of Allah," as well as the feature of having sole responsibility for shaping his Nation of Islam. He used both aspects to his advantage, as needed, as long as these perceived images did not deter the growth of the Nation of Islam.

ELIJAH MUHAMMAD
THROUGH THE EYES OF OTHERS

An April 22, 1968 FBI report from the Chicago SAC acknowledged that their COINTELPRO efforts to deny and defame Elijah Muhammad may have in fact worked in his favor.

> For years, Chicago has operated a counterintelligence program against the NOI and MUHAMMAD, along these lines; however, despite these efforts, he continues unchallenged in the leadership of the NOI and the organization itself, in terms of membership and finances has been unaffected. The possibility exists in fact that allegations along these lines, from whatever source, may well serve to enhance the status of these individuals among their peers.

In an effort to understand the mystique and intrigue associated with Elijah Muhammad, *The Man Behind the Men* will observe "the fruit of his tree." The fruit, in addition to carrying the DNA blueprint of its progenitor, it also does not fall far from its tree. Each of these four men, Wallace, Louis, Malcolm, and Muhammad Ali, though unique in their own special way, inherited from Elijah common links.

One dominant trait of Elijah Muhammad that is inherent in the men and women to whom he gave life and purpose is his courage to challenge injustices. Elijah Muhammad was a bold man who dared his following to think differently and to think big, as he worked to establish a community life for African Americans independent of Caucasian domination and obliging to the United States of America. In time this Islamic community produced shining examples of black manhood and womanhood that the world never before had witnessed in African Americans; a historical and classical phenomenon.

An in-depth study is seriously needed to understand which components Elijah Muhammad, the little uneducated man from the dust of the Deep South, used to produce these individuals, some who earned international stature, recognition and praise.

The works of Elijah Muhammad connected with the innate yearnings in the souls of the descendants of African American slaves who desired an independent identity as far removed as possible from the identity of the former slave masters. Elijah Muhammad did not fail them. He gave them a new diet, holidays, family names, and a sense of self-determining nationhood. And above all, he gave them a new way to worship.

The four men highlighted in this book rose to be the cream of Elijah's crop. Each of them uniquely represents prime examples of the aims and purposes of the mission of the Honorable Elijah Muhammad. Their individual accomplishments are noteworthy in and of themselves; yet, if not for Elijah Muhammad, history would not have been able to record them amongst the world's international personalities. Through his many followers the influence of Elijah Muhammad went far beyond the Nation of Islam into the fields of business, culture, religion, academics, sports, and many other fields of human endeavor.

Hopefully future observations can be made on Mr. Muhammad's influence upon other notable men such as his youngest son Akbar, a noted Islamic scholar; football great, Jim Brown; civil rights leader, Jesse Jackson; *The Godfather of Soul*, James Brown; and others. It is only fair and proper to present to the world a fuller and healthier picture of Elijah Muhammad, who thus far has been neglected and overlooked.

Jesse Jackson purchasing an issue of *Muhammad Speaks* from Muslim salesman. *(Muslim Journal file)*

Rev. Jackson at the 1975 Saviour's Day Convention, one day after the passing of Elijah Muhammad shared the following:

ELIJAH MUHAMMAD
THROUGH THE EYES OF OTHERS

> I, as have many of you, sat at the feet of the Honorable Elijah Muhammad and shared and was taught. I will share with you in a measure some of the lessons that he taught me that I hope will stay in your heart forever... I am here to say today that his leadership extended far beyond the membership of the Nation of Islam. For more than three decades this prophet has been the spiritual leader and a progressive force of Black identity and consciousness, self-determination and economic development. He was the father of Black self-consciousness. During our "Colored" and "Negro" days he was Black.

The number of notable African Americans who privately praised Elijah Muhammad during and after his lifetime numbers well into the thousands. However, due to his strong racial commentaries many of these same men and women would never praise Elijah Muhammad in public.

Mr. Muhammad's position on race, as taught to him by Mr. W.D. Fard, went beyond mischaracterizing all white people as devils by nature, Fard also taught that the black man was the "God of the universe." These views are racially and theologically un-Islamic in the greater Muslim world; however, they were an essential part of Elijah Muhammad's message that profoundly affected the lives of the four men discussed in this book.

Until his death Elijah Muhammad promoted to African Americans a supernatural image of the "Blackman of America," which had a definite and immediate influence upon the thinking of all his followers and the thinking of the African American community as a whole.

It is ironic and seemingly contradictory that Elijah Muhammad actually respected the white man as a dignified race. At the Armory Arena in Chicago on February 26, 1974 Elijah addressed thousands of his followers at his final Saviour's Day address. During this convention Elijah Muhammad openly praised the good qualities of Caucasians and ordered his followers to respect them. To add emphasis to his message of respect for white people, Elijah had two white Muslims from Turkey, whom he referred to as scientists, on stage with him. Not only was Elijah telling the world that his perceptions of white people had been altered over the years, more importantly he also wanted his followers to change their attitudes towards Caucasians.

> We are very happy. We have with us two or three great scientists over to my right here. They are great scientists visiting us. If we had been here worshiping the space, the atmosphere, for God, they would not have taken a seat over there. So we are happy and honored to have these great scientists sitting over here to our right. We are happy to be honored by them. We are glad that they are visiting us to know that sun, the Spiritual sun, is vice-versing itself, rising from the West!

THE MAN BEHIND THE MEN

Several times during his 90 minute long discourse Elijah gave thanks to Caucasians, explaining why his followers should follow suit. This tremendous reevaluation of white Americans by Elijah Muhammad actually was the construction of a bridge, before his passing, to help his followers cross a racial divide that he himself had previously been instrumental in widening.

> We want to thank the Chicago white people for making it possible for us to obtain the Country Club. For making it possible for us to get in such position where we can prove ourselves worthy of position.
> We thank them. They have did us a great favor. I don't think that we have nothing to do but to honor and thank them for putting us in such position. This is their house and we are here teaching the truth. They are not objecting to you teaching the truth. As we have white Muslims in America. And lots of them. We have them all over the world. And they recognize and respect you. You must recognize and respect them.
> You don't disrespect people that is trying to respect you. I remember the last time that I was out to the airport. They let me and my followers get on first. Now remember that their flag is still flying over America. Honor and respect the man. Because he still has his flag.
> God give way to them to rule. Then you're honoring their ruler. As long as they are in power to rule, then respect them. This I mean from my heart. Every where we go, respect people and people will respect you. Don't think that you are so great now just because God promised you the Kingdom. Wait until you get in it.
> I say to you, my beloved brothers and sisters, give justice to where it belongs. And don't try and rob people out of justice. If the White man, and he has, freed you and me to go to work for self... and you go all around the earth, he don't object...you can go wherever you want to, and he's not to blame today. You are the one to be blamed. This is a very sly and distraught way that we have of dumping the burden on someone else.

Imam Khalid S. Lateef of the *Americans for Justice and Positive Change* joined the Nation of Islam in 1966 in Brooklyn, NY. He believed it important that Elijah Muhammad's February 26, 1974 Saviour's Day address be transcribed for new and younger Muslims so they too could become familiar with the entire written text of Elijah Muhammad's last major public address. Imam Lateef introduced this transcript that he titled, "Look at "Self" Before Charging Others..." by noting that Elijah Muhammad spoke to his membership in unequivocal terms, telling them to respect the "White man." Imam Lateef wrote:

ELIJAH MUHAMMAD
THROUGH THE EYES OF OTHERS

The Honorable Elijah Muhammad made strong statements about the evil done by the "White Man." He was uncompromising in his attacks on their moral life and their behavior towards the "Black Man." However, there are two occasions where his comments about European-Americans seemed different from his usual theme: The first time was on the death of President John F. Kennedy, when he said, "We, with the world, are very shocked at the assassination of our President." (*Muhammad Speaks*, December 20, 1963 issue, page 3) *[sic]* and the second time was in his Last Sermon. His comments in his last sermon about the "White Man" were so different from the theme he spoke over the years that many of those who claim to represent him and his teachings have discouraged the distribution of this — the Honorable Elijah Muhammad's Last Sermon.

In his Last Sermon, Elijah Muhammad clearly instructed his followers to respect all good people, regardless of color or race, and he ordered his followers to stop blaming the "white man" for actions that they controlled. He directed African Americans to look to their own behavior as the cause of their lack of progress.

Even author Karl Evanzz, with his heavy-handed anti-Elijah stances, begrudgingly noted the changes in the later theology of Elijah Muhammad. Evanzz's biography on Elijah Muhammad includes watershed quotes from the Muslim leader. "The white man and the black man must learn to live together and to respect each other if America is to survive" (Evanzz 420). This same biography acknowledges that in 1974 Elijah told the editor of *Muhammad Speaks*, "Let's not talk no more about any blue-eyed devil" (Evanzz 421).

The last year of Elijah Muhammad's life is replete with statements suggesting a change in his attitude towards white people. In his book *Our Saviour has Arrived*, released in 1974, Elijah spoke of the righteousness of white Muslims. On page 83 he wrote, "...there are a lot of white believers in Islam. I have met many of them and they are sincere in their faith."

The waning years of Elijah Muhammad's mission seemed to focus on preparing his community for a racial shift from a total rejection of white people towards grounds of commonality. Elijah noted in *Our Saviour has Arrived* that there would be white Muslims in America. "There will be quite a few thousand in America. When the time comes you will learn of them, but you will not learn of them at the present time."

White Muslims were not new to Elijah Muhammad. Later we will discuss the few reports of non-African American members who were members of the Nation of Islam during both Fard's and Elijah Muhammad's tenure.

Elijah Muhammad's recognition of white Muslims fell short of acknowledging an integrated hereafter, but the fact that he openly recognized that white people can be sincere righteous Muslims represents a major shift in his public teachings. He further states on page 89 in *Our Saviour has Arrived*:

> There are white people in Europe who believe in Islam. They are Muslim by faith and not by nature. They believe in righteousness and have tried, and are still trying, to practice the life of a righteous Muslim. Because of their faith in Islam, Allah (God) Blesses them and they will see the Hereafter.
> There are quite a few white people in America who are Muslim by faith. Good done by any person is rewarded and these white people who believe in Islam will receive the Blessing of entering into the Hereafter.
> The white people who believe in Islam will not enter the Hereafter that is Promised to the Lost-Found Black People.
> The Lost-Found People will take on a new birth.

Before accusing Elijah Muhammad of promoting a separatist hereafter merely on skin color, caution should be taken. The two racially distinctive hereafters described by Elijah Muhammad in *Our Saviour has Arrived* is also discussed in *Message to the Blackman* that describes the hereafter as the entering into a life of "seeing and living under a ruler and a government of righteousness, after the destruction of unrighteousness."

In Elijah's mind the hereafter is an earth-bound spiritual state of righteousness that is obtainable by all races. But due to the centuries of disabling slavery and oppression that African Americans endured, he believed that a special work of rebirthing the black man was required to ready them to earn their "hereafter." Therefore, the black man's hereafter had to be different, or separate for no other races had been reduced to the mental, moral and spiritual state of African Americans.

Elijah Muhammad's concept of the hereafter as described in *Message to the Blackman* states.

> "After what?" may be the question asked. The hereafter means after the destruction of the present world, its power and authority to rule...I never felt the like before. Islam is heaven for my people. They will see their God in truth, the righteous will meet and embrace them with peace...Read the Scriptures carefully on the life in the hereafter, and try to understand it; you will find that it doesn't actually mean what you have been believing. No one is going to leave this planet to live on another. You can't, even if you try. You can't reach the moon and live on it, so be satisfied and believe in Allah, live where you are on this good earth, but be righteous. (303-304)

ELIJAH MUHAMMAD THROUGH THE EYES OF OTHERS

There are other numerous aspects of the life of Elijah Muhammad that remain unclear in the minds of many people, including questions about his extra-marital affairs that later became know as "marriages." Other individuals constantly raise the sensitive issue regarding the assassination of Malcolm X. We pray that this book adds intelligent commentary to these issues without seeking to justify, nor condemn anyone. However, to not mention controversial events such as Malcolm's death would be unforgivable.

The shrouds over Elijah Muhammad must be lifted. This book is one step towards that unveiling. This author believes that looking at Mr. Elijah Muhammad through the four men from Elijah's Nation of Islam, who achieved international status, may allow the world to get a true and clearer understanding of T*he Honorable Elijah Muhammad: The Man Behind the Men.*

-§- CHAPTER -§-
FOUR

Mr. Elijah Muhammad

October 7, 1897 - February 25, 1975
Leader of the Nation of Islam from 1933 - 1975

"My mission is to give life to the dead. What I teach brings them out of death and into life. My mission, as the Messenger, is to bring the truth to the world before the world is destroyed...I do not say that I will live so long as that, but when God comes, if it pleases Him, I may be with Him. However, if I am not with Him, this is the final. This truth I bring will give you the knowledge of yourself and of God."

— Elijah Muhammad
Message to the Blackman p. 306

Elijah Muhammad was born in a little town named Deepstep, GA, near Sandersville, in Washington County. No actual birth date was recorded for Elijah Poole but he believed his birthday was October 7, 1897. It is reported in *100 Answers to the Most Uncommon 100 Questions* that Elijah said, "I do not know exactly my birthday. I just know the month it came in (October). So when October passes, I say I am so and so old" (29).

At the beginning of the 20th century the backbone of the economy of southern states was sharecropping. This financial system obliged landowners, legislators, and southern mores to place a greater interest in

MR. ELIJAH MUHAMMAD

working young Colored boys and girls — and oft-times poor whites — in the farm fields, over providing them with a good education. Most likely young Elijah's segregated all black school held classes only for the four-to six-month period between the autumn harvest and the planting season of the following spring.

Working the soil alongside their parents began at an early age for many poor black and white youth. The preference for work over schooling rendered a southern rural education at the turn of the century inadequate and substandard for all farming families, especially for African Americans. This is the kind of inferior educational setting that Elijah Muhammad experienced; which for him only lasted until the third grade — the pinnacle of his schooling. Historian, Tom Hanchett noted the inadequacy of a southern education in the early 1900s in his book *Saving the South's Rosenwald Schools*.

> The problem was the sorry state of African American education in the South after 1900. Since slavery times, when most states had flatly forbidden teaching slaves to read, black Americans had hungered for learning. They flocked to academies set up by missionaries after the Civil War, and poured into public schools in the late nineteenth century, often attending in larger numbers than their white counterparts. The separate schools for blacks were never equal, but things got worse after 1900. That was when Southern states stripped blacks of the right to vote – Disfranchisement it was called.

Even though African American students made up 45-percent of all Georgia's students, African American schools only received one-fifth of the resources as the white schools, thus making the Georgia public school system that Elijah Poole attended probably providing some of the nations lowest levels of quality education. The three-to four-year period in which young Elijah would have attained his third grade education most likely occurred circa 1902-1906. It is important to note that according to Hanchett, in 1915 the nationwide average spent on education in the United States was $30 per child while Georgia spent only $1.67 per black child.

In 2005 Doctor Susan Williams McElroy and doctoral student Kruti Dholakia, both from The University of Texas at Dallas, prepared the *Between Plessy and Brown: Georgia School Finance in 1910* report. McElroy and Dholakia cited Dr. John Dittmer's, professor emeritus of History at DePauw University in Greencastle, IN, account of the disparity of educational resources of black schools compared with that of white schools:

> ...during the "Progressive" period, roughly from 1900 to 1920, less than 10% of the [sic] Georgia's total state budget for school buildings, equipment, libraries and maintenance was allocated to

the black schools, even though nearly half the state's population was black at the time... In 1910 the counties of Georgia spent a combined $2,212,276.40 on white schools and a combined $346,427.53 on black schools, (for each enrolled white child) Georgia counties spent $7.79 per enrolled white child as compared with $1.67 per enrolled black child, for a black-white ratio of 0.21. In other words, Georgia counties spent nearly 5 times as much per white student as they spent per black student.

The evils of Jim Crow enjoyed by many southern whites including the regular lynching of African Americans, compounded by the lack of sufficient education and employment, soon soured Elijah Poole's hopes of making a life for himself and his family in Georgia. As a young man he married Clara Evans, and the young couple joined the mass African American migration to northern cities. In April of 1923 Elijah and Clara settled in Detroit, MI to establish their family life.

Elijah Muhammad's wife, Clara *(Photographer and Date Unknown)*

MR. ELIJAH MUHAMMAD

To Elijah Poole's dismay racism also existed in the northern states. After years of working various jobs in the Detroit area, the Depression of 1930 further interrupted the lives of the Poole family. While struggling, without much optimism to support his family, Elijah soon turned to alcohol to help him escape his misfortunes and his lost pride. Circumstances did not begin to change for Elijah and his family until 1930 when he met Mr. W.D. Fard, a foreigner claiming to be from Mecca, Arabia.

Mr. Fard, purporting to be a door-to-door purveyor of silk material and housewares, actually was more concerned with selling an idea of religion that he called Islam. Fard's version of Islam was unique to Islam as taught around the Muslim world. The Islam that Fard taught gave racial superiority to the black man over all other races — a concept that has no foundation in Qur'an. Fard's black supremacist ideal of Islam also was the direct opposite of the common thinking of that era in America that promoted white supremacy.

Fard's message had a tremendous impact upon Elijah Muhammad, saving him and his family from a life of despair. Soon Elijah became Fard's number one student and his highest ranking officer in a community called the Temples of Islam, a name later changed to The Lost-Found Nation of Islam in the Wilderness of North America, or simply, the Nation of Islam. Fard gave Elijah Poole a new purpose for living; a new dedication, a new religion, and a new name — Elijah Karriem, later changed to Elijah Muhammad. Fard indeed was a savior for Elijah Muhammad in that Fard saved Elijah Muhammad from a life of hopelessness and rejection. Elijah accepted Mr. Fard as his prophet, a status later elevated to "god, in the Person of Master W. Fard Muhammad." Mr. Fard's version of Islam revived Elijah Muhammad's lost pride and restored his dignity with a new sense of self-worth. Mr. Elijah Muhammad in his book *Message to the Blackman in America* spoke of Fard's advent to the ghettos of North America:

> Allah came to us from the Holy City Mecca, Arabia, in 1930. He used the name Wallace D. Fard, often signing it W.D. Fard, in the third year (1933). He signed his name W.F. Muhammad that stands for Wallace Fard Muhammad. He came alone. He began teaching us the knowledge of ourselves, of God and the devil, of the measurement of the earth, of other planets, and of the civilization of some of the planets other than earth (16).

Fard's immigrant status made him an easy target for the police and other government officials who were dissatisfied with his racially-based teachings. Under pressure from these officials Fard was forced to leave the United States of America. Shortly before "disappearing," Fard left Elijah Muhammad in charge of the Nation of Islam and gave him a list of

104 books to study. The names of the books are unknown. Elijah said, "The Saviour gave me 104 books in the Congressional Library to study on Islam and the history of Muhammad." Elijah Muhammad was a dedicated disciple of Fard. In the estimation of Elijah, Fard's teachings were "Supreme Wisdom", knowledge that was to be studied but never doubted.

The "Lessons" or "Teachings" of the Nation of Islam consisted of small internal publications that the faithful strove to memorize from 8.5 x 11 sheets of paper. These Lessons titled, "The Problem Book", "First Student Enrollment", "Lesson No. 1" and "Lesson No. 2", "English Lesson No. 1", "14 Questions and Answers", "34 Problems", and "The Actual Facts".

For 42 years after the disappearance of Mr. Fard, Elijah Muhammad extracted numerous lessons from the teachings he had received from his teacher that he used in the process of creating a new community. From 1933 until 1975 Elijah Muhammad used the teachings engineered by Fard to prepare social and religious antidotes that could help heal the ailing souls and minds of African American men and women.

This black-oriented, quasi-Islamic community of Elijah Muhammad offered African Americans a total transformation in their food regimen, attire, and religion and gave them a totally new outlook on life. Elijah Muhammad's Nation of Islam overlooked no community need as he began establishing a nationwide independent school system and temples for worship. The Nation of Islam became a model for many other African American organizations such as the Black Panthers and other radical, yet conscious-minded youth organizations of the 1960s. Elijah Muhammad's leadership is the force behind many areas of African American progress. Without doubt, by the late 1950s Elijah Muhammad's leadership was well established and rooted in American history.

Mr. Elijah Muhammad's Nation of Islam was more than a movement for civil rights or just another social agency program set up to help blacks get a share of America. The Nation of Islam was designed to attract dissatisfied African Americans and re-orientate their whole lives so that they would hunger for more than a mere secondhand share of America. The Nation of Islam expanded the appetites and horizons of its members by teaching African Americans that the entire universe belonged to the black man.

The Nation of Islam, striving to prove its value, opened numerous businesses and small factories for manufacturing products. This progressive image of success gave Elijah Muhammad's Nation of Islam a striking edge over all other contemporary African American groups and organizations.

Whether rich, poor, or middle-class, Muslim, Christian or committed to no particular faith system at all, every African American, in some way, has been positively affected by the teachings of the Honorable Elijah Muhammad. In significant ways the teachings of Elijah Muhammad have touched the life of every African American. To this day, sociologists are studying the teachings of Elijah Muhammad for solutions for many of the problems that affect the African American mind and soul.

The question that begs to be answered, notwithstanding his errors, is what in Elijah Muhammad's teachings was so potent that it deeply touched the lives of African Americans in ways that no other leader of any race or ethnicity has been able to reproduce?

The message of Elijah Muhammad was designed to address the specific needs of African Americans. Few, if any, who joined the Nation of Islam had the willpower or desire to question the man who had given them a sense of self and a response to America's open racism of the 20th century. Imam Wallace D. Mohammed agrees:

> He appealed to the dissatisfied people in the African American, or the black public in America. He appealed to the dissatisfied ones, and he attracted those. When they heard his different teachings on God, on the origin of man, the nature of man, the white man as a race; on the black man as a race — they had no problem hearing him (with) both ears and their complete attention, and following him without suspecting.
> He didn't have to transfer his mind to them. They were fastened on him and what he was talking about. They followed him. They followed him, and did not question him. They could not question him. I couldn't question him without his help. I would never be able to question him myself, I don't think.
> I wasn't born in the church. I was born under his teaching in 1933. But I don't think I could have questioned him either if I hadn't been encouraged to think and question what he taught — by him! He encouraged me to do that.
> — Telephone interview December 2002

Elijah Poole began as a poor man in every respect — educationally, financially, mentally, and spiritually. Broken in every possible way, Elijah was unable to lift himself up until encountering the altered version of Islam of W.D. Fard. It was this altered teaching that Elijah Muhammad used to lift the lives of men and women, even to the point of international prominence.

The life-altering effect Elijah Muhammad's leadership had upon his followers and supporters cannot, and should not be dismissed as happenstance, luck, or as an unimportant occurrence. This epoch of the sojourn of the African American soul, under the tutelage of Elijah Muhammad, must be properly studied, understood and given its correct station in world history. His impact upon African Americans and America as a whole is too important to ignore or disregard as merely racism or hatred.

THE MAN BEHIND THE MEN

Immigrant Muslims who appreciated the success of Elijah Muhammad in improving life for African Americans often worked for him while fully realizing that his brand of Islam was not orthodox, in accord with the teachings and traditions of Prophet Muhammed of Arabia. Abdul Basit Naeem, who wrote the introduction to Elijah Muhammad's 1957 book *The Supreme Wisdom*, noted this reality.

> I am, of course, fully aware of the fact that some of the teachings of Mr. Elijah Muhammad, which have been included in this book, would not be acceptable to Moslems in the East without, perhaps, some sort of an explanation by the author or by someone who can interpret them well. The Moslem leader (Elijah Muhammad) himself knows this, and he is perfectly frank about it. As he told me a few months ago, "My brothers in the East were never subjected to conditions of slavery and systematic brainwashing by the slavemasters [sic] for as long a period of time as my people here were subjected. I cannot, therefore, blame them if they differ with me in certain interpretations of the Message of Islam. In fact, I do not even *expect* them to understand some of the things I say unto people here" (4).

Apparently men such as Naeem, the educator Dr. Jamil Diab, and other Muslims from overseas understood the importance of Elijah Muhammad's contributions to the African American community and the eventual importance to the international Islamic community. Naeem, writing in defense of Elijah Muhammad penned, "Despite Mr. Elijah Muhammad's 'blunt techniques' and a few controversial teachings about certain aspects of Islam, I have nothing but the utmost respect for the Moslem leader."

An important aspect of Fard's commission to Elijah Muhammad included bringing African Americans back to their Islamic heritage; accordingly, Naeem felt the same way. "I do indeed appreciate (Elijah's) efforts to bring the black people of America 'back into the fold of Islam,' which, in his opinion, as in mine is the only solution to their basic problems" (The Supreme Wisdom, 5).

Elijah Muhammad demonstrated his ability to ward off the offenses of Muslims from abroad who occasionally challenged his leadership and his black oriented form of Islam. In *Message to the Blackman in America*, Elijah Muhammad responded to an article in the *Chicago American* newspaper that indicated that Orthodox Muslims of Saudi Arabia were questioning what he was teaching. After stating that, "We are the brother of the Muslims not only of Arabia but from all over the entire world, wherever one is found," Elijah Muhammad rebuked the *Chicago American* newspaper and other

MR. ELIJAH MUHAMMAD

"white Americans and their newspapers" and charged them with spreading propaganda. In an effort to hit two birds with one stone Elijah Muhammad challenged the notion of Muslims from the Muslim world coming "to tell me and my followers in America to stop teaching what we are teaching." In his answer to the publication and to the Muslim world Elijah wrote:

> Now this is not an answer to the Muslims of Saudi Arabia, because I do not know the truth of what they have said; this is an answer to the *Chicago American [sic]* newspaper and its correspondents...But in answer to such attempt, I will say that neither Jeddah nor Mecca have sent me! I am sent from Allah and not from the Secretary General of the Muslim League. There is no Muslim in Arabia that has authority to stop me from delivering this message that I have been assigned to by Allah, anymore than they had authority to stop Noah, Abraham, Jesus and Muhammad. I'm not taking orders from them, I am taking orders from Allah (God) Himself. (329)

In the 1960s Abdul Basit Naeem was a regular contributor to *Muhammad Speaks* newspaper writing regularly in defense of Elijah Muhammad and the Nation of Islam doctrines. Naeem often lauded the progress and benefits of the Nation of Islam while strongly criticizing white Americans and "the so-called Negro integrationists and preachers of Christianity." Naeem's writing style and content was very much like any other minister of Elijah's Islamic following.

For thousands of men, the Honorable Elijah Muhammad not only became a father figure; his Nation of Islam also served as an association that brought many of them into manhood. The Fruit of Islam, the Nation of Islam men's group, provided rites of passage into manhood for many otherwise wayward African American men. Elijah Muhammad's Fruit of Islam and its discipline made many disenfranchised men for the first time in their lives feel like complete men.

Shanette M. Harris' *Black Male Masculinity and Same-Sex Friendships*, published in *The Western Journal of Black Studies*, addresses how black men interact and bond as "gang" members as a means to protect one another from racism and other societal defects. The bonding within the ranks of the Nation of Islam's Fruit of Islam was very similar to Harris' conclusions, in that the Fruit of Islam gave nurturing and protection for racially and socially abused African American males, but without resulting in the negative affects that gangs tend to have upon the African American community.

Additionally Harris discusses the way in which African American male masculinity, referred to as black male masculinity, is "learned and expressed" within male same-sex peer relationships. Harris explains:

This form of masculinity protects the self from pain and frustration associated with perceived and actual oppression and stigmatization. As a minority group member, these behaviors provide for affiliation and achievement needs not met by other social institutions, increased feelings of power and mastery, and inspired feelings of optimism and superiority. This lifestyle also serves as a channel for the release of anger and resentment towards the existing social structure.

Harris' description of male enrichment is a process not uncommon in the Fruit of Islam. Referring back to Chris Rock's Willie character, Elijah Muhammad's Fruit of Islam and the overall Nation of Islam teachings, in addition to serving as a collective catharsis for releasing anger and resentment, also brought black men into a fuller sense of manhood. The Nation of Islam's Fruit of Islam was an organization that the "Willies" of America — black men who were full of spite and hatred towards white America — could benefit from.

SPECIAL CALL MEETING of the Muhammad's Mosque No. 7 Fruit of Islam, saw hundreds of the dynamic followers of the Messenger of Allah ready to begin a concerted drive for the establishment of the National Educational Center of the Nation of Islam. The meeting was held in conjunction with a countrywide movement to see to it that the inspiring educational facility is established with deliberate speed.

New York City Fruit of Islam. *(Muslim Journal file)*

Proof that Elijah Muhammad's strategy for alleviating pent up anger from African American males worked has been shown by the fact that job performance of his followers always excelled other African Americans who worked the same job, even under the same white boss. Elijah Muhammad taught his men to hate no one. He taught them to never steal, lie, or cheat their employer out of a full days work. Elijah Muhammad's Fruit of Islam fulfilled what Shanette M. Harris observed: a black male masculinity and same-sex friendship that functioned "as a means to protect one another from racism and other societal defects."

There are other little known but important aspects of Elijah Muhammad which America and the world need to become aware. Despite the images and reports that errantly depict Elijah Muhammad as isolated and marginalized, it is important to stress that he was very much a multifaceted leader. Covering all the bases of community life for his Nation of Islam, he built bridges of relationships in business and education nationally and internationally. Often he quietly gave charity to many African American causes and concerns.

Muhammad Siddeeq, the former Director Clark X of the Nation of Islam's New York City *University of Islam* elementary school, stated that in 1968 the leading educators in the Nation of Islam had been invited to come to Chicago for a national meeting at the home of Elijah Muhammad.

At one of the evening dinners the Nation of Islam educators were joined by a group of civil rights workers led by Julian Bond, who made an appeal to Elijah Muhammad for financial assistance needed to bring a delegation from Atlanta, GA to Chicago for the *1968 Democratic Convention*.

Muhammad Siddeeq said that Elijah Muhammad told Julian Bond, "Well, Brother Bond you know I'm a poor man. I don't have any money." Elijah said, "The only money I have is the money that belongs to my followers. That is not my money; that is their money. So I cannot accommodate you." Then Siddeeq shared that Elijah Muhammad said, "But we have a representative group of them here now. If you would like for them to vote on that and make a decision, render you a decision, (then) I'm willing."

Siddeeq recalled Julian Bond's response, "Yes Sir, Mr. Muhammad! If they could do that I would appreciate it." Elijah Muhammad replied, "Well, it would be right for each one of them individually to express their opinion whether they want to support you or not."

Despite the common perception that Elijah Muhammad is often thought of or depicted as an autocratic ruler, on this occasion he demonstrated the Islamic democratic practice of group consultation, called *shurah* in Arabic. The Qur'an says in chapter 3; verse 159: "... and consult them in affairs (of moment). Then, when thou hast taken a decision put thy trust in Allah. For Allah loves those who put their trust (in Him)."

Elijah Muhammad went around the entire table stopping at each individual for their comment and whether they supported Julian Bond's request. Siddeeq and the majority of the educators gave their approval for supporting the request for financial assistance, a figure of $50,000 or more. Siddeeq recalled that after the educators from the Nation of Islam had voted Elijah Muhammad and Julian Bond had the following conversation:

> The Honorable Elijah Muhammad said, "All right, it appears that the overwhelming majority of my followers have supported that. So they choose to give you some money. So Mr. Bond, that is fine." Then he (Elijah Muhammad) went on talking to him and he said, "Now, I know you don't want a check from Elijah Muhammad?" Julian Bond said, "Well Mr. Muhammad I'll take a check from you if you want to give me a check." The Honorable Elijah Muhammad said, "No, that's okay. You come back in the morning around 10:00; you be here at 10:00 and I'll give you cash." Julian Bond said, "Oh thank you Mr. Muhammad. Thank you so very much." And he said, "No, that's okay. Thank my followers."

There are other accounts of Elijah Muhammad's charity going to others outside of the Nation of Islam, including him giving money to post bond for many who were jailed during the many civil rights movement demonstrations.

When Elijah Muhammad died on February 25, 1975, the world paused. Condolences from around the world flowed in from leaders and politicians for the man who, in his own right, had earned international recognition by evolving his community from being a "baby nation" up to the threshold of universal Islam.

Malcolm often described the Honorable Elijah Muhammad as "a man like Moses." As Moses had split the Red Sea for the Israelites as reported in the Book of Exodus, Nation of Islam members believed Elijah was splitting the sea of racism and despair to forge a way for his people to cross over to safety. But as with Moses, Elijah only could lead his people to, but not into the *Promised Land*. Elijah reached his modern-day *Mt. Pisgah*, a rugged elevation from which he saw into a "Promised Land" that his community was destined to enter, but one which he would not personally enter.

Elijah Muhammad understood the extent as well as the limitations of his purpose on earth. In an effort to prepare his followers for the completion and the termination of his mission and leadership he often would say, "My mission goes to my grave with me." This message not only meant that when he died his mission would be completed, it also meant that Elijah's role — as with Moses — was purposefully designed only to take his community to the threshold of the "Promised Land."

Over 7,000 people attended the Honorable Elijah Muhammad's funeral, creating a funeral procession over 500 cars in length. One day after Elijah Muhammad passed, Chicago's Mayor Richard Daley, Sr. proclaimed February 26th "Nation of Islam Day," a recognition that serves as another testimony of Elijah Muhammad's influence on not just black America, but on America as a whole.

MR. ELIJAH MUHAMMAD

During his lifetime Elijah Muhammad was the guest of Mecca where he made *umrah* — the lesser hajj. He also was welcomed in Egypt; Istanbul, Turkey; Damascus, Jordan and Beirut as well as Karachi, Pakistan and Mexico. Upon his passing condolences poured in from all over the world. Within the African American community condolences came from leaders such as the Rev. Jesse L. Jackson, Julian Bond, Vernon E. Jordan, Rev. Leon Sullivan, and Dr. C. Eric Lincoln. We will revisit these condolences in later Chapters.

This is the Elijah Muhammad that we will study and observe through the words and lives of four of his protégés: Imam W. Deen Mohammed (also called Wallace or Warith), Minister Louis Farrakhan, Minister Malcolm X (El-Hajj Malik El-Shabazz) and boxing great Muhammad Ali. No one can present a fuller picture of the positive contributions of Elijah Muhammad better than these four men whom he groomed - men who went on to achieve worldwide recognition, respect, and their individual places in history.

The numerous writers who have spent years chronicling and interpreting Mr. Muhammad's life, often highlighting his errors and shortcomings while downplaying his successes and strong points, still can't explain why he remains the only person in history who reshaped the lives of the descendants of African American slaves to the point of creating a new group of people on earth.

Even with the theological errors of Elijah Muhammad as he struggled with religion as taught to him by Mr. W.D. Fard, many Muslims today still are deeply grateful for his leadership as they continue to pray that God forgive him his sins and grant him the paradise. Regardless of the strong racial overtones heard in his message, Elijah Muhammad's overriding message was an orchestrated effort to address the social, spiritual, and mental ills of poorer African Americans who were seeking "freedom, justice and equality" from a fair and just God.

When looking at the results of Elijah's works, in conjunction with his claims to be the divinely appointed *Messenger of Allah*, varying opinions are drawn as to the legitimacy of such a declaration. To place too much concern on Elijah Muhammad's claim to be the divinely appointed *Messenger of Allah* may taint our ability to properly recognize his successes and see him in the best light. Nonetheless, no one can argue against Elijah Muhammad's success in bringing thousands of African Americans away from lives of hopelessness and despair to become productive and upright citizens. Regardless of whether individuals in society perceive Elijah Muhammad to be a divinely sent messenger or only as a social reformer — even if they opt to disregard him as no more than a racist — still his legacy as a strong African American leader remains intact.

This book will not focus much on Mr. W.D. Fard, the teacher of Elijah Muhammad even though Fard was a major factor in his life. Fard is not highlighted because he was not personally with Elijah Muhammad after

THE MAN BEHIND THE MEN

1933 as Elijah navigated the Nation of Islam through America's stages of maturation for more than 40 years. Hopefully in the near future a book will be written that focuses on the work and achievements of Mr. W.D. Fard, a.k.a. Professor Fard, a man who is known by a plethora of other aliases.

Our focus will be on Elijah Muhammad, a study of the four decade-plus tenure of his leadership of the Nation of Islam. This book will bear witness to a leader who was evolving and shifting his emphasis, even away from calling white people the devil as taught to him by Mr. W.D. Fard. But one unwavering emphasis of Elijah Muhammad was his attentiveness to the issues and concerns that best helped his community achieve independence and greater respect and freedom as a race of people.

Yes, Mr. Elijah Muhammad did receive the vast majority of his teachings from Mr. Fard. But when it came to preparing and grooming these four men for the international scene, Elijah Muhammad was working from his own efforts and understanding. From observing and exploring the lives of these four men, we will garner insights into aspects of Mr. Muhammad's life that have helped to put the premise of this book — *The Honorable Elijah Muhammad: The Man Behind the Men* — into perspective.

As we study the life of Elijah Muhammad through the eyes and words of four of his top students we will also include chapters that discuss aspects of Elijah Muhammad's concepts and teachings.

Elijah Muhammad was not behind these men in the sense of being their follower, but as their leader. First we'll observe what Malcolm X Shabazz has said of his former leader, followed by three-time Heavyweight Boxing Champion Muhammad Ali and how he viewed Elijah Muhammad. We'll observe Minister Louis Farrakhan and how he connected his life with Elijah Muhammad. The last of his four students observed in this book is his son Imam W. Deen Mohammed.

Mr. Elijah Muhammad and his Nation of Islam is the common thread that distinguishes these four stars from other men of the world. It was Elijah Muhammad's Nation of Islam that gave birth — and rebirth — to their minds and souls, and in variant ways and at divergent times dispatched them to serve as ambassadors to the international family of man. Therefore we argue that Mr. Elijah Muhammad, with his strategies and objectives that go far beyond his racially-charged language, deserves to be seriously studied by theologians and sociologists.

Allah, the Creator of the heavens and the earth, must have blessed the good intentions of Elijah Muhammad. Our presentation of these four successful and independent thinking, world renowned African Americans is our proof of Elijah being blessed by God. Otherwise, Mr. Elijah Muhammad could not stand, as this book proclaims as, "*The Man Behind the Men.*"

-§- CHAPTER -§-
FIVE

El-Hajj Malik El-Shabazz
(A.K.A. Minister Malcolm X)
May 19, 1925 – February 21, 1965

Malcolm X, later known as El-Hajj Malik El-Shabazz rose up to become the number-one spokesman for the Nation of Islam.
(Photograph Courtesy of Omar Farooq)

THE MAN BEHIND THE MEN

The Honorable Elijah Muhammad & Malcolm At Podium
(Photographer and Date Unknown)

"I believe that no man in the Nation of Islam could have gained the international prominence I gained with the wings Mr. Muhammad had put on me – plus having the freedom that he granted me to take liberties and do things on my own – and still have remained as faithful and as selfless a servant to him as I was."

— Malcolm X
(The Autobiography of Malcolm X, page 298)

This section highlights key interactions between Elijah Muhammad and Malcolm X that show the positive affects Elijah had upon Malcolm. Also their difficulties and some of the results are addressed as we seek to show the influence that the senior Elijah had on Malcolm. The full Islamic name for Malcolm X is El-Hajj Malik El-Shabazz. *"El-Hajj" is a titled earned after one has completed the pilgrimage to Mecca.*

Malcolm was born on May 19, 1925, in Omaha, Nebraska, the seventh child of Earl and Louise Little, both of whom were workers in Marcus Garvey's *Universal Negro Improvement Association (UNIA)*. Malcolm's relationship with his parents was painfully etched into his mind by the sacrifices his father made to preserve their family's dignity and the efforts of his mother to keep the family intact. His parents' sacrifices resulted in the unsolved murder of his father when Malcolm was six years old, and the subsequent harassment of his mother by state welfare officials until she suffered a nervous breakdown from worrying about feeding eight hungry mouths. When Malcolm was 12 years old his mother was institutionalized at the State Mental Hospital at Kalamazoo in Michigan. With the final anchor of the Little family removed, Malcolm and his siblings were scattered into detention and foster homes around Lansing, MI which resulted in Malcolm first living in the home of the Swerlins and later the home of the Lyons.

In February of 1946, after a brief life of crime and drugs in Boston, MA and New York City, Malcolm at the age of 20 found himself at the Massachusetts State Prison in Charleston serving an 8-10 year sentence for grand larceny, burglary, and breaking and entering — ironically six months before Elijah Muhammad was released from the Federal Correction Institute in Milan, MI. Two years into his sentence Malcolm's family members introduced him to the message of Elijah Muhammad. This introduction was the beginning of one of many transformations that occurred throughout the life of Malcolm Little.

Malcolm Little, police booking photo, before meeting the teachings of Mr. Muhammad

The Autobiography of Malcolm X: As Told to Alex Haley speaks of the tremendous influence Elijah Muhammad had on Malcolm's life. After prison the personal one-on-one tutelage he received from Elijah Muhammad provided Malcolm with vital leadership skills that helped to eventually raise him to national prominence. At the climax of Malcolm's tenure in the Nation, of Islam he was lifted to the coveted position of National Spokesman for the Honorable Elijah Muhammad, which included international travels and recognition as he journeyed to Africa and the Middle East on behalf of Elijah Muhammad and the Nation of Islam.

The first direct encounter between Malcolm and Elijah Muhammad occurred via mail during Malcolm's incarceration. After gathering enough courage, Malcolm, from his prison cell, wrote Elijah Muhammad a one-page letter. Malcolm's autobiography states, "At least twenty-five times I must have written that first one-page letter to him, over and over. I was trying to make it both legible and understandable."

THE MAN BEHIND THE MEN

Malcolm's letter to Elijah Muhammad required a concentration of sincerity and confidence. To begin with, he had to overcome his embarrassment about his penmanship and his limited knowledge of the English language. "I practically couldn't read my handwriting myself; it shames even to remember it. My spelling and my grammar were as bad, if not worse. Anyway, as well as I could express it, I said I had been told about him by my brothers and sisters, and I apologized for my poor letter." (172)

In most reports on Malcolm's prison life he is praised for having read the entire dictionary, writing each word and learning its definition. However, Malcolm's recognition of his insufficient grammar and spelling, and his apology to Elijah Muhammad for his poor writing skills strongly suggest that he had not begun his insatiable study of the entire dictionary until after he became acquainted with the teachings of Elijah Muhammad.

What Malcolm probably did not realize was that the earnestness and willingness he displayed in meeting the challenge of writing this letter demonstrated the type of individuals that Elijah Muhammad was looking for; disadvantaged Negroes who were sincere, but dissatisfied to the point of wanting serious changes in the condition of their life.

Elijah Muhammad's response affected Malcolm tremendously. "Mr. Muhammad sent me a typed reply. It had an all but electrical effect upon me to see the signature of the 'Messenger of Allah.' " Malcolm's humble submission of his scribbling versus Elijah Muhammad's typed reply captures a descriptive picture that shows the gaping distance between the refinements of the two men. Within a few years Elijah poured himself into the unpolished Malcolm as he had done for hundreds of other disadvantaged African Americans; reforming and reshaping Malcolm from a mere convict into a dignified, upright human being.

Additionally Elijah Muhammad impressed Malcolm with an interpretation of why he and other black men suffered imprisonment. Malcolm related in his autobiography on page 172, "The black prisoner, he said, symbolized white society's crime of keeping black men oppressed and deprived and ignorant, and unable to get decent jobs, turning them into criminals." Elijah Muhammad's explanation gave Malcolm and other African American inmates an excuse or rationale that allowed them to transfer the guilt for their crimes away from themselves and place the onus for their incarceration upon white America. Even more, Elijah's explaining away Malcolm's need to feel fully accountable for his life of crime, helped to reinforce the foundation and the bonding between Malcolm and Elijah.

In the book *Elijah Muhammad Meets the Press* Elijah offers a degree of forgiveness for African Americans while ladening blame upon the white slavemasters.

They were made unrighteous by the slave-masters. They are not even charged with it. You are forgiven everything of evil, on your accepting Islam-your Own. That is all God Asks you to do today, go back to your Own. You are forgiven for everything, because all the evil you did in the past, it was not you, it was the slave-master who made you do evil. (18-19)

This fledging relationship between Malcolm and Elijah was not only the starting point of a transformation of Malcolm Little from the hustler and criminal known as "Detroit Red" into Minister Malcolm X; in time this relationship led to Malcolm becoming a shining, and often envied, star within the Nation of Islam. The exchange of letters between Malcolm and Elijah was the nascency of Elijah Muhammad being the man behind Malcolm's development into a man of international renown.

Malcolm X Shabazz sitting on a rostrum with Mr. Elijah Muhammad and his daughter Lottie. *(Photographer and Date Unknown)*

From 1930 until 1933 Mr. W.D. Fard provided Elijah Muhammad with the basic tools necessary to reconstruct the lives of his followers. As the years progressed Elijah Muhammad precisely honed his dexterity with and application of those tools as he repeatedly reshaped the lives of thousands of men and women who had given their lives to the Nation of Islam. As the Nation of Islam grew and advanced Elijah Muhammad's work upon his immediate following also heavily impacted the thinking of millions of African Americans who were not members of the Nation of Islam. Malcolm

THE MAN BEHIND THE MEN

X Little is among these men and women who willingly were retooled directly by Elijah Muhammad; the same tools that Malcolm also applied on men such as Muhammad Ali and Louis Farrakhan.

Malcolm's autobiography states that the teachings of Elijah Muhammad transformed him into a new person, freeing his mind and spirit from the shame of a life of crime and bringing him to a life of submission — a submission that persuaded Malcolm to read and study. Malcolm wrote, "Mr. Muhammad, to whom I was writing daily, had no idea of what a new world had opened up to me through my efforts to document his teachings in books." (182)

Malcolm's and Elijah's relationship was mutually beneficial. Elijah gained by Malcolm being a devout student articulating the Nation of Islam's message better than any of Elijah Muhammad's ministers. In exchange Elijah — by intent or coincidence — offered Malcolm an open platform that before was unknown to him; a stage for Malcolm to present himself to America and to the world.

Elijah Muhammad's message together with Malcolm's oratory skills created an energizing and exciting force that captured the attention of the media, the surveillance of government agencies and the respect and curiosity — whether secretly or publicly — of many African Americans.

Malcolm X worked tirelessly as a minister for Elijah Muhammad. The number of registered mosques in the Nation of Islam grew exponentially with Malcolm's activities in and outside of the mosques. Elijah Muhammad's son Wallace and Malcolm often worked and studied together. Imam Wallace Mohammed in his book *The Champion We Have In Common: The Dynamic African American Soul*, wrote:

> Malcolm was not a workaholic but he was a man energetic and an organization man who stayed on top of all important details. He would not leave chance completely to others. He would travel to a temple and see about the situation there himself. He (Malcolm) would insist that the Minister accept that he give him some help, if he thought help was needed. If the Minister refused him, he would immediately go to the Honorable Elijah Muhammad and tell what the situation was there and get the Honorable Elijah Muhammad to give him the authority to go back there. Malcolm was a troubleshooter and a great producer for the Nation of Islam. (47)

Shortly after Wallace became the leader of the Nation of Islam, many of the community's mosques, which heretofore were identified numerically, were renamed after the men and women who had sacrificed and labored in the Nation of Islam under Elijah Muhammad. The new leader Imam

Mohammed renamed Mosque No. 7 in New York City, Masjid (Mosque) Malcolm Shabazz in recognition of Malcolm's contributions to the growth of Islam in New York City.

Malcolm devoted 12 years of his life in service to Elijah Muhammad, a devotion that developed into a form of reverence, as was common for the majority of Elijah Muhammad's followers whose once dismal lives had been vastly improved after joining the Nation of Islam. According to his autobiography, in the later years of his life Malcolm described the reverence and loyalty he once held for his former leader and teacher:

> I believed so strongly in Mr. Muhammad that I would have hurled myself between him and an assassin. A chance event brought crashing home to me that there was something — one thing — greater than my reverence for Mr. Muhammad. It was the awesomeness of my reason to revere him.
> I was the invited speaker at the Harvard Law School Forum. I happened to glance through a window. Abruptly, I realized that I was looking in the direction of the apartment house that was my old burglary gang's hideout.
> It rocked me like a tidal wave. Scenes from my once depraved life lashed through my mind. *Living* like an animal; *thinking* like an animal!
> Awareness came surging upon me — how deeply the religion of Islam had reached down into the mud to lift me up, to save me from being what I inevitably would have been; a dead criminal in a grave, or, if still alive, a flint-hard, bitter, thirty-seven-year-old convict in some penitentiary, or insane asylum. Or, at best, I would have been an old, fading Detroit Red, hustling, stealing enough for food and narcotics, and myself being stalked by cruelly ambitious younger hustlers such as Detroit Red had been.
> But Allah had blessed me to learn about the religion of Islam, which had enabled me to lift myself up from the muck and the mire of this rotting world. (293)

The strong teacher-student and the father-son affinity that formed between Elijah and Malcolm provided both men, and the Nation of Islam, with an era of great growth. Their bond seemed inseparable. Elijah was well pleased with his star student who he described as his best minister, often referring to Malcolm as "son." In many ways Elijah Muhammad fulfilled Malcolm's fatherless void, but for Malcolm, Elijah Muhammad was more than a mere father figure. As was custom in the Nation of Islam, Malcolm addressed Elijah Muhammad as "the Honorable Elijah Muhammad" or as "Dear Holy Apostle," or by the title "The Messenger." Malcolm believed Elijah Muhammad to be divine.

THE MAN BEHIND THE MEN

Malcolm served the Nation of Islam diligently, baptizing himself nonstop in the work of building the Nation of Islam. Traveling constantly for Elijah Muhammad, Malcolm established numerous Nation of Islam temples in his stead. Numerous times Malcolm traveled the breadth of the United States of America, often appearing on radio and television representing and explaining the Nation of Islam's beliefs and defending Elijah Muhammad. In 1959 Malcolm also traveled outside of America to Egypt, Sudan, Nigeria and Ghana on behalf of Elijah Muhammad.

Malcolm's source of strength, an asset he metaphorically described on page 296 in his autobiography as wings, had come from Elijah Muhammad himself. "The only way I could keep up with my job for Mr. Muhammad was by flying with the wings that he had given me."

Later Malcolm depicted these same "wings" given to him by Elijah Muhammad in antithetical terms as he described the challenging balance act that he had to constantly maintain; swiveling between his loyalties to Elijah Muhammad and his unfettered independence. "I believe that no man in the Nation of Islam could have gained the international prominence I gained with the wings Mr. Muhammad had put on me — plus having the freedom that he granted me to take liberties and do things on my own — and still have remained as faithful and as selfless a servant to him as I was." (298)

The chapter titled *Icarus* in *The Autobiography of Malcolm X* is quite appropriate for introducing the breakdown in the relationship between Elijah Muhammad and his top minister Malcolm X. Icarus was a Greek mythological boy whose father Daedalus had made him and his son pairs of wings that were fastened with wax. According to the myth the wings were designed only to allow the father and son a means of escape from prison. The father warned Icarus, "Never fly but so high with these wings." (293)

Elijah Muhammad replicated with Malcolm the same limitations that the father of Icarus had afforded his son. Elijah Muhammad, in order to assure his "son" Malcolm a means of escape from the prison of America's racism and classism, had prepared Malcolm's "wings" to navigate only limited flights. The "wings" given to Malcolm, that allowed him to soar above the other ministers in the Nation of Islam, were not wings that Malcolm himself had created. Malcolm was flying with wings fashioned by Elijah Muhammad.

The close relationship between Elijah Muhammad and Malcolm was constantly being challenged by evil factors, internal and external of the Nation of Islam. In time these negative factors took their toll on the closeness enjoyed by Elijah and Malcolm. Eventually Malcolm was forced out of the Nation of Islam and into the international arena where he had to navigate the higher stratums on his own, independent of Elijah's protection.

Malcolm's choice of Icarus, the Graecized myth, to describe his father-son relationship with the Elijah Muhammad seems to reveal two important conclusions that Malcolm had come to realize. Firstly he recognized even in the closing days of his life the value and wisdom of the guidance and leadership of Elijah Muhammad. This is confirmed when Malcolm acknowledges that he himself was dependent on Elijah Muhammad for his "wings." Secondly, Malcolm had an inconspicuous realization that he may fail, as Icarus had fatefully floundered, if he became overly engrossed with his freedom to fly with wings capable of soaring "but so high."

The dissolution of the close bond between Elijah and Malcolm compelled Malcolm to search his own soul for answers, especially as news of Elijah Muhammad fathering numerous children by his secretaries began spreading throughout the Nation of Islam. And before the extramarital affairs of Elijah Muhammad had cleared the air, Malcolm received a 90-day suspension — later extended to an indefinite suspension — for disobeying a direct order of Elijah Muhammad by commenting on the assassination of President John F. Kennedy. If anyone should have known not to speak negatively about the assassination of President Kennedy it should have been Malcolm, the National Spokesman for the Nation of Islam. When the National Spokesman speaks his words carry the weight and the implication that the whole of the Nation of Islam thinks and feels this way. Instead of registering the fact that every Nation of Islam member would be affected by his comments, Malcolm instead disobeyed his leader's directives. Malcolm's autobiography states:

> Within hours after the assassination — I am telling nothing but the truth — every Muslim minister received from Mr. Elijah Muhammad a directive — in fact, *two* directives. Every minister was ordered to make no remarks at all concerning the assassination. Mr. Muhammad instructed that if pressed for comment, we should say: "No comment." (307)

The 90-day suspension from the Nation of Islam allowed Malcolm time to perform an act that he had not taken time to do for over a decade: reflect. Malcolm had worked diligently for the Nation of Islam — eating, walking, and sleeping the vision and the program of Elijah Muhammad. Malcolm's disobeying the "no comment" directive issued by Elijah Muhammad inadvertently led to Malcolm having time to ponder and reflect during his 90-day suspension from the Nation of Islam.

This community severance, compounded by the reverberating accusations of Elijah Muhammad having fathered outside children, in addition to Malcolm's need to provide for the security and well being of his own family, all weighed heavily on his mind. These challenges allowed, maybe even forced, Malcolm to shortly thereafter take the opportunity to look outside of the Nation of Islam for religious answers and for his family's welfare. Although under the duress of survival, Malcolm realized that his days in the Nation of Islam were numbered. Malcolm's autobiography mentions this trying period that required him to assess his newfound dilemma and future plans:

> I was racking my brain. What was I going to do? My life was inseparably committed to the American black man's struggle. I was generally regarded as a "leader." For years, I had attacked so many so-called "black leaders" for their shortcomings. Now, I had to honestly ask myself what I could offer, how I was genuinely qualified to help the black people win their struggle for human rights. I had enough experience to know that in order to be a good organizer of anything which you expect to succeed — including yourself — you must almost mathematically analyze cold facts.
> I had, as one asset, I knew, an international image. No amount of money could have bought that. I knew that if I said something newsworthy, people would read or hear it, maybe even around the world, depending upon what it was. (316)

The international setting of New York City had already exposed Malcolm to other interpretations of Islam which he often pushed to the back of his mind because of his belief that the Islam taught by Elijah Muhammad was the correct Islam. The internal struggles in the Nation of Islam, plus the manifested venom of jealously against Malcolm from Nation of Islam officials that increased during his suspension, allowed him opportunities to follow his suppressed curiosities about the other variations of Islam that differed from the message of Elijah Muhammad. Malcolm had been forced into another involuntary life transition. When he left the Nation of Islam in 1964 he carried with him many of Elijah Muhammad's ideas and beliefs which he incorporated into his own organization called the *Muslim Mosque, Incorporated*. At an April 12, 1964 speech in Detroit, MI, before the communication and relationship between he and Elijah Muhammad further deteriorated, Malcolm declared:

> I'm still a Muslim. That is, my religion is still Islam. My religion is still Islam. I still credit Mr. Muhammad for what I know and what I am. He's the one who opened my eyes. At present, I'm the Minister of the newly founded Muslim Mosque, Incorporated, which has its offices in the Teresa Hotel, right in the heart of Harlem — that's the black belt in New York city.
> — Transcribed from phonograph "The Best of Malcolm X"

EL-HAJJ MALIK EL-SHABAZZ

During a March 19, 1964 interview with poet and jazz critic A.B. Spellman, a month before his trip to Mecca, Malcolm explained his split with the Nation of Islam.

> "Well, I did encounter opposition within the Nation of Islam. Many obstacles were placed in my path, not by the Honorable Elijah Muhammad, but by others who were around him, and since I believe that his analysis of the race problem is the best one and his solution is the only one, I felt that I could best circumvent these obstacles and expedite his program better by remaining out of the Nation of Islam and establishing a Muslim group that is an action group designed to eliminate the same ills that the teachings of the Honorable Elijah Muhammad have made so manifest in this country.
> But the political philosophy of the Muslim Mosque will be black nationalism, the economic philosophy will be black nationalism, and the social philosophy will be black nationalism. And by political philosophy I mean we still believe in the Honorable Elijah Muhammad's solution as complete separation. The 22,000,000 so-called Negroes should be separated completely from America and should be permitted to go back home to our African homeland which is a long-range program.

The next stage of development for Malcolm was evidenced in his pilgrimage to Mecca for hajj, the fifth pillar of Islam that was established by Prophet Muhammed in the 7th century. Encouraged by Elijah's son, the then Minister Wallace D. Muhammad and other close associates and family members, Malcolm decided to travel to the Middle East this time for personal spiritual growth.

The hajj is one of the world's best international forums where annually Muslims from every corner of the globe gather in one central location. Many in the international Muslim world already knew of the great works that Malcolm had accomplished as a minister for Elijah Muhammad. Even with his new freedom as a Muslim seeking to learn more about his religion by fulfilling the hajj rituals, still Malcolm could not avoid receiving questions from inquisitive Muslims about his 12 years as a student and minister under Elijah Muhammad.

While on hajj Malcolm refused to criticize Elijah Muhammad; instead he judiciously addressed the vulnerable relationship that now existed between himself and his former mentor by focusing on black unity. In a discourse on Mt. Arafat with the Grand Mufti of Jerusalem, Hussein Amini, and Kasem Gulick of the Turkish Parliament, Malcolm noted that, "Both were learned men; both were especially well-read on America. Kasem Gulick asked me why I had broken with Elijah Muhammad. I said that I preferred not to elaborate upon our differences, in the interest of preserving the American black man's unity. They both understood and accepted that." (351). It is interesting that the two "scientists" that accompanied Elijah Muhammad at his 1974 Saviour's Day address were also from Turkey.

Upon completing the hajj Malcolm stayed in the region and continued his international travels by visiting many African countries and being received by their respective rulers. While in Ghana the question of the split between Malcolm and Elijah Muhammad arose again. Again Malcolm refused to criticize his former teacher. He states in his autobiography:

> At a jam-packed press club conference, I believe the very first question was why I had split with Elijah Muhammad and the Nation of Islam. The Africans had heard such rumors as that Elijah Muhammad had built a palace in Arizona. I straightened out that falsehood, and I avoided any criticism. I said that our disagreement had been in terms of political direction and in involvement in the extra-religious struggle for human rights. I said I respected the Nation of Islam for its having been a psychologically revitalizing movement and a source of moral and social reform, and that Elijah Muhammad's influence upon the black man had been basic." (360)

Upon Malcolm's return to America the tensions intensified. The negative energies within the Nation of Islam, compounded by the interfering long arm of government officials and agencies, sowed dissension between Elijah Muhammad and Malcolm X until any hope of reconciliation was virtually impossible.

The depth of the father-and-son, teacher-to-student, "divine" leader-to-devotee relationships between Elijah and Malcolm is too involved to be adequately quantified and reported in this writing; nor is that the intent. Nonetheless, the shaping of Malcolm into a leading minister of the Nation of Islam and his introduction to the international world was singlehandedly the masterpiece of Elijah Muhammad. Only Elijah Muhammad, and no one else, not even Malcolm, can claim responsibility and praise for Malcolm being catapulted into his national and international status.

The impact and influence that Elijah Muhammad had upon the adult life of Malcolm X, El-Hajj Malik El-Shabazz, is immeasurable. Even the negative time that existed during the later years between the two men provided opportunities for Malcolm to learn and benefit from the many lessons he had learned from Elijah Muhammad.

Before Malcolm's departure from the Nation of Islam an undying love for Islam had been imported to him by Elijah Muhammad. Even during his departure, while in the midst of reevaluating the years of dedicated service he had given to the Nation of Islam, the love for Islam that was given to Malcolm by Elijah Muhammad never swerved.

Another quality that Malcolm gained from Elijah Muhammad's Nation of Islam was the mental challenge and exercise that every follower of Elijah Muhammad acquired from studying the "Lessons" that originated with the Nation of Islam's founder, Mr. W.D. Fard. Every member in the Nation of Islam, including Elijah Muhammad, was charged with the responsibility to "get busy and solve these problems."

Their minds were challenged as they tried to grasp and decipher the hidden messages in Fard's mythologies. One test given by Fard was the *Lost-Found Muslim Lesson No. 2*, an exercise in which Elijah Muhammad did not get a 100 percent passing grade. Elijah was Fard's top student. Still apparently the best grade he received from Fard stated "This Lesson is answered very near correct." Interestingly, although Elijah's grade was less than perfect still Fard left instructions that, "all students should read and study it until he or she can recite it by heart."

Surely Malcolm, as a minister in the Nation of Islam, studied and taught these lessons. But according to Wallace Mohammed Malcolm's methodical mind did not spend much time entertaining these Nation of Islam's catechistic styled mythologies and mysteries. Wallace knew Malcolm to be a worker and a troubleshooter seeking hands-on results. Still, just coming in contact with Fard's "Lessons" had to agitate Malcolm's mind in ways that encouraged him to approach life with curiosity and scrutiny. Even if Malcolm did not seek the possible hidden meanings in Fard's lessons, then surely it challenged him to find order and consistency in what Fard taught. The lifesaving benefits that Malcolm achieved as a studious follower of Elijah Muhammad are undeniable, as shown when Malcolm the inmate was revived and activated when he first encountered the teachings of Elijah Muhammad.

Elijah Muhammad's teachings and the lessons entrusted to him by Fard were replete with dichotomized dualities, symbolisms, and innuendos that, directly and indirectly, supported his message of lifting up black men and women in America. Often multiple meanings in his messages provided his students with a twofold benefit. On one hand Elijah's message helped to free their minds from their previous dismal state of racism and social rejection; while on the other hand, it stimulated their curiosities with legends of great blackness — even if the legends were fanciful and unscientific. As the members of the Nation of Islam studied the "Lessons" and the teachings of the Nation of Islam, their mental engaging of this novel body of knowledge stimulated and refreshed their once depraved and denied intellects. The mental renaissance that Nation of Islam members gained from studying the "Lessons" was designed to be a temporary benefit that would suffice them until they encountered universal Islam.

The challenge for many former and longtime Nation of Islam members came years later, particularly after Wallace Mohammed became the leader in 1975. After reflecting on and reinterpreting their evolving understandings on the "Lessons" of the Nation of Islam, which included revisiting and adjusting their earlier understandings on Nation of Islam doctrines such as "Yakub's History", the "Mother Plane" and "What makes rain, hail, snow and earthquakes," Nation of Islam members' appetites increased for more sound interpolations and applications of the "Lessons." The traditional race-based understandings of the "Lessons," in the face of modernity, were no longer sufficient answers for the Muslim community.

Initially, on the surface, Fard's lessons quenched a need in African Americans to claim exclusive ownership of a unique body of knowledge. However, with each member charged with the duty to solve the lessons of the Nation of Islam, it was only a matter of time before a few in the Nation of Islam would begin to see through the racial clouds that were part and parcel of Fard's teachings. While many Nation of Islam members simply learned these lessons by rote without challenging themselves to delve deeper in to standard Nation of Islam conclusions, some members sought to extend their knowledge base via hard study of the lessons, with some even attempting independent reinterpretations of the "Lessons." Independent reinterpretations sometimes carried the risk of the student moving away from the Nation of Islam towards the universal teachings of orthodox Islam.

Some used the lessons to form their own groups as was done by Clarence 13X Smith, also known by the name Puddin, who formed a group called the Five Percent Nation that placed him as the central figure instead of Elijah Muhammad. Some independent minded students of these "Lessons" may have left Islam altogether for another religion or ideology. When Elijah Muhammad gave Malcolm the wings to think and act freely, obviously he knew the risk involved of Malcolm outgrowing his Nation of Islam.

One major dichotomy in the teachings of Elijah Muhammad that would challenge a free thinker like Malcolm was Elijah Muhammad's claiming a divine-like role as the "Messenger of Allah." Publicly Elijah taught that he was not here to teach the religious aspects of Islam; in fact he described his job as that of a harbinger responsible for cleaning up the people in preparation for the one to come after him who would teach the people Islam. Also Malcolm heard Elijah say that no one would succeed him because his mission would "Go to his grave with him." These two seemingly contradictory statements only added ambiguity to the issue. For a free thinker the questions needing answers are: If your mission goes to your grave with you then for what purpose are you cleaning us up? Why are you not cleaning us up to support your mission?

Another seemingly contradictory message of the Nation of Islam was over the issue of succession. Malcolm, aware of the "my mission goes to my grave with me" statement, also had been taught that Wallace was the one designated to succeed Elijah Muhammad.

EL-HAJJ MALIK EL-SHABAZZ

Dr. E. U. Essien-Udom from Nigeria studied the Nation of Islam in the early 1960s. Dr. Essien-Udom in his book *Black Nationalism: a Search for an Identity in America* wrote of the possibility of a successor to Elijah Muhammad.

> Because of his overwhelming importance in the movement, the question of Muhammad's succession deserves comment.
> Muhammad's followers appear to think that he is the "Last Messenger." This is official doctrine; but it does not seem to be his view. One of his brochures suggests a subtle concept of his role as "Leader and Messenger I." He himself has admitted that "if I cannot accomplish this task, another will," but he would have "gathered the materials" for the completion of the task. Besides, it appears that he is training his son, Minister Wallace Muhammad, as his successor. Recently it became clear that he is next in the line of succession. Several followers have told the writer that Muhammad assured them that "Allah has chosen Minister Wallace to succeed him."
> Other ministers of Muhammad's Temples of Islam regard Minister Wallace as a possible successor. Minister Malcolm X of the New York Temple, one of the Nation's most highly regarded leaders, alluded to this in a speech at the Chicago Temple on December 12, 1958, when he introduced Minister Wallace as "the seventh son of our dear beloved Leader and Teacher who is following in the footsteps of his father." (80-81)

L-R Malcolm X., Raymond Sharrief, Wallace Mohammed/Muhammad enjoying one of their favorite snacks, corn bread and buttermilk.
(Photographer and Date Unknown)

THE MAN BEHIND THE MEN

Dr. Essien-Udom's noting of the disparity in the Nation of Islam's issue of succession deserves reflection. On the one hand Elijah states that his mission dies with him, while on the other hand leading officials such as Malcolm were promoting another opinion. Was Elijah Muhammad's twofold message regarding his possible successor one of many hints strategically inserted into his teachings to lead his followers towards a different view of Islam after his death? Surely Elijah Muhammad was aware that such an apparent contradiction regarding succession would stimulate Malcolm and other free thinkers to question its inconsistency.

If Malcolm and other curious minded members still in the Nation of Islam were to accept Elijah Muhammad's words, "I'm not here to teach you Islam," then the question that begs to be answered is, well Mr. Muhammad if you're not teaching us Islam then what exactly are you teaching us? More importantly the question to ask is, "How can you be 'The Messenger of Allah' if you are not teaching the message of Islam?" Lastly, one may conclude that since Elijah knew that he was not teaching Islam, but only a "wake-up message," then what reality or purpose were Nation of Islam members to awaken to?

Would a man as wise as Elijah Muhammad make such ambiguous statements about his mission and his succession; statements that would eventually make his followers, as it did with Malcolm, question aspects of his leadership? Undoubtedly Elijah anticipated the possibility of these inevitable conflicts and their ramifications. Probably Elijah Muhammad intentionally inculcate provocative double messages in his teachings to make his followers search for deeper meanings in his teachings that would help them move towards a more universal form of Islam? Perhaps Malcolm had woken up too early before the majority in the Nation of Islam?

While on hajj, reposed on a hill in deep reflection, Malcolm contemplated upon what he now saw as his credulous submission to Elijah Muhammad. His autobiography states:

> "In Mecca, too, I had played back for myself the twelve years I had spent with Elijah Muhammad as it were a motion picture. I guess it would be impossible for anyone ever to realize fully how complete was my belief in Elijah Muhammad. I believed in him not only as a leader in the ordinary *human* sense, but also I believed in him as a *divine* leader. I believed he had no human weaknesses or faults, and that, therefore, he could make no mistakes and that he could do no wrong. There on a Holy World hilltop, I realized how very dangerous it is for people to hold any human being in such esteem, especially to consider anyone some sort of "divinely guided" and "protected" person. (372)

EL-HAJJ MALIK EL-SHABAZZ

Malcolm's critical review of his tenure with the Nation of Islam represents a watershed experience — in fact a life altering experience — in which Malcolm would never be the same. The common simplistic misconception that the highlight of Malcolm's hajj to Mecca was his discovering "blue-eyed, blond haired" Muslims with whom he shared the same drinking cup is a red herring. Surely this was not Malcolm's first time encountering white Muslims as evidenced in his July of 1959 visit to the Middle East as an ambassador for Elijah Muhammad. Moreover, the fact that Malcolm lived in New York City, a richly cosmopolitan city that also was home for many of the world's embassies as well as the United Nations, also put Malcolm in proximal distance to Muslims who were racially diverse; Muslims from many parts of Europe and Asia. Actually Malcolm's pilgrimage to Mecca is not where he discovered white Muslims. Malcolm's hajj, after a life of crime followed by 12 years in the Nation of Islam, is when he began to rediscover his self.

Malcolm reporting that while in Mecca he discovered that there were white Muslims, appears to be only a strategy to garner media attention and enhance the popularity of his two new organizations, the *Muslim Mosque Incorporated* and the *Organization of Afro-American Unity (OAAU)*. The stakes were high but the possible yield was great. As Malcolm had realized during his 90-day suspension, the one assest he still had was media appeal. His report of discovering white Muslims in Mecca was Malcolm relying upon his belief that, "if I said something newsworty, people would read or hear it, maybe even around the world, depending upon what it was."

One definite affect achieved by Malcolm's reporting there were white Muslims in Mecca was to rattle the faith of the followers of Elijah Muhammad. After his return to the United States Malcolm was confronted by news reporters who were inquiring why he believed members of the Nation of Islam were making threats against him. A Youtube website shows Malcolm standing on the steps of the Queens County Civil Court on June 15th 1964 with a derisive smile telling reporters:

> I do know that when I wrote that letter saying that there were white people in Mecca it shook up a lot of Muslims. Because most of the Muslims who follow Mr. Muhammad absolutely believe that it was impossible, physically impossible, I should say divinely impossible for a white person to go to Mecca. And my trip there shattered that image, or that mis-concept.

There are many reports that quietly Malcolm wanted to return to the Nation of Islam, even after publicly disagreeing with "the Messenger of Allah." Malcolm missed the disciplined support, from Nation of Islam members, that he had grown accustomed to. In addition to the *Muslim Mosque Incorporated* people and *Organization of Afro-American Unity* people being at odds with one another, neither of these two groups had the organizational or devout discipline that was common amongst Nation of Islam members.

Dr. Manning Marable of Columbia University in New York City believes that Malcolm's intention even while writing his autobiography was to find a way back into the Nation of Islam. In February of 2005 Marable told Amy Goodman, the host of "Democracy Now!," that "Malcolm's objective was actually to reingratiate himself within the Nation of Islam..." Even against the great odds of combating the unproven charges against Malcolm that were being fed to Elijah Muhammad from internal and external antagonists who accused Malcolm of planning to take over the leadership of the Nation of Islam, still Marable reports that "Malcolm felt that if he could make a public — a prominent public statement to show his fidelity to the Honorable Elijah Muhammad that that might win back the good graces of the organization."

Muhammad Siddeeq, the former Director of the Nation of Islam's private school in New York, acknowledges that in either 1969 or 1970 that he and Farrakhan received a similar report stating that Malcolm had expressed interest in returning to Elijah Muhammad's Nation of Islam.

> What had happened, back when I was in New York as the Director of the University of Islam, I was out in Queens on Northern Boulevard and this brother stopped and walked along with me and said he wanted to meet with Minister Farrakhan... so I set it up so that they could meet at the shopping plaza after one of our, I think it was a Wednesday night meeting...One of the points that he brought to our attention was that he was with Malcolm while Malcolm was in Africa, and he wanted to call to Farrakhan's attention that Malcolm was trying to find a way to come back to the Nation of Islam under the Honorable Elijah Muhammad. And that he was not comfortable in his new situation outside of the Nation of Islam, and that he was definitely looking for a way to come back there.
>
> Telephone interview

Another complicated question in the Malcolm-Elijah relationship is who killed Malcolm X. No one knows for sure who killed Malcolm X Shabazz. From Malcolm's own words come suggestions that he, himself, did not know for sure who was behind the efforts to kill him. What is known is that on that fateful Sunday February 21st of 1965 Talmadge Hayer (also known as Thomas Hagan) was one of the three trigger men captured at the scene. Hayer, under the name Hagan was officially released from prison in April 2010.

The other two men sentenced for the murder of Malcolm, Thomas 15X Johnson (who became Khalil Islam) and Norman 3X Butler (who became Muhammad Abdul Aziz), served 22 years and 20 years respectively. Khalil Islam died August 4, 2009. But their involvement was refuted in 1977 by Hayer in his signing of two sworn affidavits exonerating both men of participating in the murder of Malcolm. But Hayer and his accomplices — whoever they may be — are only a small piece of the bigger puzzle; a puzzle that if ever solved will reveal who ordered, planned, financed, and actually committed Malcolm's assassination.

The many theories surrounding Malcolm's death have resulted in myriad questions, finger pointing, speculations and divisiveness that has only darkened the cloud on the issue. Malcolm's murder created separate camps with each group driving their respective stakes deeper into their own conclusions as to who was responsible for the crime.

For Elijah Muhammad, the passing of Malcolm at best could be only like a two-edged sword that cuts both ways with Elijah Muhammad left standing in the middle of the proverbial "Catch-22." Not only had he lost all possibilities for the return of his faithful general, he also had to live with an image of complicity in Malcolm's demise.

This double-edged sword also represents another duality of affection and aggravation. One edge of the blade loved Malcolm as a wayward son who had gone astray and whose absence and public criticisms of Elijah Muhammad only further agitated an already strained "father and son" relationship. The death of Malcolm in many ways was like the death of one of Elijah's own biological sons. Any possible relief that Elijah Muhammad may have gained by Malcolm's death would have been eclipsed by the fact that in the end he had lost a distanced "son" forever.

The other side of this sword viewed Malcolm as a pestilence in the side of Elijah Muhammad and the Nation of Islam. As a minister for Elijah Muhammad, Malcolm had gained international prominence. And now that he was no longer a member of the Nation of Islam and publicly expressing his change of belief, Malcolm had become a distraction for Elijah Muhammad and his Nation of Islam. One edge of the blade loved Malcolm while the other edge just wished he'd go away.

After Malcolm was pressured out of the Nation of Islam two greater challenges loomed for Malcolm: quantifying his readily accessibility to an international audience, and assessing his willingness to utilize to the maximum that accessibility.

When Malcolm began promoting the civil and human rights issues of African Americans on the global scene, he became the target of officials in the United States of America and of parties in other world governments. These governmental entities were far larger and more concerned with Malcolm than Elijah Muhammad and his American-based Nation of Islam operations.

THE MAN BEHIND THE MEN

Malcolm's efforts to internationalize the African American plight, and his petitioning of African nations to present charges before the United Nations against America, for the denial of human rights and full citizenship to black Americans, drew both negative and positive international attention to Malcolm and his post-Nation of Islam efforts.

The pro-Marcus Garvey website *http://www.uaia.org* while praising Malcolm, all but absolves Elijah Muhammad and his Nation of Islam of the charge of murdering Malcolm. Instead, this website alleges that the FBI and CIA may have had a direct hand in Malcolm's assassination because Malcolm — maybe in the spirit of his father Earl Little — was continuing Marcus Garvey's work "To further crystallize Black Nationalist and Pan-Africanist thought." Malcolm, similar to Garvey — and to a degree like his father — drew upon himself the ire of the government and leaders in society.

This *Universal Negro Improvement Association (UAIA)* website in addition to saying that Malcolm's "travels to Africa and Asia left a lasting impact on black and brown people around the world" also states the following:

> Malcolm X was assassinated on February 21, 1965 after breaking with the Nation of Islam. Though members of the Nation were convicted of the murder, it is a well-established fact that the FBI had infiltrated the Nation of Islam and was working actively to forge a divisive wedge between Malcolm X and Elijah Muhammad. It should also be noted that J. Edgar Hoover, Director of the FBI specifically called for the "prevention of the rise of a Black Messiah" as part of the COINTELPRO program. Add to this the fact that Malcolm was poisoned while traveling abroad, as well as the fact that Talmadge Hayer, who was the only assailant caught at the scene of Malcolm's murder, all but exonerated the other NOI members who were charged in the case, and the fact that the FBI *still* refuses to release all of its files on Malcolm X suggests that there was *probably* some FBI involvement in Malcolm's murder.

Malcolm's temerity, despite being poisoned while in Cairo, Egypt, as well as being followed in an intentionally noticeable manner by white men who were obviously trying to frighten him, was not discouraged. He was determined to have the plight of African Americans in the U.S. heard in an international setting. As mentioned on page 76 in his book *Malcolm X Speaks: Selected Speeches and Statements*, Malcolm, while in Cairo attended the African Summit Conference and appealed to the delegates of 34 African nations who had gathered at the summit, "to help us bring our problem before the United Nations, on the grounds that the United States is morally incapable of protecting the lives and the property of 22 million African-Americans."

Malcolm with Sheikh Ahmad Hasun of the Sudan with the Kalimah Shahadah (Islam's testimony of faith) in Arabic on the wall. *(Photographer and Date Unknown)*

After Cairo, Malcolm continued his African tour even after doctors told him he had consumed a "toxic substance" that ruled out food poisoning. Malcolm believed the poisoning was the responsibility of the white men who always showed up wherever he went in Africa in their effort to intimidate him.

When Malcolm returned to the United States the numerous telephone threats and confrontations between Malcolm and Nation of Islam faithful resulted in Malcolm initially blaming the Nation of Islam for the attempts on his life. The epilogue of Malcolm's autobiography documents the following.

> Malcolm X steadily accused the Black Muslims as the source of the various attacks and threats. "There is no group in the United States more able to carry out this threat than the Back Muslims," he said. I know, because I taught them myself. (429)

THE MAN BEHIND THE MEN

Further review of his autobiography supports that Malcolm, at this time, still believed that the Nation of Islam was seeking to kill him. In a conversation with *Life* magazine photographer-author Gordon Parks, approximately two days before his death, Parks asked Malcolm to seek police protection. Malcolm laughed before replying, "Brother, nobody can protect you from a Muslim but a Muslim — or someone trained in Muslim tactics." Then Malcolm indirectly implicated himself as the originator and the leader of past retaliatory actions that may have been used against Nation of Islam dissidents when he revealed to Parks, "I know. I invented many of those tactics." (436)

Minister Malcolm X teaching the men about the role of the husband, and the Nation of Islam's lesson that the black man was "god."
(Photographer and Date Unknown)

The next day Malcolm's thoughts changed. Whereas before, Malcolm's accusations of the ones trying to kill him were pointed solely at the Nation of Islam, one day before his assassination he shared another view point with the writer of his autobiography, Alex Haley. Malcolm X phoned Alex Haley and told him he was going to stop saying that it was the Muslims who were trying to kill him. Malcolm related to Alex Haley: "I'm going to tell you something, brother — the more I keep thinking about this thing, the things that have been happening lately, I'm not all that sure that it's the Muslims. I know what they can do, and what they can't, and they can't do some of the stuff recently going on." Malcolm explained further, "Now, I'm going to tell you, the more I keep thinking about what happened in France, I think I'm going to quit saying it's the Muslims." (438)

Circa February 5, 1965, approximately 16 days before his murder, it is reported that the French government had denied Malcolm's visa when he tried to enter France because of fear that an assassination plot against Malcolm was to unfold on French soil. Elijah Muhammad's influence was domestic. He did not wield any power or influence in France. Any plans or attempts upon Malcolm's life that were to transpire on French soil definitely were beyond the realm of Elijah Muhammad and his Nation of Islam.

The closing days of Malcolm's life witnessed, however slightly, a hope versus despair period between him and his former teacher. Sadly, despair won the contest. Claude Andrew Clegg III in his book *An Original Man* described the love-hate actions exemplified by both men as a moment that included "a window of opportunity that could have served as a safety valve for the rising tensions between Muhammad and Malcolm." (227)

Clegg noted that during this time Elijah Muhammad had expressed his willingness to forgive Malcolm, Wallace and his grandson Hassan Sharrieff. And simultaneously, Malcolm, "as late as Mid-February, had expressed regret over the prospect of 'two Black groups [having] to fight and kill each other off' and called on Muhammad to end the feud." Sadly, the more negative forces of the day prevailed.

When the news of Malcolm's murder reached Elijah Muhammad, according to Clegg's book, one of Elijah grandsons reported that Elijah "seemed genuinely shocked, even disturbed." According to this report the first words Elijah Muhammad uttered upon hearing this news is, "Oh my, God! Um, um, um!" as he fell back into his chair.

Malcolm knew that his death was at hand, but he was not sure from who or when. He correctly predicted that he would not live long enough to read his own autobiography because of his bold and outspoken style. "I know, too, that I could suddenly die at the hands of some white racist. Or I could die at the hands of some Negro hired by the white man. Or it could be some brainwashed Negro acting on his own idea that by eliminating me he would be helping out the white man, because I talk about the white man the way I do." (388)

As mentioned earlier no one knows for sure who is responsible for the killing of Malcolm. Even Malcolm himself was unsure. Before placing the blame upon the shoulders of Elijah Muhammad, all of the other possibly complicit parties, locally and internationally, must be considered, especially those entities concerned that Malcolm's message could challenge, maybe even damage their international image and interest.

THE MAN BEHIND THE MEN

Even to this day there remains strong divisions between those who have concluded in their own minds who is responsible for Malcolm's murder. Hopefully one day the whole truth will be made known to the public.

Malcolm was a brilliant mind and inspiring soul who continues to touch the lives of millions around the world in many positive ways. Without doubt had Malcolm not met Elijah Muhammad, he may not have been inspired to study and learn about Islam and world events. Nor would he have gained an international audience willing to hear his message. Therefore, it is a fact that, it is the Honorable Elijah Muhammad who remains the man behind Malcolm X; a motivating factor that led to him eventually becoming the international man, El-Hajj Malik El-Shabazz.

-§- CHAPTER -§-
SIX

On calling the White Man the "Devil"
How the Mission of Elijah Muhammad Served As a Mirror for Whites to See Their Racism

In his book *The Theology of Time* — originally released in 1972 and reprinted by Abass Rassoull in May of 1992 —Elijah Muhammad states that he was not trying to make mockery of white people by calling them the devil. Elijah Muhammad, striking a parallel with the Epistle of Paul that speaks of the innocence of the clay in the hands of the potter, indicts the black man with the onus of creating the white devil. By analogy Elijah Muhammad is saying that the white man, the innocent clay, is not responsible for his mistreatment of black people, "the potter" who shaped him into a "devil":

> This is not a mockery for Me to stand here and call the people "devil" because devil is just what they are. If any mockery should be done it should be done to us for what we have made or created. Then the God of the Black Man should be responsible for the mockery. I want to give the Truth. They didn't make themselves, we made them. Well then, you have no right to be saying that your product is no good. If you made it no good then don't blame that which you made for being no good. I know I'm coming to you in a way that you didn't think that I would. We are here to tell the truth. (167)

In the above quote, Elijah Muhammad seems concerned with debunking his own myth of white devilry. He is not teaching hatred of the white man or of any man. The many years that Elijah Muhammad spent obligating African Americans to love themselves above loving any other people is not proof that he is teaching hate. Considering the condition of African Americans up until that time, a self-love message desperately was needed, as witnessed by the success of James Brown's 1968 hit song, "Say it Loud, I'm Black and I'm Proud."

Often when one thinks about Elijah Muhammad the first thing remembered, especially among Caucasians, is that he called the white man "the devil." As with all of Elijah's religious lessons and Nation of Islam theology this devil theory was also birthed by Mr. W.D. Fard in a story dubbed, "Yakub's History"; the making of Yakub's grafted devil, the white man.

In *Message to the Blackman*, Elijah Muhammad explains the origin of the Nation of Islam belief on whites as devils. "It's what He (Fard) revealed, and what He revealed is what I am teaching and believe in, and this term "devil," or name "devil," is applied to wicked people, people who are by nature wicked." (320).

In addition to Elijah calling whites the devil, he would remind his followers that they too had the potential of being a devil. Often he warned his members to be careful of their Islamic etiquette and sincerity or risk the possibility of "turning devil overnight."

To help ensure that they remained "righteous," Elijah Muhammad issued his registered followers identification cards that included the wording, *"The Bearer is a righteous Moslem. Kindly retain this card and punish of said bearer, if found other than righteous."* Those instructions are a seemingly odd license from Elijah that permitted and encouraged the so-called "white devil" to detain and confine his errant followers.

If Elijah truly believed the white man to be "the devil" would he freely surrender and subject his followers to the arrest and detention of predominantly white police departments merely because they may have slipped or erred? The Nation of Islam had a record of serious unfavorable encounters with police departments in Detroit, New York, Los Angeles and other cities around America. If Elijah Muhammad truly believed that all white people were "devils" he would not have allowed them, whether they're a police officer or a public citizen, permission to punish his followers.

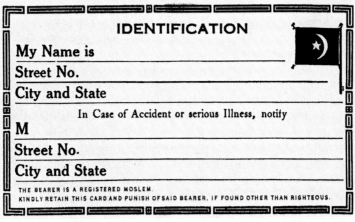

Every registered Nation of Islam member carried this card.

Upon closer examination it appears that Elijah Muhammad's calling the white man the devil indicates that he was actually addressing an immoral mentality more than the racial and genetic qualities of Caucasians.

This "white devil" language also offered African Americans a skewed view of white Americans that would offset and counteract the religiously based

ON CALLING THE WHITE MAN THE "DEVIL"

stigma that had been placed upon African Americans as the cursed seed of Noah's son Ham; a curse that doomed the descendants of Ham to the role of eternally being servants to non-black people. The European interpretations of this biblical report of a permanent curse of servility being placed upon Ham's son Canaan — merely because Ham, Noah's dark-skinned son had committed the sin of seeing his father drunk and naked — was now being countered by Fard's white devil rhetoric.

W.D. Fard originated the folk story "Yakub's History" for Elijah Muhammad and the early followers of the Nation of Islam to offer an explanation for the origin of Caucasians as well as to transfer the Hamite curse of "innate evil" from African Americans and place it upon white people. Whereas Christianity, as taught in many circles, provided Caucasians with messages of white superiority, the Nation of Islam taught that Yakub's making of the white man was his creation of a sub-human; the making of the devil.

In addition to addressing the inferiority that African Americans carried because of being taught in religion that they were divinely cursed, Elijah Muhammad also was addressing deep-seated superiority complexes that some Caucasians felt simply because of their white skin. Elijah was drawing attention to the debilitating mental and spiritual strains that accompany racially based superiority-inferiority complexes.

Elijah Muhammad is not the first one to refer to the white race as devils. Other non-whites, especially Native Americans, also called the white man the devil. The Native American Shawnee tribe had a folktale similar to "Yakub's History" for explaining the origin of white people. Lalawethika, later known as Tenskwatawa, was the younger brother of the famous chief Tecumseh and served as the tribe's spiritual advisor. Tenskwatawa, as reported in *Time-Life Books, The American Indians: The Mighty Chieftains* earned his position as spiritual advisor in 1805 during an epidemic.

> For the better part of his life Lalawethika was the polar opposite of Tecumseh: lazy, boastful, and a hard drinker. But in 1805, during an epidemic, he fell into a series of trances and emerged fundamentally changed. While he was unconscious, he said, two young men had carried him into the spirit world, where he met the supreme deity, the Master of Life, who showed him a paradise of game-rich forests and fertile cornfields — the way the earth was before the whites spoiled it. The Master of Life told him that the paradise could become a reality if the Shawnee would follow a path of virtue. Lalawethika spelled out the requirements. He had heard the Master of Life say: "The Americans I did not make. They are not my children, but the children of the Evil Spirit." According to his vision, the white race had been created on the shores of North America by malevolent powers residing either in a giant crab or in the scum that washes onto the beaches. (61)

THE MAN BEHIND THE MEN

Every society and nation enjoys its freedom and productivity. When a nation or group of people are faced with enduring hardships that result in their people being under the foot of another, explanations are incumbent to explain their downfall, especially if the suffering people have a history of greatness and independence. In the case of Elijah Muhammad, as demonstrated with Lalawethika and the Shawnee tribe, why not make the dominating rulers in your life the "Evil One, Satan"? Better yet, create a story that explains how the oppressing dominator came into existence unnaturally.

Often these accounts culminate with the oppressed group one day being free and again in control of their lives. Fard in creating the "Yakub's History" fable recognized the need to provide such a story in his effort to rebuild the African American mind and soul. Additionally Fard recognized the impact that his "blue-eyed, blond haired, white devil" message would have on Caucasians, especially the racist among them who held the Aryan belief that those two phenotypes are the epitome of beauty and indicators of superior human intellect. Fard was striking at the core of their racist beliefs.

To hearten African Americans Fard gave the Yakub catechism to his early followers. Elijah Muhammad faithfully promoted this artificial race laden story to every African American who would lend him their ear. But for white Americans Fard's "white devil theology" must have been disturbing to their individual sense of morality, and also challenging to the status quo standard of that era which promoted that blond hair and blue eyes were the highest standards for defining beauty and undefiled pedigree.

The artificiality that accompanies the superiority-inferiority complex also requires that those in power create folklores or interpretations of religious scriptures — as with the Noah, Ham, Canaan story — that justify their claims of superiority and oppressive *isms* that find expression in race, national pride, gender and class discrimination.

When it comes to historical reports on the wrongs of white racism and its gluttony for superiority, the Ku Klux Klan most likely comes to mind. Repeatedly this band of white-hooded "Christian Knights," mainly from southern states, are presented as the worst expression of white racism, with little if any focus placed upon other forms of pervasive white racism that existed in America. Whereas the Ku Klux Klan has been exposed for its sins, the other more powerful forms of institutional white racism that prevailed during the lifetime of Elijah Muhammad have not been given the same attention and scrutiny.

The Ku Klux Klan for the most part was comprised of rich and poor southern farmers, small town law officials, and civic leaders. But the overall racial superiority based on the presumptuousness of European hegemony was evident nationwide during the lifetime of Elijah Muhammad. Any public thought of another race being equal with white people oft times was ridiculed outright as nonsense, even by many white liberals.

ON CALLING THE WHITE MAN THE "DEVIL"

The regular promotion of the superiority of the Anglo-Saxon man over all other people was in many ways just as wrong, if not more errant than, the atrocities committed by the KKK. John Howard Griffin, the author of *Black Like Me* also believed that the worse racism did not come from the Ku Klux Klan but from the educated white people who displayed a "willingness to destroy and subvert values that have traditionally been held supreme in this land." Referencing P.D. East's book *The Magnolia Jungle*, Griffin wrote:

> It is perhaps the most incredible collection of what East calls "assdom" in the South. It shows that the most obscene figures are not the ignorant ranting racist, but the legal minds who front for them, who "invent" for them the legislative proposals and the propaganda bulletins. They deliberately choose to foster distortions, always under the guise of patriotism, upon a people who have no means of checking the facts. (78)

Griffin's summation that the invention of racism stemmed from regional interest seems to discount the fact that national leaders in politics, science, and education also displayed a nationwide willingness to destroy and subvert values. Nonetheless, Griffin accurately described the problem that arises when the Ku Klux Klan and poor whites are blamed for promoting white racism while rich and powerful — even liberal minded whites are excused from their role in promoting and supporting racism against non-white people.

African American leaders such as W.E.B. DuBois, Frederick Douglass, Booker T. Washington, Dr. Martin Luther King and others, in various ways all fought against such Anglo-Saxon arrogance. Elijah Muhammad chose to oppose this racial arrogance by fighting fire with fire. He waged his battle by teaching his "the white man is the devil" message; a blow to white racial pride and a social mirror reflecting to the white man of conscious the ugly arrogance and social shortcomings of racism. Elijah Muhammad's method, though stinging, got the attention of both black and white Americans and allowed both races an opportunity to reevaluate themselves individually and as racial groups, eventually allowing both races to reevaluate the true human worth of each other.

The white supremacy in Anglo-Saxonism of the 19th and 20th centuries was promoted by many college professors and often supported by some U.S. presidents. Long before the advent of Elijah Muhammad and the Nation of Islam, deep-seated racism had taken root in every level of American society. Thomas Jefferson's *Query XIV: The Administration of Justice and Description of the Laws? Notes on the State of Virginia, 1787*, clearly outlines Jefferson's position on white superiority versus black inferiority. In this writing, penned four years before his White House presidency Congressman Jefferson refers to whites as the more beautiful of the two races. He stated "The circumstance of superior beauty, is thought worthy attention in the propagation of our horses, dogs, and other domestic animals; why not in that of man? Besides those of colour, figure, and hair, there are other physical distinctions proving a difference of race. They have less hair on the face and body. They secrete less by the kidneys, and more by the glands of the skin, which gives them a very strong and disagreeable odour." He further denigrated the descendants of Africa stating, "Comparing them by their faculties of memory, reason, and imagination, it appears to me that in memory they are equal to the whites; in reason much inferior, as I think one could scarcely be found capable of tracing and comprehending the investigations of Euclid; and that in imagination they are dull, tasteless, and anomalous."

Jefferson held strongly to his views of white superiority and did not consider a change until later in life when challenged by the African American intellectual, astronomer and city planner Benjamin Banneker, a freeman of African descent. On August 19, 1791 while serving as Secretary of State, Jefferson received a letter from Banneker. The letter, accompanied with a copy of Banneker's almanac, in part asked Jefferson, "Sir, suffer me to recal (sic) to your mind that time, in which the arms and tyranny of the British crown were exerted, with every powerful effort, in order to reduce you to a state of servitude..." Building upon this reminder of how British oppression had denied Jefferson's predecessors the freedom to think and reason, and how their servitude hindered the imagination of downtrodden Englishmen, Banneker encouraged Jefferson to reconsider his opinion toward enslaved Africans in America. He asked Jefferson, "to wean yourselves from those narrow prejudices which you have imbibed with respect to them, and as Job proposed to his friends, 'put your soul in their souls' stead."

Thomas Jefferson did express his appreciation to Banneker for his letter. Nonetheless, the unpleasant ambience of white racial superiority remained a public nuisance for generations to come. When Elijah Muhammad met W.D. Fard in 1929 the assumed superiority of the white race was still deeply entrenched in the psyche of most white Americans. The night raids of terror committed by the Ku Klux Klan actually pale in comparison with the open-air artificial messages of white superiority promoted by those who believed in the unparalleled excellence of the Anglo Saxon male in particular.

At least one sitting president openly promoted the superiority of the white Anglo-Saxon over other races. President Theodore Roosevelt, caught in the spirit of the eugenic age and concerned over a possible shortfall of Caucasian babies, feared the possible decline of white babies if voluntary sterility prevailed. The scientific thinking of that time promoted a type of breeding that favored "advanced" races, an ideology that influenced the president's public

ON CALLING THE WHITE MAN THE "DEVIL"

appeal to white Americans. Fearing a "race suicide," President Roosevelt in 1903 warned that minorities and immigrants were too fertile. In a speech dubbed, "The Fertility Race: Part IV: Race Suicide," he cautioned against using birth control and "failing to keep up baby-for-baby."

In one speech Roosevelt declared, "The chief of blessings for any nation is that it shall leave its seed to inherit the land. The greatest of all curses is sterility, and the severest of all condemnations should be that visited upon willful sterility.

In order to prove that whites were superior not only mentally and morally but also physically, the aristocratic mind of Anglo Saxonism made its way into sports. When the African American boxer Jack Johnson became the heavyweight champion of the world in 1908, he sent the white racists on a vain, worldwide search for The Great White Hope. This is the racial and social milieu that Elijah Muhammad's generation encountered.

Even the monuments erected to preserve the history of the Civil War were required by 19th and early 20th century standards to use marble and higher quality materials to replicate carvings of white people. If the monument was multi-racial then the slave or the non-white figures were, in addition to being placed in a position inferior to the statue's white figures, also were often made from lesser quality materials such as bronze. Kirk Savage observed in his book *Standing Soldiers, Kneeling Slaves: Race, War, and Monument in Nineteenth-Century America* how American statues were fashioned in a way to support race-based fallacies.

> More than any of the other arts, sculpture was embedded in the theoretical foundation of racism that supported American slavery and survived long after its demise. For racism, like sculpture, centered on the analysis and representation of the human body. The concept of race emerged in the late eighteenth-and early nineteenth-century natural science as a way of explaining visible differences between bodies. Certain differences, notably of skin color, facial structure, and hair type, came to be correlated with moral and intellectual capacities thought to be inherited and therefore shared by the "race" (8).

These are a few of the forms of white racism that Elijah Muhammad's message challenged when he called the white man "the blue-eyed devil;" a highlighting of their wrong and evil ways that gave white Americans an opportunity to see their flaws.

African American leaders, even prior to W.D. Fard often publicly called the white man the devil. Frederick Douglass, David Walker, Henry Highland Garnet, Harriet Jacobs (aka Linda Brents) and the Noble Drew Ali were leaders who in their respective generations witnessed the cruel treatment that African Americans received from the hands of European Americans. They too called white people "the devil."

Frederick Douglass in his book *My Bondage and My Freedom*, on page 264, spoke strongly against the supporters of slavery. Douglass placed the wretched slave close to God; those who "were nearest and dearest to his great heart." Simultaneously Douglass referenced as devils the Christians who upheld slavery. "Those ministers who defended slavery from the bible, were of their 'father the devil'; and those churches which fellowshiped slaveholders as Christians, were synagogues of Satan, and our nation was a nation of liars."

David Walker, born in the 1780s to a free black woman, became a leading voice among slave abolitionists. In his book Walker's Appeal (circa 1848) Walker systematically chronicles his support for referring to the white man as a devil. Walker wrote, "The whites have always been an unjust, jealous, unmerciful, avaricious and blood thirsty set of beings, always seeking after power and authority." After defining the white man's presence in Greece, Rome, Gaul, Spain, Europe, Asia and Africa as that of a heathen, Walker concludes, "...and we see them acting more like devils than accountable men."

A contemporary and cohort of David Walker was Henry Highland Garnet, a former child slave. The mercilessness of slavery moved Garnet to call white people the devil in the flesh. In his 1843 address at the National Convention held in Buffalo, NY, Garnet twice titled white people with devil status. "Remember the stripes your fathers bore. Think of the torture and disgrace of your noble mothers. Think of your wretched sisters, loving virtue and purity as they are driven into concubinage, and are exposed to the unbridled lust of incarnate devils."

In his concluding comments Garnet disparagingly criticized the patience of African American slaves with their condition. "Yes, the tyrants would meet with plagues more terrible than those of Pharaoh. But you are a patient people. You act as though you were made for special use of these devils."

In 1861, writing under the pseudonym Linda Brent, the former slave Harriet Jacobs, who had learned to read and write at the age of six, penned her slave experience in hopes of building support for the abolition of slavery. In her book *Incidents in the Life of a Slave Girl*, Jacobs wrote how the 1831 insurrection of Nat Turner behooved many slave masters, "to give the slaves enough of religious instruction to keep them from murdering their masters" (59). Jacobs said the themes of the sermons were the usual "slave serve your master" orations.

During the indoctrination styled sermons that were designed to maintain the slave-to-master relationships, the slaves would sing hymns they had composed that scarcely hid their disdain for both their slave

ON CALLING THE WHITE MAN THE "DEVIL"

masters and the houses of worships that the slaves were now allowed to attend in the evenings. Jacobs wrote that the slaves would openly protest their mistreatment by singing "as though they were as free as the birds that warbled round us," double-messaged songs that called their white masters the devil. "Ole Satan's church is here below. Up to God's free church I hope to go. Cry Amen, cry Amen, Cry Amen to God!"

Elijah Muhammad was born one generation after the release of Jacob's book. As shown in her book, it was very common in many African American circles — due to their plight of slavery and subsequent Jim Crow restrictions — to refer to many white people as "Satan" or the "devil". When W.D. Fard introduced his anti-white version of Islam to Elijah Poole African Americans had already begun referring to the white man as the "devil."

The evil effects of slavery stirred in men and women such as Douglass, Walker, Jacobs and Garnet the temerity to describe white men and their behavior in the most effective term available, "devil." The immoral Jim Crow era that followed slavery also evoked a similar charge from some 20th century African American leaders, namely Elijah Muhammad.

The difference between Elijah Muhammad calling the white man the "Devil" in comparison with the African American leaders who preceded him, is that Elijah had a theology with catechisms that supported his repetitious charges of white devilry. Other factors that broaden Elijah Muhammad's resounding of "the white man is the devil" is that his mission was aided by the media outlets of his day, radio and television, not to mention public access to his audiotapes and phonographs, communication tools that were not available or accessible in the lifetimes of Walker, Garnet, Jacobs and Douglass.

Further, Elijah Muhammad had an ever growing community of followers who were able to reach a wider national audience than a Frederick Douglass or a David Walker. Lastly, another factor that accounts for America's vivid recollection that Elijah Muhammad charged Caucasians with white devilry is that chronologically he is the most recent voice in American history to charge the white man of yesteryears with being the "devil."

In Muhammad Ali's book *Soul of a Butterfly*, written in conjunction with his daughter Hana Ali, the former boxing champion shared on pages 59-60 how his personal life experiences allowed him to consider the possibility of white people as the devil. "The Nation of Islam taught that White people were devils. I don't believe that now; in fact, I never really believed that White men were devils. But when I was young, I had seen and heard so many horrible stories about the White man that this made me stop and listen."

In an effort to soften Elijah Muhammad's charge that the white man was the devil, Ali argues that Elijah Muhammad did not mean that all white people were devils. In Ali's account Elijah Muhammad "was mainly talking about some of the history of America. White people slaughtered the Indians, enslaved Black people and robbed them of their cultures so they had no real identity." Using the analogy of a snake, Muhammad Ali summarized how Elijah Muhammad qualified using the term "devil" to describe white people.

> We knew that not all White people were bad and that there were Black people who did wrong, too. Some White people wanted to help us and in their heart meant us no harm, but how were we to know who they were? The way Elijah Muhammad put it was like this: "What if there were one thousand rattlesnakes outside your door, and maybe one hundred of them wouldn't bite you, didn't mean you any harm. But they all looked alike, so you couldn't tell the mean ones from the nice ones. What should you do? Should you open the door and hope that the hundred snakes that wouldn't harm you will come together and form a shield, protecting you from the other nine hundred snakes that want to harm you? Or should you close the door and stay safe? (59-60)

Malcolm X, while still a minister for Elijah Muhammad, detailed the position that the Nation of Islam was not necessarily labeling each and every individual white person a devil. In his autobiography pages 271-72, which was completed by Alex Haley, Malcolm stated:

> Unless we call one white man, by name, a 'devil,' we are not speaking of any individual white man. We are speaking of the collective white man's historical record. We are speaking of the collective white man's cruelties, and evils, and greeds, [sic] that have seen him act like a devil toward the non-white man. Any intelligent, honest, objective person cannot fail to realize that this white man's slave trade, and his subsequent devilish actions are directly responsible for not only the presence of this black man in America, but also for the condition in which we find this black man here. You cannot find one black man, I do not care who he is, who has not been personally damaged in some way by the devilish acts of the collective white man!

Wallace Muhammad often included his clarifications to elucidate upon many of his father's ideologies. On March 13, 2004 while speaking at George Washington School — 29 years after the passing of Elijah Muhammad — Wallace offered his understanding of the serendipitous path that the followers of Elijah Muhammad traveled on their way to classical or universal Islam. This indirect pathway used an innovative language that was designed to address step-by-step the areas of weakness in the African American community. Imam

ON CALLING THE WHITE MAN THE "DEVIL"

Mohammed's review of this unusual but progressive road towards universal Islam allowed him to have tolerance with his father calling the white man the devil in the past. He told the audience:

> I believe that the strange thing that has happened to bring us to the Qur'an and to (Prophet) Muhammed — Mr. Fard and all of his strange teachings, the Honorable Elijah Muhammad the fiery preacher denouncing the white world and telling us we have been chosen and we are the original people, we are the ones who have divinity, or holiness and righteousness, and godliness and the white man does not — all of that strange teaching, that's not a truth because the truth is true yesterday and today. It wasn't a truth but it was relevant because at that time the white man was behaving as a devil. And his nation was behaving as a devil. His nation, the United States was behaving as a devil, in the international world and also in our life. Okay? So in that space of time it was justified to call the white man a race of devils; to call his nation a nation doomed for destruction. It was justified. The teacher who came, he didn't give us Islam. But he quietly, secretly, made us distinguish between the Qur'an and what he was teaching. And he distinguished between Islam and what he was teaching. He even told my father, according to my father's own words, he said "Don't worry so much about teaching them the Qur'an, someone will come later and do that."
>
> — Imam W. Deen Mohammed
> George Washington School, Newark, NJ

The fact that the mother of Elijah Muhammad's mentor, Mr. W.D. Fard, was "100 percent white" but somehow not devil is another noteworthy factor in giving understanding and clarity to the misconception that Elijah Muhammad believed all whites to be devil. W.D. Fard's mother's name was spelled either "Baby G" or "Baby Gee". The Nation of Islam taught that she escaped being a devil because her upbringing was under the care of black people and not by her own race.

Surely all whites were not to be classified as devils if the mother of "God in the Person", Fard, is a "100 percent white woman" but yet not labeled a "blue-eyed devil." Also it must be remembered that if whites were truly devils then neither Elijah nor Fard would have allowed a few whites to become members of the Nation of Islam.

W.D. Fard and Elijah Muhammad carefully crafted their words in a way to have both contemporary as well as future effects. The student of Fard's phrase the "blue-eyed devil," and his placing that burden upon the white man, must also investigate other questions. What is the status of the green-eyed or the hazel-eyed white man? Are they also a devil, or a lesser devil in light of the fact that they don't have blue eyes?

THE MAN BEHIND THE MEN

Imam Clyde Rahman of Cleveland, OH shared a report of how an altered interpretation of the "blue-eyed devil" concept worked in the best interest of the Nation of Islam. A lawyer representing the Nation of Islam was successful in convincing a judge to allow the ministers of Elijah Muhammad to teach in the prisons. The judge was reluctant to allow the Muslims access to the inmates because of the Nation of Islam's "blue-eyed devil" message until the lawyer, who noticed that the judge did not have blue eyes, told the judge that the Nation of Islam was not calling all white people devils, only those with blue eyes.

There are a variety of arguments regarding the proper interpretation of what the phrase "blue-eyed devil" actually means. A popular belief is that the color blue was not to be understood as a physical color but as a symbol of deceitfulness. Blue, in this explanation is analogous to the blue as it appears on seas, or in the daytime sky which to the naked eye appears to be blue but upon closer inspection actually are transparent. Their appearance from afar deceives the viewer.

Another analogy suggests that the "blue-eyed devil" charge is not speaking at all about the physical eye of any particular race, but is actually addressing a disease of the spiritual eye. Sura 20: ayat 102 of the Qur'an speaks of the "blear-eyed," of which some translations use the phrase "blue-eyed." Yusuf Ali's translation reads: "The Day when the Trumpet will be sounded: that Day, We shall gather the sinful, blear-eyed (with terror)." The Arabic term for blear or blue is zurq. On page 376 in *The Hans Wehr Dictionary of Modern Written Arabic* the medical description for zurq is glaucoma or blindness. In a spiritual sense this blindness is not of the physical eye but of the mental eye that is blind to the word of God.

The various attempts to give a definitive answer to why W.D. Fard and Elijah Muhammad specifically said "the blue-eyed" white man is the devil only proves that neither of them meant that all white people were genetically a devil. Elijah Muhammad's warning to his own followers to be wary of "turning devil overnight" clearly indicates that in Elijah's and Fard's mind, regardless of any individual's race, anyone one could be a devil.

Elijah Muhammad definitely was addressing a mentality that had negatively affected some white people to think themselves superior. Using this strong "devil" language he got the attention of both black and white America. A language that was a potent tool used to attract and free the thinking of disenfranchised, fearful Negroes.

-§- CHAPTER -§-
SEVEN

Muhammad Ali
(Three-Time Heavyweight Boxing Champion)

Ali, donning his Fruit of Islam uniform, speaking at a pre-1975 Nation of Islam gathering. *(Muslim Journal file)*

"And my idol was a man named Elijah Muhammad. [His] Islamic teaching is what made me so confident."

— Muhammad Ali
Reader's Digest, December 2001

THE MAN BEHIND THE MEN

Muhammad Ali was born in Louisville, KY on January 17, 1942, as Cassius Marcellus Clay, the oldest son of Odessa and Cassius Marcellus Clay, Sr. His younger brother Rudolph (Rudy) was Cassius only sibling. Rudolph later changed his name to Rahaman Ali.

Louisville was a segregated city during Ali's childhood and young adult years, yet he still loved his hometown. At the age of 12 Cassius was introduced to the world of boxing after his bicycle was stolen. During his quest to retrieve his stolen bike he was directed to Joe Martin, a Louisville policeman. "I'm gonna whup 'em!" young Clay exclaimed while seeking justice with Officer Martin. "Well, do you know how to fight?" Martin asked. "No," Cassius said, "but I'd fight anyway." Martin advised, "Why don't you learn something about fighting before you go making any hasty challenges?" With that said Martin invited Cassius to take boxing lessons at his gym. The rest is boxing history.

Young Clay's quick ascension through the boxing ranks of Golden Gloves contenders often provided him with occasions to travel outside of Louisville, which in turn, while boxing in Chicago, indirectly availed him opportunities to hear the message of Elijah Muhammad and the Nation of Islam. Clay enjoyed the message of Elijah Muhammad — this was the beginning of Elijah Muhammad being a major influence in Clay's life.

Cassius Clay encountered the Nation of Islam the same way as most other young African Americans. It was common to see members of Elijah Muhammad's Nation of Islam sharing their message and selling their publications on the streets of America's ghettoes. Conversations about Elijah Muhammad and the Nation of Islam, whether pro or con, were taking place throughout black America. Thomas Hauser, a biographer on the life of Muhammad Ali, reports in his book *Muhammad Ali: His Life and Times*, that Clay's first encounter with the Nation of Islam was in 1959 while attending a Golden Gloves tournament in Chicago where Cassius purchased a record album of Elijah Muhammad. According to Hauser, Ali said:

> The first time I heard about Elijah Muhammad was at a Golden Gloves Tournament in Chicago [1959]. Then, before I went to the Olympics, I looked at a copy of the Nation of Islam's newspaper, *Muhammad Speaks*. I didn't pay much attention to it, but a lot of things were working on my mind.
> When I was growing up, a colored boy named Emmett Till was murdered in Mississippi for whistling at a white woman. Emmett Till was the same age as me, and even though they caught the men who did it, nothing happened to them. Things like that went on all the time. And in my own life, there were places I couldn't go, places I couldn't eat. I won a gold medal representing the United States at the Olympic Games, and

when I came home to Louisville, I still got treated like a nigger. There were restaurants I couldn't get served in. Some people kept calling me 'boy. Then in Miami [1961], I was training for a fight, and met a follower of Elijah Muhammad named Captain Sam. He invited me to a meeting, and after that, my life changed. (89)

Howard Bingham, a close friend and personal photographer of Muhammad Ali since 1967 offers a different report of Ali's first encounter with the Nation of Islam. Whereas Hausers believes it was in Chicago in 1959, Bingham notes that Clay's first encounter with the Nation of Islam was in Atlanta in 1958. Quite a mesmerizing experience, the following week at school Cassius was given an English essay assignment to write on any topic about which he felt strongly. He chose to write about the Nation of Islam. Bingham, in his book *Muhammad Ali's Greatest Fight: Cassius Clay vs. United States of America*, noted the following:

> When he turned in the essay a few days later, his teacher, a black woman was livid. She marched right into principal Atwood Wilson's office and demanded disciplinary action be taken. The Principal turned the matter over to the school's guidance counselor Betty Johnston. ..."I [Johnston] went to school with his parents and knew the family quite well. It was obvious from the paper that he was well-versed in the doctrine of the Muslims and that he admired them." (Bingham and Wallace, 63-64)

Two days after dethroning Charles "Sonny" Liston to become then the world's youngest heavyweight boxing champion, Cassius publicly disclosed on February 27, 1964, that he was a member of the Nation of Islam. On that day, which is also one day after the Nation of Islam's annual Saviour's Day, Cassius, via the media told the world, "Islam is a religion and there are 750 million people all over the world who believe in it, and I'm one of them."

Prior to the first Liston-Clay fight Malcolm X was in close communications with Clay, even to the point of visiting his boxing gym. Malcolm became Cassius' close friend and tutored him on Nation of Islam teachings. However, after relations between Elijah Muhammad and Malcolm X soured, so too did the friendship between Clay and Malcolm. When Malcolm left the Nation of Islam Clay sided with Elijah Muhammad, the ultimate authority in the Nation of Islam. Elijah Muhammad, acknowledging Clay's loyalty, bestowed upon him the "holy name" Muhammad Ali. After receiving that noble distinction from Elijah Muhammad, Cassius Clay never would be the same.

On March 6, 1964 during a radio broadcast, Elijah Muhammad said, "This Clay name has no divine meaning. I hope he will accept being called by a better name. Muhammad Ali is what I will give him for as long as he believes in Allah and follows me."

THE MAN BEHIND THE MEN

Ali's response to Elijah Muhammad giving him a "holy name" was one of joy. At the age of 48, Ali related to Thomas Hauser the excitement he still possessed about receiving his Islamic name. "Changing my name was one of the most important things that happened to me in my life. It freed me from the identity given to my family by slave masters...I was honored that Elijah Muhammad gave me a truly beautiful name. 'Muhammad' means one worthy of praise. 'Ali' was the name of a great general [a cousin of the Prophet Muhammad, and the third *(actually fourth)* Caliphate after the death of the Prophet]. I've been Muhammad Ali now for twenty-six years. That's four years longer than I was Cassius Clay." (102)

When Elijah Muhammad renamed Cassius Marcellus Clay with the name Muhammad Ali, it was more than rewarding Ali for choosing to follow him over following Malcolm. With his act of renaming Clay as Ali, Elijah was giving Ali a new persona, inner dignity, and a new outlook on life as a black man in America.

Muhammad Ali found in Elijah Muhammad and his brand of Islam a resource of confidence and strength. As a superb boxer Ali already had an elevated self-esteem; but now with Elijah Muhammad giving him a new name that came complimentary with a change in his diet and attire, Ali's discipline and sense of black manhood rose even higher. The power that Ali garnered from Elijah Muhammad reassured the boxing champion that his choice to follow Elijah Muhammad instead of Malcolm was correct, a stance that in some measures Ali would later regret.

Ali, working with his daughter Hana Ali, wrote in his book, *The Soul of A Butterfly: Reflections On Life's Journey*, "I was forced to make a choice when Elijah Muhammad insisted that I break with Malcolm." Ali penned, "Turning my back on Malcolm was one of the mistakes that I regret most in my life. I wish I'd been able to tell Malcolm I was sorry, that he was right about so many things. But he was killed before I got the chance. He was a visionary — ahead of us all." (84-85)

After Malcolm's departure from the Nation of Islam he and Ali crossed paths while in Ghana, Africa. Bruce Perry in his biography on Malcolm X reported that Ali admonished Malcolm, "You left the Honorable Elijah Muhammad. That was the wrong thing to do, Brother Malcolm." Perry claims that after Ali had departed, Malcolm with sagged shoulders and in a state of "glum" responded, "I've lost a lot... almost too much." (270)

On another occasion Ali criticized Malcolm for dressing in middle-eastern garb. Elijah Muhammad's followers were well known for wearing American styled suits and bow ties. Making mockery of his former tutor, Ali said, "Man, did you get a look at him? Dressed in that funny white robe and wearing a beard and walking with a cane that looked like a prophet's stick? Man, he's gone so far out he's out completely. Doesn't that just go to show that Elijah is the most powerful; nobody listens to Malcolm anymore." (Bingham and Wallace, 102)

CHAMPION MUHAMMAD ALI

Ali over the years seems to be ambivalent regarding Elijah Muhammad and Malcolm X. Obviously he loved both men deeply for their contributions to his growth as a Muslim and as a human being. He was forced to split his loyalties between the two men while still a youngster in life and as a new convert to Islam. Furthermore, before Ali's reached maturity in either life or in Islam Malcolm was murdered, thus denying Ali the opportunity to bring a real sense of closure between him and Malcolm. As the years waxed and Ali matured in his understanding of Islam, the importance of Elijah Muhammad and Malcolm in his life took shape, especially after Imam Wallace Mohammed succeeded his father as the leader of the Nation of Islam.

But it was Elijah Muhammad who gave Ali his Muslim name. The depth of the impact of renaming Cassius Clay with the name "Muhammad Ali" had not escaped the wise planning of Elijah Muhammad, who understood the strategic and mutual benefits that the name change would bring for both he and Ali. The name change gave Ali a sense of brotherhood with every Muslim in the world, as well as a sense of freedom from his birth name, which he now saw as a slave name. For Elijah Muhammad, Clay's name change gave the Nation of Islam worldwide attention in general, but specifically it gave the Nation of Islam another connection with the entire Muslim world.

On two occasions in 1975 Ali publicly recognized how receiving the name Muhammad Ali from Elijah Muhammad helped to thrust him onto the international scene. At the annual Saviour's Day in 1975, the day after the passing of Elijah Muhammad, Ali told a throng of 15,000 Muslim faithful, "After that the world realized that I followed the Honorable Elijah Muhammad, I was a Muslim. We immediately received invitations to countries such as Egypt, Arabia, Libya, Syria, Abu Dhabi, Iran, Pakistan, Indonesia and many more countries. All the kings of these countries, such as President Gamal Abdel Nasser of Egypt, all spoke of the Honorable Elijah Muhammad. He said, 'When is Elijah Muhammad coming to Cairo?' We promised them that whenever he had time he would come."

In a 1975 interview with *Playboy* magazine Ali reflected on the importance of having a name that united him with the international Islamic world.

> I just don't think another fighter will ever be followed by people in every country on the planet. You can go to Japan, China, all the European, African, Arab and South American countries and, man, they know me. I can't name a country where they don't know me. If another fighter's goin' to be that big, he's goin' to have to be a Muslim, or else he won't get to nations like Indonesia, Lebanon, Iran, Saudi Arabia, Pakistan, Syria, Egypt and Turkey — those are all countries that don't usually follow boxing. He might even have to be named Muhammad, because Muhammad is the most common name in the world. There are more Muhammads than

there are Williamses, Joneses, Ecksteins, Smiths or anything else on earth. And he's also gonna have to say the name Allah a lot, can't say God. I know that God is the Supreme Being, but Allah is the name used most on the planet. More people pray to Allah than to Jehovah, Jesus or just plain Lord, 'cause there are about 11 Muslims in the world to every non-Muslim.

Elijah Muhammad was not interested in boxing. Actually the Nation of Islam had a long history of denouncing sports as a wrong that supports gambling and hinders one's remembrance of Allah. On April 11, 1969 Elijah Muhammad publicly admonished Ali for disobeying his order to hang up his boxing gloves and accept to be a minister for the Nation of Islam instead of seeking the white man's money through boxing.

There appears to be a misrepresentation of facts emanating from within the Nation of Islam concerning how Elijah Muhammad reacted to Ali's boxing career. Some reports indicate that Elijah Muhammad was totally against Ali boxing, but in 1966 and 1967 the Nation of Islam's newspaper, *Muhammad Speaks* regularly printed a full page with photos titled "News from the Camp of the Champ." This page was dedicated to reporting on every Ali fight as well as his training and community activities.

"News From the Camp of the Champ," regularly reported the boxing activity of Ali. *Muhammad Speaks* - November 18, 1966. *(Muslim Journal file)*

CHAMPION MUHAMMAD ALI

Despite the strict dress code of the Nation of Islam that promoted modesty and decency for both males and females, every week the *Muhammad Speaks* showed pictures of Ali scantly clad in the typical dress that all boxers wear; only boxing trunks and shoes. How this obvious contradiction between Nation of Islam modesty including the Muslim aversion to sports, blended with Ali being promoted in public in *Muhammad Speaks* as a half-nude boxer is interesting. Surely this contradiction should have presented a challenge to some of the Nation of Islam officials to explain to the faithful why Ali was allowed to do what other members were forbidden.

Apparently Elijah Muhammad had some room in his heart for Ali's boxing career. The only sport Elijah Muhammad did allow was baseball, a game that Nation of Islam members played on Tuesday nights during the years that W.D. Fard was the leader of the Nation of Islam.

Not only did Ali fight on the canvas, he also found himself fighting in a variety of venues outside of the boxing ring. The media was a constant foe that challenged him on his beliefs and his name change. Some of his immediate family members, particularly his father, openly opposed Ali's conversion to the Nation of Islam. As he had eluded the heavyweights in the boxing ring, Ali in similar fashion skillfully eluded the offense of his out-of-the-ring opponents. Applying the lessons he had learned from Elijah Muhammad, Ali was able to defend his new way of life as a Muslim in the Nation of Islam.

Ali remained devoutly loyal to Elijah Muhammad. At a moment's notice, as with all faithful Nation of Islam members, he was ready to defend his leader's character. In 1968 as a guest on *Firing Line*, host William Buckley questioned Ali about being exploited financially by Elijah Muhammad. Ali's response revealed just the opposite. Ali retorted, "I owe him money right now. $100,000!" Howard Bingham recalled the Ali-Buckley exchange:

> But the famous conservative intellectual William F. Buckley Jr., well known for his debating skills, was anxious to challenge Ali's views on race and booked him on his weekly TV show for a more serious discussion. In a memorable exchange that proved Ali could hold his own against any opponent, in or out of the ring, Buckley fired the first salvo: "You have said that 'the white man is our enemy." Well, I happen to know this is not true. I believe you have been poisoned by your leader."
> Ali jumped right in. "How can you say Elijah Muhammad is poisoning us to believe the white people are our enemy? It's you who taught us that you're our enemy. It was white people who bumped off Martin Luther King, it was white people who bumped off Medgar Evers, it was white people who bumped off Adam Clayton Powell. We didn't imagine this."
> Buckley has rarely, if ever, publicly admitted being wrong. More inconceivable still would be an admission that he was

bested by a mere athlete. But after the debate he told an interviewer, "I started out thinking he was simply special-pleading on his behalf, but I ended up thinking he was absolutely correct." (212)

In conversation Ali was apt at verbally slipping, leaning, jabbing and shuffling before releasing upon his opponents in the media a rapid succession of statements that often began with the phrase, "the Honorable Elijah Muhammad teaches us..." Then he met a Goliath of an opponent — the United States Army. Again, Ali looked to the teachings of Elijah Muhammad for strength, support, and guidance as he entered into a political boxing ring to fight in defense of his status as a conscientious objector.

Elijah Muhammad totally avoided direct involvement in America's politics. Yet it can be argued that indirectly through Ali he was a major factor in the spread of the anti-Vietnam movement in America. Elijah Muhammad's 1942 refusal to be inducted into the United States Army became the model for all other males of the Nation of Islam to follow. The same proved true with Muhammad Ali when he too refused to be drafted into the army. Elijah's influence upon the young heavyweight boxing champion's decision to refuse induction is quite obvious; the anti-war die had already been cast by Elijah Muhammad and other Nation of Islam members in the 1940s. Now it was Ali's turn to conform to the mode he inherited from his Muslim predecessors.

Philip A. Klinkner and Rogers M. Smith observed the potential political effect of Ali's resistance to fighting in Vietnam; an effect that resonated not only in America but also in developing countries. In their book *The Unsteady March: The Rise and Fall of Racial Equality in America*, Klinkner and Smith noted how Muhammad Ali's anti-Vietnam stance resounded around the world and challenged "the U.S. government to try to hold the allegiance of other nations of color abroad and of African Americans at home." Klinkner and Smith concluded that Ali in following the conscientious objector model established by Elijah Muhammad would have multiple effects that were displeasing to U.S. officials. Klinkner and Smith acknowledged the role that the Nation of Islam played in the up-rise of the anti-Vietnam war sentiments. This laid upon United States officials the obligation, according to Klinkner and Smith, to "threaten to imprison the charismatic heavyweight champion Muhammad Ali when he refused military service, championed the Nation of Islam, and spoke out against U.S. policies to admiring African and Islamic countries." (293)

After Ali publicly followed the footsteps of Elijah Muhammad by refusing induction, the world took notice and soon thereafter the Vietnam War protest rapidly engulfed the college campuses and streets of America. The seemingly apolitical Elijah Muhammad, through Ali, had become an indirect but effective political influence upon American's feelings toward the war in Vietnam. Elijah Muhammad had already served a five-year federal prison sentence for violation of the draft. Nonetheless, his teachings on Nation of Islam Muslims not participating in wars – outlined in *Message to the Blackman* – was clear as shown in Elijah's reply to Judge F. Ryan Duffy.

Minister Muhammad Ali at the rostrum in Muhammad's Mosque No. 7 in New York City. March 24, 1967 edition of *Muhammad Speaks* (Muslim Journal file)

Elijah Muhammad wrote: "The very dominant idea in Islam is the making of peace and not war; our refusing to go armed is our proof that we want peace. We felt that we had no right to take part in a war with nonbelievers of Islam who have always denied us justice and equal rights." This thinking of Elijah Muhammad is most likely the stimulus behind Ali's famous quote, "I ain't got no quarrel with the VietCong... No VietCong ever called me nigger." Elijah Muhammad continued, "and if we are going to be examples of peace and righteousness (as Allah has chosen us to be), we felt we had no right to join hands with murderers of people or to help murder those who have done us no wrong. What would justify such actions? Let the truth answer." (322)

THE MAN BEHIND THE MEN

Ali lost the first round of his fight with the United States Army, yet he still maintained his conscientious objector status as a Nation of Islam Minister for Elijah Muhammad. "How can I kill somebody when I pray five times a day for peace?" Ali argued, "Elijah Muhammad teaches us to fight only when we're attacked, and my life is in his hands."

As the days and months passed, Ali sternly maintained his conscientious objector stance. In response to a reporter who asked, "What will you do if your appeal falls through; will you then resist going into the army?" Hauser captured the Champ's answer, "The world knows that I am a Muslim. The world knows that I am a sincere follower to death of Elijah Muhammad. We say five times a day, 'My prayers, my sacrifices, my life, and my death are all for Allah.' I repeat, 'My prayers, my sacrifices, my life, and my death are all for Allah.' So this is what I sincerely believe." (166)

Howard Bingham, echoing Hauser's account reported Ali as saying, "I am sincere in every bit of what the Holy Koran and the teachings of Elijah Muhammad tell us and it is that we are not allowed to participate in wars on the side of non-believers." (126)

On two other occasions Ali would reiterate his conscientious objector status while renewing his commitment to Elijah Muhammad and to his Islamic faith. Ed Gordon of National Public Radio remembered Ali's April 28, 1967 press conference where a question was raised regarding Ali's battle with the United States draft board and his allegiance to Elijah Muhammad. Ali unequivocally retorted:

> This would be a thousand percent against the teachings of the Honorable Elijah Muhammad, the religion of Islam, and the Holy Qur'an, the holy book that we believe in. This would all be denouncing and defying everything that I stand for. Whatever the punishment, whatever the persecution is for standing up for my religious beliefs, even if it means facing machine gun fire that day, I will face it before denouncing Elijah Muhammad and the religion of Islam, I'm ready to die!
> — National Public Radio

The other occasion where Ali reaffirmed his conscientious objector's stance and his loyalty to Elijah Muhammad occurred during the 1968 Saviour's Day Convention in Chicago. "Now they want to put me in jail, cause I follow this sweet lovely man. I tell 'em they can clean out my cell and put me in jail cause I'll never denounce this man!"

For more than three years Ali endured a serious loss of income and the opportunity to fight during the prime of his boxing career. The burden of legal maneuvers, caring for his family, and standing up for what he believed to be right was a tribulation for Ali. Although he was allowed to resume his boxing career in October of 1970 — his first fight since March 22, 1967 —

the reversal of the U.S. Supreme Court in Ali's favor was not rendered until June 28, 1971, four years and two months after his refusal to step forward to be inducted into the armed forces.

When Ali's forced hiatus from boxing was over Elijah Muhammad wanted Ali to quit boxing and serve the Nation of Islam as a full-time minister and ambassador. After a long anguished contemplation and with mounting bills to pay, Ali defied his leader and teacher and publicly stated his desire to continue fighting. On April 4, 1969 Elijah Muhammad swiftly countered by suspending Ali from the Nation of Islam for one year. Elijah Muhammad was dissatisfied with Ali's decision to continue boxing to the point of trying to deny Ali the use of his Muslim name.

Just two years earlier *Muhammad Speaks* newspaper had given Ali his own page titled *News from the Camp of the Champ,* now that Ali had spurned Elijah Muhammad's request to relinquish his boxing career this same publication in its April 11, 1969 issue published Elijah Muhammad's reprimand of Ali.

> We tell the world we're not with Muhammad Ali. Muhammad Ali is out of the circle of the brotherhood of the followers of Islam under the leadership and the teachings of Elijah Muhammad for one year.... Mr. Muhammad Ali wants a place in this sport world. He loves it. Mr. Muhammad Ali shall not be recognized with us under the holy name Muhammad Ali. We will call him Cassius Clay. We take away the name of Allah from him until he proves himself worthy of that name. This statement is to tell the world that we, the Muslims, are not with Mr. Muhammad Ali, in his desire to work in the sports world for the sake of a "leetle" *[sic]* money...I gave him, The Muslim Name Muhammad Ali and removed the slave name, Cassius Clay. This made him famous all over the world. In Asia, the Muslim world recognized him to the highest, but no more when they find that he is still Cassius Clay, everywhere...Why would Asia, respect Muhammad Ali (Cassius Clay)? They respected him because of the name, Muhammad Ali. They did not respect him for the sake of the sport, boxing. They do not have prize fighting in the Muslim world. They respected Muhammad Ali (Cassius Clay), because he was a Muslim and was whipping the white man and the Black Man out of the honor of being the champion man of the fistical *[sic]* world of sport.

Elijah Muhammad wanted to lift Ali above the mere status of a pugilist to that of a full-time Muslim minister. Ali was not the only professional whom Elijah Muhammad asked to leave a profession in order to serve him as a minister in the Nation of Islam. R&B singer Joe Tex, also known as Yusef Hazziez, while at the apex of his career deferred singing and dancing to become a minister in the Nation of Islam. Louis Farrakhan also had a promising career blossoming as a calypso singer, but he too stopped performing as "Gene the Charmer" and followed Elijah Muhammad. There are hundreds of men and women who left promising careers in government, business and the corporate world to assist Elijah Muhammad in "building a nation." However, Ali never obeyed Elijah's order to stopped using his Islamic name.

The confrontation between Elijah Muhammad and Ali's desire to fight seems to contradict the numerous claims that Elijah Muhammad was out to usurp Ali's money. Elijah Muhammad's open criticism of Ali's boxing career indicates that he wanted Ali to quit boxing and give full attention to the Nation of Islam. For years Elijah Muhammad had been against sports which he described on page 246 in his 1974 book *Message to the Blackman in America* as the "cause of delinquency, murder, theft and other forms of wicked and immoral crimes."

After years of shunning Ali's fights, Elijah Muhammad showed peripheral support for Ali in his October 30, 1974 Rumble in the Jungle bout against George Foreman. Hauser reported that Herbert Muhammad, Elijah's son, and at that time Ali's manager, entered the dressing room with a message for Ali from Elijah Muhammad. Ali recalled the message. "He told me I was fighting for our people." Ali remembers. "He said I should do my best, and that if I did, Allah would be with me." (297)

Apparently Muhammad Ali absorbed the advice that Elijah Muhammad had relayed to him via Herbert. After the victory over Foreman, during the post-fight interview, Ali spoke in reciprocating terms that suggest he was responding directly to the words of support he had received from Elijah Muhammad. Ali told the international world via the media, "I proved that Allah is God, Elijah Muhammad is His messenger, and I have faith in them." Ali, in the spirit of a believing Muslim further acknowledged, "Regardless to the world and the pressure, I made it an easy night because Allah has power over all things and if you believe in Him, nothing, even George Foreman will look like a baby." On this late October day, a little less that four months before the passing of Elijah Muhammad, Ali and his grand mentor had re-established their bond. We will elaborate further on the Ali-Foreman fight in later chapters.

The influence of Elijah Muhammad upon the life of Muhammad Ali is unquestionable. Every facet of Ali's life during this Nation of Islam era reflected the teachings of Elijah Muhammad. Ali even gave credit to Elijah Muhammad for the peace and serenity that was commonplace at his boxing camp. In a November 1975 interview with *Playboy* magazine Ali noted:

And you can tell [we are] a bunch of Muslims: no violence, no hate, no cigarettes, no fightin', no stealin', all happy. It's a *miracle*. Most Negro places you be in, you see folks fussin' and cussin', eatin' pork chops and women runnin' around. You've seen the peace and unity of my training camp--it's all Elijah Muhammad's spirit and his teachings. Black people never acted like this before. If every one of us in camp was just like we were before we heard Elijah Muhammad, you wouldn't be able to see for all the smoke. You'd hear things like, "Hey, man, what's happenin', where's the *ladies*? What we gonna *drink* tonight? Let's get that music on and *party*!" And hey, this isn't an Islamic center. We're *happy* today.

Years later Ali spoke with Thomas Hauser about the 1975 passing of Elijah Muhammad; an event Ali called sorrowful. Recounting the contributions Elijah Muhammad had made to his life, as well as to the lives of millions, Ali told Hauser, "I was at Deer Lake, training, when I heard the news, and it made me sad. Elijah Muhammad dedicated his life to helping black people. Not everything he said was right, but everyone in the Nation of Islam loved him because he carried what was best for us in his heart. His life was dedicated to lifting people up, and it was his teaching that started me thinking." (294)

When addressing the loss of Elijah Muhammad in the November 1975 interview with *Playboy* magazine the question was asked, "What difference did he [Elijah Muhammad] make in your own life?" Ali answered,

He was *my* Jesus, and I had love for both the man and what he represented. Like Jesus Christ and all of God's prophets, he represented all good things and, having passed on, he is missed. But prophets never die spiritually, for their words and works live on. Elijah Muhammad was my savior, and everything I have came from him — my thoughts, my efforts to help my people, how I eat, how I talk, my *name*.

Since the passing of Elijah Muhammad in 1975 Ali has continued his growth as a Muslim following Elijah's son Imam Wallace Mohammed until Wallace passed in September of 2008. In many aspects the Islam taught to him by Elijah's son differs from that which he learned from Elijah Muhammad; nonetheless, Ali remains deeply respectful of the man who was influential in making him the international man he is today. Ali related to Hauser:

> Since then, my beliefs have changed. I don't believe in Mr. Yacub (Yakub) and the spaceship anymore. Hearts and souls have no color. I know that too. But Elijah Muhammad was a good man, even if he wasn't the Messenger of God we thought he was. If you look at what our people were like then, a lot of us didn't have self-respect. We didn't have banks or stores. We didn't have anything after being in America for hundreds of years. Elijah Muhammad was trying to lift us up and get our people out of the gutter. (97)

Ali's unique yet jovial and gregarious spirit has left open the opportunity for each of his admirers to remember him in his or her special way. Ali, speaking from his heart shared with *Playboy* magazine how he wishes to be remembered.

> I'll tell you how I'd *like* to be remembered: as a black man who won the heavyweight title and who was humorous and who treated everyone right. As a man who never looked down on those who looked up to him and who helped as many of his people as he could – financially and also in their fight for freedom, justice and equality. As a man who wouldn't hurt his people's dignity by doing anything that would embarrass them. As a man who tried to unite his people through the faith of Islam that he found when he listened to the Honorable Elijah Muhammad. And if all that's asking too much, then I guess I'd settle for being remembered only as a great boxing champion who became a preacher and a champion of his people. And I wouldn't even mind if folks forgot how pretty I was.

In a December 2001 *Reader's Digest* interview conducted by Howard Bingham, Ali readily revealed his continued admiration for Elijah Muhammad. Bingham asked Ali, "Now, after you were older, who influenced your life and the beliefs that you have?" Ali replied, "After I started boxing, Sugar Ray Robinson. And my idol was a man named Elijah Muhammad. [His] Islamic teaching is what made me so confident.

Muhammad Ali remains one of the most recognized faces in the world. Undoubtedly he is a former student yet still a product of Elijah Muhammad. Historically the two men are inextricable.

The Ali of today has taken advantage of opportunities to advance his life as a Muslim and as a human being, far beyond the limits of the Nation of Islam. Nonetheless, without the Nation of Islam Muhammad Ali may never have become as famous as he is today throughout the international world.

Surely he would have accomplished greatness in the boxing ring as Cassius Marcellus Clay. But without meeting the Honorable Elijah

Muhammad he most likely never would have challenged and championed his rights to be the conscientious objector named Muhammad Ali. Without Elijah Muhammad in Ali's life he never would have personified black manhood for African American men, nor would he have become a symbol of hope for millions in the ghettoes of Black America.

Ali humbly shaking hands with Mr. Muhammad, the man who named him and gave him confidence as a black man in America. *(Muslim Journal file)*

THE MAN BEHIND THE MEN

Elijah Muhammad was an idol to Ali for many years. He gave Ali confidence against great odds. Many want to credit Malcolm X as the one who gave Ali confidence, without recognizing that it was Elijah who had given both Malcolm and Ali their confidence. Elijah Muhammad gave Ali an Islamic name, a "holy name" that increased the furor of the already bodacious youthful braggart. Ali, even as the heavyweight champion of the world weighing over 200 pounds, was humbled by the small-framed, 5-feet, 5-inch, 150-pound Elijah Muhammad.

The Honorable Elijah Muhammad is the only man who is due the most credit for the making, developing and deliverance of Muhammad Ali to the international world. During the epoch of the 1960s the name Muhammad Ali helped to attract the attention of billions of people around the world toward that loudmouthed kid from Louisville, KY.

Who, in the 1960s, had ever heard of such!? A famous Negro with a Muslim name, *Muhammad Ali*? Not many! And with the confidence gained from being a follower of Elijah Muhammad, Ali has taken that name, *Muhammad Ali*, to international fame and acclaim. So much so that history must recognize that Elijah Muhammad is the man behind the man, Muhammad Ali; the hero, the Muslim and the humanitarian who has touched the lives of individuals of every race and nationality.

-§- CHAPTER -§-
EIGHT

Not Bearing Their Names – "Do For Self"

> All nations of the earth are recognized by the name by which they are called. By stating one's name, one is able to associate an entire order of a particular civilization simply by name alone.
> — Elijah Muhammad

Hadith Encouraging Self-Help

A man came to the Prophet Muhammed (peace be upon him) and begged for something from him. The Prophet asked the man: "Have you nothing in your house?" The man replied: "Yes, a piece of cloth, a part of which we wear and a part of which we spread (on the ground), and a wooden bowl from which we drink water." The Prophet asked the man to bring him these items. He then auctioned them off to the highest bidder and gave the money to the man who was begging, saying: "Buy food...and give it to your family, and buy an axe and bring it to me." When the man brought the ax, the Prophet fixed a handle on it with his own hands and said: "Go, gather firewood and sell it, and do not let me see you for a fortnight." The man went away and gathered firewood and sold it. When he had earned enough money, he bought food and clothing. The Prophet then said to him: "This is better for you than having begging (be held against you) on the Day of Judgment."
— Sunan of Abu-Dawood, Hadith 664

Another distinguishing mark of Elijah Muhammad that came across as strident to those opposed to his leadership, but as encouraging to his followers and sympathizers, was his call for African Americans to come out from under their "slave master's names." If you know any indigenous African American with an Islamic, and/or African name, most likely the root cause behind them receiving that name is Elijah Muhammad.

The concept of name, as used by Elijah Muhammad meant more than just the letters and sound that contained an individual's name. It was more than a mere word or title that one may respond to when they heard their personal name called. For Elijah Muhammad, your name included the social, ethnic, religious and historical connotations associated with it. When it came to African Americans wearing European names, particularly the surnames from their family's former slave masters, Elijah Muhammad understood this to be a pulsating vestige of slavery. Elijah Muhammad wanted more for his followers than a leftover reminder of servitude; something better than a name derived from slavery.

Repeatedly Elijah reminded his followers to "Do for Self." This sense of "self" intended that African Americans progress in every avenue of life in their own "original" or "holy" name, and not bearing the names of another race or ethnic group, especially that of Caucasian Americans.

For generations many immigrant Muslims, particularly those seeking to assimilate into American society, were adopting European names or Anglicizing their Arabic names while the followers of Elijah Muhammad were proudly and boldly rejecting their Americanized last names in hopes of one day receiving a righteous Arabic "holy name."

Immigrant Muslims often opted to substitute their Arabic names for more acceptable nicknames by shortening or altering their names. Some immigrants named Mohammad preferred to be called "Mo." Fareed became the more tolerable Fred, and Sami favored being called Sam. To further aid their absorption into America's culture many Muslim immigrants, in addition to the degree they were willing to abbreviate their names, commensurately altered and abbreviated their dedication to and practice of their Islamic faith.

The significance of this section, *Not Bearing Their Names*, is to show how these four men, Imam W. Deen (Wallace) Mohammed, Minister Louis Farrakhan, El-Hajj Malik (Malcolm X) El-Shabazz, and boxing champion Muhammad Ali, as products from Elijah Muhammad's Nation of Islam, shed or never donned the surname, religion, diet and persona of white American culture. Of the four men mentioned, Wallace is the only one born with an Islamic surname.

In addition to names having their unique meaning, as well as its historical, ethnic, and cultural connotations, they oftentimes indicate one's national bonds. Therefore, every name offers a description that defines important basic qualities of the bearer. According to Nation of Islam doctrine, the birth names of African Americans, usually names of European origin, were classified as "slave names." Upon becoming a registered member, the new Muslim surrendered their "slave name" in exchange for the surname name "X"; a placeholder for the "unknown" pre-slavery family name. As the "x" in algebra symbolizes an unknown number or value, the "X" as a surname represented the bearer's unknown Islamic or African family name.

Fard recognized and capitalized upon the many aspects of African American life that he deemed insufficient due to slavery. Their religious and cultural life being his prime areas of focus. Claude Clegg's biography on Elijah Muhammad outlines the effects that slavery and Europeanization had upon the enslaved African's Islamic cultural and religious past. Clegg states, "The rigors of slavery and the submergence of most blacks into a European culture that esteemed only Christianity as a religion, discouraged basic practices of Muslims such as circumcision, Islamic educational instruction, avoidance of pork, and the passing on of traditional Arabic names to children." The process of slavery removed and denied African Americans the rich Islamic culture and heritage they enjoyed in Africa.

Out of respect for their parents, members of the Nation of Islam often kept their given first names, or when possible they accepted an Arabic version of the same name; as with Yusuf instead of Joseph, or Yahya instead of John. The Nation of Islam's practice of retaining first names is a sign that it was not Europeanized names that most disturbed Elijah Muhammad, but it was the keeping of the surname that most likely came from a former slave master. Elijah Muhammad's book *Message to the Blackman* states:

> First, you must be given the names of your forefathers, whose names are the most Holy and Righteous Names of Allah. Again, I repeat, that restoring to you your identity is one of the first and most important truths to be established by God, Himself.
> All nations of the earth are recognized by the name by which they are called. By stating one's name, one is able to associate an entire order of a particular civilization simply by name alone. For example, if you take the name Lu Chin, we know immediately that this is a Chinese name, whose land or origin is China, a country that operates on an independent basis and is recognized through the world as a nation and whose people demand respect...It is only when we come to America and learn the names that our people are now going by that we discover that a whole nation of 20,000,000 black people are going by the names of white people. How can a so-called Negro say that his name is "Sam Jones," a white man's name with roots in Europe, when "Sam Jones" (Black Man) comes from Asia or Africa? (54)

Once a new Nation of Islam convert's letter was accepted they would receive their "earned" X for their surname, or better yet directly receive an Arabic "holy name" from Elijah Muhammad as done by Cassius Clay. Elijah Muhammad believed that converts earning the temporary surname "X" or renaming them with "holy names" represented a watershed moment for Nation of Islam members. Earning an "X" was honorable and a sign of renewal.

The December 15, 1972 issue of *Muhammad Speaks*, on page 3, the Nation of Islam's National Secretary Abass Rassuoll warned Nation of Islam members against freely adopting names. Only Elijah had the authority to confer "holy names," all others had to wait for the return of God to receive a "Righteous Name."

HOLY NAMES

The Nation of Islam WILL NOT recognized nor accept Holy Names adopted by persons desiring to rid themselves of slave-names. Buying names or changing them through the court WILL NOT be accepted. The rule is that only names given by The Honorable Elijah Muhammad will be recognized. Your names are not to be bought, they are free. The Honorable Elijah Muhammad gives some of his laborers names Himself, which are recognized by Allah, to keep them from being called by slavenames [sic]. He has the freedom to do this. You are very foolish to go and buy names when they are free. You make a fool of yourself when you buy these names from the devil. I am certain they laugh at your ignorance. From the reading of this notice, any one that adopt [sic] names without permission will be penalized.

You are not to put X's behind Holy Names. The Holy Name is free within itself. When you place an X behind it you are X-ing yourself out of the Holy Name. The best thing is that you keep away from trying to order and correct these names yourself. You will get a name as it is written and as Allah told The Honorable Elijah Muhammad. The Bible teaches in Revelations that the judgment cannot proceed unless you have your Holy Names.

ABASS RASSUOLL, NATIONAL SECRETARY

Elijah Muhammad taught that black people should have a family name that separates them from the residue of slavery. That was a driving force behind boxer Muhammad Ali's brutal beating of Ernie Terrell in 1967.

During their pre-fight buildup Terrell refused to call Muhammad Ali by his Islamic name, pointedly using Ali's birth name, Cassius Clay, which was being disowned by Ali as a "slave name."

Ali responded by calling Terrell an "Uncle Tom" and telling him "I'm gonna' hurt you bad!" For 15 merciless rounds Ali pounded on Terrell. Neither the referee nor Terrell's corner intervened. So until the final bell rang Ali pulverized Terrell, repeatedly chiding him by asking, "What's my name fool? What's my name?"

Kathleen Duffy for *Suite101.com* wrote about Ali's maternal great-great grandfather, John Grady. He was an Irishman from Ennis, in County Clare in Ireland. In the 1860s, John's son Abe migrated to America and married Ali's great-grandmother, a free African American (name unknown). The maiden name of Ali's mother is Odessa Grady. Ali visited Ennis in 2009 to reconnect with his Irish roots. He was warmly received as Ennis' first "Honorary Freemen."

Maybe Ali would not have pulverized Terrell in the manner he did had he known of his great-grandfather, John Grady and the kindness of Ireland, but the Terrell fight came in the context of a younger Ali who knew firsthand a segregated Louisville. It was a time during which Ali was trying to make

NOT BEARING THEIR NAMES "DO FOR SELF"

sense of an immature America still struggling to extend to African Americans even the most basic noble claims gauranteed in the U.S. Constitution.

Those challenging days resulted in young Cassius Clay being generally dissatisfied with white people. Upon hearing the message of Elijah Muhammad, Clay was renamed Muhammad Ali, and became a man with a new name and purpose. Ali was seeking an identity as far removed as possible from slavery and Jim Crow. Along the way the Ali-Terrell pre-fight hype mushroomed into serious name calling that revealed both fighter's disdain for being labeled less than a free black man.

> Address
> City and State
> Date
>
> Mr. W. F. Muhammad
> 4847 South Woodlawn Avenue
> Chicago, Illinois   60615
>
> Dear Saviour Allah, our Deliverer, Who Came in the Person of Master Fard Muhammad, to Whom Praises are due forever:
>
> I believe in the religion of Islam, as taught by Thy Servant, Elijah Muhammad. I bear witness that Muhammad is Thy Servant and Apostle. I desire to reclaim my Own. I desire a name from Thee. My slave name is as follows:
>
> Name (Mr., Miss, Mrs.)

A sample letter given to individuals desiring membership in the Nation of Islam. The applicant had to personally write an error-free duplicate of this letter, addressed to Mr. W.F. Muhammad (W.D. Fard), in hopes of receiving a "holy name."

THE MAN BEHIND THE MEN

Malcolm X, in an interview with Alex Haley for the May 1963 issue of *Playboy* magazine shared his personal experience and the benefits he received from using an Islamic name that distinguished him from being merely another typical Negro living in the overly racial sensitive America of the 1960s.

> You see, the American black man sees the African come here and live where the American black man can't. The Negro sees the African come here with a sheet on and go places where the Negro – dressed like a white man, talking like a white man, sometimes as wealthy as the white man – can't go. When I'm traveling around the country, I use my real Muslim name, Malik Shabazz. I make my hotel reservations under that name, and I always see the same thing I've just been telling you. I come to the desk and always see that "here-comes-a-Negro" look. It's kind of a reserved, coldly tolerant cordiality. But when I say "Malik Shabazz," their whole attitude changes: they snap to respect. They think I'm an African. People say what's in a name? There's a whole lot in a name. The American black man is seeing the African respected as a human being. The African gets respect because he has an identity and cultural roots. But most of all because the African owns some land. For these reasons he has his human rights recognized, and that makes his civil rights automatic.

African Americans distancing themselves from a family name because of its association with slavery was not a creation of Mr. Fard or Elijah Muhammad. John Edgar Wideman in his book *My Soul has Grown Deep: Classics of Early African-American Literature* reports Booker T. Washington's account of the many freed slaves who believed "that they must change their names, and that they must leave the old plantation for at least a few days or weeks in order that they might really feel sure that they are free." Booker T. Washington added, "In some way a feeling got among the coloured people that it was far from proper for them to bear the surname of their former owners, and a great many of them took other surnames. This was one of the first signs of freedom." (646) Although Booker T. Washington was a whole generation ahead of Elijah Muhammad, still both acknowledged that for many free African Americans the changing of one's name is "one of the first signs" of gaining independence.

The ex-slave Isabella Baumfree choosing the name Sojourner Truth is another example of a post-slavery spiritual and cultural transition that many African Americans made by taking on a new name. Sojourner Truth speaks of her name change as if it were a testimony that she was really free of the vestiges of slavery. Olive Gilbert's book, *Narrative of Sojourner Truth*, contains Truth's story that explains why she changed her name.

NOT BEARING THEIR NAMES "DO FOR SELF"

Gilbert wrote about a conversation between Truth and the famous 19th century writer Harriet Beecher Stowe. A discussion in which Truth candidly told Stowe that taking on a new name aided her assurance that she was removed as far as possible away from "Egypt" (slavery). Sojourner Truth explained: "My name was Isabella; but when I left the house of bondage, I left everything behind. I wa'n't goin' to keep nothin' of Egypt on me, an' so I went to the Lord an' asked him to give me a new name" (164).

Sojourner Truth's argument for changing her name is very similar to the rationale put forth by Elijah Muhammad when he encouraged African Americans to change their names. Albeit intermingled in a separatist message every issue of *Muham ad Speaks* printed, "We believe the black men should be freed in name as well as in fact. By this we mean that he should be freed from the names imposed upon him by his former slave masters. Names which identified him as being the slave master's slave. We believe that if we are free indeed, we should go in our own people's names - the black people of the earth."

As the four students who are highlighted in this book traveled abroad, especially in Asia and Africa, their Islamic names were positive factors that imbued their status. Other African American leaders who have traveled abroad with European names most likely were not as well received internationally as these four men who were groomed by Elijah Muhammad. The Muslims' shedding of the "slave name" not only distinguished them from other African Americans domestically, but their new names also gave them a great advantage in the eyes of the international world.

When studying the impact of Elijah Muhammad encouraging his followers to change their last names it is important to note that during this same era the world politics in Asia and Africa were in constant flux. Not only were Elijah Muhammad's followers seeking new and independent names and identities; in Africa and the Middle East many formerly colonized people were redefining their nation's identity by ridding their countries of European names in favor of traditional indigenous names. During this epoch Northern Rhodesia was renamed Zambia; and the Belgium Congo became known as Zaire, while British East Africa was renamed Kenya. Many other nations seeking to break free from European domination also followed suit. In the 1940s, just one generation before these national name changes occurred in Africa, the Middle East also witnessed the liberation and/or the creation of Pakistan, Jordan, Israel, Lebanon, Syria, and Egypt.

On March 6, 1957 Dr. King and other prominent African Americans were in Ghana supporting Prime Minister Kwame Nkrumah and the Ghanian people usher in their independence. *The Autobiography of Dr. Martin Luther King Jr.* speaks of a handsome black man walking out on the platform and announcing: "We are no longer a British colony. We are a free and sovereign people." Dr. King said:

THE MAN BEHIND THE MEN

> When he uttered those words, we looked back and saw an old flag coming down and a new flag going up. And I said to myself, "That old flag coming down doesn't represent the meaning of this drama taking place on the stage of history, for it is the symbol of an old order passing away. That new flag going up is the symbol of a new age coming into being." I could hear people shouting all over that vast audience, "Freedom! Freedom! Freedom! (112)

Today, at the expense of many other nations, the United States of America claims the status of being the world's only "superpower." When Elijah Muhammad's community was heralding its message to African Americans the political, economic and cultural disparities between the United States and other countries were stark, particularly when comparing America to many third world countries that were shrugging off the burdens of European colonialism and other forms of oppression that came as a result of western domination. Therefore, when the Nation of Islam gained worldwide attention because of their unique way of shrugging off white authority, third world nations took note.

The Nation of Islam, being a de facto "nation in a nation" that emanated from the loins of America's former slaves, offered the international world access to a voice and a community that was solidly fixed within the borders of the United States of America. Many people in the Muslim world took a special interest in Elijah Muhammad's Islamic prototype, a community that already had an image and public presence that openly articulated a message rejecting the superpower status of the United States of America. Many oppressed and weaker nations, including many Islamic countries who may have disagreed with Elijah Muhammad's racially based version of Islam, still appreciated and identified with the boldness and temerity that Elijah displayed without relent against western influences.

Elijah Muhammad's strategy for liberating African Americans, called Negroes at that time, from the injustices of America was to invite them to a way of life that not only challenged injustice but also accused and reminded the political and religious powerbrokers of their guilt of abusing African Americans and the weaker nations of the world. One of the benefits of this strategy resulted in many smaller or poorer nations warmly and sometimes extravagantly welcoming Elijah Muhammad and his protégés when they visited such countries.

Elijah Muhammad's separatist effort — commensurated with America's overall racial immaturity of that era — was a public display of the way many African Americans, of all sectors of society, felt in private. The non-Muslim African American, particularly those who preferred to assimilate and integrate into America in that racially and socially unjust era, were often perceived by Nation of Islam members as clones of the white power structure, in dark skin. The Nation of Islam's separatist, independence-driven message strongly distinguished its members from other African Americans in that Nation of Islam members were clearly individuals not seeking to assimilate western or European values.

Elijah Muhammad was not the first African American leader to encourage a course of progress void of assimilation. Booker T. Washington also understood the necessity for African Americans to establish their own hegemony of culture and identity. Washington, reflecting a disdain for assimilation, stated "...no white American ever thinks that any other race is wholly civilized until he wears the white man's cloths, eats the white man's food, speaks the white man's language, and professes the white man's religion."

Arthur Huff Fauset, author of *Black Gods of the Metropolis* wrote in 1944 about the early developments of African American religious life. Fauset's assessment of African American Christianity in large agrees with Elijah Muhammad's charge that the Christianity of black America is not the original property of Africans, just merely a replication.

Fauset noted that, "It is safe to assume that not one Negro in the original cargo of slaves landed at Jamestown, VA, in 1619 was a member of the Christian faith..." Without being date-specific, Fauset asserts that due to slave owners discouraging slaves away from Christianity that:

> It is not until relatively late in the Negro's experience in the United States that we have trustworthy records of practices among Negro slaves which we may be certain are to be included within the general framework of their religious beliefs and practices. By this time the basic elements in these practices are frequently difficult to distinguish from those of various European forms, to which in large measure they undoubtedly owe their derivation. (2-3)

The internal need in the souls of African Americans to be mentally and spiritually free from white society's norms and values was voiced by many African American leaders. Elijah Muhammad was not alone on many of the goals and aspirations that he outlined for his people. He is one of many leaders who worked diligently on totally freeing his people.

Elijah Muhammad's identification with the people of Africa and of the Middle East is monumental. Though all African Americans are descendents of Africa only a few have sought to reconnect with their motherland. Elijah Muhammad was careful to teach his followers that they are brothers and sisters to all black-skinned Africans and people of color all over the world.

THE MAN BEHIND THE MEN

To better appreciate this discussion on *Not Bearing Their Name* it is pertinent to contrast Elijah Muhammad's cognizance of Africa versus that of many African Americans who, even to this day, still proudly carry the names and mannerisms, and sometimes even the arrogance of the European supremacy that was forced upon darker nations. Such African Americans, in the eyes of many Africans prompt reminders of European encroachment upon Africa and many other nations of the world.

According to some accounts the Ali-Foreman 1974 "Rumble in the Jungle" World Boxing Association championship fight exemplified the contrast between the Nation of Islam's love for blackness, compared to the love for blackness shown by other African Americans. The Ali-Foreman fight also displayed how changing one's name affected Ali and gave him a positive attitude toward African black people and them toward him. The stark contrast between Ali's image in the minds of the people of Zaire compared to their appreciation of George Foreman was as far apart as night and day. Yes, physically George Foreman was just as black and African as Muhammad Ali; however, Ali's strong suit in relating to the people was the Nation of Islam's mental and spiritual blackness that he exuded to the Zairian public.

Ali walked the streets and talked with the people while Foreman walked around with his pet Belgian Shepherd dog, that most likely, unbeknownst to Foreman was the same type of canine that the Belgian police used to patrol the public before Zaire gained her independence. Surely the several weeks of discomfort and travel, compounded by living in a third world country wore on both fighters. But Ali's open display of care for Zairians earned him their trust, while Foreman by and large shunned them.

Ali's acceptance of an Islamic name aligned him with a sense of liberation that the citizens of Zaire were familiar with. Their relatively recent freedom from European control, which resulted in changing their country's name from The Congo to Zaire in 1971, was comparable with Muhammad Ali changing his name from Cassius Clay. There is not much of an African representation in the name George Foreman, but his name did carry a strong European aura and possibly a reminder to the people of Zaire of their recent colonialism under Belgium rule.

Thus the stage was set; Ali, possibly because of Elijah Muhammad's foresight, became the symbol of the world's weaker nations while big George Foreman symbolically represented the world's superpowers; a Goliath-type in the minds of Zairians. Expressing their admiration for Ali over Foreman the Belgian Shepherd dog lover, the Zairians released a united spontaneous chorus of *Ali, Ali Bom a ye*, which means "knock him down, kill him dead." George Foreman was totally innocent of any wrong that the Belgian government had committed against the people of Zaire, but symbolically

NOT BEARING THEIR NAMES "DO FOR SELF"

Foreman came to represent the oppressor, the Belgians in effigy. The Zairian praise given to Ali was a direct benefit of him applying the teachings that he had learned from Elijah Muhammad who taught him that African Americans are brothers and sisters with the peoples of Africa and Asia.

William Strathmore in *Muhammad Ali: The Unseen Archives* notes how Ali took advantage of every opportunity to express his appreciation for being in Zaire. Strathmore wrote, "To the press, Ali made much of being in a country run by black people – at a function at the presidential palace, he said, 'Mr. President, I've been a citizen of the United States of America for 33 years and was never invited to the White House. It sure gives me great pleasure to be invited to the Black House.' " (231) Ali's proud expression of gratitude was a direct result of Elijah Muhammad's black consciousness message

The Ali-Foreman paradigm is repeated often by others who were influenced by Elijah Muhammad, including Minister Louis Farrakhan's *Million Man March* that numerically eclipsed the *1963 Civil Rights March on Washington*. The *Million Man March* also went further in reestablishing qualities of black manhood in many African American males than any other mass gathering in American history. The *Million Man March* addressed a longing in many African Americans who felt the need in their soul to show America and the world that "I am somebody"; that "I too am a man." Through the *Million Man March*, led by Farrakhan, a student of Elijah Muhammad, millions of African American men — and women — found renewal for their souls.

The resiliency of Elijah Muhammad's appeal was amplified when the success of the *Million Man March* came without the support of the black church or the support of the majority of the white community, that is, if any Caucasian support was ever given at all. It was the coming together of black men without the approval of white America that gave the *Million Man March* one of its most unique qualities. The large numbers in attendance testifies to the fact that there remains, even to this day, a void in the soul of African American males. Farrakhan's *Million Man March* were black men uniting to fill that void with a sense of value, purpose and destiny.

Regardless of whether one agrees or disagrees with the mission of the *Million Man March*, one would be hard pressed to disagree with the fact that the march was done bearing the name of Elijah Muhammad. The *Million Man March* did not bear the name of another race or ethnicity other than that of African American men. For the organizers and participants this independent quality was expected, needed, and enjoyed.

Even with the attendance at the 1995 *Million Man March* outnumbering the 1963 *March on Washington* by at least a 4 to 1 ratio, both events achieved great advances for African Americans and the less fortunate in general. Whereas the *March on Washington* directly affected civil rights legislation, voter's rights and influenced the U.S. labor force, the Farrakhan-led *Million Man March* made an historical impact on African American males that translated into better African American families and increases in black membership in many groups and organizations, including an increase in black men attending churches and mosques.

Both Washington D.C. mass movements were honored by R&B singer Curtis Mayfield. In 1965, while singing with the Impressions, Mayfield released their gospel-R&B hit song *People Get Ready*, a tune that was inspired by the 1963 *March on Washington*. The key refrain said, *"People get ready, there's a train a-comin'. You don't need no baggage, you just get on board. All you need is faith to hear the diesels hummin', Don't need no ticket, you just thank the Lord."*

Thirty years later in recognition of the *Million Man March*, Mayfield wrote the song *New World Order* for Hollywood movie director Spike Lee. Mayfield's soundtrack for Lee's movie, Get on the Bus (1996) seems to deem the *Million Man March* as "a fulfillment of prophecy." One chorus reads. *"Operation influx and it's on the way. We just marched a million plus the other day. Look we all witnessed the sweat rolling down Ms. Liberty's head. She knows the sleeping giant is no longer sleeping dead. Oh what a fulfillment of prophecy. Let us teach the children freedom's never been free."*

Admittedly, the *Million Man March* came in an age in which the world had greater access to the media which facilitated Lee's ability to make a movie Get on the Bus. Nonetheless, it seems that Louis' Farrakhan's march spoke more to the need in the African American community to see a resurrected black man. Another verse in Mayfield's song *New World Order* indicates that he too recognized the *Million Man March* as a resurrection, or a new birth for many African American males. Mayfield penned, *"Mother Earth's given birth to a brand new man. Sister I know you're misunderstood. But hold on to your man 'cause the future looks good. It's a new day."*

The teachings of Elijah Muhammad, notwithstanding their racial underpinnings, provided his followers with ideals and programs for uplifting African Americans without seeking the approval or acceptance from anyone, except God. There are many other leaders in contemporary and historical African American communities who sought God as their main source of help and security; but few had a functioning community life that was as independent and well equipped as Elijah Muhammad's "Do for Self" Nation of Islam.

Wallace, Elijah Muhammad's son also applied the "Do for Self" philosophy wherein one proceeds forward toward an objective regardless if it satisfies the status quo. It is through Wallace that Elijah Muhammad's influence indirectly reached the minds and souls of the world's religious leadership. Imam W. Deen Mohammed, the heir-successor of Elijah Muhammad, quietly yet effectively introduced many Qur'anic-based solutions to many problems in America and around the world; contributions that often reflect a conscious connection to the teachings and disciplines he learned from his father.

Members of CRAID in Los Angeles, CA including boxer Muhammad Ali promoting the message to remove all racial effects from worship. (Circa 1981-1982).
(Photographer Charles Muhammad - Courtesy of Matthew Ali)

Without seeking permission or approval from any race or established religion, Wallace set out to remove the crippling effects that resulted from using racial images to portray the divine. He created a movement called *CRAID (The Committee to Remove All Images that attempt to portray the Divine)*. The specific purpose of CRAID was to question and arrest the damaging psychological effects suffered by African Americans who Sunday after Sunday, worshipped a Caucasian image as divine. When CRAID began, America's dominant iconic images of "God" were white, Caucasian. The angels were depicted in white skin. Jesus and all of the prophets were depicted as white. Even the "hand of

THE MAN BEHIND THE MEN

God" descending from the clouds was white. The only dark-skinned images in Christianity were sinners as exemplified in the artists' renderings of Judas, the one who betrayed Jesus.

The August 5, 1983 issue of the *American Muslim Journal*, page S8, reported that in cities and towns around America, Bermuda, and throughout the Caribbean Islands, CRAID groups were established to peacefully carry signs and pass out literature that asked:

> What would happen to the minds of Caucasian people if Bilalian (African American) people would suddenly come into power with their mentality, with their love for their religion? What would happen if nappy-headed, black Jesuses were put all over their land and throughout their homes and in all of their churches? What would happen to their minds over a period of three hundred years if they kept coming to churches and seeing our image as their redeemer, seeing our image as their prophets, their apostles, their angels? They would be reduced to inferiority because the image before them of the supreme model of superiority would be "black" and not "white." If we don't want dope in our communities, how much more should we be against a Caucasian image of God that makes Bilalians (blacks) think inferior and act inferior, and that makes Caucasians equally artificial?

Wallace Mohammed was striking a death blow to what many considered the ultimate form of white racism: God depicted in Caucasian flesh. In a 1982 booklet titled *Racism in Religion* he said, "Islam asks white people to stop putting God in their image and to stop putting angels in their image. That is too much for a people with a racist mentality to accept. It's been too comfortable for them. It has served them too well for them to put it down." The Imam added, "But thanks to Allah, Islam is growing faster and gaining more territory among the Caucasian people." (33)

Another question Imam Wallace Deen Mohammed constantly asked was, "What would happen if people would sit in churches throughout the world for centuries with the image of an African American man as savior of the world before them?"

Nor was CRAID the Imam's effort to establish a black god. The stated end goal of CRAID was to remove *all* images that attempt to portray divine. In addition to scrutinizing the unnatural race-consciousness in Christianity, CRAID also targeted the image of Elijah Muhammad's savior, Mr. Fard; a man who had strikingly Caucasian features. Wallace's intellect, set free by his parents to question and investigate all things, eventually became a freedom that questioned accepting W.D. Fard, a man, as God.

While yet a teenager Wallace had made a parallel of Fard's status as "God in the Person" with the Christian belief that presented Jesus Christ as "God in the Flesh." In addition to both of these anthropomorphic figures having Caucasian-like features, the young Wallace also questioned their iconic status as representations of the Divine.

From May 10-12, 2007 a select group of religious and social leaders and educators convened at Wisdom University in Tulsa, OK to explore the topic *"Sacred Activism and the Power of Inclusion — A Heartland Summit."* Wallace Mohammed was invited to address this assembly and part of his presentation addressed his coming to terms as an adolescent with the concept of God in the Person, or God in the flesh.

> As I grew older, some of my friends, who would confide in me, were carrying burdens too in not understanding the Nation of Islam concept of God. But one day I shared my thoughts with them on God, and I said, "If we are not to believe that Jesus Christ is the son of God, that God has no son, then why should we believe that Mr. Fard is God or the son of God? We know he was born, he was not that old. He was not a thousand years old. So who is his father? It seems to me that we are saying the same thing and got it more confused.

Believing in the encouragement that he had received from his parents to follow his own mind without fearing the consequences of not toeing the line, Wallace forged ahead with CRAID, an entity that created public discussions on racial imagery in religion. CRAID served as a help to free and heal both African Americans and Caucasians of the burdens that accompanied seeing the divine racially. CRAID in a quiet yet powerful way helped to liberate Christian communities as well as Islamic communities of their respective spiritually-based racial divides.

Many leaders in Christianity agreed with Wallace Mohammed's CRAID message. In 1983 the initiatives of Wazirudin Ali and James Sharif working under Imam Mikal A. Rasheed in Atlantic City, NJ grew into a working relationship with Rev. H. Edward Burton of the St. James A.M.E. Church, an institution that traditionally did not condone images in their worship services. The *A.M. Journal (Muslim Journal)* printed Rev. Burton's stance regarding racial imagery in worship:

> I, Rev. Burton, Pastor of St. James A.M.E. Church, am in agreement with the members of CRAID (the Committee for the Removal of All Images that Attempt to portray the Divine) and I base my agreement on the fact of a revelation in the Bible and in the African Methodist Episcopal Church Discipline, 1980 Section II Under Special Declaration, Page 18. The Bible, Exodus 20:3-5: "Thou shalt have no other gods before me. Thou shalt not make unto thee any graven image, or any

likeness *of any thing* that *is* in heaven above, or that *is* in the earth beneath, or that *is* in the water under the earth. Thou shalt not bow down thyself to them, nor serve them."

The A.M.E. Church Discipline, 1980 Section II Under Special Declaration, Page 18: "We strenuously deny that the presence and use of heavy and prosy ritualistic images and services in our public congregations will in any sense increase their spiritual interest and we depreciate any and all efforts that favor the introduction of extreme ritualism in connection with public services.

— Reverend H. Edward Burton Sr.,
Pastor of St. James A.M.E. Church

It is important to note that without abandoning the sense of independence he developed as a student and member of the Nation of Islam, Wallace did abandon the racial hindrances of the Nation of Islam that differed with the Qur'an and the life exemplified by Prophet Muhammed of Arabia. He did his work in the name of God, not in the name of another race, ethnicity, nor in the name or sway of foreign investors. In the Nation of Islam's spirit of "Do for Self" Wallace took on the challenge that CRAID presented and began the effort to remove all images that attempt to portray the divine.

As the leader over the same community that formerly followed his father, Wallace achieved success as an Islamic leader without seeking the approval of Muslims abroad. He was quick to give praise and thanks to God for his successes while also recognizing the contributions and sacrifices made by his father in establishing a strong foundation for the Nation of Islam; a foundation upon which he now stood as a free and independent leader in Islam, a religion that now had become the fastest growing faith in America.

Leslie Goffe in a September 19, 1999 *(IPS) Global News Agency* article titled *Islam on the Rise Among African Americans* noted, "But it is Wallace D. Mohammed, the soft spoken leader of the moderate Muslim American Society who is regarded as the most influential voice among America's black Muslims." Additionally Goffe pointed out that "Mohammed's Muslim American Society, which has 200,000 members and a following of more than 2 million people is, by contrast, a racially mixed, mainstream Muslim organization."

After his release from prison in 1946 Elijah Muhammad was no longer on the run for his personal life, which allowed him to begin instituting business ownership amongst his membership while still focusing on their mental and spiritual exodus. To achieve a financial "Do For Self" community Elijah Muhammad recognized another hurdle that many African Americans had to overcome; the challenge of showing one face to the white public of America while living an opposing life internally. This is not

NOT BEARING THEIR NAMES "DO FOR SELF"

the type of two-facedness discussed earlier in our Chris Rock and Joe Brown scenarios where the public feigning of love and the private spiteful hate was verbalized. This hurdle was the quiet and internal struggle any minority people will encounter as they struggle to reconcile disparate values and seek comfort in the majority society.

No one can ever charge Elijah Muhammad with being two-faced. Yes, over the years he evolved and adjusted his emphasis in accord with society's overall treatment of African Americans. But he never was a participant in living a double-faced life. He instead chose to mentally migrate himself, taking as many African Americans as would follow him on an exodus away from the influences of America's mid 20th-century racism.

Dr. Robert Staples in his book *Introduction to Black Sociology* on page 67 spoke of a biculturation duality within African Americans. A disposition he described as a type of unnatural duality. Staples references W.E.B. DuBois book *The Souls of Black Folk* that describe these two sets of social forces as a "double consciousness" that African Americans had to live within. DuBois explained that this double consciousness obligated African Americans to relate to the social process of American life as well as relate to their experience as African Americans within America. "One ever feels his twoness – An American, a Negro; two souls, two thoughts, two unreconciled strivings; two warring ideas in one dark body." (214)

Elijah Muhammad's Nation of Islam provided its members with a "Do For Self" mentally that removed them from this duality, thus freeing them of needing white approval. The Nation of Islam's psychology freed African Americans from this "twoness" described by DuBois.

The Islam presented by Elijah Muhammad purposefully aimed at every pain of African Americans in order to get their attention and call them out of "the wilderness of North America" on an exodus away from the mental and spiritual grip of white America.

The Do For Self mantra of Elijah created an environment for developing these four men and the other Nation of Islam members. Whereas the Civil Rights Movement was perceived by many as a form of assimilation, the Nation of Islam was making bold and often disturbing statements and attention-getting claims of the greatness of being black — independently black.

The popular "Do for Self" slogan of Elijah Muhammad was intended for every aspect of African American life. It stimulated in many African Americans an awakening from a dormancy that was induced by slavery and maintained by written and unwritten racist Jim Crow laws. The "Do For Self" theme offered opportunities for Elijah's followers to sate their unfulfilled needs for an independent and productive life; the undying yearnings that are innate in all human beings. When watered with the words of encouragement to "Do For Self," the human urge in many African Americans to independently accomplish what other races had already achieved was powerful. Elijah Muhammad's "Do for Self" message was similar in many ways to Booker T. Washington's "pick yourself up by your bootstraps" and "be patient and prove yourself first" viewpoints.

The spin that *Black Entertainment Television (BET)* put on the "Do For Self" slogan, in their hit series *American Gangster* that was narrated by Ving Rhames, does no justice to the true meaning of the slogan as it was intended by Elijah Muhammad. *BET*, wittingly or unwittingly, gave license and ownership of the Nation of Islam's "Do for Self" creed to a criminal element that had taken cover under the umbrella of the Nation of Islam for selfish criminal gains. It would have been more proper if BET had shown also the great benefits that came from the use of the slogan. *BET's* carefree use of this Nation of Islam slogan is another example of why there is a need for a book such as, *The Honorable Elijah Muhammad: The Man Behind the Men*.

When Nation of Islam members obeyed Elijah Muhammad's "Do for Self" concept, it allowed them to stand proud and compete as men and women contributing to their black nation and to humanity as a whole. Being a positive factor in sustaining their own lives while bearing an Islamic "holy name" gave Nation of Islam members a great sense of dignity and pride. Nation of Islam members accepting Arabic "holy names" in place of European names was another unspoken statement telling whites, "I'm no longer your slave; therefore, I do not need your name, nor your acceptance, or validation in order for me to be a free human being." By adopting Islamic names the followers in the Nation of Islam were sending a message to America and the world proclaiming that they too can achieve in life bearing their own name — a righteous name. The Nation of Islam's message to white America was clear. "I'm no longer your 'boy' or 'gal'; in fact I am a free man and a free woman able to provide for our life without the white man's name."

This is one of the reasons many converts to the Nation of Islam happily received their "X" in place of their former "slave names." In addition to their seeking to be removed from a surname associated with slavery, their name changes also signaled their intent to change everything about them that was a vestige of slavery. Therefore, anything done independent of Caucasians, or Caucasian influence was very much welcomed by all in the Nation of Islam.

This mentality and spirit for total independence from dependency upon whites spread rapidly amongst many African American groups in the 1960s and 1970s. For groups such as the Black Panthers and other pro-black organizations, full independence — especially from white America — became their common theme in black America.

NOT BEARING THEIR NAMES "DO FOR SELF"

During this "Do For Self" era many African American business, educational, and social institutions and organizations adopted non-European sounding names in an effort to demonstrate a new sense of independence. These institutions chose African and Islamic names that in addition to offering an awareness of black heritage, also gave these African American associations a sense of purpose and destiny.

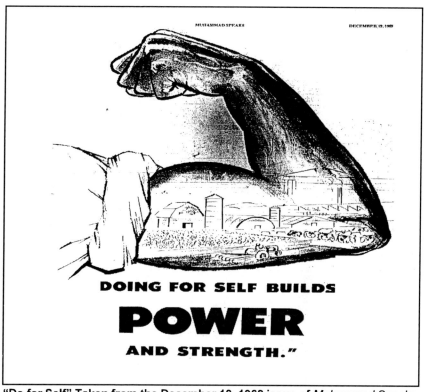

"Do for Self" Taken from the December 19, 1969 issue of *Muhammad Speaks*.
(Muslim Journal file)

African American professionals began to form black organizations and associations within their respective fields in order to proclaim a sense of independence. With the rise of black consciousness that grew commensurate with the popularity of the Nation of Islam, African American lawyers, doctors, government officials, educators, police and fire service personnel — practically every field of employment that had African American employees was soon witnessing the formation of black-oriented associations, societies, or organizations.

THE MAN BEHIND THE MEN

Black student unions flourished around America at many large and small colleges and universities. Elijah Muhammad's "Do for Self" message resonated throughout black America striking a cord in the African American soul that is still vibrating, even unto this day. No, Elijah Muhammad was not the only voice encouraging black consciousness. But as the Rev. Jesse Jackson said, "He (Elijah Muhammad) was the father of Black self-consciousness."

The Nation of Islam under Elijah Muhammad also was a factor in parents naming their newborn. As Nation of Islam members adorned their children with Islamic and African names many non-Muslim parents began to give their children similar names. It can even be argued that the current trend that became popular amongst African Americans in the 1980s – to create unique names for their babies; names with spellings and pronunciations heretofore unknown to humanity, may be an unconscious effort on the part of young African American mothers to replicate the same independence and sense of self determination that Nation of Islam members found in naming their babies with new and unique names.

In addition to reigniting a naming trend in the African American community similar to that described in Booker T. Washington's account of the newly freed slaves who also felt compelled to choose any surname other than their former slave master's name, Elijah Muhammad also recognized the importance of acquiring a name that connected the African American with a new beginning. The concepts of "not in their name" and "Do for Self" represent a type of African American genesis that was full of opportunities to achieve and progress while not bearing the name of their former slave masters.

In closing this portion of this book it is important to reiterate the importance that Nation of Islam members placed upon relieving themselves of surnames that they considered a remnant of U.S. slavery. Their preference for donning the letter "X", in anticipation of one day receiving a "righteous Arabic holy name," in place of their birth "slave names" was more dignified than having "the slave master's name." Even though the surname, "X", which essentially means "my true original last name is unknown," for Nation of Islam brothers and sisters, "receiving my 'X'" was like earning a badge of honor.

Native Washingtonian, Amatullah Sharif, the former Georgetta Stokes remembers the joy and excitement she felt upon finally receiving her "X" in 1970. Repeatedly she had unsuccessfuly written her acceptance letter to Nation of Islam officials. She recalled:

> I was really frustrated because I thought I was always writing my letter real well. And then they would send it back and say "No, write it again." Finally, I received a letter that said, "...take this to the

mosque and present it to the minister, you have received your "X"." I screamed and hollered. It was so exciting because the process of working for it, and working toward it was, you know, it was intense. The thing I remember about it the most is that the following Sunday was Easter Sunday, and I felt like I was resurrected. I felt like, you know, I just felt like, Wow! On Easter Sunday and I get my "X." That was the best thing that could ever happen to me. I was really, really excited. I took it to the mosque and people were very happy. I came up there and they called me "Georgetta X". I was the first X under the name Georgetta. I was just walking on cloud-nine.
— Telephone interview, October 6, 2008

The Nation of Islam consisted of Bible-minded people. The many examples of key biblical figures that changed their names are also models for Nation of Islam members. Abram and Sari became Abraham and Sarah, Saul of Taurus' changed his name to Paul, Jacob's name was changed to Israel, and Simon, the son of Jonah becoming known as Peter.

As these biblical figures could not continue in their previous names after being assigned by God to complete a task of significant consequences — nor could the Nation of Islam members pursue the liberation of the "17 million lost-found Negroes" if they too were still bearing the names of their former slave masters.

Elijah Muhammad told his followers to come out from under the names of the former slave master and to replace that name with a holy name, a righteous name of dignity in order to be free to "Do for Self" while not bearing another's name.

-§- CHAPTER -§-
NINE

Minister Louis Farrakhan
Leader of the Million Man March

(Photographer Saahir Communications)

"So when I gave up music and became a follower of the Honorable Elijah Muhammad, my love for music, my love for my craft just was transferred to my love for Allah, my love for the Messenger, my love for Islam."

— Farrakhan interview with Jabril Muhammad

MINISTER LOUIS FARRAKHAN

Louis Farrakhan was born in the Bronx borough of New York City on May 11, 1933, as Louis Eugene Walcott. He is the son of Percival Clark from Jamaica, and his mother, Sarah Mae Manning, is from St. Kitts in the eastern Caribbean.

Raised in Roxbury, MA, where he attended St. Cyprian's Episcopal Church, young Louis sang in the choir and played violin at Sunday concerts after service. He was encouraged to play the violin by his mother, which earned him an opportunity to appear on television in May of 1949 on *The Ted Mack Original Amateur Hour*.

A brilliant honor student whose high school education exposed him to four foreign languages, a wide array of histories, and the studies of mathematics, Louis was well prepared for college. Louis acknowledged in an April 2002 interview with Jabril Muhammad, the former Bernard Cushmere, "My high school education was so superior, that when I went to college, I never bought a book. I never was mentally challenged by anything that was being offered as a course of study. I went there because my mother desired that I have a fall-back position, in case music failed."

In addition to excelling in academics, Louis also stood out in sports where he tied the state record by running a 10 second flat 100 yard dash. Graduating from high school just one month after his seventeenth birthday, his coaches agreed that one year of college prep school — apparently not to improve his academics — would give him more time to strengthen and increase his foot speed and help him acquire a track scholarship.

Before building a career as a calypso singer under the stage name *Gene the Charmer*, Walcott breezed through three years at Winston-Salem Teachers' College in North Carolina excelling in the study of English. Success in the entertainment field provided Louis, who now had married, with opportunities to perform weekly.

In 1955 he met Nation of Islam Minister Malcolm X and soon thereafter joined the following of Elijah Muhammad. Louis Eugene Walcott became Brother Louis, adopting the Nation of Islam's customary "X" as his last name to replace his "slave-name" Walcott.

Even with all of his mental acumen, Brother Louis X was mesmerized by the message of Elijah Muhammad taught to him by Minister Malcolm X. Other ministers of the Nation of Islam who also influenced Louis X's early development in Islam included Minister Lucius of Washington D.C.; Minister Karriem of Baltimore; and Minister George of Philadelphia.

The words "study" and "student" had neither challenged or deterred Louis in elementary, high school or college; however, now those same terms were treasured by him after he joined the Nation of Islam. Eagerly accepting the obligation incumbent upon every member of the Nation of Islam to study the "lessons" provided Louis with a stricter, yet refreshing discipline that enhanced his cultured upbringing. The teachings of Elijah Muhammad were so different and exciting to him that sitting under the feet of his new-found teachers, most of whom had not even finished high school, did not disturb the college-educated and talented calypso singer.

> Even though there were people over me in authority who may not have had a high school education, they were so well-studied in the teachings of the Honorable Elijah Muhammad, it meant nothing to me that they did not have the amount of school time that I had, or the quality of preparation that I had. They had what I was trying to get. That was an understanding of the message of Islam, as taught by the Honorable Elijah Muhammad.
> — Interview with Jabril Muhammad

Not only did Louis' encounter with the message of Islam as taught by Elijah Muhammad press his mind and soul forward, the message of Elijah Muhammad also made his high school and college studies more viable and applicable. He studied everything associated with Elijah Muhammad that was within his reach. He told Jabril Muhammad, "By immersing myself in his message, then everything that I learned in high school, prep college and college took on greater significance."

Louis X ascended quickly through the ranks of the Nation of Islam. It wasn't long before Minister Malcolm X recommended to Elijah Muhammad that he make Brother Louis the minister of the Boston mosque. Elijah Muhammad balked at Malcolm's proposal. Elijah wanted to first observe Louis X's ability as a Nation of Islam captain. Louis served as captain under the supervision of another minister at Boston's Mosque No. 11 while Malcolm served as his mentor. Malcolm X and Louis were extremely close friends.

Farrakhan adjusting mic for Elijah Muhammad
(Photographer and Date Unknown)

After demonstrating his abilities as a captain in the Nation of Islam, Louis X became a minister around 1957. Malcolm X spoke favorably of Louis X in his autobiography. Malcolm noted, "The Boston Temple's outstanding young Minister Louis X, previously a well-known and rising popular singer called "The Charmer," had written our Nation's first popular song titled "White Man's Heaven is Black Man's Hell." (254).

Minister Louis X's dedication and loyalty to the leadership of Elijah Muhammad was demonstrated later when Malcolm was forced out of the Nation of Islam. The growing mistrust of Malcolm by Nation of Islam officials – of which Louis may have participated in — and the external manipulations conducted by United States governmental agencies that agitated the strife between Elijah and Malcolm culminated to a point of no return. Malcolm was on the outs and Minister Louis X, boxing champion Muhammad Ali and other Nation of Islam officials castigated Malcolm X, their former mentor and friend.

When Malcolm was no longer in the Nation of Islam, Minister Louis X was chosen by Elijah Muhammad to fill the office formerly held by Minister Malcolm X in Harlem, NY. This opportunity offered Minister Louis X the challenge of rebuilding the mosque in New York City which had been torched by arsonists, apparently angered when Malcolm X was assassinated. Circa 1966, shortly after Minister Louis X arrived in New York, Elijah Muhammad designated him with the surname "Farrakhan," a name that Elijah described as a "modern name" from God.

Steven Barboza in *American Jihad: Islam After Malcolm X* asked the Minister, "What does the name Farrakhan mean and how did you get it?" He answered, "The name Farrakhan was given to me by the Honorable Elijah Muhammad. When I asked him what it meant he said it had very many good meanings. It was one of the modern names of God. He said, 'I have the meaning upstairs, and one day I will give you its meaning.' I never did get the knowledge of its meaning. So I can tell you in truth, I really don't know." (142)

Elijah Muhammad was transforming and retooling Minister Louis X with this transfer to New York City. Under the obligation of the new name, *Farrakhan*; working in a new city "New York," that pulsated with an international ambience; serving under a title and role as the *National Spokesman for the Honorable Elijah Muhammad*, a title and role designed to fill the void created when Malcolm left the Nation of Islam; it was amongst this combination of changes and new challenges that Farrakhan began the arduous task of "rebuilding" New York's Mosque No. 7. To achieve this objective he brought in men such as Larry 4X Prescott, and Clark X Moore of Pittsburgh, who he assigned as the director of the local University of Islam elementary school.

After the assassination of Malcolm X in February 1965 many in the African American militant community became very distant from both the Nation of Islam and Minister Farrakhan. When Farrakhan joined the Nation of Islam he and Malcolm were extremely close; however, at the end of their relationship the animosity between the two was intense.

The post-Malcolm X era that isolated the Nation of Islam from the African American militant community was short-lived, lasting about five years. Relationships began to heal in the late summer of 1970 when Elijah Muhammad was invited to participate in the *Congress of African People (COAP)*, an international Pan Africanist organization that met in Atlanta, GA on September 3, 1970, convened by Amiri Baraka, the former LeRoi Jones, the founder and chairman. The international strength of this Congress was evidenced by the presence of representatives from 27 African nations, the Caribbean nations, four South American countries, Australia, and the United States.

Elijah Muhammad sent Farrakhan, accompanied by Minister Larry 4X Prescott, who later changed his name to Akbar Muhammad, and the former Clark X Moore, who lat r changed his name to Muhammad Siddeeq. Elijah Muhammad sent the trio to Atlanta to prepare for his arrival. At the time of the COAP Larry 4X was the minister of the Nation of Islam mosque in Corona, N.Y.

September 11, 1970 issue of *Muhammad Speaks* promoting the Atlanta Congress.
(Muslim Journal file)

MINISTER LOUIS FARRAKHAN

Siddeeq recalls the exchange and culmination of events surrounding the Nation of Islam's involvement in the COAP as a succession of events that catapulted Farrakhan into the international spotlight.

> In the year 1970 Minister Farrakhan basically had been in leadership from 1965, which is the period of the death of Malcolm. He was a popular person in the Muslim community and known in some local (places) in New York and some major cities with Afro-centric organizations but not anybody in the national or international field.
> It was at that point that the Honorable Elijah Muhammad was invited to the *International Congress of African People*, held in Atlanta, GA in 1970. He in turn designated Minister Farrakhan to go as his spokesperson. And when the participation of the Honorable Elijah Muhammad was upgraded from a workshop to a major speaker in the congress, Minister Farrakhan went as a participant in that congress in Atlanta.
> — Telephone interview

Elijah Muhammad in support of the COAP instructed the editor of his newspaper *Muhammad Speaks* to carry in bold block fonts the headline: "Atlanta Congress," resulting in the attendance of a large nationwide indigenous African American throng.

Due to the dominant Afro-centric spirit of the crowd, explained Siddeeq, a number of speakers and participants were rejected. Whitney Young, Jr. representing the Urban League, an organization with a large Jewish, Caucasian board of directors, and singer Jerry Butler who had a Caucasian drummer, were turned down by a chorus of boos. Siddeeq explained that in order to fill in the gaps in the program created by the crowd's rejections of Young and Butler, Minister Farrakhan's speaking time was increased from 3 minutes to almost a whole hour. "The crowd was not in any kind of mood to accept anything short of people who represented and lived their lives as spokespersons for African American justice and what was right." (Siddeeq)

The role of education, especially a model of independent education, was a key element of the Congress of African People conference and Elijah Muhammad's nationwide University of Islam school system fulfilled that need. The Nation of Islam school in New York City, with an enrollment of more than 400 students, that later grew to an enrollment of 1,500, helped secure Minister Farrakhan favor with this international gathering. Serving as the director of the New York City University of Islam, during that time, provided Siddeeq with this firsthand account:

THE MAN BEHIND THE MEN

The one thing everybody was looking for at the congress that was on everybody's mind was a strong black educational component that would be at the foundation and the base of anything that would be done in an African nation. The one thing we (Nation of Islam) had that no one else had was a school system that represented that. In New York City where the major people would come and visit because of the United Nations and the international flavor of New York City, there was a model — we had just built a school in the heart of Harlem. The people would see the school, and as a result of that, the majority of the invitations that came asking for a spokesperson to come, they wanted someone from the school, and Minister Farrakhan was the spokesperson for the city of New York, period!

He was invariably given all the invitations that came to the school, which were in the hundreds; they came in by the tons. So as a result of the Congress of African People and as a result of our (Nation of Islam) educational effort, Minister Farrakhan was given invitations around the country and outside of the country. (Siddeeq)

Taken from the October 22, 1971 *Muhammad Speaks*. *(Muslim Journal file)*

Farrakhan's representing Elijah Muhammad at the Congress of African People convention provided numerous benefits for Elijah Muhammad and the Nation of Islam as a whole, both locally and internationally.

One nationwide benefit was an increased acceptance from nationalistic minded African Americans who had soured on the Nation of Islam since the assassination of Malcolm X. Internationally the Nation of Islam gained status by having a model of education that was appreciated by visitors from abroad.

A Final Call newspaper website captures the international importance of Minister Farrakhan's COAP address.

> The Honorable Elijah Muhammad instructed Minister Farrakhan on how to go after his subject that evening in Atlanta. He said, "If you say it as I have told you, you will be successful." The Minister did as he was instructed and his speech was received overwhelmingly. This speech was broadcast repeatedly on PBS stations across America and the world. The Honorable Elijah Muhammad told Minister Farrakhan that, after this speech, it would be written of in 40 nations and for that one speech, he (Minister Farrakhan) was more valuable to him than a truck load of diamonds and gold.

Ironically it was Malcolm's 1959 ambassadorship to Africa and the Middle East on behalf of Elijah Muhammad that may have been the seminal event that inspired such organizations as Amiri Baraka's COAP. But by time the Atlanta congress took place Malcolm had been dead more than five years. As a result of Elijah Muhammad being invited to participate at the COAP and Farrakhan serving in Elijah Muhammad's stead, Farrakhan over the years has reaped the benefits of this international exposure.

Farrakhan remained the minister in New York City while often traveling around the United States on behalf of Elijah Muhammad and the Nation of Islam until Elijah's death in 1975. His charismatic and magnetic personality and oratory skills, accompanied by his dedication to promoting the message of Elijah Muhammad, continued to draw thousands to listen to Farrakhan's presentation during the closing years of Elijah's life.

With the 1975 passing of Elijah Muhammad, one day before the Nation of Islam's annual Saviour's Day Convention, the Muslim community's leadership, which included Farrakhan's support, unanimously voted in Wallace, the son of Elijah Muhammad, to lead his father's community. Promising full allegiance, Minister Farrakhan pledged to "Submit, and yield and give of myself, and all that I have, and all within my power" to help Wallace as the new leader of the Nation of Islam.

Any public display of disunity, even with the internecine struggles that sometimes dogged Nation of Islam officials, was taboo. Maybe this same communal taboo was resounding in Farrakhan's conscious when he vowed unity at the 1975 Saviour's Day convention and pledged his undying support to Imam Wallace Mohammed. Minister Farrakhan vowed:

And so I close saying that we have learned the lesson of history. And that those who sit around waiting for fractions and split-offs, waiting for those who would be hungry for leadership and hungry for power; I want you to know this afternoon that our father, Elijah Muhammad did not make us that kind of people. The Honorable Elijah Muhammad loved unity. He lived for unity. He fought for unity. And we today will fight that same fight and will keep the faith of Muhammad. And only in that faith will we find the unity and the strength that we need to help Minister Wallace D. Muhammad, the leader of the Nation of Islam, carry on in the noble work of his father.
— Saviour's Day February 26, 1975

As the new "Supreme Minister" of the Nation of Islam, Wallace Muhammad introduced changes that began to move the followers of the Nation of Islam away from the black-only oriented message of his father towards compatibility with the universal message of traditional Islam as practiced by Muslims around the world.

Other changes introduced by Minister Wallace included changing the community's name from the Nation of Islam to the World Community of Al-Islam in the West. Additionally he opened the Nation of Islam's membership to Caucasians and changed the titles of the mosque leaders from "minister" to the Islamic title of "imam." In addition to changing the spelling of his last name to *Mohammed*," Wallace also offered Farrakhan the first name Abdul-Haleem which means "servant of the Fore-bearing One," a name that Farrakhan temporarily accepted while he served as a minister under the leadership of Wallace Mohammed.

Louis Farrakhan charged that the many changes that were being introduced by his new leader were coming too fast. In particular he had difficulty when Wallace diminished the divine status of Elijah Muhammad from being the "Messenger of Allah." Furthermore, Wallace removed the deification that had been given to the Nation of Islam's founder, W.D. Fard. Instead of deifying Fard as "God" and Elijah as the "Messenger," Wallace preferred to refer to his father and Mr. W.D. Fard as "great social reformers."

After three years of wrestling with the theological and organizational changes, amid the whispering rumors of jealousy because he had not been chosen to succeed Elijah Muhammad, Minister Farrakhan left the leadership of Imam Wallace Mohammed to "rebuild the Nation of Islam." In 1978 Farrakhan vowed to return to the language and institutional structure used by Elijah Muhammad, reviving the black-centered Nation of Islam teachings that promoted the black man as god and the white man as the devil. With Elijah Muhammad no longer alive, Farrakhan named himself the spokesman for the deceased leader, thus becoming the central figure of his version of a resurrected Nation of Islam. The split that Farrakhan discouraged on February 26, 1975 had indeed happened. His pledge to fight for unity, waned.

Other former followers of Elijah Muhammad, such as his brother John Muhammad of Detroit and Silas Muhammad of Atlanta, also revamped their own versions of the Nation of Islam with limited success. They too claimed dissatisfaction with the changes ushered in by Wallace. Without doubt, of the three, Farrakhan by far has been the most successful even though he has yet to rebuild his Nation of Islam to the membership level or the financial status that Elijah Muhammad had achieved in his lifetime. Nor has Farrakhan's membership reached the following of Wallace's Islamic community. Nonetheless, he has had huge success in reaching millions of youth with his message, even converting thousands to his message, while providing a place of retreat for other former Nation of Islam members who also were dissatisfied with the changes introduced by Imam Wallace D. Mohammed.

After receiving numerous reports that Farrakhan was asking people to return to the black consciousness as taught prior to 1975, Imam Mohammed appealed to Minister Farrakhan to rethink this position. During a Friday Jumah service held on March 24, 1978 Wallace addressed the Muslim community about the reports of Farrakhan's apparent dissent. The April 28, 1978 issue of *Bilalian News* carried the following:

> I don't like to come to you with this kind of thing, but I'm afraid that if I don't some people will be made to behave in the wrong way. Almost every week or so there's a clipping, a report or something, telling me about Minister Farrakhan's activities. That he spoke somewhere, or said something about his changes or about our direction that we have now. I thought maybe I should speak to you because it's a chance that you might be getting some of this too. As I have told you, if the information I'm getting is correct, Minister Farrakhan is asking people to go back to the same things exactly that were being taught before in 1974.

In concluding this Friday Islamic prayer sermon Wallace included a challenge to Farrakhan to see which framework could produce more, the former Nation of Islam ideologies or the new program that Wallace envisioned. "This is not a challenge to him as my enemy. This is my challenge to him as my friend. I want to show my friend that I have a better way than he has." Then Wallace turned his anger towards those who he suspected had neither his nor Farrakhan's best interests at heart. "Now here's my word to my enemy and Farrakhan's enemy: 'You bastard! You'll never pull me out in the street to do one ounce of harm to Minister Farrakhan! You go to hell, you bastard!"

With the aid of Minister Larry 4X Prescott, Farrakhan began rebuilding their version of the Nation of Islam based largely on the racial and nationalistic teaching formerly espoused by Elijah Muhammad. It would be 22 years before the two men, Imam Wallace Deen Mohammed and Minister Farrakhan, would officially mend the rift caused when Farrakhan opted to "rebuild the Nation of Islam." We will discuss the reunion of these two leaders later.

Minister Farrakhan's message, delivered in his gracious-to-fiery oratory style, had instant appeal to many African Americans. Farrakhan's assessment of the racial, political, and social ills of American society resonated with African American youth and young adults, many whom had minimal understanding of Qur'anic based Islam. Over the years Farrakhan's Nation of Islam grew to a reported 10,000 followers and exponentially his image grew. Two key factors played into Farrakhan's resurgence. The media swarmed on his comments that were deemed by many as an anti-Semitic and anti-white "hate message." Another vital reason for his resurgence, particularly in the African American community, was due to the young men in his Fruit of Islam selling Farrakhan's *Final Call* newspaper, and audio cassettes of his lectures, on the street corners of black America.

The shining moment in Farrakhan's renewed Nation of Islam occurred on October 16, 1995 when over one million men responded to Farrakhan's call to come to Washington D.C. The official estimate reported by the United States Park Police said the crowd size was 400,000 participants. But Professor Farouk El-Baz of Boston University using satellite remote sensing techniques estimate the *Million Man March* crowd to be around 878,587 marchers, with a plus-minus of 25 percent.

Minister Farrakhan and the *Million Man March* organizers believe they far surpassed their goal of gathering one million black men. *Cable News Network (CNN)* in a report titled "Minister Farrakhan Challenges Black Men" cite Farrakhan expressing a strong sense of fulfillment and satisfaction. Farrakhan proudly said to the massive multitude.

> Look at you. Oh, I don't know what the number is. It's too much for me to count. But I think they said it's a million and a half, or two. I don't know how many. But you know, I called for a million. When I saw the word go out my mouth, I looked at it. I said, "Oh my God!" It just came out of my mouth. I didn't know. And after it came out, I said, "Well, I got to go with it." And, I'm so glad I did. People told me you better change that figure to one more realistic. And I should have changed it to the three Million Man March.

In a July 31, 1996 interview titled *One in a Million*, with the late John F. Kennedy Jr., a co-founder of *George* magazine and the son of former United States President John F. Kennedy Sr., Minister Louis Farrakhan spoke about how Elijah Muhammad's words had inspired him to call for the *Million Man March*.

MINISTER LOUIS FARRAKHAN

> **Kennedy:** I want to talk to you about the *Million Man March*. Where did the inspiration for the march come from? There's a story that you were watching Martin Luther King's "I Have a Dream" speech with the Honorable Elijah Muhammad and he was displeased. True?
>
> **Farrakhan:** That's true. He had reservations, not about the march but about the frivolity of the march when the quest for justice and jobs was such a serious issue. He said, "One day I will have a march, and it will be of a very serious nature." I wanted to give the world a different image of the black community — and the black male in particular — so I traveled around this country for two years promoting this day. Promoting black men, promoting atonement, a change in the conduct of black men. I didn't know how we were going to do it, but I had said it, and so we had to set about trying to do it.
> — John Kennedy, Jr.

After the *Million Man March*, Minister Farrakhan completed a very successful *50-Nation World Friendship Tour* in which he met with world leaders and students thus permanently engraving in the annals of history his status as an international figure. The website *http://www.noi.org/mlf-bio.html* notes that the tour included Iran (for an Islamic conference), Iraq, Kuwait, the United Arab Emirates, Saudi Arabia, Syria, Israel, Palestine, China, Malaysia, Singapore, North Korea, South Korea, the former Soviet Union, 20 countries in Africa including Libya, and nations in the South Pacific, the Caribbean and South America.

The stated purpose of the *World Friendship Tour* was an opportunity for Farrakhan to take his *Million Man March* message of atonement and healing throughout the world. "I would like to demonstrate how diplomacy and friendly relations should be carried out," Farrakhan said, explaining how the U.S. and other world governments have strayed from the path to peace.

However, there remained another more important bond of friendship that still needed mending. The mental and spiritual weight of splitting with Imam Wallace D. Mohammed, the special son and "seventh child" of Elijah Muhammad, must have presented a quandary for Minister Farrakhan. Not only had Elijah Muhammad taught and shaped Farrakhan and other top Nation of Islam officials, Elijah Muhammad had also taught these officials the importance of maintaining a unique regard for his son Wallace.

Farrakhan and Wallace had at least one ray of hope despite their years of differences since the passing of Elijah Muhammad. Louis Farrakhan and Wallace Mohammed had agreed to always remain friends. They always left open a door of communications.

THE MAN BEHIND THE MEN

During the life time of Elijah Muhammad, Farrakhan's high regard for Wallace was strong, as evidenced at a January 1975 Fruit of Islam meeting held in New York City. Minister Farrakhan introduced the then Minister Wallace D. Muhammad to the Fruit of Islam, the paramilitary arm of the Nation of Islam. Standing before a body of more than 1,000 men, Farrakhan, in his excitement, said of Wallace Muhammad.

> This brother is the seventh child of the Honorable Elijah Muhammad. I can only tell you of him that which I know and that which I have heard from the mouth of the Messenger. And since Messenger Elijah Muhammad is a man who does not tell other than the truth — he told me some years ago, he said 'Brother, my mouth was not made to speak idle words. My mouth was made to speak the will of God.' Then I listen to what that mouth said. I would like to tell you what that mouth; that divine mouth has said of this one. And if he never said it, if we look hard enough we could see it. Uhm! I'm so happy this morning! Boy! (Applause) That's right!
> ...If you want the Messenger's presence, you should want to hold onto one who has him inside, very deep inside.
> Years ago, when Minister Muhammad first began teaching, those of us who heard him we marveled at him. He is different from any other minister of Islam. He always had a depth that none of us had. He always had the ability to inspire us to greater heights of wisdom because of the depths to which he had been blessed to go. So whenever he spoke we all listened because we knew that here was something different, yet the root of it was still the father's teachings but its height and its depth was so that we could see greater horizons from listening to his mouth. And he began to marvel us all. We would sit at the Messenger's table when he was absent and talk about him; we were great backbiters. The Messenger would say, "If you think he is great now, wait until you see him ten years from now." That was in 1963; its twelve years. Messenger Muhammad told me personally. I don't know who was around to witness. I can witness for myself — and the truth is a witness of itself. The Messenger told me, and I don't want you to think in any way other than the way I'm saying it. He said that when the germ left him that was to be the base of this man (Minister Wallace), he said, "The Saviour was in that germ." And while he was being formed in his blessed mother's womb the Saviour told the Messenger to name him after himself. The Saviour told him to "name him Wallace D. Muhammad."

The mid-to-late 1990s show a Farrakhan who is very much conscious of reconciling the many unresolved issues that had lingered since the assassination of Malcolm X. In 1995 Farrakhan reconciled with Betty Shabazz, Malcolm's widow. The necessity and gravity of the Shabazz-Farrakhan reconciliation is heavily underscored by the failed assassination plot against Farrakhan that had been planned by Malcolm's daughter Qubilah. Farrakhan, instead of blaming Qubilah, asserted in the *Final Call* newspaper that she was "the victim of an orchestrated plot to entrap her in a complex U.S. government surveillance program."

With the success of the 50-Nation World Friendship Tour behind him Farrakhan began to redirect his attention to reconciliation with Wallace and the other children of his mentor. Past reunions between Farrakhan and Wallace (Warith) Deen Mohammed were followed with short-lived success stories. Fortunately each attempt to come together yielded more hope that one day the two Islamic leaders and their respective communities would work closer together. Sadly, in 1999, this long-anticipated reunion was delayed another year as Farrakhan overcame a serious battle with prostate cancer.

Of the four internationally acclaimed men that this book highlights it is important to note that Farrakhan is the one student who kept to Elijah's initial lesson plans longer than the other three, only re-interpreting the lessons of his teacher as compelled by the necessity of modernity.

One example of Farrakhan wisely reinterpreting the teachings of Elijah Muhammad occurred when he altered the spelling of Saviour's by transposing the apostrophe to the right of the letter "s," thus rendering *Saviour's Day* to read *Saviours' Day*.

Minister Farrakhan's modification in the spelling of the Nation of Islam's most sacred observance, the annual Saviour's Day, occurred in 2000, the year in which his reconciliation with Wallace Mohammed finally was fully realized. A year had passed since Farrakhan's 1999 battle with prostate cancer and now the two Islamic leaders enjoyed a successful reunion.

Quite appropriately the reunion occurred at the traditional Saviour's Day weekend, a time that also recognized the birthday of W.D. Fard. The reunion began with the traditional Islamic Jumah prayer on Friday February 25, 2000, and was well attended by followers of both Imam Mohammed's and Minister Farrakhan's Islamic communities.

Minister Farrakhan's altered spelling of "Saviour's Day" (shifting the apostrophe to the right after the "s") made the term non-personal, thus transferring the ownership and responsibility of saving the downtrodden black man and woman from the sole shoulders of Mr. W.D. Fard and distributing the obligation and the blessings of being a "saviour" to everyone. Now, instead of Fard standing alone as a special "saviour," everyone was to accept to become a savior.

Pluralizing the spelling of the title saviour exponentially altered Fard's traditional god-like status. This modified spelling also opened opportunities of comfort for Muslims, who were not members of the Nation of Islam, to attend future Saviours' Day assemblies without the burden or fear of Fard being presented as a divine savior.

That slight alteration of the spelling from Saviour's to Saviours' was ingenious and courageous. More importantly, this change was liberating in two ways. First it would help to free Nation of Islam Muslims who were under Minister Farrakhan's leadership from the serious Islamic sin of shirk; the associating of another entity as a partner with God. Second, this new spelling provided a bridge to strengthen the connection between Wallace Mohammed's and Louis Farrakhan's Islamic communities.

Since the passing of Elijah Muhammad in 1975 and Farrakhan's subsequent 1978 return to "rebuild the Nation of Islam," the Minister has often been criticized for what many Muslims have interpreted to be his wavering on his declaration of faith. They question whether Farrakhan is committed to the universally accepted Islamic declaration of faith that declares — as outlined in chapter 112 of the Qur'an — that there is only one God without partner. They question if he is still quietly promoting the Nation of Islam declaration that Allah appeared in the form of a man, namely Mr. Wallace Fard Muhammad who reportedly was born on February 26, 1877.

Notwithstanding the fact that Farrakhan's *Final Call* newspaper was still promoting the concept that Fard is Allah, nonetheless, at the 2003 Saviours' Day observation he made another bold step towards bringing his community closer to the international community of Muslims. Repeatedly he cautioned his audience to carefully listen to his distinguishing between Allah, the God and Wallace Fard Muhammad the man.

> Are you listening? February 26, 1877 could never have been the birth of Allah. Allah has no birth record. But His khalifah, the man that He made to represent Him, to carry His mind, to carry His spirit, to execute on His will and wisdom – all of us human beings have a birth. So we are not celebrating the birth of Allah, we are celebrating the birth of a man who came to us from Allah. A man who came bringing to us that which got us started into a magnificent growth. Listen! No matter how great any of us as human beings may be, none is worthy of worship but Allah, God. He has no rivals. He has no partners. Everything that is in existence came into existence by His active or permissive will. So that which comes into existence by the permission of God is yet less than He Who allowed him to come into existence. A man that is born of a woman can become a master. A man that is born of a woman, who will seek knowledge and has a pure heart, God can grow that man into Himself — meaning grow him into a perfect reflection of Himself. And even that which is a perfect reflection of God is not worthy to be worshipped. You do not worship any reflection. You worship Him Who created the reflection."

MINISTER LOUIS FARRAKHAN

A review of many of Minister Farrakhan's lectures, including his talk at the *Million Man March* are sprinkled with instructions that can suggest that he is slowly guiding his community towards Islam as known throughout the Islamic world. He is careful to give these instructions in a fashion that does not remove his community from the day-to-day struggles of the African American community. Still the minister is scrutinized, often criticized for not being more direct with denouncing Mr. Fard outright, and completely removing Fard from any connection with a god-head.

At the reunion of Wallace Mohammed and Louis Farrakhan in the year 2000, thousands of Muslims from both communities traveled from near and far to witness the reunion. Other American Muslims, both immigrant and indigenous, as well as Muslims from overseas also came to witness this occasion as American and international newspapers reported the great reunion of Minister Louis Farrakhan and Imam W. Deen Mohammed. Following is one website account of the reunion titled *The Healing of the Split in the African-American Muslim Community* posted by the *Pluralism Project* of Harvard University:

> On February 26th, 2000, *The Washington Post* reported on the announced unity between Muslim American Society leader Wallace Deen Mohammed, son of Nation of Islam founder Elijah Mohammed (sic), and Nation of Islam leader Louis Farrakhan at the 2nd annual Saviours' Day conference sponsored by the Nation of Islam. ...Mohammed spoke to the crowd at Friday's prayer services: "Dear Muslim brothers and sisters, it's not difficult for Minister Farrakhan and Wallace Deen Mohammed to embrace each other...for this is too big a cause for personal differences." Farrakhan stated: "Twenty-Five years later, I know your father wanted this...From this day forward, the Imam Mohammed and I, no matter what our little problems are, will work them out for the glory of Allah." Farrakhan openly declared, "we bear witness that there is no prophet after the prophet Mohammed," which is a change from the Nation of Islam doctrine that held W.D. Fard, Elijah Mohammed's teacher, as God incarnate and Elijah Mohammed as the final prophet to mankind.

The March 14, 2000 *Special Edition* issue of the *Final Call* — Minister Farrakhan's media arm — on pages 20-21 printed the Minister's words of delight he expressed about the reunion between himself and Imam Mohammed; words that also addressed a need for God's help to make this reconciliation and healing complete.

> There was great joy in Imam Warith Deen Mohammed, myself, our families and communities reuniting with each other. Imam Mohammed and I were young men together and the love that Allah (God) put in our hearts for each other could not

be destroyed even though we had serious differences, but, Allah (God) says in the Qur'an, "He will settle the differences between those of us who believe."

It is clear to me that Allah (God) is helping us in the settling of our differences and we have agreed to continue this dialogue, moving closer and closer to one another, sharing information, knowledge, experience and collaborating wherever we can in promoting the rise of our people and the promotion of the righteous values as taught by all of the Prophets. (Pg. 20-21)

Imam W. Deen Mohammed making comments at 2000 Saviors' Day Sunday program.
(Photographer Saahir Communications)

The Friday Jumah prayer service was led by an Palestinian imam. Afterwards Imam Mohammed spoke giving Allah the credit for the union.

> It's easy for me to embrace Minister Farrakhan. Our families are together. We are really one family. Our friendship has not died, and it will not die. And the little problem, the small problem, that we've had along the way, struggling to present ourselves as God willed that we present ourselves, it's not bigger than the word of God, the Qur'an, and it's not bigger than Muhammad, the model for all human beings, for all people of faith. It's very small. So we see, we think, what have we done to bring about this togetherness? What have we done to bring about this closeness that we have this minute? What have we done to free our hearts so we can hug each other and kiss each other, as I did kiss my

brother? What have we done to bring that about? Nothing but tried to find the way in the path of Islam, and Allah did the rest. Allah did the rest.

On Sunday February 27, 2000 Minister Farrakhan spoke to an audience comprised of 28,000 diverse Muslims who had gathered at the United Center in Chicago. Minister Farrakhan spoke in obvious reconciliatory terms yet maintained his due respect to Elijah Muhammad, as he reached out to touch every Muslim in attendance. The crowd responded with thunderous approval as He shared:

> I love Prophet Muhammed and I know that he is the end of the prophets, and I know that the Qur'an is the final book that was brought to the human being to prepare us for the life of the hereafter; but I don't think that Allah would be pleased with me if I embraced the Prophet Muhammed and disrespected the man that suffered to bring me up to a position where I could see the prophet, respect the prophet, follow the prophet and be a true servant of the prophet...Thanks to the Honorable Elijah Muhammad, who no one can deny has done a great work in North America, for the upliftment of Black people. So much so that many scholars, scientists and thinkers who have benefited from the wisdom of the Honorable Elijah Muhammad are now getting a richer, more vibrant knowledge of our history which is causing us to begin to love ourselves. And now the love of our neighbor is gradually becoming easier.

The powerful influence that Elijah Muhammad has had upon the life of Louis Farrakhan is inestimable. Farrakhan baptized his whole life, thoroughly submerging his mind and soul into the teachings of Elijah Muhammad. In the book *Back Where We Belong*, a collection of Farrakhan's selected speeches, discusses the significant effect Elijah Muhammad had on him as his teacher. At a 1987 speech given in Washington D.C. the Minister shared, "Now here I am a student of the Honorable Elijah Muhammad, a man who performed this service for us. He cleaned us up; he stood us up; he united us; he made us love ourselves and love our people" (212). In this testimony of Farrakhan we are reminded that Elijah Muhammad was a man who made men over and over again.

The international prominence enjoyed by Farrakhan today is due greatly to the lessons and opportunities he received from Elijah Muhammad. Yes, Minister Farrakhan's oratorical skills have assuredly kept him in the international eye. But if not for Farrakhan coming into contact with the strength, vigor and courageous voice of Elijah Muhammad, the world perhaps would have heard the calypso performer "Gene the Charmer" singing his song Belly to Belly, Back to Back. However, without the Honorable Elijah Muhammad the world would have never known a Minister Louis Farrakhan.

-§- CHAPTER -§-
TEN

Was God With Elijah Muhammad?

> I look at my father's life, his preaching, his words, his actions, and I know God intervened. He could not do that by himself. He could not have done that by himself, on his own limited education, thinking and mind. In fact, if he had been the most educated black in America, he couldn't have done it, unless God assisted him and intervened in his life. I know that for a fact, after looking at his words and his life and how it grew over the many years of his leadership and where he left off. He left off where all people should start.
>
> — Imam W. Deen Mohammed
> First Sunday Address Nov. 5, 2006

Studying Elijah Muhammad's life and leadership within the context of the unjust racial era in America that restricted the free expression of his soul and mind, compounded by the fact that he was born only 32 years after the end of chattel slavery, cannot be reiterated enough. If his life is reviewed in light of these factors perhaps a better appreciation and understanding of Elijah Muhammad can be garnered.

If we reflect on the devastating effects of African American bondage and the fact that its burdens crippled a race of people for generations, then maybe we can realize the role and purpose of Elijah Muhammad — a man who was a brazened product of that unjust period in American history.

For centuries downtrodden African Americans met the challenge of praying and waiting for the justice of God to come. The slavery and Jim Crow segregation forced upon the vast majority of African Americans during the lifetime of Elijah Muhammad may lead one to ponder if God is obligated to answer the cries of such suffering?

When Elijah Muhammad met Mr. W.D. Fard his life was at an all time low. Alcoholism and unemployment during the Great Depression of 1929 resulted in Elijah's family being dependent upon welfare assistance. Elijah Muhammad, almost depleted of his manhood because of his poor financial and mental state, was a prime candidate for the well crafted message of Fard.

For any human being in the indigent and dejected state that Elijah was in at the time he first heard Mr. W.D. Fard's teachings, any help, whether pure or tainted, freeing or enslaving, would have been considered manna from heaven. Elijah Muhammad was in no position to question the validity of Fard's message that promised him a brighter future. Nor was Elijah a man of letters familiar with the sciences and disciplines of the world. At best Elijah was a poor Negro masking the shame of his current state of affairs with alcohol until Fard introduced himself as "the Prophet."

WAS GOD WITH ELIJAH MUHAMMAD

Elijah had fled the transgressions of southern racists in an effort to remove himself and his family from the sins of oppression, only to find himself unemployed and trapped in the ghettoes of Detroit, MI. A man who falls into sin and error while living under such duress — as Elijah and most other urban Negroes were caught in — may sometimes be excused for the errors they commit under the pressures of living in survival mode. The following Qur'anic verses offer forgiveness from God for people who find themselves in situations very similar to that which Elijah was facing — a life of weakness with no hope or favor.

> *When angels take the souls of those who die in sin against their souls, they say: "In what (plight) were ye?" They reply: "Weak and oppressed were we in the earth." They say: "Was not the earth of Allah spacious enough for you to move yourselves away (from evil)?" Such men will find their abode in Hell, – What an evil refuge! – Except those who are (really) weak and oppressed – men, women, and children – who have no means in their power, nor (a guide-post) to their way. For these, there is hope that Allah will forgive: For Allah doth blot out (sins) and forgive again and again.*
>
> Holy Qur'an Chapter 4; Verses 97-99

The condition of African Americans entering the 20th century was very much that of a "weak and oppressed" people. They had "no means in their power, nor a guidepost." There are no verses of the Qur'an that can establish Elijah Muhammad as the "Messenger of Allah," but the fact has to register that no Qur'anic verse precludes the strong possibility that God was with the sincere efforts of Elijah Muhammad. These few verses of chapter four of the Qur'an extends to Elijah Muhammad the strong possibility of receiving the mercy and forgiveness of God simply because of his position of powerlessness in the 1920s and the helplessness of his people for decades to follow.

The origin of Elijah Muhammad's title "Messenger" is discussed on page 18 in his book *Message to the Blackman in America*. Before Fard's departure he had promoted Elijah Muhammad to the envied position of Supreme Minister of the Nation of Islam. Afterward, with Fard no longer on the scene, Elijah Muhammad's position was elevated to a divine-like status, "the Messenger of Allah."

Many of Elijah Muhammad's critics, even to this day, have difficulty with him possessing a title that suggests divinity of any degree. The descriptions "Dear Holy Apostle" and "The Messenger of Allah," even the reference to Elijah Muhammad as "honorable," generates in many of his critics various degrees of resentment and disgust. But in the minds and hearts of his devout followers and admirers these titles inspired reverence and respect for Elijah Muhammad, even a type of awe.

A daring question to entertain is: Was Elijah Muhammad divinely guided? The argument here is not whether Elijah Muhammad was the "Messenger" of God in the traditional Biblical or Qur'anic sense of a divine messenger, but rather, was God's hand, that of the Creator of heaven and earth, working through Elijah Muhammad and W.D. Fard?

Three of the four men observed in this book evolved to publicly state that Elijah Muhammad was not a divinely sent "Messenger" of God. But all four men, including Louis Farrakhan, have clearly stated that Elijah Muhammad definitely is not the Prophet of God. And it is important to note that Elijah Muhammad himself never claimed to be a prophet, he only claimed to be a messenger. Nonetheless, even Elijah Muhammad's claim of "messenger" doesn't eliminate the possibility that he was guided by God.

Additionally it is important to note that Elijah Muhammad may have seen Fard's role in the Nation of Islam's theology as a duality. On one hand Elijah portrayed Fard as "God in the Person." But he often presented Fard as a man who believed in and prayed to God, hinting that the physical man Fard was not actually God the Creator of the heavens and earth. In *Message to the Blackman in America* Elijah makes a clear distinction between God and Fard: "We, the Muslims, are sure of help from Him (Allah) who has visited us in the name of Master Fard Muhammad (God in Person), the long-awaited Mahdi..." (259). It is clear from the above quote that Elijah is speaking about two separate entities that are working together for one cause. Elijah Muhammad's two portrayals of Fard are very similar to the Christian dichotomy of Jesus the Christ juxtaposed to God the Creator — both Jesus and Fard only serves as representatives of the God who used them as a conduit for His message. Note that Elijah said that Allah "visited us *in the name of* Master Fard Muhammad...," thus making a distinction that Fard was only a medium.

If we judge the possibility of God working through Elijah Muhammad, especially in light of Elijah's successes; or, if we judge Elijah by the rule that God's mercy is with the oppressed, then yes, it can be concluded that God was with Elijah Muhammad. According to Ibn Abbas, the first-cousin and young companion of the 7th century Prophet of Islam, Muhammed ibn (son of) Abdullah said, "God is with the oppressed." In one report Prophet Muhammed said, "and be afraid of the curse of an oppressed person as there is no screen between his invocation and God." In another report Prophet Muhammed said "the invocation of the oppressed is responded to (by God)." Without question when W.D. Fard made himself known in 1929, the life of Elijah Muhammad and African Americans was that of an oppressed people.

African Americans, since slavery days, have always believed that God, in a very special and unique way, was on their side. They held a belief that God did not allow their race to endure the evils of slavery unless He was with them during their centuries of slavery, and the subsequent generations of restrictive human rights. Additionally, African Americans in general believed that after these epochs of suffering that God's promise of a brighter future awaited them. Elijah Muhammad was of this same belief; that God was on his side as he sought to usher in a better tomorrow for African Americans.

Many African Americans felt as Elijah Muhammad did when it came to blaming white Americans for the evils of racism. The only difference is that most of them were not as publicly frank, therefore, not as offensive with their blaming as Elijah Muhammad was for the vast majority of his life. Most African Americans of Elijah Muhammad's era saw the United States power structure as oppressive and destined to be punished by God for the sins committed against African Americans. As recently as the late 20th century it was common to hear African Americans speak with pride when certain natural disasters bypassed their locale but damaged nearby Caucasian neighborhoods. They'd whispered amongst themselves, "Did you see where it hit?" Speaking as if God was especially on the side of African Americans they would say to their family and friends, "It passed right over us and hit them white folks."

In this same vein it be must be understood that God was with Elijah Muhammad, a man who was a vocalized response — albeit to the extreme — of the racism of his day. The difference between Elijah and other African American leaders is best seen in two areas. First, was his boldness to say in public what others would only say behind closed doors. Second, was his racially separatist methodology for uplifting his people. He was not the first to advocate separation of the races, nor was he the first to attempt to publicly expurgate the evils of racism in America. Nonetheless, he became the one best known for applying such techniques.

Dr. Martin Luther King Jr., Frederick Douglass, Harriet Tubman, Sojourner Truth (born Isabella Baumfree), Noble Timothy Drew Ali, Marcus Garvey and others believed that God was with them in a special and unique way. They held in common a belief that the Lord of all the worlds would serve as a merciful intervener in the cause of uplifting African Americans.

Kate Clifford Larson in her book *Bound for the Promised Land* notes Tubman's "confidence in the voice of God, as spoken to her soul...and her faith in a Supreme Power truly was great." Also as noted by the great Reverend Richard Allen, founder of the African Methodist Episcopal Church, "We wish you to consider, that God himself was the first pleader of the cause of slaves."

Some of these African American leaders noted that the Christianity practiced by many white Americans perpetuated racism and other forms of oppression against African Americans. They surmised such Christianity as practiced by racist whites as a "hypocritical" expression of religion. This is the line of thinking that Elijah Muhammad was working in: a belief that religion as taught by white people, particularly by the white racist, had not met the spiritual and social needs of African Americans. In fact, such teachings had failed African Americans completely.

THE MAN BEHIND THE MEN

An even stronger argument advanced the possibility that the religion of the slave master never could benefit the slave even after emancipation; that such a religion — by its very nature — was designed to uphold the evil ways of the slave master, therefore obligating the God of heaven and earth to intervene and send a special response to the downtrodden Negro of North America.

Mr. Fard wanted the white western world to see their shortcomings. Working through his top student, Elijah Poole, Fard instituted a type of reverse psychology that Elijah used to harshly criticize the American white man by appealing to his moral conscience, accusing the white man of being unable and unwilling to do right by the descendants of America's former slaves.

Elijah Muhammad, serving as a link in the chain of men such as David Walker, Henry Highland Garnet, Marcus Garvey and others, opted to label white Americans as morally inept. Daring the white man to obey God was one strategy employed by African American leaders in an effort to secure more freedoms for African Americans. Another tactic that Fard gave Elijah Muhammad was a form of reverse psychology that publicly charged the white man with being incapable of obeying God.

Marcus Garvey applied this same strategy of issuing a warning and a challenge to white Americans with his poem "Halt America", written in 1934. Garvey's disfavor with the white man's version of Christianity is quite evident, yet his belief that God was with downtrodden African Americans is clear.

"Halt! America!"

America of white men's rule,
The God of Heaven calls to you;
You used the black man as a tool,
And proved of faith and love untrue.
Your Christian faith is all a lie,
If you do not some changes make;
You brought us here to make us die,
But God will save us for His sake.
There is a call to make things right,
And to your conscience we appeal:
For peace we are, we want no fight,
We ask you but the wound to heal.
We've laboured long in many fields,
To clear your waste and barren lands:
We fought your wars with manly shields,
But you've cast us off your hands.
America will flourish great,
If love and truth abide within;
And so we call upon the State,
To free itself from deadly sin.

WAS GOD WITH ELIJAH MUHAMMAD

> The Negro's cause is holy word,
> And God proclaims the mighty truth,
> The angels speak with flaming sword,
> And it is so to man forsooth.

Circa 1841 Frederick Douglass, in the narratives of his life as a slave, wrote about his disillusionment with the type of "hypocritical" Christianity practiced by slaveholders.

> What I have said respecting and against religion, I mean strictly to apply to the *slaveholding religion* of this land, and with no possible reference to Christianity proper; for, between the Christianity of this land, and the Christianity of Christ, I recognize the widest possible difference — so wide, that to receive the one as good, pure and holy, is of necessity to reject the other as bad, corrupt and wicked, To be the friend of the one, is of necessity to be the enemy of the other. I love the pure, peaceful, and impartial Christianity of Christ: I therefore hate the corrupt slaveholding, women-whipping, cradle-plundering, partial and hypocritical Christianity of this land. Indeed, I can see no reason, but the most deceitful one, for calling the religion of this land Christianity. (115-116)

Whereas Frederick Douglass called the Christianity practiced in his day "most deceitful," Elijah chose to describe this "hypocrisy" in stronger terminology such as "falsehood," or, in his effort to attract African Americans to join him, he simply labeled Christianity as "the white man's religion." As shown in the leadership of Douglass and Garvey and other African American leaders who preceded Elijah Muhammad, many expressed serious difficulties accepting Christianity at face value as taught to them by white people. In spite of this general distrust of Christianity as practiced by whites, particularly white racists, still these African American leaders maintained a strong belief that God was with the African American struggle for justice.

Sojourner Truth recalled her mother reassuring them that no matter how difficult slavery was, that God was on their side. John Edgar Wideman's book *My Soul Has Grown Deep: Classics of Early African-American Literature* explains how Sojourner's mother had prepared her offspring with survival tools to help them endure the hardships they would surely encounter in life as a slave.

> In the evening, when her mother's work was done, she would sit down under the sparkling vault of heaven, and calling her children to her, would talk to them of the only Being that could effectually aid or protect them. Her teachings were delivered in Low Dutch, her only language, and, translated into English, ran nearly as follows:—

'My children, there is a God, who hears and sees you.' 'A God, mau-mau! Where does he live?' asked the children. 'He lives in the sky,' she replied; 'and when you are beaten, or cruelly treated, or fall into any trouble, you must ask help of him, and he will always hear and help you.' She taught them to kneel and say the Lord's Prayer. She entreated them to refrain from lying and stealing, and to strive to obey their masters. (376)

Other African American men of the cloth spouted similar thoughts that openly suggested that God was with the black man's struggle for justice even to the point of promoting vengeance against the white man. Dr. Edward Curtis in his book *Islam in Black America: Identity, Liberation, and Difference in African-American Thought*. on page 66 notes three such men of the cloth — described as pre-millennialist — those who "posited that a great battle between God and Satan would occur before Christ's triumphal reign of a thousand years."

Curtis illustrates James Theodore Holly, the first African American Episcopalian bishop, as one describing the black race as Noah's son Ham, the ones who had endured "Christ-like suffering for four thousand years." Curtis notes that Holly also describes descendants of Africa as the race "morally capable of replacing Japhetic (white) control of ecclesiastical and social institutions."

Another pre-millennialist whom Curtis highlights is Theophilus Gould Steward, who promoted the belief that "the end of the world would be coterminous with the halt of Anglo-Saxon supremacy." Steward also predicted in 1888 that future immigration of Europeans to the United States would make America a searing cauldron, "whose only hope would be to embrace the black prophets of a bigotry-free Christianity." Was this a premonition of the coming of men like Dr. Martin Luther King?

Neither was Elijah Muhammad the first to promote that God was a black man. Curtis also notes in his book that prior to the Nation of Islam there existed in black liberation theology the promotion that God was not a white man. In 1895, speaking at a Baptist convention, AME Bishop Henry McNeal Turner promoted an Afro-centric belief in a "Black God." Curtis wrote:

> Turner said that African Americans had "as much right biblically and otherwise to believe that God is a Negro, as you buckra or white people have to believe that God is a fine-looking, symmetrical, and ornamented white man. For the bulk of you and all the fool Negroes of the country believe that God is white-skinned, blue-eyed, straight-haired, projecting nosed, compressed lipped and finely robed *white* gentleman, sitting upon a throne somewhere in the heavens. (67)

WAS GOD WITH ELIJAH MUHAMMAD

There is no record of young Elijah Poole ever meeting or hearing these men speak. Nonetheless, the expectancy of a racially laden *Armageddon* was common in African American circles during the time of Elijah Muhammad's youth.

The success of Elijah Muhammad during and after his lifetime strongly supports the belief that God must have been with him, not necessarily because of Elijah's understanding of Islam proper nor because of his familiarity with world history. God would have been with Elijah Muhammad because of his sincere efforts to help improve the condition of the black man and black woman in the United States of America.

The Qur'an chapter 4; verses 97-99, apply to oppressed people of any race, whether they are Muslim or of another faith system. These verses offer hope to any people who are oppressed regardless the quality or quantity of their contact with, or their understanding of, Islam. The fact that the vast majority of Elijah Muhammad's followers eventually evolved to practice traditional Islam in unison with Muslims worldwide, serves as a testimony that God was with the sincere efforts of Elijah Muhammad. The Nation of Islam members who evolved out of Elijah's racially inhibited community into the wider expanse of universal Islam, have already received a great forgiveness and mercy from God; a hope of forgiveness promised to them partly because of their pre-Islamic state as oppressed human beings.

According to the above Qur'anic verse even the most despicable African Americans during the time of Elijah Muhammad, because of their hopeless situation, had hope of forgiveness and receiving God's mercy. The dismal condition of African Americans at the advent of Elijah Muhammad's mission, qualified them to be prime candidates to receive direct help from the hands of God.

The fruit yielded from Elijah's tree is a good crop of good Muslims. Each of these men is a testimony to the Bible verse Luke 6:43 that read, "For a good tree bringeth not forth corrupt fruit..." Whether his followers evolved from their black race-conscious practice of Islam during his lifetime or after his death, still Elijah gets credit for starting them on their journey to universal Islam. This includes individuals who became Muslim post-1975 under Louis Farrakhan, Silas Muhammad of Atlanta, John Muhammad of Detroit, or individuals who joined one of the other versions of the Nation of Islam that developed after Elijah Muhammad's death. Actually, Elijah Muhammad, directly or indirectly may singlehandedly be responsible for orientating more Americans towards converting to universal Islam than any other person on earth.

Elijah never claimed to receive revelation directly from God. He always established Mr. Fard as a buffer, or intercessor between himself and God. He often said "Allah (God), *in the Person* of Master Fard Muhammad."

THE MAN BEHIND THE MEN

Elijah Muhammad never said that Fard was God the creator of heaven and earth, but Elijah Muhammad did say that he received his understanding of God from the person, the individual, named Fard. Actually, Elijah's claim to be the "Messenger of Allah," may be more fitting titled as the "Messenger of Fard."

In *Message to the Blackman in America*, Elijah Muhammad stated on page 237 that "In 1877 a Saviour was born..." He further explains that this Saviour, Mr. W.D. Fard, was "...born, not to save the Jews but to save the poor Negro." However, in this same publication on pages 73-74, after quoting sura (chapter) 112; which Elijah Muhammad errantly numbered as sura 114, his commentary on the oneness of God does not resemble Fard:

> A Muslim is one who believes in One God. It is forbidden by Allah (God) for us to believe in or serve anyone other than Himself as a god. He warns us not to set up an equal with Him, as He was the One in the beginning from whom everything had its beginning and will be the One God from which everything will end. He is independent, having no need of anyone's help, but on the other hand, upon Him we all depend. It is the highest of ignorance for us to choose a God or attempt to make something as an equal to Him. Foolish people all over the earth have been for the past 6,000 years, and still are, trying to make an equal to Allah (God). He has no beginning, nor is there any end of Him. How, O foolish man, can you make an equal for such a One? How foolish we make ourselves, serving and worshipping gods other than the One God, Allah.

The contrasting irony in these two concepts of the deity is that Fard had a beginning in 1877, whereas Elijah Muhammad's comments on the oneness of God clearly states that "He has no beginning, nor is there any end of Him." Additionally sura 112 of the Qur'an states that God was never born; however, Elijah Muhammad said that, "In 1877 a Saviour (W.D. Fard) was born."

Allah, the one God was with Elijah Muhammad the same as He is with any and all oppressed people. Islam teaches that God judges one by the intention of their hearts. The multiple success stories of Elijah Muhammad and his Nation of Islam stand alone as a testimony that God must have been with him as He was with other African American leaders who struggled against oppression, men and women such as David Walker, Sojourner Truth, Harriet Tubman, Frederick Douglass, Dr. Martin Luther King and others. When studying the topic of whether God was with Elijah Muhammad, maybe the best standard was given in the words of Prophet Muhammed Ibn Abdullah when he stated, "God is with the oppressed."

-§- CHAPTER -§-
ELEVEN

Imam Wallace Deen Mohammed
(Successor of his father Mr. Elijah Muhammad)

(Pentagon - February 05, 1992)

"I don't owe my cleanliness to my new understanding of what Islam is. I owe my cleanliness to the teachings of the Honorable Elijah Muhammad. I owe my moral obedience to that teaching. I owe my success to the person of that teaching."

— Imam W. Deen Mohammed
Forest Park Community College - St. Louis, MO
Feb. 4, 2000

THE MAN BEHIND THE MEN

Wallace D. Mohammed was born on October 30, 1933 in Hamtramck (Detroit), MI, the seventh child of Elijah and Clara (Evans) Muhammad. As an adult Wallace changed the spelling of his last name to "Mohammed," noting that was the spelling on his father's driver's license. Wallace D. Fard, the founder of the Nation of Islam, also used the spelling "Mohammed" on a postcard, post marked October 18, 1933 that he had sent to Clara Muhammad after his departure.

Elijah Muhammad moved his family to Chicago, IL while Wallace was still a toddler. Wallace was educated in the Nation of Islam's elementary and high school called the University of Islam. As a youth he was constantly reminded of his responsibility to be a helper to his father's messianic mission that was dedicated to the rise of the black man of North America.

His mother, family members and friends closely guarded Wallace's childhood as instructed to them by Fard. Upon succeeding his father as the leader of the Nation of Islam in 1975, Wallace was crowned the Supreme Minister by the Muslim community's officials; the same title that Fard had bestowed upon Elijah Muhammad in the early 1930s.

Often Wallace had heard the report that Fard, while using the alias W.F. Muhammad, had named him before birth. Shortly after his inauguration as the leader of the Nation of Islam, Minister Wallace gave an interview for *Muhammad Speaks* titled, *"First Official Interview with the Supreme Minister of the Nation of Islam."*

During this lengthy interview that was conducted by his brother Herbert, Wallace spoke of his upbringing, and described himself as being "a child for the Mission." Correlating his physical birth with his father's messianic birth, Minister Wallace stated, "I have also heard my father, himself, say that when I was born or I was conceived in my mother, he (Elijah) had been born as the servant — the "messenger" of God, who manifested himself with W.F. Muhammad; and by me being born at the time when he was in contact with his saviour, the 'God in person,' helped to form me, not only as a child of his loins, but a child for the Mission."

Fard, who Elijah believed was divine, had ordered both parents to watch over Wallace's growth and development. Wallace noted, "My Father, watched over my religious development and He [sic] has done that for as far back as I can remember." While Wallace was very young Elijah Muhammad began giving his son special attention.

The influence of Elijah Muhammad in the life of Wallace had to be tremendous. In addition to being his father, for young Wallace, Elijah Muhammad also was the "Messenger of Allah" who represented the final word of God, and Elijah was not to be contradicted.

The Nation of Islam can also be described as a womb that was energized for the development of the mind and soul of Wallace and his siblings. His nightly bedtime stories told to him by his mother were recollections of catechisms left with the Nation of Islam by Fard; stories of Fard's version of the origins of creation and the beginning of racial distinctions. From the cradle Wallace was reared to be an exceptional product of the Nation of Islam.

The impression of Elijah Muhammad upon Wallace and his siblings, particularly those close to Wallace in age, must have been more intense compared to the effect Elijah had upon other Nation of Islam members because the younger ones were suckled and nurtured with the teachings of the Nation of Islam from infancy. Therefore, they did not have to erase previous mindsets, habits, and religiosities in order to receive Elijah Muhammad's message. For the youngsters who were born into the Nation of Islam, Elijah Muhammad's teaching shaped their infant minds and became their daily routine and their only religion. Wallace and those closest to his age are the first unadulterated, fertile minds of the Nation of Islam to have the mental and spiritual seed of Elijah Muhammad's message invested into them. These youths of the early 1930s became the first original harvest and original yield that was reared from birth, breast fed, and tutored on the Nation of Islam's theology, schooling and etiquettes with no, or very little interference from non-Nation of Islam influences.

As a teenager Wallace quietly began to question his father's doctrines, especially the role of Fard, whose status in the Nation of Islam after 1933 had been elevated from "Prophet" to "God in the Person." Steven Barboza in his book *American Jihad* asked Wallace about his childhood understanding of Farad's (Fard) divine status. Imam Mohammed compared the large portrait of Fard displayed in his childhood home with the church's figure that shows a Caucasian man crucified on the cross. "As I grew as a young man, and I got in my teens — at fifteen, sixteen — I started to wonder why this man looking so white was supposed to be black and a black god. I started to see similarities between the way Jesus is portrayed in Christianity and the way he was portrayed." Reflecting on his adolescent years that included studying the Qur'an, Wallace shared with Barboza, "Maybe the Qur'an had started to influence my thinking without me knowing." (100)

It wasn't long before Wallace questioned his father on Fard's divinity. Standing on the edge of Nation of Islam heresy, the adolescent Wallace exposed his views to his father stating that he'd prefer to see his father as a "savior" instead of W.D. Fard. Very few adult members in the Nation would dare openly question Elijah Muhammad even on the basic tenets of his teachings, not to mention question him about the sacredness the Nation of Islam had associated with Fard.

Young Wallace questioning his father on such a sacrosanct issue was courageous. Such theological inquiries that questioned the norms of the Nation of Islam's dos and don'ts could carry earth-quaking consequences.

THE MAN BEHIND THE MEN

Now the dilemma before Elijah Muhammad was reconciling how the one who W.D. Fard had specially designated to help him, could also be the same person to doubt and question the divine status of Fard.

Elijah Muhammad still had to fulfill his charge of raising Wallace with "special care" so that he would be a helper to himself and Fard's works; however, the special attention given to Wallace by Elijah Muhammad was producing in Wallace a mind that approached the teachings of Fard in ways unexpected, even to the point of questioning Fard's divinity.

A young Imam W.D. Mohammed (holding Qur'an) poses with his father Elijah in the "Pine Room" with portrait of Mr. W.D. Fard in background.
(Photographer - Gordon Parks)

IMAM WALLACE DEEN MOHAMMED

Often Elijah had recounted for Wallace and other family members and Nation of Islam officials the importance of Wallace being named after W.D. Fard. Elijah Muhammad must have been perplexed by his son's confession. Wallace was the special child who was named after Mr. W.D. Fard, by Fard himself. The "W" in Fard's name stood for both the name Wallace and Wali, and now Wallace was questioning the sacred role of his namesake and spiritual predecessor. The quandary that Elijah Muhammad faced was challenging: Wallace had shaken the foundation of the Nation of Islam by expressing a different belief regarding Mr. W.D. Fard as being "God in the person." Imam Yusuf Shah of Chicago, a special assistant and confidant of Elijah Muhammad, recalled a conversation he had with the leader of the Nation of Islam. Yusuf Shah said that Elijah Muhammad revealed to him that Wallace, while rejecting Fard as his savior said, "Daddy I'd rather see you as my savior." The wise and potent statement demonstrated, without Wallace denouncing his father or the Nation of Islam, that he supported his father's works but, with all due respect, he could not worship Fard, a man, as God.

Below is a fuller account of the 1975 interview that Wallace gave to *Muhammad Speaks* newspaper, conducted by his brother Herbert (Jabir). He spoke about how he received his name and the importance his father placed upon that name.

MUHAMMAD SPEAKS: What did Master W.D. Fard Muhammad tell your father about you before your birth and when was this first revealed to you and by whom?
SUPREME MIN.: I couldn't truthfully say who revealed it to me first, but I can only remember my mother, because she kept it before me. She told me that before I was born, while I was growing in her, my name was put on the door, on the back of the door in chalk by Master W.F. Muhammad (Fard).
He told her and my Father that the baby would be a boy (and a) helper to his Father. I (recall) also my father telling me many times that He asked for a boy and was told that He would get a boy. He wanted a boy to help Him in His work. He was asked to give the promise that if He received a boy, He would let the boy help him in His work.
MUHAMMAD SPEAKS: Did this knowledge make your early childhood different in any way? What fears or joy did you experience as a result of this knowledge?
SUPREME MIN.: I can't say that this knowledge influenced me or influenced my early childhood in any certain way or influenced me to become different. But looking back at my childhood, as an adult, now, I do know that it did influence me. But I was not aware of the influences then. It was a kind of subtle influence. It was intended for my protection and for my growth. It was not given to make me aware of myself as any special person.

> I did not think of myself as any special person. I only, now, think of myself as a special person because I have come into a Special Office. (13)

In 1942, at the age of 45, which coincidentally was the cutoff age for World War II draftees, Elijah Muhammad was imprisoned at the Federal Correctional Institution (FCI) at Milan, MI as a conscientious objector for his refusal to serve in the United States military, a violation of the Selective Training and Service Act. He was released from prison in 1946, two months before his 49th birthday. Although World War II ended in August 1945 Elijah Muhammad wasn't released from prison until one year later. His imprisonment and that of other Nation of Islam members presented a challenging time for Elijah's Islamic community. When Elijah Muhammad was released from prison, government officials reminded him of the reason for his incarceration. As reported in his book *The Theology of Time* a disgruntled Elijah Muhammad recalled what the government official told him as Elijah got out of the car in Chicago's downtown Loop District:

> "We are not trying to stop you from your Teachings, but President Roosevelt doesn't want you out there in the public with that kind of Teaching while America is trying to prosecute the war between her, Germany and Japan. That's all we are putting you in jail for, to keep you out of the public." "well," *[sic]* I said, "it is a terrible thing to set a man up in jail to wait until the war ends to free him." (18)

While in prison, through mail correspondence and visits from his wife Clara, Elijah continued to lead the Nation of Islam. She kept him abreast of the day-to-day operations of the Nation of Islam and relayed his directives to the faithful. During one visit Elijah forwarded a letter, via Clara, to Wallace that contained chapter 31, verses 13-15 of the Holy Qur'an:

> "Behold, Luqman said to his son by way of instruction: "O my son! join not in worship (others) with Allah, for false worship is indeed the highest wrong-doing." And We have enjoined on man (to be good) to his parents: in travail upon travail did his mother bear him, and in years twain was his weaning: (hear the command), "Show gratitude to Me and to thy parents: to Me is (thy final) Goal. But if they strive to make thee join in worship with Me things of which thou hast no knowledge, obey them not; yet bear them company in this life with justice (and consideration), and follow the way of those who turn to Me (in love): in the end the return of you all is to Me, and I will tell you the truth (and meaning) of all that ye did."
> — Yusuf Ali translation

IMAM WALLACE DEEN MOHAMMED

Wallace remembers receiving that Qur'anic message from his father when he was 11 years old.

> He was in prison. I'm a boy now about eleven years-old. She said, "Your father sent something from the Qur'an, and he wants me to read it to you." So she read it. And it was from chapter Luqman, Luqman's advice to his son. Its exact wording was, "If your parents strive with you to get you (inaudible) accept something that you can find no support for, then don't accept it; but keep good company with them in this world." That's in the Qur'an, Luqman's advice to his son. That is what my father sent.
> — Interview Summer July 03, 2005

Wallace believes Fard told his father to send that message to him. "I think Mr. Fard reached him and told him to send that to me. And he did it. I kept if for a long time." Wallace reasoned that Fard wanted him to receive that verse on Luqman to "help influence me on towards the right understanding in Islam about God; who God is, what God is. So when the Qur'an started influencing my thinking then I'm going to remember what Daddy said."

In later years Wallace's encounter and endearment to the verse "Luqman's advice to his son" would serve as a source of solace, especially when Wallace and his father did not see eye-to-eye religiously. Wallace explained that whenever he was "wondering, feeling bad about differing with my father" he would remember, "Daddy told me that if the parent strives to get you to believe something (and) there is no support in what God gives for it, (sic) says don't obey them in that but keep good company with them in the world." With that Qur'anic message in his heart about Luqman's advice to his son, Wallace, to the best of his ability and as the laws of the Nation of Islam allowed, kept good company with both his parents for the rest of their lives.

Despite Wallace's propensity to think differently from the other members of the Nation of Islam, Elijah Muhammad continued to groom his son as instructed by his teacher W.D. Fard. Wallace, as required by all Nation of Islam members, had to retain the community's "Lessons," and a conglomeration of astronomical figures and physical science data that Fard dubbed as the "*Actual Facts*." Additionally Nation of Islam members were kept busy trying to solve the questions in the "Problem Book".

For African Americans with little or no schooling at all, learning the "Actual Facts" and mentally engaging "The Problem Book" was emboldening and exciting. As the youth of the Nation of Islam matured, some seeking to solve "The Problem Book" encountered another challenging problem; the reality that on face value, as it was written, a lot of the information Fard had constructed for his followers did not make sense nor was it consistent with the world's sciences. This obligated these students to either accept Fard's information as written or to pursue a path of serious inquiry, seeking to find and extract possible deeper or hidden meanings that may be contained within Fard's mystical and esoteric writings.

At the Whittenmore House on the campus of Washington University in St. Louis, MO in October of 1996, Wallace spoke of another childhood experience that led him to question and seek interpretative explanations for the lessons W.D. Fard left with his father. Elijah Muhammad could not read Arabic but he encouraged the younger members to learn their "original tongue." Nation of Islam schooling included studying Arabic along with regular studies. Wallace and his younger brother Akbar became very efficient in the Arabic language.

Elijah Muhammad wrote in his book *The Supreme Wisdom*, page 51: "...to get a real Holy Qur'an one should know the Arabic language in which it is written." By exposing his two youngest sons to Qur'anic Arabic Elijah also was introducing them, wittingly or unwittingly, to other Islamic teachings that challenged and contradicted the teachings of Fard.

Before his 1933 departure Fard had entrusted Elijah Muhammad with a copy of a Qur'an that supposedly updated the 7th century revelation given to Prophet Muhammed. One day, Elijah decided to compare the Arabic of this "special Qur'an" with the other Qur'ans they regularly used. Wallace and Akbar, both students of the Arabic language were asked by their father, "Look, can you all read this Arabic in the Qur'an?" Wallace recalled his father bringing down that special book that was put away under careful wrapping. "He had taken the green wrapping off of it and he handed it to us and said, 'can you read anything in here?' So we looked at it. He said, 'What does it say?'" After comparing the two Qur'ans and finding the Arabic in both books identical, Wallace's eyes and Akbar's eyes met with both sons quietly realizing — without voicing a single word — the loud reality that, "We don't have anything new to tell Daddy."

Now, with this exposé Elijah Muhammad realized that W.D. Fard had not given him a special Qur'an that was different from the Qur'an that Prophet Muhammed had left with the Muslim world. As late as 1957, in his book *The Supreme Wisdom*, Elijah Muhammad wrote about what he believed to be a special holy book, a "new" Qur'an. He taught his followers, "Both the present Bible and the Holy Qur'an must soon give way to that holy book which no man as yet but Allah has seen." He differentiated this special book explaining that, "The teachings (prophecies) of the present Bible and the Qur'an take us up to the resurrection and judgement [sic] of this world but not into the next life. That which is in that holy book is for the righteous and their future only; not for the mixed world of righteousness and evil."

Upon hearing the report from Wallace and Akbar that this special Qur'an and the other Qur'ans that are common throughout the Islamic world were the same, not only were Elijah and Clara's two youngest sons amazed that Fard had not given them a different Qur'an to usher in the correct Islam, Elijah himself was amazed thus forcing him to begin reevaluating what his teacher Fard had taught him. Wallace recalled his father's reaction after they informed him that Fard had not given him a new or a different Qur'an. "When he (Elijah) found out the truth he accepted it, but I think Mr. Fard was getting smaller and smaller in his eyes."

Wallace following his freedom to "question everything" plus the weight of having a name that united him forever to the Nation of Islam, presented a predicament for him that was created by the recurring inconsistencies within the Nation of Islam's theology. Which of the two religious philosophies should he give allegiance to? Or could a birthright that obligated Wallace to aid a theology that gave him more questions than answers ever be correlated? In his book *The Champion We Have in Common*, Wallace explains that it was the message bequeathed to him from his parents to "question everything" that provided him relief from his dilemma of correlating Nation of Islam doctrinal irregularities with universal Qur'anic concepts.

> The Honorable Elijah Muhammad conditioned me to question that theology. Those who were in the Nation of Islam for a long time know that he said, "Brother and sister, don't just look at the surface. Study it. There are answers that Allah wants us to get." So he told me to study and look under the surface, and that is what I did whenever something did not look good to me (on its surface). When I did that, it helped me to deal with the surface. The Honorable Elijah Muhammad conditioned me to have those curiosities. (6)

Wallace held a number of jobs within the Nation of Islam ranging from working in his father's businesses, to serving the community as a common foot-soldier and lieutenant in the Nation of Islam's Fruit of Islam. Beginning in 1958 through 1960 Elijah Muhammad assigned the 24 year-old Wallace to be the minister of Temple No. 12 in Philadelphia, PA. During the times he was expelled from the Nation of Islam, Wallace worked various jobs which included painting, working in a poultry market and scrap iron yard, and as a welder.

As a minister Wallace ran the Philadelphia temple with the same independence of mind that had accompanied him since childhood. Steven Barboza reports in his book *American Jihad* on page 103 that Minister Wallace went against Nation of Islam policy by relaxing the requirements of members to pay weekly charity or sell newspapers. Over a three year period Minister Wallace's policy resulted in Temple No. 12 growing from 67 to 500 members.

Elijah Muhammad began to give Minister Wallace more room to think differently as long as it did not interfere with the overall operation of the Nation of Islam. In his book *Growth for a Model Community in America* Wallace explained, "The Honorable Elijah Muhammad tolerated me being different." Wallace viewed this allowance as his father's way of preparing the pathway for him to succeed him. "He could have exposed me before his community as someone who had different ideas in his head. He could have told his national leaders to beware of me and never give me any support. But instead, he did things to help me get into the position once he was out of it." (16)

The five years Yusuf Shah served in Chicago, as one of the leading ministers and special assistants, obligated him to regular visits to the home of Elijah Muhammad. He said, "I had to be at the house (of Elijah Muhammad) every day." During one of his many one-on-one conversations that he enjoyed with Elijah Muhammad their discussion turned to Wallace's understanding of Fard's divinity status. As the two men talked, Elijah Muhammad pointed to a portrait of Fard and shared that Wallace didn't accept Fard as a god. Minister Shah related, "...the Messenger told me 'Wallace don't believe that is God'." It was common knowledge among many Nation of Islam officials that Wallace didn't believe Fard to be God or even "God in the Person."

Elijah Muhammad resolved within his individual self that Wallace would not accept Fard as God. Maybe, quietly in Elijah's heart he was at peace knowing that his message from prison that was sent to Wallace about Luqman's advice to his son had taken root and blossomed in Wallace's mind.

The times that Wallace was excommunicated from the Nation of Islam were exclusions not initiated by Elijah Muhammad. Wallace's dismissals, although sanctioned by his father, were actions fueled by grumblings from among a few of the top Nation of Islam officials.

Wallace always loved the Nation of Islam, even when his beliefs resulted in him not receiving the good graces of his father. He even loved the Nation when he was excommunicated from the community. One expulsion from the community occurred after Malcolm was silenced by Elijah Muhammad, after Malcolm disobeyed his orders not to comment about the assassination of President John F. Kennedy. After Malcolm left, the Nation of Islam officials turned their accusations towards Wallace, saying that he was the one who had influenced Malcolm's thinking, and even worse he did not represent W.D. Fard according to their standards.

IMAM WALLACE DEEN MOHAMMED

Ministers Wallace Muhammad (Mohammed) and Malcolm X at Uline Arena in Washington D.C. on June 25, 1961. *(Photographer Unknown)*

During interrogations led by Nation of Islam officials Wallace remained true to his beliefs that Fard was not divine. The closeness of Wallace and Malcolm as companions and confidants further jeopardized Wallace's security in the Nation of Islam when Malcolm began reporting Elijah Muhammad's private affairs in public. In order to safeguard the integrity of Nation of Islam policies, decorum and order, Elijah Muhammad had no other choice but to excommunicate Wallace D., the one who Fard had promised would be his helper.

Wallace and Malcolm often studied Islam and the "Lessons" of the Nation of Islam together. Malcolm shared in his autobiography the strong respect he had garnered from studying with Minister Wallace. When Malcolm had to make a serious decision regarding traveling to Mecca, he was very selective in choosing the individuals with whom he spoke about his intentions. He readily trusted the opinion of Wallace. In his autobiography Malcolm shared, "Once in a conversation I broached this with Wallace Muhammad, Elijah Muhammad's son. He said that yes, certainly, a Muslim should seek to learn all that he could about Islam. I had always had a high opinion of Wallace Muhammad's opinion." (325)

THE MAN BEHIND THE MEN

Wallace reciprocated his love and appreciation for Malcolm's friendship. In honor of the years of dedicated service that Malcolm X had given to the Nation of Islam while he was minister in the New England area, Wallace, after becoming the leader of the Nation of Islam, renamed the Harlem, NY mosque Masjid Malcolm Shabazz.

Wallace maintained that both he and Malcolm loved Elijah Muhammad and the Nation of Islam as noted in his book *The Champion We Have In Common*:

> Let me let you in on this: W.D. Mohammed and Malcolm X, who later came to be called Malcolm Shabazz, we loved the Honorable Elijah Muhammad. We loved the Nation of Islam and our brothers and sisters, the manners and the disciplines of the Nation of Islam. We loved the morals and decencies that were sometimes hard on us and would cause someone to be thrown out for violating something that others just would ignore.
>
> Malcolm and I were not boys — we were men. We were not average men; we were extraordinary men when it came to wanting to exert our manhood. Not only that, but we also loved the food of the Nation of Islam, we loved our bean soup and bean pies so much that we had to tell all of the African American people about our bean pies. We did not want to break from that. We did not want to separate from the Nation of Islam. (3)

However, as with most friendships there were times of disagreement. One involved a public speaking engagement in which George Lincoln Rockwell was present. The other occasion was over a dispute regarding divulging the private affairs of Elijah Muhammad.

In addition to Malcolm and Wallace studying together, often Malcolm would invite Wallace to accompany him on speaking engagements. On one particular speaking engagement in 1961 Elijah Muhammad personally instructed Wallace to accompany Malcolm. Wallace recalls his father saying, "Son, I want you to be there at that meeting. I want you to be with Malcolm on the podium, and I want you to speak to the crowd."

Upon their arrival Wallace learned that Malcolm had also invited George Lincoln Rockwell, the leader of the American Nazi Party, to speak. Wallace was very displeased with Rockwell's presence, especially after Rockwell praised Elijah Muhammad as "a man like our leader Adolph Hitler." When Wallace spoke he lambasted Rockwell. At a July 29, 2001 public address Wallace recalled his 1961 onstage encounter with Rockwell. Imam Wallace recalled telling Rockwell "You're not welcomed here, Mr. Rockwell...I can't understand it. I don't know why you are here."

Wallace explained to his July 2001 audience his sentiments toward Rockwell and his dissatisfaction with Malcolm for inviting Rockwell. "Here's the worst of the devils sitting down there and made comfortable. I burned him up buddy. He wasn't comfortable any more. And I looked at Malcolm and Malcolm wasn't comfortable either." Wallace said that he looked at Malcolm as if to say, "Well you just have to burn baby with that devil over there...if you're angry then just be uncomfortable along with that devil I'm looking at over there."

Many individuals such as Dr. Manning Marable have criticized the Nation of Islam for having close secretive ties to many of America's white racist groups. But none of this criticism has been tied directly to Elijah Muhammad. Nonetheless, as the leader of an all black organization, at a minimum, he should have known or been suspicious of the possibility of secret meetings with white separatist groups. Most reports point to John Ali, the former National Secretary for the Nation of Islam, and sometimes to Malcolm X, as the individuals associated with holding secret meetings with Rockwell and other white separatist organizations.

The white supremacy group Stormfront's website has recorded two dates for Rockwell attending Nation of Islam meetings. *www.stormfront.org* indicates that the first meeting, apparently where Wallace Mohammed condemned Rockwell, was held on June 25, 1961, at Uline Arena in Washington D.C. Rockwell's second visit to a Nation of Islam gathering was at the February 1962 Saviour's Day convention; an invitation that seems to have came from the Nation of Islam's secretary John Ali, not from Elijah Muhammad. Karl Evanzz in his book *The Messenger: The Rise and Fall of Elijah Muhammad* (pp 241-242) gives an interesting account of the events that day.

Evanzz states that even while Rockwell waited for a microphone, "booing filled the room," and "hundreds left." The chorus of boos continued throughout Rockwell's brief statement that said:

> "We don't want to integrate. When we come to power, I promise you we will help you get what you want....Elijah Muhammad has done some wonderful things for the so-called Negro. Elijah Muhammad is to the so-called Negro what Adolf Hitler was to the German people. He is the most powerful black man in the country. Heil Hitler!"

Evanzz notes that the booing only ended and "changed to thunderous applause" when Elijah Muhammad made his way up to the microphone as Rockwell was returning to his seat. Elijah rejected Rockwell's offer for assistance stating, "We don't need no help from you. We want to help you keep your race all white. We also want to keep ours all black."

THE MAN BEHIND THE MEN

Another weightier issue of disagreement between Wallace and Malcolm occurred while Malcolm was out of the Nation of Islam, when he claimed that Wallace was the one who first divulged to him that Elijah Muhammad had fathered children by women other than Clara Muhammad.

The documentary *Brother Minister*, created by Jack Baxter in association with Jefri AalMuhammed, contains a clip of Malcolm giving an apparent impromptu interview to a flock of news reporters in front of the Queens County Civil Court. It was June of 1964 and Malcolm was at the court seeking the right to stay in his residence that was owned by the Nation of Islam. One reporter asked Malcolm why he believed that his life was being threatened by the Nation of Islam. Asked, "Why are they threatening your life?" Malcolm replied:

> ...I will tell the real reason that I'm out of the Black Muslim movement, which I've never told, I've kept to myself. But the real reason is Elijah Muhammad, the head of the movement, is the father of eight children by six different teenaged girls; six different teenaged girls who were his private personal secretaries. Four of them had one child apiece by him, two of them had two children, and one of those two are pregnant right now in Los Angeles with their third child. The one who first made me aware of this was Wallace Muhammad, Mr. Muhammad's son.

Apparently Wallace missed seeing this news clip; that is if it ever was aired on television or radio. Additionally other Nation of Islam officials made this same allegation that Wallace was the one who had told Malcolm of the outside children — one of the allegations that resulted in Wallace being excommunicated during the same period in which Malcolm was out.

Wallace refused to believe that Malcolm had accused him of spreading news about his father's private affairs. To set the record straight Wallace requested that he and Malcolm meet with his father for a hearing. However, Malcolm was forced completely out of the Nation of Islam, and the hearing never happened.

In a December 2002 interview Wallace shared, "I was charged with that. I was charged with supporting him and publishing my father's affairs. But that was incorrect too. I didn't support him (Malcolm). I didn't make him aware of that. He asked me questions and made me aware that I had been pushing things in the back, out of my mind. And I said "Yes, I saw these things, but I didn't want to think about them."

Wallace's account of events seems to coincide with Malcolm's autobiography which clearly indicates that Malcolm already knew of Elijah's family discrepancy issues even before he talked with Wallace. Malcolm's autobiography seems to acknowledge that Wallace was not the one who first disclosed to him Elijah's extramarital affairs. According to Malcolm the rumor mill was already churning when he brought the issue to Wallace:

> ...But by late 1962, I learned reliably that numerous Muslims were leaving Mosque Two in Chicago. The ugly rumor was spreading swiftly – even among non-Muslim Negroes...
> There was no one I could turn to with this problem, except Mr. Muhammad himself. Ultimately that had to be the case. But first I went to Chicago to see Mr. Muhammad's second youngest son, Wallace Muhammad... And Wallace knew, when he saw me, why I had come to see him. "I know," he said. I said, I thought we should rally to help his father. Wallace said he didn't feel that his father would welcome any efforts to help him. I told myself that Wallace must be crazy. (302-303)

According to Malcolm, since 1955 he had been ignoring reports and hints that Elijah had fathered children outside of his marriage to Clara, until he received a reliable account in "late 1962." Ironically, in late 1962 Wallace was away serving a 14½-month sentence at the Federal Correctional Institution (FCI) in Sandstone, MN for selective service violations until his release on January 10, 1963. Wallace Muhammad also clarified that at no time during his incarceration did he and Malcolm have any correspondence.

It took Wallace more than a decade to finally confirm that Malcolm did tell Elijah Muhammad that Wallace was the one who had made Malcolm aware of Elijah's other children. Wallace explained, "I didn't know it until ten years or more after his death. I'm still believing that Malcolm, my friend, did not say that to my father." It was in Washington D.C., as a guest on the Gil Noble show "Like It Is," while Wallace was once again defending Malcolm that Noble confirmed that Malcolm had also made the same allegation against Wallace to him.

Wallace recalled sharing with Noble his account of events. "...I was accused, but I never got the opportunity to have Malcolm sit with my father and I. Because Malcolm, I don't believe he would..." Before Wallace could complete this sentence Gil Noble interrupted him and informed Wallace, "He (Malcolm) did say it. He said it on my show." Wallace, taken aback by this unexpected confirmation that Malcolm had spread this inaccurate information to others admitted, "I was so surprised and hurt too."

Wallace's incarceration in late 1962, the time that Malcolm gives for when he received his "reliable account," eliminates Wallace as the responsible party. The actual reason or possible strategy that Malcolm may have had in accusing Wallace of being the first who told him of Elijah Muhammad's extramarital affairs may never be known. Maybe it was to create a stronger reaction from the media?

There were other times when Wallace was excommunicated from the Nation of Islam. Writing about one of his expulsions, Wallace penned in his book *The Champion We have in Common: The Dynamic African American Soul*. "The first time I was separated from the 'Nation,' it was because someone said I was saying things about the concept of God that was not approved in the Nation of Islam. For we were told in the Nation of Islam that Fard was Allah in the person, the man who taught my father. So I was rejected when this complaint was forced on my father. And I say 'forced' on my father, because my father knew that my mind was developing differently and he never bothered me." (4)

Surely the promise Elijah and Clara made to Fard to give Wallace special attention was always on Elijah's mind, even when he had to expel his son from the Nation of Islam. Wallace was not above Elijah Muhammad's laws, and in the minds of some Nation of Islam officials Wallace's thinking was heretical, if not outright blasphemous. When Elijah Muhammad's tolerance of Wallace's differing opinions and conclusions reached the point of disturbing Nation of Islam progress, Elijah willingly or unwillingly enacted the law and expelled Wallace during which times Elijah remained informed of his son's well being through Wallace's siblings.

Whenever Wallace would return from his forced expulsions, their father and son friendship always blossomed, especially in the later years of Elijah Muhammad's life. In the December 2002 telephone interview Wallace spoke of the special closeness he shared with his father. "I recall him as a friend, a friend that would find comfort in my presence and I would find comfort in his presence. We had a spiritual bond unlike what I had with any other person. And I believe that my spiritual bond with him was unlike what he had with any other person except for his teacher, his saviour Mr. Fard."

Less than a year before Elijah Muhammad passed the relationship between him and Wallace crossed a major threshold. Minister Yusuf Shah, according to the book *Prayer and Al-Islam* in an attempt to expose Wallace before his father, played a recording of a talk that had been given by Minister Wallace that was not in keeping with traditional Nation of Islam sermons.

> Yusuf Shah played a recording of a lecture given by Imam Muhammad to the Honorable Elijah Muhammad. When he heard the text which his son had skillfully worded to bring his followers to the true teachings of Al-Islam, he was overjoyed. His face brightened, and though he was in the last stage of his terminal illness, he jumped to his feet, his face blushed, and with tears in his eyes, he said before his top officials, family, ministers and laborers, "I thank Allah for my son. This is what we (his wife and himself) prayed for." (xviii)

IMAM WALLACE DEEN MOHAMMED

Obviously the message of Minister Wallace on the tape Yusuf Shah carried to the house was not in accord with the traditional message of Elijah Muhammad. According to the report above Minister Shah was seeking to expose Wallace as one teaching other than that which Elijah himself had taught; however, to the surprise of Minister Shah, the Muhammad family, and the other Nation of Islam officials at the table, Elijah Muhammad praised Wallace's message while acknowledging it as a long awaited prayer being fulfilled.

On other occasions Nation of Islam officials tried to create a wedge between Elijah and his son Wallace. Minister Yusuf Shah apparently didn't remember himself as being one of the individuals who scurried to Elijah Muhammad with tape recordings of Minister Wallace. Shah recalled, "Imam W. Deen Mohammed, whenever he would speak in the Temple No. 2, at that time, the officials would always have a tape there recording everything he said because what he was teaching was (that) his father was a lie. He was contradicting what his father was teaching... and the minute the meeting was over he'd take that tape and go straight to the house for the Honorable Elijah Muhammad to hear it."

Following is a fuller account from Minister Yusuf Shah given on April 25, 1992 on how Elijah Muhammad responded to Wallace's sermons:

> The minute that it was over they grabbed that tape and rush straight to the house. Zoom! All the officials they come to the house to see Imam W. Deen Mohammed get a whipping'; that is what they were coming to see. Everyone sat down for dinner. They put the tape on. The Honorable Elijah Muhammad came in and sat down and he began to play the tape and they got around to what he (Wallace) had said. He said, "I know what my father taught you all about the Black man being first, the Maker and the Owner and all that." He said, "The Black man is not first, the woman is first." Everybody looked right down to the head of the table to him, the Honorable Elijah Muhammad. They were looking for him to jump up, you know, and cut that tape off and jump on Imam Mohammed. He (Wallace) was at the table too. The Honorable Elijah Muhammad dropped his head. We were still waiting. He said, "Well, that's right." That is what (Elijah) said, "That's right." Then they (the officials) kind of livened back up (thinking) "He didn't get a whipping that time." The ones on pins and needles were myself and Imam Mohammed, because everything we said they would record and bring back and give it to him. They would play it at the table and if there was anything wrong he would jump on you. But I have my first time to see him jump Imam W. Deen Mohammed on anything he said within the three times he came in and out of the community. I have my first time to see him stop that tape and jump him.
>
> — Audio recording

THE MAN BEHIND THE MEN

Yusuf Shah recalled another one-on-one conversation he had with Elijah Muhammad wherein he praised Wallace's "gospel". Shah related, "When he heard Imam Mohammed. He said, 'Brother Minister, he got it!' He said, 'He can go anywhere and teach *that* teaching.' He didn't say teach my teaching. He can go anywhere and teach that teaching anywhere in the world. He can go down to Mexico, anywhere and teach that, what he's teaching.'"

Death certificate of Elijah Muhammad

IMAM WALLACE DEEN MOHAMMED

On February 25, 1975 at the age of 77 years-old Elijah Muhammad passed. The next day, Mr. Fard's birthday, when the Nation of Islam celebrated its annual Saviour's Day, bore witness to another birth — the birth of Minister Wallace D. Muhammad as the Supreme Minister of the Nation of Islam. Chosen by the Nation of Islam's leadership, Wallace was presented to the general membership as the one to succeed Elijah Muhammad. Building upon the 40-plus years that his father had sacrificed in building the Nation of Islam, the new Supreme Minister initiated a new focus for the "Nation," by introducing the Holy Qur'an as the main source of Islamic knowledge in place of the racially-based teachings of Mr. W.D. Fard.

Minister Wallace Muhammad being lifted at the 1975 Saviour's Day.
(Muslim Journal file)

The tens of thousands of Muslims who had gathered in Chicago for Saviour's Day witnessed all of the top officials in the Nation of Islam, accompanied by boxing champion Muhammad Ali and guest such as the Reverend Jesse Jackson, acknowledge the contributions that Elijah Muhammad had made toward uplifting their lives, and each of these men — one after the other — pledged their support to Wallace Muhammad as the new leader of the Muslim community.

Reverend Jackson stated, "The Black community, the city of Chicago, the nation and the world are less because of his passing, but more because of the training of Brother Wallace." Muhammad Ali drew a thunderous applause from the audience when he stated, "I also make my pledge here today. And that pledge is, that I will be faithful and loyal and honorable to the Honorable Wallace Muhammad. And I'm sure that everyone here today who feels the same will be happy to stand up right now and let the world know that you are behind this man."

Before taking his seat, Ali shared with the Saviour's Day gathering what he had learned from Elijah's son Herbert, who also was Ali's boxing manager. "I have one more thing I would like to say to put the icing on the cake. Why did the brother tell me this? Brother Herbert told me that his father, the Messenger, told him constantly that Allah told the Messenger when Wallace was in his 40s, that Allah, Himself, would visit Brother Wallace Muhammad. And he is now 41 years old today. I repeat, Allah, God Himself, would visit Brother Wallace Muhammad."

Minister Farrakhan, before pledging his allegiance to Minister Wallace, sought to ease any misgivings that may have risen in the minds of the faithful due to the passing of Elijah Muhammad. Minister Farrakhan explained, "Allah did not leave us comfortless. He knew that we would need a comforter. He gave us one from the Messenger's family to comfort us." Minister Farrakhan followed up these words by praising the Honorable Elijah Muhammad as one who, "...never spoke an idle word. Every word he spoke had meaning for not only today but for tomorrow and the many tomorrows to come." Then Minister Farrakhan began to acknowledge Minister Wallace Muhammad as he led up to his oath to "submit and yield" to the Nation of Islam's new leadership. Farrakhan, with tears flowing, recalled what he had learned from Elijah Muhammad about Minister Wallace.

> He told me about his son. And I rely on his words. He said his son would help him. He told me that Allah promised him a son. And he told me, and all of you that know the Messenger, know that he said that Wallace would one day help him. That day has arrived.
> And I, like all of the rest of Messenger Muhammad's followers submit, and yield, and give of myself and all that I have, and all within my power to see that the work of Messenger Muhammad is carried on to its completion behind the leadership of his son, the Honorable Minister Wallace D. Muhammad and the family of the Messenger and all of his followers. I greet you in peace.
> — Saviour's Day February 26, 1975

IMAM WALLACE DEEN MOHAMMED

The late Dr. C. Eric Lincoln, Ph D., professor of religion at Duke University and author of *The Black Muslims in America*, was known as America's leading expert on the Nation of Islam. In a 1992 publication titled *A Look at W. Deen Mohammed*, that was created by Imam Earl Abdul-Malik Mohammed, Dr. Lincoln described the new focus for the Nation of Islam ushered in by Wallace Muhammad:

> The world stood in astonishment when Wallace Deen Mohammed renounced the political leadership of the Nation of Islam with its plush securities and emoluments and chose rather the spiritual leadership of the Muslim Community in the West. His was not merely a gesture of symbolism, but a clear clarion commitment to a religious investment reaching far beyond the accidents of the world today and tomorrow, and anchoring the well-being of his followers in the solid rock of classical Islam.
> It is at this time juncture in his young life that the qualities for serious and responsible leadership became unmistakable, and a concern of service unbound by any of the limits of previous constraint began to unfold. (2)

The Nation of Islam's unique combination of a black-oriented religiosity, ideologies, and myths, plus the Nation of Islam's deliberate grooming of its members to excel as black men and women, were elements which form the bases upon which Wallace's leadership was developed. These factors also are key ingredients that helped to make him a leader who defies typical religious leadership. The diligent work performed by his father, a mantle that he inherited, and the fact that he was reared in a racially separated religious community, only strengthens the impact of him evolving into a world leader who welcomed dialogue and interfaith exchange. The separatist environment that helped to shape Wallace's youth and maybe even influence his imam-ship, is historical especially in light of the path that he chose after emerging from that nationalistic setting. This aspect of the Nation of Islam's history that culminated in the world having an Imam W. Deen Mohammed is rooted in the Honorable Elijah Muhammad providing opportunities for Wallace to succeed him.

As the new leader, Wallace relentlessly met the local needs of his Islamic community. In particular he fulfilled the key role of opening doors of opportunity for the establishment and growth of Islam in America, including him being the first Muslim to offer the invocation prayer for the U.S. Senate in February of 1992. Even before these accomplishments Wallace's leadership had opened many doors internationally. He was enthusiastically welcomed in Kuwait, Palestine, Egypt, the Sudan, and as a special guest in Mainland China, and numerous other countries.

THE MAN BEHIND THE MEN

Throughout Wallace's leadership the community evolved through many changes. Yet he never denied the importance of his father to the growth of Islam in America. The influence that Elijah Muhammad had on him as a father and as a leader was never forgotten by Wallace.

Peter Skerry stated in the 2005 autumn issue of *Wilson Quarterly* in an article titled, "America's Other Muslims," that Imam Mohammed and his followers "routinely invoked...with the utmost respect" the formal title of "Honorable" when referring to Elijah Muhammad. Skerry noted that "W.D. Mohammed took over the Nation of Islam — a curious amalgam of freemasonry, Christianity, and Islam ... upon his father's death in 1975." Skerry said:

> (Imam Mohammed) immediately brought its adherents to Sunni Islam. Not only did the son change the name of the organization, he transformed its ideology, eliminating its antiwhite racism and embracing the political institutions of the United States. And he did all this while continuing to honor his father's memory. (17)

In 1976 Wallace Muhammad, serving as the Supreme Minister of the Nation of Islam upgraded the title for the heads of the mosques from "minister" to the traditional Islamic title *imam*. With the racial barriers removed the Nation of Islam was renamed the *World Community of Al-Islam in the West* (WCIW). With surgical precision Wallace — now called Warith Ud-Deen (the inheritor of the religion), but preferring the shortened spelling "W. Deen," began to remove from the minds of his followers the mysteries in the language of the teachings of Mr. Fard.

Wallace held on to the social building blocks that Fard had given to his father but reinterpreting, even at times disregarding the racial and mystical teachings of Fard. While Elijah Muhammad was alive Wallace maintained peace with his father by avoiding disagreeing over Fard's teachings. During a 2005 lecture in Homewood, IL, Wallace Mohammed explained how he avoided arguing with his father even though he disagreed with much of the race-based theology of the Nation of Islam.

> I'm not a Muslim because my father taught me ""Yakub's History"." I'm not a Muslim because my father told me the black man was god. I never could understand it; how he could be god and can't do anything. Or how could he be god and can't compete with white people. I couldn't understand it. I didn't argue with my father, I didn't want to hurt his feelings.

Wallace began his mission as the imam who was now responsible for teaching Islam to millions of people. In the first year of Wallace's leadership

IMAM WALLACE DEEN MOHAMMED

of the Nation of Islam he was faced with a challenge, which he later called "conflicts in darkness." While knowing that the two ideologies would never fully agree, the Imam began the seemingly impossible task of reconciling Mr. W.D. Fard's teachings with the message of the Qur'an.

"Strain your mind and follow me." As the new leader of the Nation of Islam Imam Mohammed introduced concepts that challenged his followers to expand their understanding of Islam, culture, and history.
(Photographer and Date Unknown)

THE MAN BEHIND THE MEN

Wallace's feat of addressing the contrasting religious concepts between the messages of classical Islam, and the "Islam" taught by his predecessors W.D. Fard and Elijah Muhammad, while maintaining a love and respect for these two men, was quite a undertaking. To synthesize the teachings of Fard with the message of the Qur'an obligated Wallace to reinterpret 40-plus years of religious and mythological teachings. That created another dilemma for the Imam as he revamped the original Nation of Islam because everyone, including himself, loved and owed a serious debt to Elijah Muhammad for the multifaceted contributions he had made to their individual and collective enhancement.

Twenty-six years later, in a July 29, 2001 public address at Jackson State University titled "The New Millennium: Tolerance a Must, Islam the Model," Imam Mohammed acknowledged this indebtedness, "...For me this is important because I'm looking at Muslims and most of you I'm looking at you know my father and most of you are indebted to my father in some way. I know I am."

With a sense of expediency the Imam added, "I don't want to die and not attend these sensitive areas for us." The particular sensitive area the Imam was addressing was the potential conflict within those individuals who he identified as believers who "want to follow me as their leader but they also are appreciative and feel indebted to my father." Wallace explained that such conflict was not necessary. Consolingly he added, "And I don't want that either. I want you to feel at peace loving and appreciating my father, and, if you will love and appreciate me too. That's what I want. That's why I work on these areas in the understanding."

Even after addressing this conflict, another larger struggle loomed because of the conflicts between the message of the Qur'an and the message of Fard. Imam Mohammed acknowledged to the Jackson State University audience, "I came to the conclusion that certain things I had to break from and I couldn't understand it." He added, "I tell you the truth, at the time I couldn't understand it. When I started out in 1975 I couldn't understand why these terrible conflicts had to be." He added:

> I believe that there was good intent in the teacher of my father. And I believe that my father was a faithful, sincere, obedient servant of his teacher. I believe that. I saw that, so I accepted that. But here I am seeing something in his teachings now that with my understanding of the Holy book Qur'an now, I can't accept it. Then I looked at the picture of his teacher. The only picture he left to be available to us is a picture of him holding the Qur'an. And he is looking down in it. Looking down upon its pages very piously with great respect; his poise, his picture tells me when I look at it that here's a man having a great respect for the book he's holding.

IMAM WALLACE DEEN MOHAMMED

Fard's photo of piousness.
(Photographer and Date Unkown)

In hope of shedding enlightenment Imam Mohammed explained the impetus, progression and importance of addressing and resolving these "conflicts in darkness." The concepts that teach that Allah came in the form of a man and that the black man was god, were two of the many ideas that Fard taught that directly contradicted what Wallace had read in the Qur'an. During this same lecture at Jackson State University he addressed how he approached this quandary.

> I began to see things that told me that the only way you're going to be at peace you're going to have to either find a way to explain the things that are conflicting or going against what this holy book is saying, that your father have taught you or the Nation of Islam gave you, or you're going to have to just completely just drop it and say all of this stuff is not for Islam, not for Muslims and just throw it aside. At one point I almost came to that point in my own life, or the development in my progression in my life studies and development, but something wouldn't let me do it. I just put it aside. I put the problems aside.

A key that helped Wallace figure out Fard's contradictions with the Qur'an was the reward that Fard offered for any of his followers who properly solved the Nation of Islam's esoteric lessons. The Imam noted that in Fard's own teachings he said, "Work out certain problems and your reward for working out these problems will be this, will be that, but the greatest reward, he (Fard) said is a family Qur'an. A family Qur'an! A Holy Qur'an!"

THE MAN BEHIND THE MEN

The fact that Fard presented the Qur'an as the highest reward for his students did not escape Wallace's attention. In addition to the photo of Fard posed piously while reading the Qur'an, another factor that aided Wallace in finding peace with the contradictions was his recognition of his father's sincerity. All of these factors were instrumental in helping Wallace's seeking of a synthesis of the two ideologies that initially seemed at odds.

As the successor to his father Wallace knew that it was imperative to address these "conflicts in darkness." If his own exposure to the message of the Qur'an had caused personal disparity in his soul because of the Qur'an differing with fundamental Nation of Islam teachings, then surely the other members who now followed his new vision and leadership would endure similar disparities.

Imam Mohammed told the Jackson University gathering:

> So here is a man (Fard) that looked up and he thought it was the highest prize — for his student to get — is a Holy Qur'an. So I can't accept that this man is intentionally going against the Holy Qur'an. So I lived with these conflicts for all of those years. Ten, fifteen years I lived with all those conflicts and finally came to devote myself to studying his works and his mind. His mind! See, you can know a man's mind by examining and studying his works. So I came to study his works but with an aim of really understanding his mind. And God blessed me to unlock the locks, or to solve the puzzle. And I came to accept him then as a person who created darkness to make us fight our way into the light. Or created darkness to make us struggle for the light. Does that make sense to you? It does to me.

A review of Fard's lessons reveals that he had provided a number of contradictory messages in his own teachings as if he intentionally incorporated a type of distanciation; a practice that would force the thinking members in the Nation of Islam, in due time, to distance their minds from his teachings — thus free to analyze his message and compare it with other Islamic teachings. As part of his plan to capture "steal" the hearts and minds of black folks from white domination, Fard also incorporated this distanciation into his message in order to propel the minds of his adherents away from his captivating mysticism and towards universal Islam.

The fact that Fard had established the Qur'an as the best and ultimate award for a Muslim and his family is significant because much of Fard's message did not measure up to the standards of the Holy Qur'an. Therefore, Fard knew that the Qur'an would serve as a positive ticking "logic-bomb" that would detonate releasing productive results whenever the time arrived for the Nation of Islam to receive a full introduction to the Qur'an.

IMAM WALLACE DEEN MOHAMMED

Imam Mohammed's July 29, 2001 Jackson State University lecture gives a clear description of his own developmental struggle within the conflicting theologies and loyalties that affected him and his followers. Wallace concluded, and rightfully so, that Fard's ultimate objective was for the Holy Qur'an to one day overtake and eradicate his temporary black version of Islam.

Among the "lessons" W.D. Fard offered was an allegorical explanation for the "grafting" or the making of the white race through a type of genetic engineering. In his report titled ""Yakub's History"" Fard outlined a 600-year process that began with 100-percent black babies. Through selectivity and elimination Yakub's experiment reportedly resulted in 100 percent white babies, or devils, that were depleted of all originality and blackness; therefore the white babies were weak, wicked, and mentally inferior especially when compared to the original black babies.

Other teachings of Wallace's namesake W.D. Fard included the memorization of astronomical numbers for the measurement of the square inches of the earth, the weight of the earth's atmosphere, and the weight and the population of the earth. This information was designed to give the Nation of Islam members a sense of having superior knowledge, and to serve as proof that black people were not mentally inferior to whites and other races in the human family. Occasionally Fard would intertwine true Islamic concepts with his message, as well as use Islamic terms and Arabic greetings to ensure that his community would have an Islamic connection with other Muslims. Nonetheless, as with "Yakub's History", in each of Fard's "lessons" there was the oft-repeated motto of white devilry and black superiority.

When Fard was teaching Elijah Muhammad in the early 1930s there were many reports in the media of flying saucers and UFOs. Fard used these news reports to his advantage. A mythological Mother Plane or Mother Ship, according to Fard, was hovering in space 40 miles above the earth. This Mother Plane, manned by original black men, was waiting for the time to destroy America, "the Great Mystery Babylon." The Nation of Islam faithful studied the skies in search of this Mother Plane while keeping mentally and physically fit in order to qualify for embarking upon this space ship of salvation.

Mr. Fard designed his mystical message to engage the curiosities of poor, uneducated African Americans who had tired of traditional religious and social norms. Elijah Muhammad proved himself to be Fard's best student and was chosen by Fard to carry the community forward after his departure. Fard wanted serious students. After answering all of the questions on Fard's "Lost Found Moslem Lesson," Elijah Muhammad received the remarks, "This Lesson is answered very near correct and all students should read it and study until he or she can recite it by heart," signed by "Prophet W.D. Fard." For some unknown reason Fard never told Elijah which questions he had gotten wrong.

THE MAN BEHIND THE MEN

As Fard's successor Elijah held on to Fard's basic teachings of cleanliness and righteousness. But as Elijah evolved over the years he changed the Nation of Islam's emphasis from esoteric teachings towards social and nationalistic interests.

The late Imam Muhammad Armiya Nu'Man of Jersey City, NJ, in his book *Who is Imam W. Deen Mohammed?*, noted one of the changes Elijah made:

> Fard Muhammad's Nation of Islam was changed by Elijah Muhammad's Nation of Islam. While Fard's was more esoterical *[sic]* and metaphysical, Elijah made it more social and nationalistic. If you rightly understand the teachings of the Honorable Elijah Muhammad, you will discover that the majority of his message was about social reform. Changing the conditions of his people. He brought in the idea, "Black man, do something for self." You are a nation. Love yourself. (12)

Wallace continued the task of transferring the minds of his followers from Fard's esoteric explanations of life and religion to Qur'anic based interpretations and applications. To achieve this mental and spiritual paradigm shift, Wallace Mohammed had to take his followers on a journey that revisited each of Fard's teachings and lessons in a way that meticulously neutralized and redefined each of Fard's concepts. The task was challenging but each time one of Fard's concepts was redefined — many that were racially burdened — Imam W. Deen Mohammed's community moved closer to universal Islam.

Fard introduced his own definitions and terms to facilitate his objective of eradicating white domination from the thinking of African Americans. One term he redefined was *Colored man*, which according to Fard was the white man, not the American black man. Whereas Fard left Nation of Islam members with understandings that were merely racial in purpose and conclusion, Wallace strove to add meaning and reasoning, or give new direction to Fard's definitions.

Imam W.D. Mohammed, speaking in Chicago, IL on November 14, 2003, explained Fard's reason for shifting the title Colored man to white people:

> He (Fard) called the white man "colored man," but he didn't mean it nice, like colorful; like we are of all these beautiful colors we have. He didn't mean it that way. To color in literature means to falsify, or to lessen the purity or the correctness or truthfulness of what you are presenting. To color something means to falsify it. That's the meaning of color Mr. Fard was giving the white man. He was saying that, "You're a liar. You misrepresent the truth. You color things. You color the truth."

Wallace also addressed Fard's claim of a Mother Plane hovering in space, waiting to initiate the dreaded day of *Armageddon* upon white America while also serving as a rescue ship to save African Americans who were blessed to be members of the Nation of Islam. The Imam explained in his book *As the Light Shineth from the East* that the Mother Plane was a parable designed to give Nation of Islam members a sense of assurance. "So we had assurance. We had a promise that something in the sky was watching over us. And many of us were of such minds that we could believe that. We felt safe down here even in the worst times...we were told that we were all taken care of, we were well watched over and to worry about nothing."

The Imam on another occasion struck a parallel with the Mother Plane and the thinking ability of human beings. The Nation of Islam's Mother Plane was reported to have the ability to travel faster than the speed of light. Some reports stated it was even possible for the Mother Plane to travel at the unhurried cruising speed of 282,000 miles per second in the earth's atmosphere, yet routinely travel at a million miles per second in outer space. Even at these speeds the Mother Plane could change directions without slowing for turns or curves, regardless of whether the move was a 180-degree turn.

Wallace offered a more down to earth perspective to explain to his community a meaning for those astronomical numbers and lightning speed manuevers. The Imam explained that this parable was not referring to the movements of an actual space ship but the movement of one's thinking. The ability of one's thinking to travel quickly, or as indicated with the 180 degree turn, the ability of an individual to change their mind in a split second and began thinking in a different direction without slowing down for the change.

In building these channels for safe passage from Fard's mystical teachings into a universal understanding of Islam, Wallace claimed that he "could leave no stone unturned." Accordingly, one by one he redefined Fard's teachings on topics such as "the deportation of the moon," and Fard's explanation for black folks having kinky hair.

Wallace offered the following closure on Fard's assessment why descendants of Africa had nappy or kinky hair. Fard was aware that by and large African Americans were dissatisfied with having kinky hair. Imam Mohammed noted in his book *As the Light Shineth from the East* that "Professor Fard was very shrewd. He studied the problems very carefully and he knew that Marcus Garvey had made a mistake in trying to give us a sense of identity and greatness in a reconnection or reunion with African ancestry."

Wallace struck at the root of Fard's intent. "He (Fard) knew we wanted straight hair." Mohammed added that Fard taught that before the black man went into the uninhabited jungles of Africa, the black man's "face was black but his hair was straight." To avoid repeating Garvey's miscalculating the African American disdain for their motherland, Fard's strategy carefully gave the black man a pre-existence in a place other than Africa. Fard taught Elijah Muhammad that black Americans are the "Asiatic Blackman." Thus Fard shrewdly disassociated black Americans from Africa, which in their minds was the home of Tarzan and apes, by getting them to believe that their real ancestral home was Asia.

Elijah Muhammad, echoing the message taught to him by Mr. Fard, wrote in *The Supreme Wisdom*, page 33: "The origin of our kinky hair came from one of our dissatisfied scientists, fifty thousand years ago, who wanted to make all of us tough and hard in order to endure the life of the jungles of East Asia (Africa) and to overcome the beast there."

The fact that Africa is west of Asia, not east as told by Fard to an illiterate Elijah, could suggest that Fard himself was uneducated. Or maybe he was implanting a hint that his whole premise for explaining the origin of black folks having kinky hair was Fard's way to help African Americans deal with the dominating European ideas of beauty. Whatever Fard's plans may have been, it is evident that his incorrect data would one day make future Nation of Islam members do as Wallace Mohammed did, and seek the real message behind Fard's fable that sought to explain why African Americans' hair is naturally nappy.

The breadth and depth of the issues Imam W. Deen Mohammed spent tireless hours sharing with his community is vast. The fact is that the majority of followers he inherited from his father's Nation of Islam were, by both Islamic and non-Islamic standards, scripturally and culturally illiterate. Nonetheless, Wallace painstakingly shared with them his knowledge by borrowing examples from myriad of sources. While constantly pointing his community to the Qur'an and the model life of Prophet Muhammed, Wallace was not shy about extrapolating conclusions from Qur'anic and Biblical text, science, the field of entertainment, nursery rhymes, Greek or Egyptian mythologies and other sources of knowledge. Nor was he reluctant to arrive at novel conclusions and understandings that challenged tradition or historically sanctioned understandings in both social and religious arenas.

For example Imam Mohammed taught that Noah's three sons, *Ham*, *Shem* and *Japheth* are not the racial forefathers, respectively, of African, Semitic, and European peoples of the planet. Instead, Wallace taught that these sons represent three types of societies. Wallace, as the imam of millions, reinterpreted many religious terms, essentially creating a new body of knowledge that his followers call "the Imam's language." He defined the word *freedom* by first identifying it as a compound of the words *free* and *dome*. He explained that this "dome" is referring to the head, or the ability of the human being to think. According to this interpretation a free dome, or "freedom," is a direct reference to the ability to think freely, or being liberated in one's thinking.

Wallace gave his followers new interpretations or meaning for colors. He explained that *green* represented growth and production as seen in plant life, and that *blue* represents deception as noted in the blueness of the daytime sky that is seen by the eye but is actually non-existent. The color *red*, he taught, represents passions and lack of inhibition in one context, yet in other contexts symbolizes blood or the social life of man.

Other colors — whose meaning varied depending on their contextual applications — included both *black* and *white*. He taught that black used in a positive way could represent faith, innocence, the original human nature, or it may mean peace. In a negative context the color black may mean darkness or ignorance; two forms of an absence of light, or knowledge. In the language that the Imam shared with his community, white in a positive application represents purity or that which is untouched, but in a negative connotation can mean death or the absence of life as exemplified in the Biblical account of the Book of Revelations 6:8; Death riding a "pale horse."

Christ Jesus, he explained was a special body of knowledge, a *blessed word* of God sent for the benefit of humanity. Every prophet of God, Imam Mohammed encouraged, was to be seen not merely as an individual but seen in plurality; as a community. He taught that it is best to see these individual prophets as representations of a special type or special development that is common in every human being.

Adam represents humanity's original nature. Idris, Enoch in the Bible, represented mankind's hunger for knowledge and the human being's ability to write. Abraham, Imam Mohammed explained, represents the human urge to use a rational-based faith instead of emotional or blind faith. In the "language" established by Wallace Deen Mohammed the meanings and understandings that were common and traditional in religious and social circles were offered a renewal. And since 1975 his community of followers have adopted the Imam's new interpretations and formulated an Islamic religiosity for their worship services and the education of their membership.

Wallace Mohammed successfully made headway on the arduous undertaking of reinterpreting the lessons of Fard that Elijah Muhammad had safeguarded. He accomplished that mission without taking his followers away from their love and appreciation for Elijah Muhammad and Wallace D. Fard.

Imam Mohammed's intellectual approach and discernment has earned him respect from Muslims and non-Muslims alike, as evidenced, for example, at Morehouse College in Atlanta, GA on April 4, 2002. There he received the *Gandhi, King, Ikeda Award* in the Martin Luther King, Jr.

THE MAN BEHIND THE MEN

International Chapel, on the 34th anniversary of the assassination of Dr. King. This award and its significance is discussed fuller later.

Thousands of Muslims who adhere to his leadership have formed many study groups for the specific purpose of studying "the Imam's language." Many religious and social groups seek his commentary, both domestically and internationally. He served as the president of the *World Conference on Religions and Peace* and he represented Muslims at the *Parliament of World Religions*. Ironically, maybe even more amazingly, with all of this international acclaim, Wallace Mohammed at the time of his death resided in a typical African American neighborhood in Chicago's southern suburbs and drove a late model sedan as he pursued his daily routine.

Throughout his three-plus decades as an Islamic leader Imam Wallace D. Mohammed repeatedly diverted attention away from himself. In a 2003 Brothers Only meeting Imam Mohammed laid great emphasis on his desire not to be the center of attention. In dissent of being followed as a personality or as someone seeking self glorification, he told his followers, "God chose me because of my thinking." Placing more importance on the community's advancement, the Muslim leader told the assembly of Muslim men, "So don't think I'm here for your worship, I don't want your worship. When I finish I wish you would forget me and not see anything but what we have to do, and just do what we have to do."

Wallace had expressed that same dissonance with personality worship while speaking in St. Louis, MO on February 4, 2000, at Forest Park Community College. While praising the work of his father Elijah Muhammad and Mr. Fard in preference to drawing attention to himself the Imam said:

> I don't want you to look at me... and give me some credit. No! That would make me very uncomfortable, if you start to give me some credit. I don't want any credit. I'm not important at all. What has been done is what is important; that has affected my life, and is affecting now the Christian world and the Muslim world.
> Do you think these learned people in Islam, among what we call the "ulema," the learned scientists or learned people in Islam — in Islamic leadership, Islamic schools of thought — do you think those persons are not attracted to what has happened in America to make me the man I am, from my father Elijah Muhammad, who says W.D. Fard was his teacher; "God in the person"? Do you think they haven't studied this? Do you think they are not studying this now?
> Do you think that the learned in Christian churches are not looking at this? Not only the learned, (but also) the half-learned

African Americans. Do you think they are not secretly studying what has happened here? A marvelous thing has happened here that has never happened on this earth perhaps — so that the whole world could see it — but maybe two times or three times (before). And now it has happened again."

On numerous occasions Wallace Mohammed would remind his audiences of the influence that his father had upon his life and the debt he owed him. Page 105 of his book *Islam's Climate for Business Success* reads:

> I owe a lot to the Honorable Elijah Muhammad. He insisted upon us being responsible — responsible for ourselves and for everything in our charge. This was Islamic. He got this from the Qur'an and the life of our Prophet. We were taught by Elijah Muhammad to respect our families, our children, our women, our homes, and our property. We were also to be responsible to those who trusted us with something. The Honorable Elijah Muhammad said that if you worked for a boss, even if he were a White man, give him an honest day's work. Don't cheat him.

Also at the Forest Park Community College public address, Imam Wallace Mohammed spoke about the liberating effects that his father's teachings had for African Americans. It was during this talk that the Imam shared the deep esteem he possessed for his father Elijah Muhammad, the man who influenced him, thus resulting in him being internationally reknown:

> This is Black History Month, isn't it? I'm talking about a man who *Channel 11 Magazine* in Chicago recorded among ninety-nine other persons as the persons who most influenced the history of Chicago in the past century, the last 100 years. That's the man I'm talking about.
> I'm talking about the man who shocked *The Chicago Sun-Times*, (they said) he is one of 100 persons who are most influential during the last 100 years. That's the man who I am talking about. I'm talking about the man who is responsible for Malcolm X — Malcolm Shabazz coming from a prison life, a nobody; to the man we have come to know. I'm talking about Elijah Muhammad, the man, who took a Louis Walcott and made him a Minister Farrakhan. I'm talking about the man who raised me to be the man I am today. So I know the power of the message of the Honorable Elijah Muhammad. I know the power of that magnetism, it's powerful. It can draw you in and snatch you from other things that are powerful and holding you — like drugs, like alcohol, like gambling, like lying, like stealing, like committing fornication or adultery or something. Yes! I don't

owe my cleanliness to my new understanding of what Islam is. I owe my cleanliness to the teachings of the Honorable Elijah Muhammad. I owe my moral obedience to that teaching. I owe my success to the person of that teaching.

For the remainder of his life Imam Wallace Mohammed always mentioned his father's contributions to the growth of Islam in America. In October of 1999 Pope John Paul II invited 200 world religious leaders, including renowned leaders such as the 14th Dalai Lama of Tibet, Tenzin Gyatso, to the *Interfaith Conference on the Eve of the New Millennium* at St. Peter's Basilica in Vatican City, in Rome, Italy. The event generated a crowd of over 400,000 observers, many of whom had come from abroad, in addition to millions more who witnessed the Interfaith Conference around the world via television.

William Cardinal Keeler of Baltimore, MD introducing Imam W. Deen to Pope John Paul II at Vatican City in 1996. *(Vatican Photo)*

Six speakers from among the 200 religious leaders were selected to speak to the international gathering. Imam Wallace Mohammed was the third to speak. With admiration in his voice Imam Mohammed acknowledged the influence his father had upon him as he addressed Pope John Paul II and the huge throng on the theme of unity of the human family.

> ...I have devoted my life to building bridges. Inclusion was in my heart. I believe I wanted that and I think my father conditioned me to want that. That it is not to be separated, but to be with all good people. I wholeheartedly accept and embrace with you the ideal of mutual sharing and love for one another...

IMAM WALLACE DEEN MOHAMMED

Wallace Deen Mohammed, also known by the names W. Deen Mohammed and Warith Ud-Deen Muhammad, is the one person influenced by Elijah Muhammad who was able to delve into the teachings of his father and extract from those teachings a new religious and social language that was rooted in the universal teachings of the Qur'an. This socio-religious combination resulted in a body of knowledge that gave birth to a new intellect for thousands of Muslim Americans. The message of Wallace, while respecting the good contributions of his father, was a language free of the racial dominance, symbolisms and mysteries that accompanied the teachings of Elijah Muhammad and W.D. Fard.

Probably Elijah Muhammad's greatest influence on Wallace was freeing him to be a thinker and to sincerely question all things. Wallace explained. "He taught us to be curious and not take all of his teachings literally, but there were deeper meanings to be found. He taught us to question everything, and I am quoting him, 'Question everything'." Imam Mohammed continued: "Although I caused him a lot of pain when I differed with him — I told him, Daddy, you are responsible for me doing this. You told me that the Qur'an was our book. I told him that he made me this way. He couldn't dislike me. He liked me a lot." *The Champion We Have in Common*, page 42.

The love that Elijah Muhammad had for his followers was profound and had a deep effect upon those who, after accepting his message, reconstructed their lives. However, some who received their first exposure to Islam from Elijah Muhammad later shunned him after moving on to other understandings of Islam. Wallace Muhammad is one of many who never forgot the contributions his father made and the influence he had upon the overall Muslim community of America. Wallace stated in his book *Growth for a Model Community in America*:

> I always loved God, Allah. I always loved the Prophet Muhammed. I loved the Honorable Elijah Muhammad and all the Muslims who supported him and loved him. They became dear to me just like close relatives in the home, and I still feel that way about them. I also loved the life of a Muslim under the Honorable Elijah Muhammad and I still love it. I have retained what he taught. He taught us not to drink, not to lie, not to steal, not to be dishonest, to respect authority, to respect ourselves and others. The Honorable Elijah Muhammad taught us a lot of wonderful things. He taught us to be thrifty. He taught us to be industrious. He taught us to take our affairs into our own hands and be responsible for them. I loved it and I still love it, and I thank Allah that I haven't departed from any of those teachings. And that's why I'm the man I am now. (14)

THE MAN BEHIND THE MEN

It is clear that the Honorable Elijah Muhammad had a profound effect upon his son Wallace Deen Mohammed, not only as a father but also as a leader and a mentor. Elijah Muhammad is the man that is singlehandedly responsible for creating a hunger in Wallace for knowledge, reconciliation, and the freedom to think and inquire until he was mentally and spiritually satisfied. It is upon this foundation that Imam W. Deen Mohammed was able to stand up and ascend into the international world — a foundation built by none other than the Honorable Elijah Muhammad.

Wallace Deen Mohammed proudly displays a picture of his father the Honorable Elijah Muhammad. *(Photographer and Date Unknown)*

-§- CHAPTER -§-
TWELVE

Students achieved their individuality

The stimulus behind these four Muslim stars becoming internationally renowned was none other than Elijah Muhammad. El-Hajj Malik El-Shabazz (Minister Malcolm X), Boxing Champion Muhammad Ali, Nation of Islam Minister Louis Farrakhan, and Muslim American Spokesman Imam W. Deen Mohammed, were all groomed by a good man, the Honorable Elijah Muhammad. That grooming process alone makes Elijah Muhammad worthy of honor and recognition.

As with the adage that honors the good woman who often is not readily seen or even remembered — whether she be mother, grandmother, wife, aunt or another female — still her dedication and contributions are her way of influencing and affecting all who come in contact with her man. In time her man may continue to advance in life, maybe even excelling her in many ways. Nonetheless, as with the four men discussed in this book, the man is always indebted to the good woman or women who stood behind him. Exponentially, the more her man advances in life she also is witnessing an extension of her influence working on all who her man encounters, because in most instances she is the one who made him the man he is.

This same indebtedness that the man owes to his good woman applies with each of these four men who excelled because of having been personally touched by Elijah Muhammad and receiving from him special support. Without Elijah these four stars would not have had the stage on which to shine in the international world of humanity.

The potency of Elijah Muhammad's influence upon his four disciples is displayed in their ability to advance beyond the womb of the Nation of Islam and establish themselves independently, in their own right, while keeping the essence of Elijah Muhammad in their own lives even after coming from under his direct leadership.

It is impossible to study Malcolm X, Muhammad Ali, Louis Farrakhan, W. Deen Mohammed — individually or collectively — and not trace the root of their success back to Elijah Muhammad. Even when trials and difficulties may have disrupted their relationships with Elijah Muhammad, still important elements of their individual success are rooted in Elijah.

Each of these men made substantial contributions not only to the advancement of the African American struggle for human and civil rights, but also advancements to the betterment of humanity as a whole. Their contributions to the world are another testimony of the effect that this one man, Elijah Muhammad, had on their respective lives. Through these four individuals Elijah Muhammad has touched and helped to shape the world.

THE MAN BEHIND THE MEN

Elijah Muhammad, fulfilling the role of a master psychologist, purposefully worked on removing the core fear of the white race from the minds and souls of his every follower. The tactics he received from W.D. Fard were race-laced, hard-hitting, and designed to counter that ugly era of America's past that was burdened with a public racism that worked to trouble and weaken the soul and spirit of the collective African American community. Elijah Muhammad worked diligently to eradicate all forms of fear from the black man and woman. Once that fear was removed from their lives no endeavor was beyond reason, possibility, and fulfillment. Not only were these life endeavors achievable, they also were viewed as something to be improved upon.

As mental and spiritual offspring of Elijah Muhammad — and in the case of W. Deen (Wallace) Mohammed also being his physical offspring — each of these men was strongly influenced by the theology and the social order of the Nation of Islam. When they applied the lessons they learned from their Nation of Islam upbringing as they entered the general society, each of them distinguished themselves by surpassing others who were in the same line of work or a similar profession.

Muhammad Ali's natural boxing ability was greatly enhanced by the confidence he garnered from the teachings of Elijah Muhammad. Before meeting Elijah Muhammad, Ali already believed he was the "greatest" boxer. But after joining the Nation of Islam he was taught to believe that God was definitely on his side. Therefore, in Ali's mind not only was he "The Greatest," he now believed he was invincible. As reported in the December 2001 issue of *Reader's Digest*, Ali made it clear that Elijah Muhammad's teachings "is what made me so confident."

Another direct benefit Ali received from the message of Elijah Muhammad, that set him apart from other boxers, was a belief that his success as a fighter was also success for all of the suffering people in the world. Only Joe Louis and maybe Arthur John (Jack) Johnson, the first African American boxing champion, are the other boxers who can claim that the pride and dignity of the African American rose and fell with their every victory or defeat.

In and outside of the boxing ring, Ali's ability to connect with and verbalize the pain and suffering of African Americans and the down-troddened, truly made him "the people's champion." The Nation of Islam's reputation for speaking out against the injustices suffered by African Americans was a reputation that followed Ali into the boxing ring, to talk shows, and on his daily encounters with boxing fans. In time his outspokenness found appeal with America's anti-Viet Nam protesters, both on and off college campuses. In the international boxing world no boxer can come close to achieving what Ali accomplished. His ability to connect with people of all races and walks of life enabled him to surpass the sport of boxing on his way to earning worldwide acclaim and respect.

STUDENTS ACHIEVE THEIR INDIVIDUALITY

Malcolm X, a.k.a. Malik Shabazz, was able to excel above many who found themselves in debate with him. His God-given ability of crisp articulation was reinforced by the courage he received from following Elijah Muhammad; a courage that made him and all members of the Nation of Islam fearless in defending their beliefs and the honor of Elijah Muhammad.

For Malcolm, a man who never went to high school or college, the Nation of Islam provided an environment for obtaining the higher education that had eluded him for so long. With Elijah Muhammad as his personal tutor and professor, the Nation of Islam provided a new classroom setting for Malcolm. The adoration of the common African American for the words espoused by Malcolm were actually the words and wisdom of Elijah Muhammad. Though some may disagree, until the two men parted company, Malcolm, at best, only was Elijah's fearless mouthpiece.

Malcolm's reliance upon what he had learned from the teachings of Elijah Muhammad enabled him to successfully silence many who agreed to debate him. As the National Spokesman for Elijah Muhammad, Malcolm began all of his statements with the refrain, "The Honorable Elijah Muhammad teaches us..." Whether his opponent came from Harvard, Yale, or the African American church, Malcolm X — the former hustler and convict — using the teachings he had received from Elijah Muhammad, stood toe-to-toe with the best debaters in America.

Louis Farrakhan's tutelage began under men such as Malcolm X. But as with all members of the Nation of Islam the only voice he strictly adhered to was that of Elijah Muhammad. Farrakhan, unlike Malcolm, was better educated before accepting the teachings of the Nation of Islam. Still, Mr. Muhammad was able to infuse a new spirit into Farrakhan. Very few members in the Nation of Islam, even up to the passing of Elijah Muhammad, had any college education. Elijah Muhammad's relationship with Louis Farrakhan also demonstrated the ability of Elijah Muhammad's message to reach and influence even educated African Americans.

Of the four men discussed in this book, Farrakhan's display of independence, as an individual, may appear on the surface difficult to detect because he has maintained some of the physical effects, dress and grooming codes from Elijah Muhammad's Nation of Islam. Also Farrakhan still finds occasions to use some of the racial overtones of Elijah Muhammad; nonetheless, Farrakhan's individuality that sets him apart from Elijah Muhammad is still quite striking.

Farrakhan's effort to "rebuild" the Nation of Islam in the 1980s obligated him to use the language, lessons and much of the literature of Elijah Muhammad. But social and racial improvements that occurred in the 1960s and 1970s in American society and the world necessitated that he also bring his followers closer toward the universal teachings of Islam as practiced by Muslims worldwide. Farrakhan's creativity was challenged by modernity and African American societal achievements in economics, education and employment. The America that Farrakhan faced in the 1980s had matured socially enough to distinguish herself from the racially arrogant America that Elijah Muhammad had reckoned with especially during the early years of his tenure. As mentioned in the chapter *Elijah Muhammad Through the Eyes of Others*, during the waning years of his life Elijah himself had began to publicly recognize a social maturity on the part of white America.

In the mid-1960s the United States government relaxed immigration laws, which allowed more Asians and Africans from Islamic countries to enter America. The "Immigration Act of 1965", also known as the "Hart-Cellar Act [1]," was signed by President Lyndon Baines Johnson on October 3, 1965 as he stood in the environs of the Statute of Liberty. This legislation allowed individuals from third world countries to enter the United States. This influx of settlers provided African Americans with an increased contact with Muslims from around the world, thus an increase of correct information on Islam that challenged the racial overtones of Nation of Islam theology and rhetoric. The number of Muslims from abroad during Elijah Muhammad's tenure is scant compared to the number that Farrakhan encountered.

Another change affecting how Islam was presented in America after the passing of Elijah Muhammad, is the effect of many imams along with Imam W.D. Mohammed presenting the message of Islam in a more palatable, non-racial manner that was more inclusive for all Americans.

An unforeseeable challenge to old mindsets and status quos began quietly in 1969 with a movement called *ARPANET (Advanced Research Projects Agency network)*, the infant state of today's worldwide Internet. The growing popularity of personal computers in the 1980s and 1990s provided all Americans easier access to an abundance of information on Islam and other world values. The information-overload and high-tech communication age of satellite television also availed Americans with other means of access to Islamic information. In contrast, during Elijah and Fard's era, widespread media access to proper Islamic knowledge was unheard of.

These world changes began to obligate Farrakhan to interpret the message of Elijah Muhammad in a way that respected both the original Nation of Islam as well as the principles of universal Islam. The balancing of these two seemingly opposite forms of practicing Islam, required Farrakhan to demonstrate an independent style of leadership that allowed his followers to absorb and practice universal Islam, while maintaining a language with Nation of Islam terminologies that was extensions of what Elijah Muhammad taught.

In line with the societal changes highlighted above some observers may question whether Farrakhan's role as a Muslim leader is a true sign of independence, or is his leadership an acquiescing to modernity. Many students of the Nation of Islam remember the report of Farrakhan's declaration that, "I would die first" before denouncing any teachings of Elijah Muhammad.

Nonetheless, Minister Farrakhan's leadership skills can be seen in his eventual introduction to his followers of Friday Jumah prayer, fasting during the month of Ramadan, and him giving his followers the "holy" surname Muhammad. He even allowed his members to register, vote, and run for office in American politics even though Elijah Muhammad stated in 1964, in reference to Senator Barry Goldwater's bid for the presidency, "I'm not going to vote for either one because I can't see my way in voting for an enemy to rule me. And I want independence. I want to vote for myself and my people." The 1992 re-release of Elijah Muhammad's *The Theology of Time* quotes Elijah saying, "We don't want to follow America's way of politics" (439). On page 37 of his book *The Fall of America* Elijah wrote, "I still say, as I have said for many years, vote for Allah (God) to be your ruler and come follow me."

Farrakhan, in his 1995 *Million Man March*, took a giant independent step when he spoke words that seem to recognize that the race conscious message of Elijah Muhammad was seasonal. After strongly criticizing white supremacy and black inferiority as being conditions that are repulsive to God, the Minister began to describe the black pride message taught by Elijah Muhammad as a time sensitive medicine. Farrakhan said, "Black had to be taught to give us root in loving ourselves again. But that was a medicine, a prescription. But after health is restored we can't keep taking the medicine. We've got to move onto something else. Higher and better."

Farrakhan's ability to make these changes in the Islamic life of his community while maintaining the veneer of the original Nation of Islam is commendable because it demonstrates his ability to distinguish himself as a leader and as an individual. As mentioned earlier one of Farrakhan's biggest changes — while seeking to maintain a continuity of what Elijah Muhammad established — was the altering of the spelling of *Saviour's Day* when he moved the apostrophe to the right of the letter "s."

Farrakhan clearly articulated his message and attracted the minds of thousands of otherwise idle, mostly African American youth. Standing upon the message of Elijah Muhammad, Farrakhan's success in instilling hope into the lives of youth and millions of other African Americans must be recognized and appreciated.

The *Million Man March* is a testimony of Farrakhan's individual identity as well as a recognition of the influence of Elijah Muhammad upon Farrakhan and America as a whole. Begrudgingly, many of the leaders in America stood in silent amazement as his voice resulted in a million-plus African

THE MAN BEHIND THE MEN

American men coming to the nation's capitol, eclipsing the amassment of labor leader A. Phillip Randolph's 1963 *March on Washington* that featured Dr. Martin Luther King Jr.

For Wallace Deen Mohammed his sense of independence began as a youngster who was encouraged to ponder and question all that his mind encountered. This led to him — first silently then publicly — questioning the message his father had received from W.D. Fard. Wallace's independence led him on a mission of constant search for clearer understandings of the Nation of Islam's myriad of questions. The routine of inquiry continued to grow, developing in him a strong tendency to scrutinize other religions, ideologies, and belief systems.

The disciplines he received as a student of Elijah Muhammad had embedded in him the ability to diligently study religion and philosophy in an independent and systematic way. In time Wallace's study regiment produced a greater appreciation of, and yielded deeper insights into, various scriptures, philosophies and other areas of human development.

On February 26, 1975, the world witnessed for the first time, the teachings of Wallace Mohammed that many in the Nation of Islam had known for years. Wallace's approach to religion — all religion — separated him from all other religious teachers. It had been noted within the Nation of Islam for many years that Wallace's independent thinking at times had resulted in him being ostracized. But also it freed him from being limited to his father's racial and nationalistic interpretations of Islam. Now, as the new leader of the Nation of Islam, Wallace immediately began explaining to his followers the universal message of Islam and introducing them to the exemplary life of Prophet Muhammed of Arabia. It was Wallace's propensity to think and act in ways distinctive from the usual regimented mode of the Nation of Islam that first established Wallace's independence as a leader.

No other minister or member of the Nation of Islam demonstrated the insights into the Nation of Islam teachings as those extracted by Wallace. Some ministers and members initially disagreed with the policy changes that Wallace began introducing in 1975, including his allowing of Caucasians to openly join the Nation of Islam. Very few in the Nation of Islam challenged his insights into scripture or "The Lessons" of the Nation of Islam.

Following the mode of his father, Wallace boldly delivered his message to America and the world. The world's religious leaders soon took notice of Wallace's new leadership and message. Kings, prime ministers and other world leaders traveled to America to meet him and to extend invitations to him from abroad, and nations as far away as Mainland China.

Wallace, until his death continued to be recognized as the most influential Islamic leader in America. The impact of his leadership may continue for generations in the nationwide Islamic communities he established amongst numerous autonomous mosques and Islamic centers. His continual influence is evident in mosques around America renaming their houses of worship *Warith Ud-Deen Mohammed* in his honor.

Wallace's humility, which is magnified by the fact that he as the leader of millions of Muslims, he preferred staying out of the public eye. When he inherited the leadership of his father's Nation of Islam he also inherited the mansion where Farrakhan now resides, nice cars, and the other amenities that accompanied being the leader. He removed himself from all of these comforts, settling for a livestyle commensurate with the level of the average member in his Muslim community.

Peter Skerry in the August 2005 issue of *Wilson Quarterly* captures the ordinariness of Wallace Mohammed, and the office where they met, to conduct an interview.

> We met in a Spartan, slightly shabby, one-story brick building on the outskirts of Chicago. It seemed a place to meet a plumbing contractor, not a spiritual leader. But this is a very down-to-earth, unassuming man. The imam arrived in a late-model but nondescript SUV, accompanied only by his daughter — without the male entourage of assistants and bodyguards that many such leaders have. He was well dressed but casual, and definitely not flashy, in a tailored suit and knit polo shirt. As he had reminded his audience at the Hyatt Regency, he once worked as a welder and still considers himself "an ordinary man, in fact a very ordinary man."

The years of following the disciplines of inquiry and respect gave Wallace the proper disposition to approach life, religion and scripture with a special and sacred regard that produced for him many insights into the character of human beings. With the constant reminder from his parents resounding in his mind to "question everything" made it easier for him to read the Bible and the Qur'an, as well as other religious books and mythologies, and extract keen building blocks for edifying the good in human beings.

This unique scriptural insight quality demonstrated in Wallace's leadership remained consistent over the years, reaching beyond the boundaries of his immediate Islamic community. An example was in April of 2002 when Wallace Mohammed was inducted as a member of the Martin Luther King, Jr. International Chapel Board of Friends, and received the *Gandhi-King-Ikeda Award* from Morehouse College. This distinguished honor was delivered by the Reverend Dr. Lawrence Edward Carter Sr., Ph.D., dean of the Martin Luther King Jr. International Chapel, archivist and curator at Morehouse College.

THE MAN BEHIND THE MEN

Dr. Carter praised the Imam in glowing terms as he recounted Imam Mohammed's national and international effect upon the world's religious leaders.

> I have followed your career for 30 years. Your unforgettable courage arrested the Nation when you announced that you would not be bounded by the limits of religion. I next heard you address the *American Academy of Religion* and the *Society of Biblical Literature* in New Orleans in the early 70s, where you held the Nation's religion professors spellbound...This past summer, when I was in the Alps of Northern Italy, in dialogue with the Dalai Lama I saw an enlarged color photograph; in fact I saw more than one of you with Pope John Paul II and Chiara Lubich of the Focolare Movement. Your sincere interfaith actions have established your name as one who knows the difference between religion and spirituality. You do not just preach or teach peace. My good sir, you are Peace...I am pleased to forever link your name and nature with Mohandas Karamchand Mahatma Gandhi, Martin Luther King, Jr., and Daisaku Ikeda.

Each of these four stars, Wallace, Louis, Malcolm X and Muhammad has evolved into their own person and image. Yet each of them has inherited strikingly similar characteristics of Elijah Muhammad. The restricting confines of the Nation of Islam also created in each of these men a pressurized but powerful yearning to express to the world the knowledge they had learned from Elijah Muhammad. The bold courage of this one man, Elijah Muhammad to publicly challenge white America and the blatant racism of his day became embedded in the soul of each of these disciples, as well as the other hundreds of thousands who joined the Nation of Islam.

Elijah Muhammad's desire to bring African Americans into a new mind that was totally independent of white rule meant that nothing was too sacred for his review and critique as he pursued that mission. Every member of Elijah's Nation of Islam was re-introduced to social etiquettes, dietary laws, and religious catechisms and practices. Often he offered new understandings and applications of scripture as solutions that were custom designed to heal the social, economic, spiritual, and political wounds of African Americans. Elijah's revolutionary approach to the black man's problems led to another benefit these four students had in common: They all benefited from Elijah Muhammad's daringness to reinterpret, without fear of repercussion, Biblical text for the purpose of explaining the dismal state of African Americans.

Elijah Muhammad left none of his students feeling comfortable with their pre-Nation of Islam understanding of the Bible, a book that he

STUDENTS ACHIEVE THEIR INDIVIDUALITY

dubbed as "poisoned." After analyzing, researching, and accepting the methodology of Elijah Muhammad's approach to the Bible, each of his students developed an ability to revisit their former religious upbringings from a position of strength and confidence, with intent to extract and render new understandings, even where none existed before.

Again, Elijah Muhammad is walking a well trodden path. Dr. Carter G. Woodson had seriously questioned accepting a form of Christianity that was "dominated by the thought of the oppressors." In *The Mis-Education of the Negro* Dr. Woodson charged, "In the church, however, the Negro has had sufficient freedom to develop this institution in his own way; but he has failed to do so. His religion is merely a loan from the whites who have enslaved and segregated the Negroes; and the organization, though largely an independent Negro institution, is dominated by the thought of the oppressors of the race.... In chameleon-like fashion the Negro has taken up almost everything religious which has come along instead of thinking for himself." (57-58)

As J.W. Schulte Nordholt, the Dutch author who penned the book titled, *The People that Walk in Darkness*, wrote, "Perhaps the greatest wonder in the whole history of the Negroes in America is that these people, who suffered so much at the hands of their masters, adopted the same religion as those masters (75).

Many pre-Emancipation African Americans and early 20th-century blacks did not readily accept the interpretations and presentations of the Bible they received from America's white religious communities. Nancy Ambrose, the former slave and grandmother of the renowned theologian and civil rights leader, Dr. Howard Thurman, through selective reading of Bible text, remonstrated against her slave master's presentation of the Bible.

Thurman on pages 30-31 in his book *Jesus and the Disinherited* shares how his grandmother's slave experience shaped her approach to the Bible. As a nine year-old Thurman read the Bible to his illiterate grandmother two or three times a week. For some unknown reason she never let Thurman read to her the Pauline verses of the Bible. Finally one day Thurman learned why.

> When I was older and half through college, I chanced to be spending a few days at home near the end of summer vacation. With a feeling of great temerity I asked her one day why it was that she would not let me read any of the Pauline letters. What she told me I shall never forget. "During the days of slavery," she said, "the master's minister would occasionally hold services for the slaves. Old man McGhee was so mean that he would not let a Negro minister preach to his slaves. Always the white minister used as his text something from Paul. At least three

or four times a year he used as a text: 'Slaves, be obedient to them that are your masters..., as unto Christ.' Then he would go on to show how it was God's will that we were slaves and how, if we were good and happy slaves, God would bless us. I promised my Maker that if I ever learned to read and if freedom ever came, I would not read that part of the Bible."

The ability to read and study the Bible in a manner different from the typical Sunday preacher became a standard feature that was common in Elijah's four stars and his hundreds of ministers. In their public discourses these four men would speak on religious matters that culminated with novel exegeses that were preached with assurance and certainty. Such revolutionary voices were refreshing to many African Americans and valued by many as proof that the Nation of Islam had something special to offer black America that no other person or organization could provide. Many African Americans dissatisfied with the *whiteness* of Christianity quickly accepted this new voice in religion that resonated with blackness. A common premise held by many Nation of Islam members was brunt and arrested one's attention with one question: "If a man won't treat you right, why would he teach you right?"

For years leaders around the world, especially in Islamic societies, kept a close eye on the works of Elijah Muhammad and his top students as they developed in the Nation of Islam. Even though traditional Islamic leaders recognized that Islam, as taught by Elijah, was not consistent with the universal teachings of Prophet Muhammed, nonetheless, they held great respect and admiration for the work he was accomplishing in the ghettoes of North America.

Without question, many of the social and community building traits of Elijah Muhammad that he passed on to these four internationally recognized men have also been passed on to their respective students and admirers. Each of these four men, being blessed by God to make a contribution to humanity in their own special way, has passed on some of the quintessence of Elijah Muhammad to future generations.

There is no other person, of any race or nationality, who can claim to have groomed African Americans from common black men to the international status that Elijah Muhammad has boosted these four men as respected leaders.

Arguably, Muhammad Ali is the most recognizable face in the world. If not for Elijah Muhammad giving Ali his Islamic name, would he be just another boxing champion tucked away in dust-covered sports magazines and reels of shelved film, waiting to be resurrected from the tombs of forgotten statistics? When Elijah Muhammad inspired Ali to stand up for more than mere boxing, to stand up for justice — as witnessed with his conscientious objector stand — it was only after Ali's refusal to fight in Viet Nam that the international world took a special interest in the former Cassius Clay.

Malcolm "X" Shabazz, although he and Elijah Muhammad never settled their disputes, is also a product of Elijah Muhammad. Even with all of his prison-honed oratory skills, if Malcolm had not been introduced to the message of Elijah Muhammad he would have remained only a street-smart hustler, going in and out of prison, instead of being the witty debater who often beset well-schooled scholars on Ivy League campuses. If not for Elijah Muhammad, Malcolm never would have been known or received by the international world as a voice for freedom, justice, equality, and Islam.

Minister Louis Farrakhan, a voice that articulated the hurt of black America so well that black men from every walk of life traveled to America's national capitol for the *Million Man March*, signaling to America and the world that they were responsible for their families, communities, and selves. If not for being a student of Elijah Muhammad he would not have gained the honor and recognition given to him by kings and rulers throughout the international world.

Imam W. Deen Mohammed, commonly called Wallace, was more interested in electronics and welding which were hopes that he had to set aside in order to take on the nobler task of helping his father. If reared in any other family setting Wallace may have been a career welder or electrician. But being raised in the house of Elijah Muhammad created for him other obligations. Elijah challenged and induced in him an intellect and nourished his soul so that Wallace would be prepared to reinterpret old understandings while extracting refreshing insights from the Qur'an and Bible. Wallace Mohammed's insights have intrigued the world's religious scholars and social scientists to study the development of Muslims in America with intense interest and with a speculative eye. If not for his father, Wallace would not have been placed on the international scene in February of 1975.

It is important to remember that none of these men ever forgot the contributions Elijah Muhammad made to their lives which helped them to be leaders on the world scene. As each of these four men grew into their own sense of individuality, the benefits from and their indebtedness to Elijah Muhammad was undeniable. Even with the strained relationship between Malcolm and Elijah taken into account, none of these men could forget the womb that bore them, the Nation of Islam, or their "father" the Honorable Elijah Muhammad, the man behind their greatness.

-§- CHAPTER -§-
THIRTEEN

Elijah Muhammad's Mental and Spiritual Genealogy

Elijah Muhammad spiritually and mentally "fathered" these four stars and thousands of other men and women who joined the ranks of the Nation of Islam from 1933 to 1975. From the minds and hearts and the loins of these thousands of faithful followers, it is clear that Elijah Muhammad is the intellectual and spiritual "grandfather" and "great-grandfather" of millions of people who now represent a multitude of races.

He is the ancestral patriarch who fathered a new mind and spirit for African Americans that the world never before had witnessed. The fact that Elijah Muhammad gave thousands of African Americans renewed hope in their individual potential makes him not only the "man behind the men," but also the man behind the creation of a new people on earth. Those who actually joined the Nation of Islam are direct spiritual descendants of Elijah Muhammad, while others were distant admirers or individuals whose lives were greatly affected by those who were Nation of Islam members.

One such African American who meets the standard of how one may indirectly be a mental and spiritual descendant of Elijah Muhammad is William C. Rhoden, the author of *Forty Million Dollar Slaves* and a sports columnist for *The New York Times*. Writing on the problems of the conveyor belt "slave" system of collegiate and professional sports, Rhoden speaks honorably of such pioneering African American athletes as Jackie Robinson, Paul Robeson, and Lusia Harris Stewart, the unsung "shero" of women's basketball. Two other athletes of whom Rhoden speaks admirably are direct products of Elijah Muhammad: Muhammad Ali and former New York Knicks National Basketball Association all-star Larry Johnson. Johnson never joined the Nation of Islam, but he acknowledged a belief in the message of love for black people that was espoused by Elijah Muhammad.

Rhoden admirably described Ali as one who "triggered an odd transformation in the country, in my household, and within the African American community." (17) Rhoden noted that "Ali became the first universal, seemingly omnipresent black man. He said things we only imagined saying, did things many of us had never conceived of doing...He shunned his slave name, Clay, for Ali; he refused to be inducted into the U.S. Army and risked everything, including the heavyweight championship, for principle."

Rhoden may not have personally sat at the feet of Elijah Muhammad, or even heard him speak — at least not to the degree that Ali had. But without question it is because of Elijah Muhammad's influence upon Muhammad Ali that Rhoden was able to appreciate Ali as that "odd transformation" that caused Rhoden to be imbued with a new sense of black pride and independence. Ali's brazenness seemed a novelty to Rhoden and others. However it is in this sense that Ali and other members of the Nation of Islam served as a conduit through which many African Americans became a mental and spiritual descendent of Elijah Muhammad's teachings.

Similarly, Rhoden cites Larry Johnson as another athlete who is a direct mental descendant of Elijah Muhammad. Although Johnson isn't a Muslim he still was greatly influenced by the teachings of Elijah Muhammad through the message of Louis Farrakhan. "Once I heard the teachings of the Honorable Elijah Muhammad; that really touched me. It was something I could relate to and made me do better." Even as an undeclared Muslim, Johnson asserted in the April 28, 2000 issue of *Muslim Journal*, "Once you have heard the teachings (of the Nation of Islam) and know the knowledge, there is no turning back."

Johnson's interest in Islam received national attention on June 5, 1999 during the National Basketball Association playoff series between the New York Knickerbockers and the Indiana Pacers. Johnson hit an improbable three-point shot that sent him to the foul line and culminated in a four point play with 5.2 seconds left in the game. In a post-game interview Johnson celebrated his game winning shot by exclaiming to millions of television viewers, "All Praise is due to Allah for that shot," and reciting the Islamic phrase, "Allah-U-Akbar! (God is greater!)"

Again the mind and spirit of Elijah Muhammad was evidenced in Larry Johnson's comments. In his book, Rhoden acknowledges Johnson's refusal to be "a slave" to sports, whether to team owners or to the sport in general, even though Johnson was enjoying the benefits of an $11 million-per-year contract. Johnson drew the ire of many non-African American sport enthusiasts when he emphatically said, "No one man can rise above the condition of the masses of his people. Understand that!" In *Forty Million Dollar Slaves*, Rhoden further emphasized Johnson's position with the quote: "So I am privileged and honored by the situation that I'm in, no question. Here's the NBA, full of blacks, great opportunities, they made beautiful strides. But what's the sense of that…when I go back to my neighborhood and see the same thing? (243)"

Rhoden's citing of Johnson's temerity may actually be an unidentified respect that Rhoden and many other African Americans have for Elijah Muhammad, a respect apparently shared by Larry Johnson. Rhoden also quoted Johnson's Elijah Muhammad-styled assessment of the African American struggle: "For a black man here in America, there is a struggle and you're either in it, or you're not. You [can] go about your life like it's peaches and cream, and not better the condition of black men and women here, and better our lives and better our community here, or not." Critical of successful African Americans who don't return to help the communities from which they have come, Johnson pointedly surmised, "You're trying to just do well by you." (243)

THE MAN BEHIND THE MEN

Elijah Muhammad's mental and spiritual message was inherited by millions of Americans, both African American and Caucasian. The minds of both white and black Americans were impregnated via the seminal broadcasting of the black-oriented message of Elijah that was pollinated throughout America via his thousands of followers.

The response of the non-Nation of Islam individual who may have been listening to or observing the works and message of Elijah Muhammad varied. The initial reaction of most white Americans to the message understandably was one of disdain, anger, or just fear. When a white person got an opportunity to better know a follower of Elijah Muhammad however their fear and disdain often changed to acceptance and very often a good friendship was formed.

In the early 1960s, Joan Visosky was a self-described white liberal Catholic who was concerned with spouting peace, brotherhood and love for all peoples. In 1962, when she met Nation of Islam member Eaustria "X" McNair — who later became Eaustria Sabir of Atlanta, GA — the two were co-workers at a department store in Johnstown, PA. Joan unknowingly had crossed paths with one of Elijah Muhammad's faithful followers and her views on life would soon change and never again be the same. Their friendship soon blossomed and the exchange between Joan and Eaustria X demonstrates how the message of Elijah Muhammad was passed on to many white Americans in a sometimes tense, but positive and effective way.

Joan knew Eaustria X by his middle name, Dale. When he began working at the department store she noted that Dale was a hard and diligent worker who kept both his conversations and company private. She shared that as she and another co-worker named Peg, "got to know him we learned that he was a student of Elijah Muhammad and Islam. This was scary to some at the time because 'Black Muslim' suggested anti-white or black militant which meant 'us versus them.' I didn't understand what it meant at all but I wanted to learn. Here was someone who could, and I felt would teach me. He was neither scary nor unfriendly."

These two individuals appeared to be as far apart as the north and south poles. She viewed Dale as frustrated, angry but enlightened, while Dale viewed Joan as an opportunity to remind her about the evils of white folks. Joan said:

> I wanted to forget the past, begin anew; he wanted to make all aware of the past and what it had done to an entire race — humankind. I wanted to bring folks together in harmony by spreading the good news of the gospel. I wanted to see integration. Here was this man who spoke of separation from the white devils who had created this mess.

ELIJAH'S MENTAL AND SPIRITUAL GENEALOGY

Joan, a former novice of the Sisters of St. Joseph at Baden, PA may not have realized it at the time but the hard working, disciplined Dale X excelled as an employee because of the teachings of Elijah Muhammad. Furthermore, the premise and objective of all of his conversations was to disseminate the message of his leader. In time Joan began to understand Dale X's point of view. Joan said, "I saw no connection between those who made slaves of Dale's ancestors and myself, because I was ready to scrap the past, but he made me come to realize that just as he could not erase or create a past that had been taken from him, I could not deny or ignore the negative past that was mine through my ancestors."

In time Joan conceded, "But it was a truth. My eyes were opening. It was this new fellow who was turning the light on for me to see things I just was too ignorant to recognize." Dale, applying Elijah Muhammad's message, challenged Joan's perception of life, especially on black-white issues. For Joan her encounter with Dale was both demanding and exhilarating. She recalled:

> What I was learning was that I did *not* know all of the answers. I hadn't even begun to touch on the basic questions! Of course I thought that I understood issues based on what I'd read in books plus the ideas I'd formed based solely on my own personal moral code. Now I was being challenged to open my eyes to see not just the black and white world of the written word in books, but to understand the black and white world that is the daily struggle of real people in real life. It was a revelation to me!

Their friendship continued to grow. Not only did Joan evolve, but Dale also grew into a more universal and racially inclusive understanding of Islam after Elijah Muhammad passed in 1975. Joan explained, "Our talking out all of these things, and more, led us to a path of understanding — neither of us changing our beliefs, but seeing others in a new light."

Throughout America, with varying degrees of success, the followers of Elijah Muhammad have replicated similar exchanges with both black and white people who were not members of the Nation of Islam. Regardless of the degree of amicability that may have accompanied these exchanges, each encounter offered opportunities for the message in Elijah Muhammad's version of Islam to impregnate the thinking of both black and white individuals.

Elijah Muhammad has also been an influencing factor in the music field, most recently in the 1990s black conscious "Golden Era" of rap music that preceded the negative bling-bling "Gangsta" style of rap.

THE MAN BEHIND THE MEN

The North Star, an online publication, issued an article by Charise Cheney of California Polytechnic State University under the section *A Journal of African American Religious History*. Her paper was titled, "Representin' God: Rap, Religion and the Politics of a Culture." Cheney, focusing on rap's "Golden Era," recognized the common inclusion of the racial aspect of the teachings of Elijah Muhammad into rap music. In the Fall of 1999 Cheney wrote:

> In Digable Planets' 1994 single "Dial 7 (Axioms of Creamy Spies)," Sara Webb, a featured vocalist and apparent cultural critic, demystifies white power and dismisses social constructions of white supremacy with one line: "The Man ain't shit." In this critique, Webb takes her cultural cues from the Black and urban working class community and denounces the representative of white domination — "The Man" — thus expelling him from his center of power. According to this verse, he is a devil ("your tongue is forked we know") whose days of deception ("your double-dealin' is scoped") and conspiring ("The Man's game is peeped") against the disempowered Black masses are over. ("It's Nation Time, Nation Time"). Racially-conscious brothers and sisters, the "creamy spies," inspired and informed by the teachings of Elijah Muhammad ("we are sun, moon and star").

Based upon Cheney's assessment the voice of Elijah Muhammad reached millions by way of artist such as the Poor Righteous Teachers, X-Clan, Public Enemy, Brand Nubian, KRS-One and other rap artists. Arguably this musical outreach sired more mental and spiritual offspring for Elijah Muhammad. Dr. Martin Luther King and other leaders also have their spiritual and mental "genetic markers" encoded into the minds and souls of the generations who succeeded them. But with the rap artists mentioned above Elijah Muhammad genes are without question the dominant trait.

The voice and influence of Elijah Muhammad also reached other generations of both Muslim and non-Muslim African American musicians. Some of the musicians in the R&B and jazz group Kool and the Gang were active members of the pre-1975 Nation of Islam. The band's leader, Robert Bell (a.k.a. Kool) and his brother Ronald come from a large Islamic family. Their Islamic names are Muhammad and Khalis Bayyan, respectively.

Kool and the Gang's 1974 album, *Light of the World* featured the tunes *Whiting H&G* (named after the Nation of Islam's popular fish program), *Higher Plane*, and *Hereafter*. Those musical compositions constituted a virtual salute to the many positive contributions of Elijah Muhammad and the Nation of Islam upon black America.

ELIJAH'S MENTAL AND SPIRITUAL GENEALOGY

The opening lyrics in Kool and the Gang's tune *Hereafter* were replete with words very common within the Nation of Islam. A smooth yet determined voice, with jazz and African-style music in the background, recite:

> Hereafter: Where freedom, justice and equality will ring in the hearts and in the minds of all men. Hereafter: Where men have consumed knowledge, wisdom, and understanding from what he has overlooked for so long. Yes, there will be peace for all, Hereafter. As-Salaam Alaikum.

In the 1970s Ronald (Khalis Bayyan), while donned in the traditional Nation of Islam suit and bowtie attire would captivate the group's audience with his ability of circular breathing; a feat he would display by blowing non-stop the note B-flat for more than five minutes. Khalis would inform the audience that the length of time he held the B-flat note represented the centuries of slavery and suffering endured by black people in America.

There are indications that Elijah Muhammad's message influenced the Sound of Philadelphia International, a music label founded by Kenny Gamble (Luqman Abdul Haqq) and Leon Huff. The 1975 hit song by the O'Jays written by Huff and Gamble, *Give the People What They Want* — which also was the title song of the album — has one verse that resonates with the Nation of Islam's theme of "freedom, justice and equality":

> Well, it's about time for things to get better
> We want the truth, the truth and no more lies
> We want freedom, justice and equality
> I want it for you and I want it for me

Another popular singer influenced by Elijah Muhammad was Joe Arrington, who performed under the stage name Joe Tex. He joined the Nation of Islam in 1968 and later changed his name to Yusuf Hazziez. In 1972 he quit his flourishing solo music career to serve as a minister for Elijah Muhammad. After the passing of Elijah Muhammad, Hazziez returned to his music career and later recorded his 1977 hit song *I Ain't Gonna Bump No More (With No Big Fat Woman)*; a reference to African Americans' entanglement (bumping) with the "big fat woman" that Hazziez said symbolized an overweight greedy America.

We also see the influence of Elijah Muhammad upon the Philadelphia based R&B singing group The Delfonics, famous for their hit songs *La La Means I love You* and *Didn't I (Blow Your Mind This Time)*. Some members of the Delfonics sold the Nation of Islam's newspaper *Muhammad Speaks*. Abdul-Wahid Taha, the former Clayton X, remembers selling with two brothers, William and Wilbert Hart, who were members of the Delfonics.

THE MAN BEHIND THE MEN

Taha said, "I was a member of the Nation of Islam's Fruit of Islam in the West Philadelphia area. It must have been late 1972 or early 1973. A couple of the members of the Delfonics used to regularly attend the Temple in West Philadelphia; Temple No. 12-C." Speaking on how the experience of selling the *Muhammad Speaks* newspaper with members of the Delfonics affected him Taha recalled:

> It sort of increased my sense of pride and sense of conviction in the N.O.I. to see men who I had admired even before coming into the N.O.I. That I had admired before really knowing that much about the Nation of Islam. I had admired them as entertainers and then to find that they too shared the same conviction that I had, and they were members of the Nation, and were not too proud or too haughty to just go door-to-door like I was going and the rest of us was going, pushing the program of the Nation of Islam.
> — Telephone Interview

According to Karl Evanzz there are very strong indications of Elijah Muhammad's social influence on James Brown, the "Godfather of Soul" and Motown's The Temptations, in their hit songs, respectively, *Say It Loud, I'm Black and I'm Proud* and *Message from a Black Man*. The presence of the Nation of Islam in America's African American community in the 1960s and 1970s had a tremendous affect on many cultural and entertainment expressions. Even the most conservative African Americans, particularly after listening to such songs, finally found comfort in calling themselves a black man or black woman.

There is no African American today who has not been influenced in some way by Elijah Muhammad. The number of non-Muslims of any race who have been positively influenced by Elijah Muhammad is innumerable. Even people who did not subscribe to his racial or separatist views would incorporate Elijah's economic and social commentary. Untold numbers of individuals recreated his model of self-help and opened independent schools with African American-specific curricula.

In the business world and in many other professions the creation and evolution of thousands of black-oriented associations most likely were motivated by Elijah Muhammad's message of "Do for Self." Many of these black only associations are — directly or indirectly — mental descendants born from the influence of the thinking of Elijah Muhammad.

It is through these music artists and other black-oriented professional groups and associations, many that still exist today, that Elijah Muhammad is the mental and spiritual grandfather of millions of African Americans; people whose individual, family, and community lives were reshaped and infused with a revitalizing spirit that emanated from the message of the little man out of southern Georgia. If any African American would retrace the origins of their thinking process, particularly thinking that has resulted in them having a love of self and a strong desire to "buy black"; if they were to research their mental and spiritual genealogy, one of their recent forefathers will definitely be the Honorable Elijah Muhammad, the man behind the men.

Hopefully in the near future African American social scientists will revisit the entire life of Elijah Muhammad in search of the many positive influences and contributions of this one man upon the mental and spiritual life of the African American community. This, I believe is a debt that is owed not only to Elijah Muhammad but to African Americans specifically and to Americans and the world collectively.

-§- CHAPTER -§-
FOURTEEN

Non-African Americans Influenced By Elijah Muhammad
Caucasians, Hispanics, American Indians, and Immigrant Muslims

> "(Islam) is the only unifying religion known and tried by the races and nations of earth."
>
> — Elijah Muhammad
> Message to the Blackman p. 131

In the minds of most people, diversity in any of its forms never would be synonymous with or remotely connected to the nationalistic black-oriented Nation of Islam. On the contrary, among members attending the 1974 Saviour's Day convention, when they heard Elijah Muhammad recognize and praise Caucasians for having their own land and flag while publicly acknowledging the two white Muslim "scientists" who had accompanied him onstage, some longtime Nation of Islam members were not surprised by Elijah Muhammad's racially inclusive words and actions. For years the Nation of Islam had allowed a very minimal number of non-African Americans into the pro-black community, as well as employing others who were from racially and culturally diverse backgrounds.

Karl Evanzz's book *The Rise and Fall of Elijah Muhammad* states that Elijah Muhammad also hired white people. Evanzz points out that the Lerner family, a Jewish family, printed *Muhammad Speaks*, and that Elijah hired Caucasians to handle the finances of the Nation of Islam. According to Evanzz, Elijah defended this action by saying, "I can get along with both...and the white people know their country, know their government, know their buildings, their material. And if my people would build those houses over there [referring to his new mansions], they would have to buy the material from the white people."

Another aspect of racial diversity was injected into the Nation of Islam from its inception. As mentioned earlier, not only was W.D. Fard's mother "100 percent white," many people also believed that Fard himself was a white man. The reality of Fard's racial makeup, compounded by the fact that Fard was not a product of the African American experience, must have influenced the thinking of Elijah. These realities may also explain why the conscience of Elijah Muhammad allowed him the freedom to provide opportunities of employment to white Americans and membership to a few non African Americans.

NON-AFRICAN AMERICANS INFLUENCED BY ELIJAH MUHAMMAD

The following section of this book, which deals with non-African Americans who were influenced by Elijah Muhammad, is probably the one aspect of his leadership that is most overlooked. Traditionally everyone has accepted that the Islam articulated by Elijah Muhammad and Nation of Islam officials was a message created exclusively for the "original Black man." This widespread perception revealed no indications that non-black people were also members of the Nation of Islam. Even the occasional reports and rumors of white members in the Nation of Islam did not affect the pervading view that the Nation of Islam was 100 percent African American.

This shocking and seemingly implausible revelation may be difficult to comprehend given the overall racial climate of America from the 1930s through 1975. Try to conceptualize African Americans openly attending Ku Klux Klan meetings and reshaping their lives according to Klan tenets and doctrines. Nor can one imagine a Jewish or Hispanic family being open and active members of the Aryan Nation or the Skinheads. But such racial and ethnic interfacing did occur within the Nation of Islam during Elijah Muhammad's tenure as the "Messenger of Allah," even as far back to the time of W.D. Fard's leadership, even though Fard soon soured on allowing white membership.

Additionally Elijah Muhammad often entertained white Americans at his home. According to his son Wallace he even served his white guests dinner on their finest china. Never would one glimmer a thought of former Alabama Governor George Wallace or Birmingham, Alabama's police commissioner of the 1960s, Eugene "Bull" Conner, ever inviting the Rev. Dr. Martin Luther King or other Civil Rights Movement members into their home for dinner, conversation, and friendly exchange. No! Never! However, Elijah Muhammad regularly entertained people of many races at his home.

The popular commercialized "Elijah Muhammad" who has been fed to and readily consumed by most Americans is an improperly prepackaged image that describes him as a man full of antipathy and ill will, especially towards white people. In order to show a fuller picture of the Honorable Elijah Muhammad it is important to explore a few of these little known interracial exchanges and relationships in the pre-1975 Nation of Islam.

For years Elijah Muhammad allowed non-African Americans, however sparsely, to either enjoy membership in the Nation of Islam or gain influential positions of employment. He hired non-African American Muslims to teach Arabic in his elementary school called the University of Islam as well as hiring Muslim writers from abroad who wrote regular columns in his newspaper *Muhammad Speaks*.

Before he found satisfaction in the late 1940s with the Palestinian-born Dr. Jamil Diab, Elijah Muhammad had tried a litany of Muslims from abroad to teach his University of Islam students Arabic. Elijah first met Diab through arrangements that were made through his son in-law Raymond Sharrief. One report states that despite dissuasions from the FBI, Diab served as an Arabic teacher for Elijah Muhammad's school for eight years, until the two men disagreed briefly over Islamic tenets in 1956.

One of Diab's former students from the University of Islam, Darnell Karim who now serves as an imam in the Chicago area, shared that in addition to Arabic, Diab also taught them the five daily Islamic prayers and how to properly read the Qur'an. Diab's students included Elijah's two youngest sons, Wallace and Akbar, as well as Karim's sister Zahirah and his future wife Gloria. Karim stated that Dr. Diab eventually taught them math and science, much of it instructed in Arabic. Karim stated that "we learned the linguistics of the Arabic language; we also learned Qur'anic Arabic, the most of it reading, writing, and translation." Other subjects taught by Diab included hadeeth (Islamic reports on the life of Prophet Muhammed), and Arabic proverbs.

Professor Jamil Diab teaching at the University of Islam. Students include Wallace and Akbar Muhammad, Isaiah Thomas, Darnell, Carl Jr., Zarifah, and Gloria Karim.
(Courtesy of Darnell Karim)

In a personal interview with Dr. Diab, Karim discussed with his former instructor two of the objectives Elijah Muhammad intended when he

NON-AFRICAN AMERICANS INFLUENCED BY ELIJAH MUHAMMAD

hired Diab. Karim related, "This is the story that Jamil told me in Arizona about a year before he passed. He said that Elijah Muhammad told him that he wanted him to teach his people the Arabic language so that they would better understand the Qur'an and better understand the religion." The second purpose for which Elijah Muhammad hired Diab to teach the students Arabic was because he wanted his followers "to get away from the devil's language." Jamil Diab passed on January 9, 2005.

Fard had taught Elijah Muhammad that Arabic was the "original" language of African Americans. Although Africans had many native tongues before the influx of Arabic, noted historian John Hope Franklin observed in his book *From Slavery to Freedom*, the importance of Arabic on the African continent:

> The use of Arabic by educated Muslim Africans after the fourteenth century was rather extensive and made possible the reduction of some of the oral literature to permanent form. Examples of this are the Tarikh-es-Soudan, a history of the Sudan, written by Es-Sadi and Tarikh-El-Fettach, written by Kati, a Sudanese. Some African scholars even sought to adapt the Arabic alphabet to the writing of one of the African languages by adding diacritical marks to represent sounds that do not exist in Arabic. This extremely difficult feat made possible the more extensive use of Arabic in developing a written literature among Africans. (28-29)

Surely Elijah Muhammad's third grade southern education did not afford him access to the proper history of Africa. Nonetheless, Fard's assertion that Arabic was the black man's original tongue served well in giving African Americans an attainable goal of reclaiming what they understood to be their pre-slavery mother tongue.

Another non-African American influenced by the success of Elijah Muhammad during the mid 1950s was Abdul Basit Naeem from Pakistan. He worked diligently in service to Elijah Muhammad even to the point of writing the Introduction to Mr. Muhammad's February 26, 1957 booklet titled, *The Supreme Wisdom: Solution to the so-called NEGROES' Problem*.

As indicated before, for many years Naeem published a regular column in the Nation of Islam's *Muhammad Speaks* newspaper. Naeem's topics ranged from discussing international affairs of Islamic and African nations to periodically writing articles addressing America's racial disparities. Naeem's writings adhered to the typical language and style of the Nation of Islam. He often referred to Elijah Muhammad as the "Little Lamb without spots and blemishes" and to non-Muslim African Americans as the "Lost-Found" people. (See *Muhammad Speaks* Feb. 03 and Mar. 17, 1967 issues.) Naeem was also the editor-publisher of *Moslem World & the U.S.A.*

THE MAN BEHIND THE MEN

Naeem was knowledgeable of Islam as taught throughout the international Islamic world, yet he on more than one occasion justified his support of Elijah Muhammad's unorthodox version of Islam. In his own words, while acknowledging that Elijah Muhammad was not teaching Islam properly, Naeem loyally defended Elijah Muhammad's methodology of teaching an altered brand of Islam that Naeem accepted as temporary and designed especially for improving the conditions of all African Americans. In the introduction of *The Supreme Wisdom* Naeem also stated:

> As far as I am concerned, I consider the differences between Islam of the East and teachings of Mr. Elijah Muhammad to be of relatively minor importance at this time, because these are not related to the SPIRIT of Islam, which, I am sure, is completely shared by all of us. A Moslem from Pakistan, Indonesia, Iran or Egypt only has to meet some of Mr. Elijah Muhammad's followers to be convinced of their love, utmost devotion and passion for all that is *true* Islamic Spirit.

However, Karl Evanzz in his book *The Rise and Fall of Elijah Muhammad* cast a dark shadow on Abdul Basit Naeem by stating that he was actually one of the informers that "the FBI considered reliable sources." (278 and 317)

The Palestinian-American Ali Baghdadi is another non-African American who was greatly influenced by Elijah Muhammad and his mission. Baghdadi was the publisher of the Arab Journal and like Naeem also was a regular columnist in *Muhammad Speaks*. Baghdadi's column was titled Middle East Report. It was laden with accusations against white Americans and Europeans while being sympathetic and supportive of "dark-skinned people" around the world.

In the March 21, 1975 issue of *Muhammad Speaks*, Baghdadi's weekly Middle East Report states, "The racist mentality of the Europeans and North Americans, and the Crusades wars and other military conflicts between Christendom and Islam, still play a great part, consciously or unconsciously, in determining Western attitudes in regard to the heritage of Black people in general and Muslims in particular." Baghdadi later would write for Louis Farrakhan's media arm The *Final Call*, a name adopted from W.D. Fard's 1930 newspaper publication.

Surely Diab, Naeem, and Baghdadi saw possibilities and promise for the overall growth of universal Islam in America via Elijah Muhammad and his Nation of Islam. Likewise, obviously, Elijah Muhammad saw the benefits of having access to the education these men offered to his community, not to mention the benefit that Elijah Muhammad gained by having Diab, Naeem, and Baghdadi as proof that race was not the only motivation and objective working in the Nation of Islam. More importantly

NON-AFRICAN AMERICANS INFLUENCED BY ELIJAH MUHAMMAD

the public presence of these Middle East gentlemen working in the Nation of Islam provided Elijah Muhammad proof that the Nation of Islam was a community of Muslims united with Muslims all over the world.

It was Elijah Muhammad's success as an effective leader that influenced these men to sacrifice convenience while under pressure from United States government officials who may have been displeased with their supporting the Nation of Islam. These men easily could have done as many other Muslim immigrants to America had done — ignored the Nation of Islam and shunned the inner city while quietly trying to assimilate into white America's suburban life.

Some white Americans also supported the message of Elijah Muhammad to the point of seeking membership. The fact that these Caucasians were seeking membership in the Nation of Islam shows that they were not racial separatists, but rather white people who related strongly with Elijah's assessment of America's racial problems. The white Americans influenced by Elijah Muhammad were not the type like George Lincoln Rockwell, the American Nazi Party leader; instead, they were sincere seekers of what they understood to be the truth. Rockwell's self-serving efforts to personally connect with Elijah Muhammad failed miserably (As discussed earlier in this book).

For many white Americans, at a minimum, Elijah's assessment of America's race issues correlated with their thoughts and aspirations on race, freedom, and justice; values that were dear to them. Regardless of the rationale that any of these white Americans stood upon that allowed them to adhere to Elijah Muhammad's program, collectively they all agreed that what he offered as a solution to life's challenges and concerns also was best for them.

Many have dubbed Dorothy Blake Fardan as the "first white member" of the Nation of Islam. But it has been recorded that when W.D. Fard began his mission in the ghettoes of Detroit he temporarily allowed white members to join. Jalal Najjar Sharif and his mother joined Fard's Nation of Islam in 1932. Sharif was eleven years-old. He readily recalls that there were Caucasian Muslims who followed Fard.

Muslim American writers and researchers Hameed El-Amin of Huntsville, AL and Marvis Aleem of Washington D.C. interviewed Jalal Najjar Sharif in May of 2002. El-Amin and Aleem recounted Sharif's acknowledgement that at first there were Caucasians in the Nation of Islam under Fard. The Muslim school had two Caucasian teachers, one called "Brother Wali" and the other called "Brother Sam" who was married to a German woman who also belonged to the community. In all there were a handful of Caucasians. Sharif explained, "Caucasians were eventually excluded from membership in the Nation of Islam since they had a tendency to take over."

THE MAN BEHIND THE MEN

Imam Clyde Rahman of Cleveland, OH, quickly pointed out that initially no 100 percent white person was ever allowed to join the Nation of Islam. In contradiction to Jalal Najjar Sharif's report Imam Rahman noted, "We didn't have no pure white people in the Nation of Islam for the first thirty years...It wasn't no [sic] full Caucasians in the Nation of Islam."

Fardan did not join the Nation of Islam until shortly after the passing of Elijah Muhammad when his son Wallace opened the membership to all races in 1975. The May 28, 2008 issue of *Muslim Journal* newspaper printed a transcript titled, *Life: The Final Battlefield*, wherein Wallace Mohammed recalled giving Blake the name Fardan:

> There was a sister named Dorothy something X and I gave her the name Fardan, before I even saw her. Some brothers were asking me for names for different ones, and I said to tell her that I think her name should be Fardan.
> I was told she was a Catholic before she converted to the Nation of Islam, and I was told that she was a White woman. I knew she was not stupid or naïve. She was a catholic sister in the church, and I knew she would think about the name I gave her.
> So I gave her that name "Fardan," which meant a person influenced by Mr. Fard. Finally, I met her in my office. She came to my office and wanted to speak with me. When I saw her, she said "AsSalaamAlaikum," and I said the same to her.
> Before she got started, I said, "You joined the Nation of Islam and you were a Catholic and a White person?" She said, "Yes." I said, "Actually, that was a concern for me and I could not understand that." She said, "I know I am not a devil."
> And that was enough for me. She didn't have to say another word to me. I knew she was sincere and she was coming from the heart. She said, "I know I am no devil."

Apparently still very much influenced by Elijah Muhammad, Fardan in 1991 (with a 2nd edition in 2001) penned a book titled *Message to the White Man and Woman in America: Yakub and the Origins of White Supremacy.* In her Introduction Fardan wrote, "Somehow as I incorporated Elijah Muhammad's teachings into my own consciousness I knew they were meant for others (Black people) but I felt they applied to me too. It was like being between two shores; while the message spoke to black people in its own way, it spoke to white people in another."

An internet website citing her book promotes that white people are trapped in "illusions of greatness" that was fabricated to fill a historical void.

> It is a historical vacuum; a chunk of time which has been severed from its origin point and reconstructed in terms of fabricated accounts

NON-AFRICAN AMERICANS INFLUENCED BY ELIJAH MUHAMMAD

and falsified documents. Such an historical and truncated worldview has allowed the illusion of white supremacy to become not only a general mind-set, but an insidious underlying strategy which informs and constitutes every institution within American society.

Fardan's commitment to the newly revised community structure of the Nation of Islam under the leadership of Imam Mohammed was short-lived. Fardan seemed to prefer a confrontational style of challenging white America. The effects of the teachings of Elijah Muhammad upon Fardan apparently lingered into the 21st Century. Today Fardan is a writer and speaker for an organization called CURE *Caucasians United for Reparations and Emancipation*, a group of white Americans supportive of African American reparations.

Cincinnati, OH Muhammad's Mosque No. 5 had a Caucasian member for many years from 1952 through 1969. Sister Pauline X Williams, formerly of Somerset, KY was the wife of Cincinnati's Nation of Islam minister Asbury X Williams. Musa Abdullah, the former Moses X, served as secretary of the Cincinnati Mosque from 1967 to 1968 before he was promoted to the rank of lieutenant in the Fruit of Islam. Abdullah remembers talking with Pauline X on many occasions. "She had blond hair and grayish blue eyes and thin paper lips." Some alleged that Pauline was mixed with American Indian, thus not 100 percent Caucasian; a factor that could have eventually led to her being allowed membership into the Nation of Islam.

Abdullah remembers that for four years Pauline X had perfect attendance. "She was there every Sunday for four years." He noted that her attendance only waned after her health began to fail in 1969. Although Pauline "stood out" because of her stark Caucasian features, Abdullah said, "We just treated her like any other member."

It has not been ascertained whether Pauline X Williams was mixed with Indian ancestry. No American Indian tribe has been specifically identified in her family lineage. But of a surety Elijah Muhammad knew of the attendance and full membership in his Nation of Islam of the Muslim sister with "blond hair and grayish blue eyes and thin paper lips."

Seifullah Ali Shabazz, born Kevin Burke in Passaic, NJ is a Caucasian American who was strongly influenced by Elijah Muhammad's message. Shabazz (Kevin X) claims that his membership in the Nation of Islam began in 1963 as a teenager while incarcerated at the New Jersey State Home for Boys in Jamesburg.

He notes that his involvement as a member in the Nation of Islam while incarcerated was without hindrance and afforded him full access to all meetings. However, due to him being Caucasian he was not allowed to attend the regular meetings at the Mosque in Newark after he was released from the State Home for Boys.

A young Seifullah Ali Shabazz, the former Kevin Burke selling *Muhammad Speaks* in the Newark-Passaic area in the early 1970s. *(Courtesy of Seifullah A. Shabazz)*

This restriction did not deter his commitment to Elijah Muhammad and the Nation of Islam. Whatever Islamic activities he could observe or participate in, even under restrictive conditions, Burke diligently pursued. Many times his performance excelled that of African American men in the Nation of Islam. Shabazz spent a lot of time at the local Muslim restaurant where he would wait until the brothers came there after the mosque meetings. In addition to assisting with unloading the *Muhammad Speaks* newspaper from the delivery truck, Shabazz would obtain bundles of *Muhammad Speaks*

NON-AFRICAN AMERICANS INFLUENCED BY ELIJAH MUHAMMAD

newspapers from various brothers and sell them to the public. Shabazz declared "I became the number one *Muhammad Speaks* salesman." Imam Yahya B. Muhammad of Baltimore, MD, formerly Captain John X of Newark, who presided over the Newark-Passaic area, vouched for Shabazz. "He did sell the *Muhammad Speaks*. Now, that I do know."

Shabazz maintained his close association with the local Muslim Minister James Shabazz and Captain John X, both of whom he often met at the Muslim restaurant. Shabazz shared that the minister was concerned for his well-being and the pressures that would accompany a Caucasian who sold *Muhammad Speaks* newspaper. "I had to convince Minister James Shabazz that I could absorb the abuse. That was a tough sacrifice. I wasn't able (allowed) to respond to any abuse." Another big challenge for Shabazz came from within the Nation of Islam from those who distrusted his genuineness. "Some in the Nation of Islam called me the police or the FBI."

Seifullah Ali Shabazz in his bookstore. Note photos of Elijah Muhammad and Wallace Mohammed on the wall in background. *(Courtesy of Seifullah A. Shabazz)*

Being raised the only Caucasian in his community Shabazz (the former Kevin Burke) bonded more with his environment than with the complexion of his skin. Shabazz, who was also known by the moniker "Red," did not allow his skin color to interfere with him acknowledging the leadership of Elijah Muhammad and relating to the plight of African Americans. Nor did the racially based membership restrictions and the occasional accusations that he was the police or the FBI discourage his commitment to being a Muslim under the leadership of Elijah Muhammad. Apparently Shabazz's conversion to Islam was deeply personal; therefore, he didn't allow his skin color to be a determinant in his choice to follow Elijah Muhammad. He said, "I was converted in my heart."

> "I'm proud of my environment. That Caucasian thing, I have that complexion but that's not who I am. I'm a product of my environment. The birth of who I am as an individual identifies my environment. So I don't have that connection with the Caucasian. When you talk about Caucasian to me you're talking about somebody who in mind and body is a devil. They took their mind and they wrapped their minds around the benefits that their physical complexion gave them in the society."
> — Telephone interview

Even the phrase "The white man is the devil" did not daunt Shabazz's dedication to the program of Elijah Muhammad. "That didn't affect me one way or the other because I didn't associate myself that way. They wasn't talking about me. I didn't see myself as the 'white man' that they were talking about even though my complexion is Caucasian, but from the influence in the environment I saw myself as a black man. That's still my position."

The Honorable Elijah Muhammad's message of self-sufficiency resonated with oppressed people in many parts of the world. One of his closest friends was a Mexican-American named Henry Almanza who had migrated from Pueblo, Mexico to Detroit, MI. Almanza's association with the Nation of Islam was similar to that of Seifullah Ali Shabazz in that he too was allowed access to all Nation of Islam activities except for entering the temple and joining the Fruit of Islam.

Henry's wife Mary and all of their children were members of the Detoit Nation of Islam temple, but due to Henry being of Mexican descent Mr. W.D. Fard personally told him that only African Americans who were descendants of slaves could attend the temple. After Fard's departure Elijah Muhammad continued the practice of Almanza's restrictive membership; nonetheless, this impediment did not stop Almanza from fully supporting Elijah Muhammad. After every temple meeting Henry would patiently wait for his family to return home so that he could be updated on the message that was delivered that day.

Osman Sharieff Almanza, Henry's youngest son has vivid memories of his father's love for the Muslim teachings. "He would ask my big brothers and sisters after they came back from the temple, 'What did the Minister say?' And you had to tell him what the Minister said. He would get his information from us."

NON-AFRICAN AMERICANS INFLUENCED BY ELIJAH MUHAMMAD

Mary Almanza-Islaam and Henry Almanza. *(Courtesy of Osman Almanza)*

Osman remembers Elijah Muhammad's regularly visiting his father. The two men often talked about Islam while they worked together on various projects. Osman said, "And when Elijah Muhammad would come they would get through their work and they would go to Brother Muck-mud's (Muhammad) house or they would go to Sister Addie's house, and they would be there all day."

During the earlier years of the Nation of Islam the name Muhammad was unintentionally mispronounced as "Muck-mud." It was not until Elijah Muhammad hired Dr. Jamil Diab that this mispronounciation was corrected.

Osman recalled the strong influence that Elijah Muhammad had upon his father:

THE MAN BEHIND THE MEN

He was a maximum influence upon him. They used to sit and talk about the conditions of Mexico and the Catholic Church. A lot of things that Elijah Muhammad taught him increased his belief in Allah. (Elijah Muhammad) was a tremendous influence upon him because he believed what he was taught, that Allah came and that Master Fard was that person. Elijah Muhammad; he loved him, he loved him dearly. He made sure that whatever we had, they had, and sometimes more because he believed that he was the Messenger of Allah. He accepted that and my mother accepted, and they worked towards that.

Henry Almanza was dedicated to the mission of Elijah Muhammad to the point of even going to jail. Even though his Hispanic ancestry kept him from joining, Almanza still made sure his family enjoyed full membership in the Nation of Islam. When the Detroit public school authorities tried to make the Muslims send their children to public schools, Henry obeyed Elijah Muhammad's request that Nation of Islam children not be placed in public schools. Osman shared, "He went to prison for not putting us in public schools. He went to DeHoCo, the Detroit House of Corrections. He served either three or six months."

The Funeral of Elijah Muhammad February 28, 1975.
(Photographer and Date Unknown)

Henry Almanza died in 1959. Elijah Muhammad delivered his eulogy. Recalling his father's funeral Osman remembers one statement of Elijah Muhammad that surprised the Muslims who were in attendance. Some Nation of Islam members errantly believed Elijah, the "Messenger", was invincible. Osman related, "One of the main things he (Elijah Muhammad) said that caught everybody's attention was when he said, 'One day I too shall lay there where Brother Almanza lay.'"

NON-AFRICAN AMERICANS INFLUENCED BY ELIJAH MUHAMMAD

Another Hispanic American to join the Nation of Islam under the leadership of Elijah Muhammad was Benjamin Perez. He earned the title and name Imam Hajji Benjamin Perez. He also added the name Mahomah, a Spanish version of Muhammad, as his surname. Perez became the president of the Berkley based *California Latino Muslim Association* in 2005, and is the former CEO of the *America Spanish-Speaking and Native American Islamic Outreach* that was held in 1972.

Perez learned about the Nation of Islam from a fellow Muslim employee named Ralus while employed at the Calo Pet foods in 1955. The two men regularly commuted together to and from work. As a result of Ralus being harassed for his religious beliefs, Perez became interested and expressed an interest in attending a Nation of Islam meeting. Ralus, knowing that Perez was non-African American realized that he first had to obtain permission from the local Nation of Islam officials for Perez to attend.

His first meeting captured him. "I went to the meeting and I sat there and the topic was Cain and Abel; those who 'cain't' (Cain) and those who were 'un-Abel.' " It was related to, more or less, the story of Cain and Abel in the Bible. I liked it because I was prone to learn about religion. I thought I would benefit by going and learning more about it. I continue going to the meetings."

Perez became an active member in the Nation of Islam with one exception — even though he was allowed to attend the temple meetings he was not allowed, at that time, to become a member of the Fruit of Islam. Twice when the local minister appealed to Elijah Muhammad to let Perez join the Fruit of Islam their request was denied. Perez stated that Elijah Muhammad's reply was, "No, I'm only teaching my people, the lost-found nation in the wilderness of North America."

Even with the two previous denials Perez still remained faithful to the Nation of Islam; however, the third request was accepted when Bernard Cushmere was assigned to Phoenix, AZ. Perez recalls that Cushmere "wrote and the reply came by way of National Secretary Abass Rasoul of Chicago. It came to San Francisco. I was walking on Fillmore Theatre Street and he (Cushmere) came up to me and asked me, 'Are you Brother Benjamin?' I said, 'Yes.' He said, 'Well, I have a message for you from the Honorable Elijah Muhammad. He has told me to inform you that you can come and help him reach his people. You can attend the Fruit of Islam class.' "

Perez unmistakably was non-African American. He described himself as "just a regular Hispanic brother". He was a native Mexican from Carlsbad, NM. Perez's father was from Sierra Mojada, Mexico, and his mother's father, a man who Perez described as "light complexed, more like German features" was from the area around Guadalajara, Jalisco Mexico.

Perez explained, "As a child I always wanted to have friends in every ethnic group that existed…there was prejudice going on, and I never wanted to be a part of it." It was Perez's openness to all people that allowed him to easily connect with the Nation of Islam, which is quite ironic in light of the fact that the Nation of Islam practiced forms of racism and prejudice against him by initially restricting his membership. Still he remained faithful.

Benjamin Perez Mohamah (Muhammad) - top rear with San Francisco Fruit of Islam (men) and Muslim women. *(Courtesy of Benjamin Perex Mohamah)*

Identifying strongly with the Nation of Islam's moral teachings, and being conscious of the dissipating condition of Hispanics, Perez recognized that within the Nation of Islam existed a model that could be emulated by the Hispanic community. He noted, "In the sense that the Nation of Islam was an all black organization I felt that I could possibly help by learning Islam and teaching it to the Latinos and Native Americans." Perez was impressed with how Elijah Muhammad taught a belief in God with emphasis on avoiding eating pork as well as any personal contact with the opposite sex. "In my case I really took it to heart when they said no drinking, no smoking, etc, etc. I believe that Islam is the message God has sent to man."

Probably one of Perez's biggest sacrifices when he joined the Nation of Islam was the repulsive response from his family. "They thought I was crazy." He had to endure taunts such as, "You're going over there with those black people." The verbal abuse also came from Hispanics who lived in his hometown. The audacity of exposing himself to a religion other than Christianity was problematic in and of itself, but Perez noted that for many of his family members and friends, "associating with blacks and much less being a part of their activities was quite a bit overboard." Perez recalled, "One of them was so bold that he said, 'Hi part-

NON-AFRICAN AMERICANS INFLUENCED BY ELIJAH MUHAMMAD

Nigger.' I said, 'You son-of-a-gun, I should pop you in the mouth.'" Through all of these difficulties Perez adjusted to these negativities by concluding, "These are people I grew up with. You know, so, you just lump it."

At one junction in his Nation of Islam years Perez was with a group of Muslims who established a Hispanic Nation of Islam temple during the leadership of Elijah Muhammad that was recognized by the Nation of Islam Headquarters in Chicago. Perez remembers, "When we ventured to have our own meetings we had reports that we had to write in."

Perez passed December 8, 2009. During his lifetime he served as an imam in the Oakland, CA area and participated in many conferences including the annual Muslim conventions that were sponsored by the late Imam W. Deen Mohammed. He also has traveled to Mecca, Saudi Arabia for the Islamic pilgrimage completing the sacred rites of the hajj.

He always maintained great respect for the Honorable Elijah Muhammad and believed that Elijah "should be recognized as the one to bring Islam to the black people in America." Perez supported this statement by adding, "This is due to the fact that everyone in the world knows that black people were enslaved and brought to America and treated as animals."

Elijah Muhammad's resonance with people of color also found connections with members of America's Native American communities. Diane Williams' paternal grandfather was an Irish immigrant, and her mother an "Athabascan" Indian from Alaska; Native American roots that Diane identifies with closely. She said, "I consider myself Indian, I look more Indian than white."

Being raised in an all-white community on Long Island in New York was challenging for Diane due to the dark hue of her skin. Although her father married her mother, who obviously was non-white still Diane's childhood memory of her father is that of a racist. "My father belonged to a real racist white country club on Long Island. My mother wasn't welcomed and basically I was told to stay out of the sun." The effect that Diane's racially charged childhood may have had upon her adult decisions may be a dominant factor in why the message of Elijah Muhammad caught her attention. The racial divide in Diane's young life was quite evident. In Diane's mind the racial overtones seems to have extended from her father on down to her siblings.

> My father was a white Irishman. My mother is a dark-skinned Indian. I just so happened to come out dark. I have sisters who came out — they must be whiter than my father was, for God's sake. They just came out really, really white. My oldest sister was like that (white-skinned). Sometimes we'd be out together and nobody would see our parents and then they would say to my older sister, because I was, you know...(dark). "Who is that?" She would make a joke and say, "Oh that is Dede." That is what they called me. "She's adopted."
> Telephone interview

THE MAN BEHIND THE MEN

In the early 1970s Diane heard the message of Elijah Muhammad and subsequently joined the Nation of Islam. Her first curiosity with Islam began with Malcolm X and the Nation of Islam in the 1960s; however, it wasn't until after marrying her African American husband Larry Williams from South Bend, IN that the Nation of Islam came into Diane's life. After moving to California she and her husband were approached by a "couple of Muslim men" who invited them to a meeting.

Before moving to California, Diane had earned a bachelor's degree from Indiana University, but the Nation of Islam connected for Diane what her college education and her other life learning had not achieved. For Diane, Elijah Muhammad's message gave continuity to her thinking. "I had just come out of college. I was well educated and all this different stuff. I knew what oppression and racism was; I had an idea, and the Nation of Islam seemed to just pull it together."

Note the Native American, African and Middle-Eastern dressed men among those called "your people." *Muhammad Speaks* - July 16, 1971.

(Muslim Journal file)

It only took one Nation of Islam meeting and Diane and Larry joined. At the conclusion of her first Nation of Islam meeting she recalled, "It was so clear when they said, 'If you believe what you heard and think it is good for the people, then stand up.' You know, and we just kept standing. It was quite a step to take."

Diane was impressed by the "unique group process in the Nation of Islam. How men and women learned to behave and try to treat each other with respect." She earned the rank of lieutenant in the MGT-GCC (Muslim

NON-AFRICAN AMERICANS INFLUENCED BY ELIJAH MUHAMMAD

Girls Training — General Civilization Class). Diane had to make adjustments to the new way of life that the Nation of Islam offered her. "The racial part was a little bit difficult for me, to be quite honest, but it wasn't real difficult because with everything that they said I could easily agree to. It was just one thing after another; it was easy to agree to."

However returning home to visit her family on the east coast was a bit more challenging. Diane arrived in New York in the Nation of Islam's attire for Muslim women with her hair covered, modestly dressed, completely covered from her head to her toes. "I wore that on the plane." She remembers her family being in a state of shock. "Well they must all have had a heart attack. It was just too much for them all together. My poor dad...he was just silent on it." She acknowledged, "There's just no doubt that that was a challenge. My father is deceased. I have to give him credit for not acting like the really rather racist, you know, conservative Republican that he was."

A close friend of Diane was Nation of Islam member Yolanda Thompson, now known as Yolanda Shuaibe. "I became a close friend to Diane because we both became pregnant at the same time and as a rule, after a sister starts showing she could not attend the temple, due to safety concerns. So that's when Diane and I became close. She gave birth to a little Girl, Sabah in April, 1973 and I gave birth to a girl, Kamilah in June 1973. After that Diane and I shared a lot of time together helping and supporting each other as sisters in the Nation of Islam would do."

Yolanda acknowledged that Diane was an active member of the Oakland, CA Nation of Islam community. Yolanda shared, "As I can remember Diane attended the Muslim Girls Training classes when she was permitted and maybe at times she stood post for the sister check room. I can remember distinctively that she was very quiet and helped out only when she was approached by those sisters that were in charge."

Yolanda said that everyone was conscious that Diane was a non-African American member of the Nation of Islam. "It was common public knowledge among the Nation of Islam membership because she was the only person that had the appearance of a white woman." Diane identified herself as Eskimo. Yolanda added, "I remember her saying that her mother was an Eskimo and her father was European. However, during those times we were always covered so she typically looked European unless she took off her scarf."

At one junction during Diane's tenure in the Nation of Islam her sense of comfort and security was troubled. The Oakland Nation of Islam Mosque membership had accumulated a growing number of non-African Americans, and everyone knew that Diane was Native American. Diane's husband Larry had a bad run-in with the law, and shortly afterwards she and all other non-African Americans were asked to leave the Mosque. "The Honorable Elijah Muhammad basically put me out of the Nation." She explained that he didn't put her out personally, but for a brief period Elijah Muhammad put all non-African Americans out. Diane shared that she received a letter from Elijah Muhammad that said for her to go back to her own community and teach; advice that she now practices in Oakland, CA. "So since that time that's exactly what I've been doing. But what I've been teaching is exactly what I learned in the MGT-GCC in the Nation of Islam."

Before Elijah Muhammad passed Diane and the other non-African Americans were allowed to return to the Mosque in time to attend the 1974 Saviour's Day address in Chicago. She says that she accepts Elijah Muhammad's decision to temporarily excommunicate the non-African American members. Without elaborating Diane defended Elijah Muhammad's decision. "He had a perfectly good reason; when I look back on that time."

Diane Williams of Oakland, CA wearing the traditional Nation of Islam "Star and Crescent" necklace in the early 1970s.
(Courtesy of Diane Williams)

Diane continued her education, earning a master's degree in public health. Yet she still gives the majority of the credit to Elijah Muhammad for having a successful career. "I tell people again, and again, and again that I know what I know not because of anything U.C. Berkeley (University of California at Berkeley) taught me, but because I learned what I learned in the Nation of Islam. I learned it from the sisters who learned it, basically, from Elijah Muhammad — and it worked! It changed a people, who just like my Indian people, had a terrible diet." Diane also noted that, "Still a lot of work needs to be done in the African American community, but Elijah Muhammad was successful in alerting, millions probably, of African American people about pork and leading a healthier life."

NON-AFRICAN AMERICANS
INFLUENCED BY ELIJAH MUHAMMAD

Diane hopes that one day Elijah Muhammad will get the credit he deserves. Very much aware of how the current world of professionalism operates and the reality that most in the professional world are unfamiliar with the excellent work achieved by Elijah Muhammad, Diane acknowledges that the name "Elijah Muhammad is still a 'dirty' word and a 'dirty' name." In the professional world and other sectors of society, there still exists an inaccurate perception of Elijah Muhammad that Diane Williams believes makes it difficult for many former Nation of Islam members to receive the "understanding and respect for the time that we spent in the Nation." She further explained, "In other words, it's not something you put on your resume in the professional world. I'm just saying it like I see it out this way."

Today Diane is not a member of any particular Islamic community, instead she has found solace in Native American traditions and the spiritual message of Native American medicine men; nonetheless, she still considers herself to be Muslim. "I will always be peaceful." She acknowledged, "There are so many things that came to me after my exposure at the Nation of Islam, that if I didn't go through the Nation and clean myself up and learn something about how to eat to live, and have really something of value to share with the people; if I hadn't been put on that path, and if I had chosen to be stuck with that of Christianity, I don't think that I would have been able to hear and understand and accept the real mystical magical teaching of these medicine men that I've been around."

Robert Steed of Rosebud, SD, or Dream Horse, has been the most influential medicine man in her life. In many ways Dream Horse seems to be a surrogate in Diane's life for Elijah Muhammad. Noting striking similarities between Elijah Muhammad and Robert Steed, Diane shared, "Steed was a short man in stature and he was very humble like Elijah Muhammad. He had piercing eyes like Elijah Muhammad. He would tell the truth in a low voice like Elijah Muhammad. He had a lot of the same mannerisms about him."

These non-African Americans influenced by Elijah Muhammad may only be a small portion of the under-reported and overlooked interracial and cross-culture relationships that took root and developed in Elijah Muhammad's Nation of Islam.

These pockets of diversity within the Nation of Islam, not well publicized then or now, surely existed while Mr. W.D. Fard was leader and also throughout the duration of Elijah Muhammad's leadership. As mentioned, the long-time members attending the 1974 Saviour's Day Convention were not surprised when they heard Elijah Muhammad recognize and praise Caucasians, nor when he introduced to the audience the two white Muslims that he called "scientists" who had accompanied him onstage. The influence of Elijah Muhammad, through the non-African American members who had membership in the Nation of Islam, affected a multitude of societies and cultures. This too is a fact that history must recognize and record about the Honorable Elijah Muhammad, the man behind the men.

CHAPTER FIFTEEN

THE IMPORTANCE OF "LAST SERMONS"

The last major address of Elijah Muhammad, held at the 1974 Nation of Islam's Saviour's Day observation concluded his mission with an ironic message that seemed to absolve the white man of guilt for the bad conditions of African American life. In this one speech Elijah Muhammad transferred the onus of responsibility from white America and placed it onto the shoulders of African Americans.

Was Elijah Muhammad implementing a new strategy after 42 years of singling out the "blue-eyed devil" white man as the beast? The question that needs to be answered is why was he now praising this same white man — even to the point of blaming black people for making the white man "the devil"?

W.D. Fard's "Yakub's History," an allegorical theory that offered an explanation of how the "white devil" was genetically engineered by a black scientist named Yakub, was weakened when Elijah Muhammad told his followers that the black man was the blame for the white man's creation. Elijah chided, "He did not make himself. It was our kind that made him. So if you want to make mock of that which you have made, he could easily tell you that 'I am not responsible for my make, you made me yourself, your kind.'"

Was this ironic change in Elijah's message, especially his indemnification of the white man for his 400 years of oppressing and sinning against African Americans, an indication that the Nation of Islam had completed its purpose on earth? Many of Elijah Muhammad's followers and Nation of Islam leaders such as Minister Yusuf Shah of Chicago have shared that they personally heard him say, "When I die, my mission goes to my grave with me." Had the aging 76-year-old Elijah now realized that perhaps his "white man is the devil" message had fulfilled its purpose and outlived its usefulness?

Maybe this last major address was designed to open a way for his son Wallace to succeed him in leadership? Yes, Wallace had differed religiously with his father but that didn't change the fact that Elijah's immediate family and all of the top Nation of Islam officials knew that Wallace, since before his birth, had been favored by Mr. Fard. In Elijah's waning years it seems he was focusing on a way to prepare for his son to begin a new era for the Nation of Islam.

Whatever objective Elijah was pursuing with this racially conciliatory public address, one must believe that he knew that the words delivered at the 1974 Saviour's Day were bringing to a close a mighty chapter in the African American drive for freedom justice and equality. Not only did he

THE IMPORTANCE OF "LAST SERMONS"

obligate his followers to respect the white man and the American flag, Elijah Muhammad also obligated his followers to strive to prove themselves worthy of being called righteous.

It may behoove the historians who study the life and works of Elijah Muhammad to place an equal amount, if not more, attention on his last Saviour's Day address than they place on his 42 years of calling the white man the devil. The final address of any leader summarizes and captures the essence of his or her particular leadership while simultaneously setting the stage for the future leadership that is to succeed them.

A review of other great leaders' "last sermons" reveals similar forethoughts as those seen in Elijah Muhammad's final major address, wherein the outgoing leaders carefully select the words of their final texts, conscious of their historical impact. The preparation and delivery of their last major communication to their followers reveal their concern for setting straight the record regarding their own leadership while they are alive, an act carried out in tandem with opening the door for future leadership and hope for their followers.

The "last sermon" of Muhammed, the 7th century prophet of Islam, specifically addresses the issues of racism, sexism, nationalism and the respective and interactive roles of husband and wife. He began his sermon stating, "O People lend me an attentive ear, for I know not whether after this year I shall ever be amongst you again. Therefore listen to what I am saying very carefully and take these words to those who could not be present here today." After giving details on the key subjects of his sermon, Prophet Muhammed concluded his message by asking his companions, "Have I conveyed the Message of God to you?" The audience answered in one voice, "You have. God is the witness."

The words and topics highlighted by Prophet Muhammed in his last sermon were precise and well selected in order to have the best impact, both contemporarily and for future generations to come. He made his community aware that he had seen his time with them on earth coming to an end, and as with the "last sermon" of all great leaders, Prophet Muhammed was concluding one epoch with words that also were ushering in a new day. The Prophet advised:

> "O People, listen well to my words, for I do not know whether, after this year, I shall ever be amongst you again. Therefore listen to what I am saying to you very carefully and take these words to those who could not be present here today...Remember, one day you will appear before Allah and answer your deeds. So beware, do not stray from the path of righteousness after I am gone...All those who listen to me shall pass on my words to others and those to others again; and may the last ones understand my words better than those who listen to me directly.

THE MAN BEHIND THE MEN

The final sermon of Christ Jesus, commonly referred to as *The Lord's Prayer*, is augmented by the establishment of communion, an act for the remembrance of Jesus after his passing. It is quite apparent that Jesus' words to his disciples were designed to soothe the sorrow they would share upon learning of his departure. As with other great leaders whose going away is imminent, Jesus had to undergo a self-preparation for the impending events, then he embarked upon a similar preparation for the benefit of his followers.

Jesus informed his disciples. "But now I go my way to him that sent me; and none of you asketh me, Whither goest thou? But because I have said these things unto you, sorrow hath filled your heart. Nevertheless I tell you the truth; It is expedient for you that I go away: for if I go not away, the Comforter will not come unto you; but if I depart, I will send him unto you." (John 16: 5-7 KJV)

In Jesus' final communication to his disciples was the closing of one door that concluded his leadership on earth whilst preparing his followers for the Comforter to come and guide them "into all truth." Jesus informed his disciples, "I have yet many things to say unto you, but ye cannot bear them now. Howbeit when he, the Spirit of truth, is come, he will guide you into all truth: for he shall not speak of himself; but whatsoever he shall hear, [that] shall he speak: and he will shew you things to come. He shall glorify me: for he shall receive of mine, and shall shew [it] unto you." (John 16: 12-15 KJV)

Elijah Muhammad was one of history's many leaders who realized and accepted that their role on earth had reached its fulfillment. As shown in Jesus' departing message, the towering challenge that accompanies their "last sermons" is sharing with their followers the promising possibilities of the future without losing the cohesiveness and continuity of their following, or losing ground on the good work they had achieved thus far.

Dr. Martin Luther King's "I've Been to the Mountaintop" speech delivered less than 24 hours before his assassination is another paradigm of how a leader, sensing their imminent demise, finds the best words and spirit that will help preserve the progress of the past while preparing and inspiring future productivity after they have died.

Although ill with a terrible cold, Dr. King delivered his last sermon at Bishop Charles J. Mason Temple on April 3, 1968 before a standing-room-only crowd in Memphis, TN. An excerpt of Dr. King's last sermon taken from *The Autobiography of Dr. Martin Luther King*, edited by Clayborne Carson, states:

> Well, I don't know what will happen now. We've got some difficult days ahead. But it doesn't matter with me now. Because I've been to the mountaintop. And I don't mind. Like anybody, I would like to live a long life. Longevity has its place. But I'm not concerned about that now. I just want to do God's will. And He's allowed me to go up to the mountain. And I've looked over. And

THE IMPORTANCE OF "LAST SERMONS"

> I've seen the promised-land. I may not get there with you. But I want you to know tonight, that we, as a people, will get to the promised-land. And I'm happy, tonight. I'm not worried about anything. I'm not fearing any man. Mine eyes have seen the glory of the coming of the Lord. (365)

Each of these great leaders, envisioning a time soon to come when they no longer would be present amongst their followers, recognized the reality that life will continue on after their death. Discriminating wisely these leaders carefully selected the words of their sensitized "last sermons" as they sought to prepare their communities for their inevitable and seemingly eminent death and the future success of their respective missions. Dr. King's words, "I may not get there with you. But I want you to know tonight, that we, as a people, will get to the promised-land..." was his passing of the mantle of leadership to future generations. He was letting his people know that I'm leaving; but nonetheless, we as a people will be successful.

Elijah Muhammad followed these same footsteps in preparing his Nation of Islam for his inevitable death. As mentioned earlier, Elijah Muhammad's final sermon was a preparatory speech for the new direction he foresaw for the Nation of Islam; a change that he emphatically drove home with positive recognitions of the white man's achievements, while expunging the white man of the devil rhetoric he had levied upon them for 40-plus years. The same white man he formerly blamed as the cause of the oppressive state of black people in America.

It is important that key statements from Elijah Muhammad's last major address be studied in the context in which he spoke. It is obvious he was intentionally presenting a new image of himself that would hopefully benefit his followers and America as a whole. The on stage presence of Caucasian Muslims and his reappraisal of whites, compounded by him underscoring that the white man has "freed you and me to go work for self," are noteworthy changes. Judging from Elijah Muhammad's new tone, apparently in February of 1974, slavery and its ugly aftermath, in his mind, was over and done with.

Another revealing portion of Elijah Muhammad's last sermon that shows without a doubt that a change was in process for the Nation of Islam is his statement, "We want you to know that you are at the setting of the sun... But that sun is rising again." The fact that these words were delivered at Elijah Muhammad's final Saviour's Day seems to suggest that he understood that the sun of his leadership was setting, but a future leadership was on the horizon.

When Elijah Muhammad's statement, "My mission goes to my grave with me," is considered, the importance of his final sermon is greatly magnified. He had reached a point of closure, while yet successfully opening the future for his followers.

-§- CHAPTER -§-
SIXTEEN

An Exodus:
From Slavery to Freedom, Justice and Equality

The Nation of Islam's red colored flag, called "The National."

Pledge to the National Flag of Islam

In the Name of Allah, The Beneficient *[sic]*, The Merciful. Let us give Praise to Allah, our God, for His Love, Mercy, and Blessings upon us in this wilderness, for giving to us a Flag that represents the Universe, the Sun, Moon, adn *[sic]* Stars. It also means that we are Free, Justified, and made Equal of all mankind.

— Elijah Muhammad

In many African American Muslim communities there exists a belief that the turn of the 20th century witnessed many sub-cultural movements operating in northern urban cities. Movements designed for the express purpose of reconnecting African Americans with a lost or stolen Islamic past. The 1913 *Moorish Science Temple of America* is considered the first popular influx of Islamic influence within the African American community. However, due to Marcus Garvey's close association with Duse Muhammad Ali of London, England, some Islamic African American thinkers promote the belief that Marcus Garvey's *Universal Negro Improvement Association (UNIA)* movement, founded in 1914 was another, more subtle effort to reconnect African Americans with their pre-slavery Islamic past. Another Islamic-based group, the Ahmadiyya Muslim Community attracted a limited number of African Americans, but still must be recognized as an important subculture that attracted black people to Islam.

The Nation of Islam was devised upon Mr. W.D. Fard's observing and highlighting the denials of African American's human and civil rights. Religiously, the Nation of Islam's premise included addressing the racial disparity that was rooted in the whiteness of Christianity. These racial overtones often led many African Americans to quietly question the Caucasian images of divinity that were very prevalent in their worship.

Fard's studying of contemporary and historical factors of African American life, especially areas that caused African Americans difficulty, allowed him to create a uniquely black-oriented response that he could peddle to African Americans in hopes that they may acquire a different perspective and resolution that could improve their depressing post-slavery lives. Elijah Muhammad proved himself to be the top student of Mr. Fard when he wholeheartedly purchased Fard's religious package; a blueprint that offered direction in every area of human endeavor whether it be religious, social, educational, or financial. No aspect of human development was off limits in Mr. Fard's plans.

Elijah Muhammad, following the mold of his mentor, re-interpreted and offered new solutions to every concern of African American life in a fashion that conformed to Nation of Islam theology and rhetoric. When Mr. Fard was working the ghettos of Detroit, MI, the whole African American life was in limbo, between shaking off the painful shackles of slavery and trying to find a place in America to carve out a home — and maybe even a citizenship — that would feel comfortable in their souls.

In the ghettos of America, Fard encountered a people who were perplexed by their overall state and condition. What reason or justification existed that explained their plight? Even to this day, in the conscious and subconscious minds of many African Americans there remain burning questions. Why did Europeans enslave Africans? More specifically, what was the state of the European's mind that supported, or allowed them to believe that such cruelty committed by man upon man could be sanctioned by God? What crime did Africans commit that justified their being enslaved in a foreign land? For African Americans, the cursed seed of Noah's son, Ham didn't provide a satisfactory answer as to why Africans were enslaved. Nor had any other rationalizations been offered to African Americans, except maybe avarice, to explain the past cruel system of U.S. chattel slavery.

The early 20th century introductions of Islam to African Americans often spoke of Africans living in refinement in advanced societies as "kings and queens." Sure every African enslaved was not from royalty, but historian John Hope Franklin on page 49 of his book *From Slavery to Freedom* notes that slavers only wanted to enslave the better Africans. Franklin noted:

> The expatriation of millions of Africans in less than four centuries constitutes one of the most far-reaching and drastic social revolutions in the annals of history. It is to be remembered

that the traders would have none but the best available natives. They demanded the healthiest, the largest, the youngest, the ablest, and the most culturally advanced. The vast majority of the slaving was carried on in the area of West Africa, where civilization had reached its highest point on the continent, with the possible exception of Egypt.

Surely the enslaving of Africans wasn't to Christianize them — at least not initially. Slaves were forbidden to read or hold church services unless supervised by a white man. In Julius Lester's book *To Be A Slave*, a former slave name West Turner narrated how the paddyrollers, a posse organized to catch slaves who were secretly attending prohibited slave-led church services, would try to catch them worshipping God. The punishment for this offense was an unmerciful beating with a whip. Turner reported on page 105, "All this was done to keep you from serving God and do you know some of them devils was mean and sinful enough to say, 'If I catch you here servin' God, I'll beat you. You ain't got no time to serve God. We bought you to serve us.'"

W.D. Fard claimed that he came to North America to reconnect African Americans with their Islamic past. Little, if any research has been conducted to substantiate whether Fard's efforts among African Americans was to reunite them with an Islamic past, or was his efforts actually his personal response in opposition to white hegemony in America and in colonies around the world — particularly what many believe to be his homeland, modern-day Pakistan, the former India.

If Fard's working with poor blacks in the ghettoes of Detroit, Chicago and Milwaukee was in fact an attempt to reunite African Americans with an Islamic past, then he may have been responding to the negative Christian dogmas and social norms of the slave era that preferred only the enslavement of non-Christians.

One of Fard's most impacting messages claimed that all African Americans were descendants of Muslims. He went further to state that every enslaved African was Muslim at the time of their capture. History does not substantiate this second claim, but there exists a strong likelihood that every African American, who descends from American slavery, also descends from an Islamic heritage.

For centuries the Church established and maintained doctrines stating that only Muslims and Africans who followed tribal communal worship could be enslaved. *The Ontario Consultants on Religious Tolerance's* website states that from 1452 to 1454 Pope Nicholas V granted to the kings of Spain and Portugal "the right to reduce any *'Saracens [Muslims] and pagans and any other unbelievers'* to perpetual slavery."

AN EXODUS FROM SLAVERY

The practice of enslaving only non-Christians continued with the American slave trade. Two Virginia laws of the 17th century reveal the prevalence of enslaving only non-Christians. Enslaved Africans hopeful of gaining their freedom by converting to Christianity were thwarted by a 1667 Virginia law, Act III, that read: "Whereas some doubts have arisen whether children that are slaves by birth [...] should by virtue of their baptism be made free, it is enacted that baptism does not alter the condition to the person as to his bondage or freedom; masters freed from this doubt may more carefully propagate Christianity by permitting slaves to be admitted to that sacrament."

Other Virginia laws effecting the enslavement of non-Christians continued into the 18th century. Aloyisus Leon Higginbotham's book *Shades of Freedom* notes on page 48 that in 1682 and 1705 enslavement laws were passed that read, respectively:

> It is enacted that all servants [...] which shall be imported into this country either by sea or by land, whether Negroes, Moors [Muslim North Africans], mulattoes or Indians who and whose parentage and native countries are not Christian at the time of their first purchase by some Christian [...] and all Indians, which shall be sold by our neighboring Indians, or any other trafficking with us for slaves, are hereby adjudged, deemed and taken to be slaves to all intents and purposes any law, usage, or custom to the contrary notwithstanding. — 1862

> All servants imported and brought into the Country...who were not Christians in their native Country...shall be accounted and be slaves. All Negro, mulatto and Indian slaves within this dominion...shall be held to be real estate. — 1705

The majority of enslaved Africans came from the western parts of Africa known as the Gold Coast, the Grain Coast and the Ivory Coast. The modern countries that occupy those areas include Ghana, Togo, Benin, Senegal, Guinea, Sierra Leone, Liberia, Nigeria and Angola. Islam and animist religions were the dominant faith traditions of these countries at the advent of the Americas' involvement in the slave trade.

John Hope Franklin also notes in his book *From Slavery to Freedom*, page 26 that the area in Africa where the majority of America's slaves came from had an Islamic presence as early as the 7th century, almost 900 years before Christianity. By the 10th century Islam had become entrenched in West Africa. Franklin wrote, "Also the followers of the Prophet accepted Africans as social equals and gave them an opportunity to enjoy the advantages of education and of cultural advancement that the religion offered. Even as a slave, the black Muslim was considered as a brother."

THE MAN BEHIND THE MEN

African Christianity has two distinct periods. The early church fathers of the first century A.D. who lived in the extreme northern portions of Africa, and the later Sub-Saharan influx of an European version of Christianity that arrived in the 16th-century. Franklin, on page 27 explained that, "In West Africa, where the population was especially dense and from which the great bulk of slaves was secured, Christianity was practically unknown until the Portuguese began to establish missions in the area in the sixteenth century."

Islam had centuries of being established in West Africa when the trans-Atlantic slave trade began, while Christianity was still unknown in this region. Franklin explained that, "It was a strange religion, this Christianity, which taught equality and brotherhood and at the same time introduced on a large scale the practice of tearing people from their homes and transporting them to a distant land to become slaves."

At the January 22, 2006 program titled, "A Service in Honor of the Birthday of the Rev. Dr. Martin Luther King, Jr." that was held at St. Bartholomew's United Church, Hanover, PA, John M. Pawelek shared, "Africans weren't Christians when they first came to America. Of course, they had their own religions. Virginia law in the 1660s stated that it was acceptable for Christians to enslave non-Christians. And when slaves began converting to Christianity, the laws were soon changed to be based on skin color rather than religion. It became legal to enslave someone who had dark skin, Christian or not." (ii)

Historian Albert Raboteau, while stating that "by far the greatest number of those Africans who fell victim to the Atlantic trade came from peoples who held the indigenous and traditional beliefs of their fathers," still Raboteau acknowledges a very strong Islamic presence among the African enslaved in the Americas. In his book *Slave Religion: The "Invisible Institution" in the Antebellum South*, on page 5 Raboteau wrote:

> Among the Africans who became slaves in the Americas were those, such as the Wolof, Serer, Mandinke, Bambara, Fulani, and Hausa, who were Muslim or at least had been influenced by Islam. The ancient kingdoms of Ghana, Mali, and Songhay had been centers of Muslim influence in the western Sudan. South of the Sahara, along the coasts of "Guinea," and through inland kingdoms, people had been exposed to Islam through trade with North African Muslims, through conquest, through colonization, and through conversion. In fact, the first black Africans with whom white Europeans came into contact on the coast of West Africa were "black Moors" (as distinguished from "tawny Moors," i.e., light-skinned Berbers).

The scholarship of Franklin and Raboteau offer support for W.D. Fard Muhammad's claim that African Americans have a great Islamic past. It was through Fard's top student, Elijah Muhammad, that today millions of African American Muslims owe their reconnection to an Islamic identity and religious life. Fard's message — notwithstanding the un-Islamic concepts he interwove into his teachings — is the individual who must be credited with offering a palatable explanation to African Americans that answer why they were forcibly taken from an Islamic past and given a European version of Christianity as a substitute. Fard proposed that Christianity as taught to African Americans was designed to deny them full rights as a human being in order to subjugate them to a life of servitude.

American history shows that even dignified free black men and women, such as the Reverend Richard Allen, founder of the African Methodist Episcopal Church, were treated as second-class church members by white Christians. Even when slavery ended, the religious life of African Americans, at best, was a black man's replication of the religion of the slave's most recent slave master. If the slave master was Baptist then most likely the slave worshipped as a Baptist. The same as many slaves adopted the slave master's surname, likewise, freed slaves most often adopted the religious and social fabric of their former slave masters.

The Christianization of slaves was an afterthought and of less importance to the slave owner's interest in financial gain and dominance. A review of the American slave trade, especially in the eyes of African Americans, shows a system of slave owners who seemed more interested in dehumanizing a whole race of people, rather than trying to elevate the well being of the slave.

Elijah Muhammad, heeding the teachings of W.D. Fard, strongly promoted that Christianity — in particular the Christianity taught by European Americans — was not the natural religion of African Americans, a premise supported by Virginia law and the overall historical attitude of white Christians towards the enslavement of Africans, namely non-Christian Africans.

With the negative energies of past slavery and the Jim Crow laws of his generation in full force, Elijah Muhammad penned in his book *Our Saviour has Arrived* on page 156, "You must remember and never forget that the white Christian race made slaves of our fathers and will not allow you now to rise above the status of a free slave!" Later in this same publication on page 185 Elijah wrote, "They separated us from our Original People of Asia and Africa in order to do a thorough job of making us other than ourselves, the Original Black Man."

When Elijah Muhammad met Mr. Fard the enduring question of why Africans had unjustly been reduced to slaves remained unanswered. For many former slaves and their descendants any attempt to quantify and understand why their race had been put in such a plight was overbearing.

THE MAN BEHIND THE MEN

Even some African American leaders wanted to put the history of the cruel institution of slavery behind them without investigating the harmful effects that may have lingered from centuries of abuse. Elijah Muhammad was one of the African American leaders who preferred to place emphasis on the cruelty of past slave history as a means to remind African Americans of their current predicament and future obligations. Elijah dissected slavery and its ills, associating its pain with the daily ghetto life of African Americans, in a way that led one to conclude that nothing had changed for African Americans — mentally you are still existing as captured slaves.

Capitalizing upon the efforts of leaders such as W.E.B. DuBois, Booker T. Washington and Marcus Garvey, Elijah Muhammad continued to address how slavery produced a deep yearning within the African American soul for dignity as a race, and independence from waiting on white Americans to fulfill their basic needs. Elijah Muhammad believed that in order for African Americans to reconcile themselves with the essentials of life that would give them independence, an exodus, more mental than physical, was necessary.

In August of 1920 in Harlem, NY, ten years before Elijah first met Mr. W.D. Fard, Marcus Garvey's *Universal Negro Improvement Association* (UNIA) and his African Communities League (ACL) had ratified in convention "The Declaration of Rights of the Negro Peoples of the World." Garvey's convention inaugurated him the "Provisional President of Africa" in addition to presenting many nationalistic proposals, including that the Negro colors be red, black and green, thus a flag. The convention also introduced the *Universal Ethiopian Anthem*.

The preamble of "The Declaration of Rights of the Negro Peoples of the World" stated:

> Be it Resolved, That the Negro people of the world, through their chosen representatives in convention assembled in Liberty Hall, in the City of New York and United States of America, from August 1 to August 31, in the year of our Lord, one thousand nine hundred and twenty, protest against the wrongs and injustices they are suffering at the hands of their white brethren, and state what they deem their fair and just rights, as well as the treatment they propose to demand of all men in the future.

Garvey's 1925 deportation from the United States of America, after serving a short sentence in federal prison for mail fraud, created a void in the African American community for a major black consciousness movement. Elijah stepped in to fill that void with a bold call for complete independence, a message that resonated with many who had heard the voice of Garvey and his "Back to Africa" message.

AN EXODUS FROM SLAVERY

As noted in Robert C. Smith's book *We Have No Leaders: African Americans in the Post-Civil Rights Era*, by the late 1930s Elijah stood alone in calling for an African American independence. Speaking on the Nation of Islam's contributions to Black Nationalism, Smith wrote, "The Nation was also responsible for helping to foster among blacks a sense of race pride and for keeping the ideology of Black Nationalism alive." Smith further argues, "Indeed, the Nation of Islam represents the largest nationalist formation since Garvey's *Universal Negro Improvement Association* of the 1920s." (100)

The Nation of Islam's call for black independence was a form of exodus that Elijah Muhammad used to get the attention of all African Americans. Elijah's approach for achieving black independence often stimulated in many African Americans a new sense of nationhood as well as a love and reverence for him.

DuBois in his book *The Souls of Black Folk* supported the idea that there was a need for a sabbatical styled exodus in which African Americans should isolate themselves for self-improvement and renewal. Recounting the impoverished and ignorant state of the slave, DuBois wrote:

> Nor was his burden all poverty and ignorance. The red stain of bastardy, which two centuries of systematic legal defilement of Negro women had stamped upon his race, meant not only the loss of ancient African chastity, but also the hereditary weight of a mass of corruption from white adulterers, threatening almost the obliteration of the Negro home. A people thus handicapped ought not to be asked to race with the world, but rather allowed to give all its time and thought to its own social problems. (12)

The Nation of Islam was successful in creating that environment described by DuBois by becoming a "nation within a nation." The Nation of Islam became an identifiable "nation" within the larger nation of the United States of America. Elijah Muhammad's Islamic community served as a womb, or an isolated place for development in which African America could retreat and "give all its time and thought to its own social problems."

The Nation of Islam was that isolated and insolated nation, a "womb" that sheltered and protected the development of its babe from outer influences, while providing the new life a place for independent growth and nourishment. The Nation of Islam welcomed all African Americans who were seeking an exodus from their negative situations — only returning to intermingle with the general American society after having the needs of the total African American life addressed. This domesticated styled exodus is evidenced by Elijah Muhammad himself. During his January 14,

1972 interview to an assembly of 16 news reporters who had gathered at his home he said, "I do not mean to say they go out of America, but out of the evil of America."

In 1965, 32 years into his leadership, Elijah released a compilation of his articles in a book titled "*Message to the Blackman in America*," in which he addressed the African American need for independence and ownership of land. He wrote, "In order to build a nation you must first have some land. From our first generation of slaves to the present generation of our people, we have been unable to unite and acquire some land of our own due to the mental poisoning of our former slave masters, who destroyed in us the desire to think and do for self and kind."

(Muslim Journal file)

Elijah Muhammad often spoke of African Americans having their own states, "...some land that we can call our own." Elijah Muhammad's newspaper, *Muhammad Speaks*, carried in every issue a list of *What The Muslims Want*. Number four on that list reads as follows:

> 4. We want our people in America whose parents or grandparents are descendents from slaves to be allowed to establish a separate state or territory of their own, either on this continent

or elsewhere. We believe that our former slave masters are obligated to provide such land and that the area must be fertile and minerally rich. We believe that our former slave masters are obligated to maintain and supply our needs in this separate territory for the next 20 or 25 years, until we are able to produce and supply our own needs.

Since we cannot get along with them in peace and equality after giving them 400 years of our sweat and blood and receiving in return some of the worse treatment human beings have ever experienced, we believe our contributions to this land and the suffering forced upon us by white America justifies our demand for complete separation in a state or territory of our own.

Elijah's request, whether symbolic or literal, created an aspiration in the minds of his followers for a separate environment where the goals opined by DuBois could be fulfilled. It is clear that in Elijah Muhammad's thinking separation was necessary in order to provide an environment where an independent African American thinking could be cultivated.

It is quite evident that Elijah Muhammad never expected white people to physically give him and his followers any of the states of the United States of America. He was well aware that one of the main reasons for the U.S. Civil war was to deny secession by white Americans who lived in southern states; therefore, surely that same government would not allow descendants of former slaves secession to live on their own in separate states.

The U.S. government did support the 1815 African American exodus that was led by Paul Cuffee, an African American maritime entrepreneur who promoted that Africa was more conducive for African Americans to "rise to be a people." The 1815 establishment, that later was renamed Liberia, "the land of the free" on the west coast of Africa, had already served as an earlier attempt to fulfill African American's request for separate land.

However, the Liberian model of an independent African American homeland may not have sated Elijah Muhammad's proposed plans for a separate land for a variety of reasons. Liberia began as a new African community that actually was an American colony. The former African American slaves who settled into Liberia were called "Americo-Liberians"; immigrants who imported the mentality of their American slave masters. At best Liberia was a black microcosm of white America, even to the point of the establishment of an elite class enjoyed by the African Americans over the indigenous Africans of the region.

When Liberia gained her independence in 1847 the indigenous Africans living in Liberia had to endure labor abuse from the hands of the Americo-Liberians; former black Americans who seemed to have quickly forgotten that they too were recent recipients of abuse as laboring slaves in America. The African Americans who settled in Liberia were aristocratic to the point of denying the indigenous Africans in Liberia suffrage rights until 1946.

In 1819, two years after Cuffee's death, the United States committed $100,000 dollars to this colonization experiment; however, the investment yielded little successful results. Cuffee's desire to see African Americans "rise to be a people" on African soil did not come to fruition. Cuffee's efforts were not in line with Elijah Muhammad's ideal for acquiring land to establish a free black homeland. Elijah's aspiration was for a mental and spiritual liberation and exodus.

Within the borders of the United States of America there are other examples of mass movements of African American exoduses; mainly southern blacks seeking to improve their living conditions by migrating to escape poverty and racism in search of better employment opportunities, secure living environments, and to obtain better educational opportunities for their children.

The 1879 African American exodus to Kansas was stimulated by the failure of the post-civil war Reconstruction era which carried the fear of a return of chattel slavery in the former Conferate states. Thereafter each successive mass exodus migrations of African Americans (with the exception of movements caused by natural disasters such as the Great Mississippi Flood of 1927 or Hurricane Katrina in September of 2005) were fired by a deep burning need within the African American soul to express their God-given potentials in an environment that was free of racism and social deprivation.

The largest exodus of African Americans occurred over a 60-year period that includes the two Great Migrations from 1910 to 1970; mass movements of approximately 7 million Southern blacks to California and Northeast and Midwest cities such as New York, Philadelphia, Detroit and Chicago, with many migrants finding a sense of refuge and jobs in midsize cities along their treks from the South. No matter where African Americans physically migrated they still faced the harsh reality that the America of that generation was strategically designed to oppress African Americans in favor of uplifting European-Americans.

Elijah and his family were part of that Great Migration. As with many African Americans he too discovered that his physical exodus from Georgia to Detroit, MI yielded for him and his family no sustainable progress, especially during the Great Depression of 1929. It was only after meeting Mr. W.D. Fard that Elijah was given the Nation of Islam, albeit a mental and spiritual place, where he and later hundreds of thousands of other African Americans could enter into a "Promised Land;" a spiritual and mental exodus away from the racism of white America.

AN EXODUS FROM SLAVERY

Elijah Muhammad's requesting physical land was a strategy to stimulate and nourish a mental exodus in which African Americans could purge themselves of the stigma of being a mere "Negro" in America. It is important to note that he made the physical acquisition of land a prerequisite for African Americans demanding human rights. "The Blackman has been actually worthless when it comes to exercising the rights as human beings in an ever-advancing civilization," chided Elijah Muhammad. "So remember, we cannot demand recognition until we have some land that we can call our own."

With or without ownership of physical land Elijah still wanted his people to think independently of the white man. Elijah Muhammad knew that the physical separation from white America would never occur, but he understood that by repeatedly asking for separate land he would be successful in stimulating a type of mental and spiritual exodus in the psyche of his followers that could help to shield them from some of the blatant racism that existed in America during that era.

Juxtaposed to the Civil Rights Movement's methods for dealing with racism, the Nation of Islam initiated a mental exodus away from white America, providing its members an alternative to, and even a deeper purging of, the evil effects of racism. Rather than seeking validation from white America the Nation of Islam opted instead to abandon white America.

Elijah Muhammad's form of Islam was structured to mentally and spiritually remove his followers from the dominating value system of white America. To accomplish this task Elijah created within his message to black America, a road map charted to lead the minds of black folks out of the "wilderness of North America."

Historical religious writings provided Elijah Muhammad with many models of how to complete an exodus. The scriptures of Jews, Christians, and Muslims are full of reports of the righteous opting for migration as a means to escape oppression. In the Old Testament Abraham left Ur, his place of birth, and Moses led the Israelites on a major exodus from Egypt to Canaan. In the New Testament the parents of Christ Jesus, Joseph and Mary, made their exodus from Bethlehem to Egypt. In the Qur'an, Muhammed the Prophet made his exodus, also called *Hegira*, from Mecca to Medina. These scriptural reports of people leaving a debilitating situation in search of favorable conditions did not escape the attention of Elijah Muhammad. But it was Moses' biblical exodus that seemed to appeal most to Elijah Muhammad.

Another distinction between Elijah Muhammad and other African American efforts for human and civil rights is evident in their different appeals to white America. In one popular Negro spiritual "Let My People Go," the followers of the Civil Rights Movement seemed to be expecting relief and equality to come from the same racist who was oppressing them. The method of Elijah Muhammad, while also recognizing white racial oppression against African Americans as a Pharaoh prototype, went one step further. Rather than appeal to or beg the oppressor for equality, Elijah refused to solicit "Pharaoh's good side" or even demand that this Pharaoh "let my people go." Instead Elijah's technique for escaping "Pharaoh" was simple; he encouraged African Americans to totally abandon "Pharaoh" and his way of life. Don't ask Pharaoh to let you go — just leave and never look back.

In the eyes of Elijah Muhammad every biblical story was interpreted in a way which explained the condition of African Americans and their promised success against their oppressors. It is important to note that even though Elijah Muhammad taught that Islam is the natural religion for African Americans, the vast majority of his teachings, as exemplified by the Pharaoh story, were based on biblical teachings, not Qur'anic instructions. His reason for placing more emphasis on biblical stories over Qur'anic scriptures is that African Americans were "mentally dead," with their minds buried in misunderstandings and errant Eurocentric hegemonic interpretations of biblical scriptures. That spiritual diet, Elijah Muhammad believed, supported Caucasian domination and African American inferiority.

In his book *The Supreme Wisdom* on page 13, Elijah Muhammad refers to the Bible as being a "graveyard." He wanted to resurrect and lead his people on an exodus out of this mental cemetery of scriptural darkness. He wrote:

> The Bible is the graveyard of my poor people (the so-called Negroes) and I would like to dwell upon it until I am sure that they understand that it is not quite as holy as they first thought it was. I don't mean to say that there is no truth in it. Certainly, plenty of truth, *if understood*. Will you (the so-called Negroes) accept the understanding of it?

The vast majority of other African American religious groups and social organizations did not connect the condition of their members' lives with a belief that the Bible was a specifically designed blueprint — "if understood" — of their historical journey and their future African American life.

African American scholars such as Dr. Howard Thurman made biblical connections in his book *Jesus and the Disinherited* that struck parallels with the African American struggle; however, it seems that Thurman's message found more expression in seminaries among intellectuals. Elijah opted for a more direct grassroots approach and connection.

Without hesitation Elijah Muhammad openly declared a divine status for himself, "the Messenger of Allah," to support his religious interpretations. In the eyes of his followers and admirers this divine assertion not only elevated the status of Elijah and offered an affirmation for his interpretations; this special title also served as an encouragement to his followers in their belief and their willingness to take a bigger step and think independently of white America. In the minds of Elijah Muhammad's followers when "The Messenger" spoke it was as if God Himself was speaking. Therefore, whatever interpretations Elijah Muhammad rendered to bible stories, in the minds of his followers and many admirers he was speaking 100 percent truth. He told his followers, "Everything written in the Bible is written to give us a picture of what is happening today."

To complete the mental and spiritual exodus of black Americans the stories of Lazarus, the Prodigal Son, the Children of Israel as "Lost Sheep," and other biblical stories, were studied and taught as if these parables were specifically foretelling the life of black people in America. Often after hearing Elijah Muhammad's interpretations of these scriptural reports members of the Nation of Islam would claim, "Yeah Brother, that verse is talking about us, the black man in America."

In many of his writings Elijah Muhammad equated the name Jesus with one of Captain John Hawkins' slave ships that reportedly was named, "The Good Ship Jesus." The actual name of this slave ship was Jesus of Lubeck. This particular slave ship, in the language of Elijah Muhammad, explained why African Americans were waiting so dearly for the return of "Jesus;" not the expectant return of the typical white-skinned representation of Jesus to take them to heaven, but instead the return of the "Good Ship Jesus" to take them home to Africa.

Elijah Muhammad received from Fard interpretations of many biblical verses that were designed to give specific significance to Nation of Islam members. In the October 20, 1956 issue of the *Pittsburgh Courier* Elijah Muhammad wrote that the 144,000 mentioned in the Bible who are promised a protecting grace in the book of Revelations, chapter 7, verse 4, represented "the first (Negro) converts" to Islam.

Similarly, according to the Nation of Islam tenets all evil biblical characters were paralleled or analogous to white people, especially white Americans. Such biblical exegesis gave the members of the Nation of Islam a belief that God had sanctioned their movement over and above other African American movements that did not seek to support themselves, or the personal lives of their members, with interpretations of the Bible that paralleled their struggles.

As the students of Elijah Muhammad baptized their minds with his methodology of life and religion, it allowed them a path away from the typical African American life into a new life that the Nation of Islam called coming into "your own." It is due to Elijah Muhammad's unorthodox approach to scripture and life that the lives of many downtrodden African Americans

THE MAN BEHIND THE MEN

— Muslims and non-Muslims — had an opportunity to blossom into new ways of thinking, and to entertain opportunities to become productive individuals and respected leaders.

Most exoduses that we read of in history serve as temporary wombs of development, as was the case with Elijah Muhammad. While away on the exodus (in this temporary womb), the formerly oppressed person must be recreated into a stronger creation that has, as a minimum, developed to a level equal to that of their former oppressors. The best way to prove that the purpose of the exodus has met its intended objective is to have the former victim, who was once dependent on a particular society, to return to that same society from which they were self-deposed. Their return is as a resolved, independent and focused individual who is now reestablished and able to navigate that society.

It was a well developed Prophet Muhammed who returned to Mecca after completing his exodus. Christ Jesus victoriously returned to Jerusalem riding on a donkey to be received by the people who paved his return with palm leaves. Moses returned and overcame the power of Pharaoh. The purpose of any exodus — whether big or small, mental or physical — is not only to exit the environment, but also to return to the same society that treated them as a reject, now able to demonstrate the ability to face their former oppressor while earning the respect that they and their people are long due.

Elijah Muhammad led thousands of people on a mental and spiritual exodus out of the "wilderness of North America" before returning them to America as dignified and independent men and women; a rare, if not unique achievement for most African Americans. His following, by and large, was constituted of poor people who had very little sense of industry, pride, strong family life or hope. However, when they returned to their neighborhoods and former environs as members of the Nation of Islam — accepted or rejected — everyone knew that this person had made an exodus from an old lifestyle into a new way of living. These descendants of slaves had completed Elijah Muhammad's exodus out of one America and had returned as a new people — to a new America.

-§- CHAPTER -§-
SEVENTEEN

Elijah Muhammad on Salat (Islamic Prayer)

The Islamic prayer performed five times daily by Muslims worldwide was not a regular practice of the Nation of Islam during the lifetime of Elijah Muhammad. Few, if any members knew the words and ritual of the Islamic prayer called *salat* in the Arabic language. Malcolm was embarrassed by, and with a hint of resentment, noted this fact in his autobiography. Recalling his April 1964 hajj (pilgrimage to Mecca) experience in which he was led in prayer by a young Muslim guide, Malcolm wrote, "With gestures, he indicated that he would demonstrate to me the proper prayer ritual postures. Imagine, being a Muslim minister, a leader in Elijah Muhammad's Nation of Islam, and not knowing the prayer ritual." (333) Further expressing frustration with his inability to pray as the other Muslims on hajj prayed, Malcolm wrote, "I was angry with myself for not having taken the time to learn more of the orthodox prayer rituals before leaving America. In Elijah Muhammad's Nation of Islam, we hadn't prayed in Arabic." (335)

One easily can understand Malcolm's frustration with his ignorance of not knowing the Islamic prayer in Arabic. But Malcolm not knowing the rituals of the orthodox Islamic prayer cannot be blamed on Elijah Muhammad. As the National Spokesman for the Nation of Islam, the second in command, it is reasonable to assume that in 1964 Malcolm knew that on February 26, 1957, at the annual Nation of Islam's Saviour's Day, that Elijah Muhammad released, albeit in English, a 24 page Islamic prayer booklet titled *Muslim Daily Prayers*.

In that same year Elijah Muhammad also released another book, *The Supreme Wisdom*, in which Malcolm wrote the preface. This publication that Malcolm was involved in producing with Elijah Muhammad had more than two pages on the orthodox Islamic prayer. He taught that "Muslims pray five times a day, not once a week or once a year." He further instructed his followers on the cleansing steps of the ablution that the Muslim completes before he steps "on his prayer rug or mat, and faces toward the ONLY HOLY SPOT on our planet — the Holy City of Mecca" (45). How could Malcolm have written the preface for this booklet yet claim in 1964, "I was angry with myself for not having taken the time to learn more of the orthodox prayer rituals"?

Also, in Elijah Muhammad's book *Muslim Daily Prayers*, he describes the Islamic prayer according to the tradition of Prophet Muhammed of Arabia. Not only did this prayer book include the times of the five daily prayers, it mentioned the *sunnah* prayers, also called the additional supererogatory prayers, that accompany the five daily obligatory prayers.

Page five of the *Muslim Daily Prayers* displayed the opening chapter of the Qur'an in Arabic script. The remainder of this prayer book describes the objective of the Islamic prayer, as well as the preparation and significance of the Islamic ablution and the importance of and proper responses to the *adhan*, the Islamic call to prayer.

Maybe in Malcolm's zealousness and the countless hours he expended in building up the Nation of Islam he was distracted from learning the basics of the Islamic prayer. That doesn't change the fact that Elijah Muhammad had made available an English version of how to perform the Islamic prayer. The prayer book produced by Elijah Muhammad included the steps of making ablution, as well as lessons on the physical positions of bowing, sitting and prostrating in the exact same manner that Malcolm's young guide was demonstrating for him by way of gestures.

The foreword of Elijah Muhammad's *Muslim Daily Prayers* states:

> Here, my beloved people who Believe, is the Book of Muslim Daily Prayers I had promised some time ago to make available to you. Allah, your God and mine, says in the Holy Qur'an Sharrief (29:45): "Surely prayer keeps (one) away from indecency and evil; and certainly the remembrance of Allah is the greatest (force that restrains evil.)" The knowledge and practice of these prayers will earn you great reward with Allah and bring about great spiritual advancement in you.
>
> These prayers, of course, are only a part of your duties as Muslims and as Believers in Allah and His Messenger Muhammad [sic] Keep up your prayers, but be mindful of your Duties as well. Be completely RIGHTEOUS. At present it is sufficient that you learn these prayers as we have printed them here. Some day in the near future, however, you will learn them in your own language and that of your Righteous fore-parents – Arabic.
>
> May Allah bless you and keep you on the Right Path.
>
>   ELIJAH MUHAMMAD

It is important to note that even though Elijah Muhammad's prayer book was teaching the Islamic prayer only in English, it is clear from his foreword that he intended for his Nation of Islam to one day pray as all Muslims pray worldwide. These prayers not only were to be learned in English, but "in the near future" his followers would learn these prayers in Arabic, the language of their "righteous fore-parents."

Why Malcolm, and surely other officials of the Nation of Islam, had not learned and practiced the prayers as offered by Elijah Muhammad can best be answered only by those individuals. One speculation is that Elijah Muhammad, himself, may have retreated from further promoting the practice of salat, Islam's prayer that is performed five times every day, in favor of encouraging his followers to pursue the amassing of land, property, and businesses — attainable material goals that he felt poor people needed more, at that time, over spiritual advancements.

ELIJAH MUHAMMAD ON SALAT - THE ISLAMIC PRAYER

Some have theorized that if Elijah Muhammad had put too much emphasis on praying in the style and manner as observed by all Muslims worldwide, that his followers — whom he often described as a "baby nation" — may have begun to adopt and imitate Arab and Middle Eastern customs and cultures that would result in him and his followers not giving the diligence due to resurrecting the black man and woman of America.

Regardless of which of these speculations one may be inclined to accept as a reason why five prayers a day were not popular in the Nation of Islam, one thing is known for sure: that Elijah Muhammad in 1957 made available a book that discussed fully the proper way that Muslims worldwide perform prayer five times daily.

Elijah Muhammad was a balanced leader who was interested in the total human makeup of his followers. "Be completely righteous," he said. The popular image of him is that of a man who did not give attention to prayer and other areas of spiritual development. Maybe to a degree this perception is true in light of his statement, "I am not here to teach you Islam..." Nonetheless, Elijah Muhammad was carefully preparing his followers for the time when Islam, in its fullness, would come to the community he called the Nation of Islam.

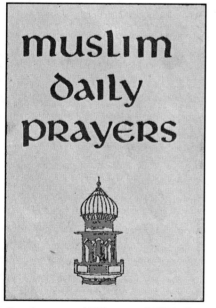 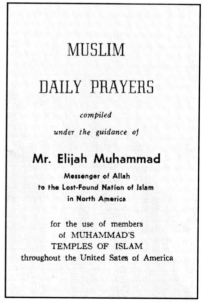

Front cover and title page of Elijah Muhammad's 1957 book *Muslim Daily Prayers*

-§- CHAPTER -§-
EIGHTEEN

Elijah Muhammad
A Man of Non-Violence

"Not one of us will have to raise a sword. Not one gun would we need to fire. The great cannon that will be fired is our unity."
— ELIJAH MUHAMMAD

The historical reports, as they have been compiled to date, have forced the legacy of Elijah Muhammad into a biased depiction of only a man of hatred and violence. A review of his many lectures, books, and his public and private discourse do not support that mischaracterization. Students of history must follow the fair standards of research to accurately determine whether Elijah Muhammad taught hatred of white people, the sector of society that for the majority of his 42-year mission he publicly condemned as "devils."

Elijah Muhammad's offensive description of the racial and social shortcomings of white people as "devils" doesn't necessarily equate to hatred of them. When he was known as Elijah Poole, he was a very dissatisfied African American, the archetype "angry young man" disturbed by the myriad economic, political, and religious injustices and disparities that had resulted in him and his people being America's super-underclass — a "so-called Negro."

The strategy that Mr. W.D. Fard offered for uplifting the black man and for addressing America's racial illness and subjective class-consciousness, was a plan wholeheartedly accepted by Elijah. Fard's approach was highly controversial and aggressive; nonetheless, it was a nonviolent response to many of the problems that every African American faced to one degree or another. The highly rhetorical but nonviolent approach that Fard gave to Elijah Muhammad was a tactful strategy for struggling against white rule and African American despondency.

A clear example of that non-violent strategy is given in the book *Elijah Muhammad Meets the Press*; a transcript of a January 14, 1972 interview wherein a reporter asked Elijah Muhammad. "You do not feel that members of the Nation of Islam will have to take up guns?" Elijah responded:

> No, they would not have to do that, if they obey Allah, anymore than, I would say, Moses and Aaron had to take up arms against Pharaoh. You have been fighting us with guns and what not ever since John Hawkins brought us here, over four hundred years ago. We have to find something more effective and the most effective are the forces of nature. (26)

ELIJAH MUHAMMAD A MAN OF NON-VIOLENCE

Oppression upon any human being is like the load placed upon a depressed coiled spring. If the pressure pushing down on the spring is ever triggered, upon its release the spring will uncoil according to the degree or intensity with which it has been depressed. Elijah Poole was a loaded spring that had been depressed mentally, spiritually and physically. When Mr. Fard gave Elijah a methodology that enabled him to release himself from his depressed state of inferiority, Fard triggered and released the tense recoiled human aspirations of an oppressed black man. Fard knew — and time has proven him to be right — that the dissatisfied, frustrated and oppressed spirit of Elijah Poole, once it was triggered, had the potential to uncoil with such velocity that within a few decades it would have a profound affect upon all of black America. That affect, personified in Elijah Muhammad, eventually would resonate around the whole world.

Elijah Muhammad was not the author or originator of his oppressed condition, nor was he the originator of his road to freedom. To the extent that he despised his unearned oppression, to an even higher magnitude Elijah loved the freedom that he inherited from the man he now accepted as his new-found *Saviour*, W.D. Fard.

Elijah Muhammad's deep appreciation for Fard manifested itself in an unquestionable dedication that was reciprocated by Fard. Elijah didn't question Fard's teachings or his claim of being a divine savior, and Fard didn't doubt Elijah's fidelity. This union of Elijah and Fard during the Great Depression resulted in the dawn of America's first major, public Islamic presence.

Fard detected in Elijah Muhammad two desirable qualities: naivety and courage. Elijah was naïve to world history and events, yet courageous enough to boldly repeat to the world whatever Fard taught him. In *Elijah Muhammad Meets the Press* Elijah Muhammad stated, "It was Him (Fard) that I have learned all that I am now teaching. I do not know anything of myself. It is what He Has Given *[sic]* me." (12)

Elijah Muhammad's meager Deep South education and his socially oppressive life had left him vulnerable to everything that Fard offered. To Elijah all that Fard taught him was good as gold. Fard inflated the ego of the uneducated men and women who joined his Temple of Islam. Until Fard "disappeared" in 1933 he fed stories of black greatness to poor ghetto inhabitants, even teaching them that the black man was god.

In 1933 Elijah Muhammad became the faithful caretaker of Fard's creation. It was only after Elijah went to prison, and later traveled to the Middle East, that he was able to begin to question Fard's teachings in ways that allowed him to see Fard in a more human and less divine context. It was Elijah's post 1933 life experiences that gave him other perspectives of Fard's purpose, thus providing him with a better appreciation of Fard's role in uplifting black Americans.

In the late 1920s and for decades thereafter, America was caught off guard by the aggressive and angry young African Americans that Fard had created. The burden upon white people of publicly being classified as a race of devils must have been daunting, especially for the non-racist white person. Nonetheless, Elijah's voice was unrelenting and in many sectors of the African American community his white devil message found acceptance. The easy way out, particularly for the whites really guilty of blatant racism and class-ism, was to try assassinating Elijah's character or charging him with teaching hate, even if the unfounded charges resulted in Elijah appearing deceitful and complicit in murder and violence.

While facing those unproven charges Elijah Muhammad never yielded from describing white hegemony as the enemy of black people, but as previously stated, in the later years of his mission he significantly decreased the language that indiscriminately condemned all white people to devilry. As mentioned, Elijah's charge of devilry was not a sign of hatred in him. Instead, the "white devil" concept was Elijah's and Fard's encapsulation of the collective historical mistreatment received by the descendents of Africa from the hands of the descendents of Europe. A conclusion reached by other pre-Nation of Islam African American leaders, due to their own oppressive state, gave similar descriptions of white devilry to describe the treatment they had received from the evil white people of their respective eras.

Elijah Muhammad was perplexed by the strong dissatisfaction among African Americans with the way that God had created them, yet hankering to be like those who were mistreating them. In his mind the conduct of the depraved white Americans toward African Americans was repulsive to the point that he asked, why and how black Americans could "love an open enemy?"

In his book *Message to the Blackman* Elijah noted this strong multi-generational dislike of even resembling the children of Africa. He wrote, "One of the gravest handicaps among the so-called Negroes is that there is no love for self, nor love for his or her own kind." Elijah charged that this lack of self-love is the root cause of many problems in the African American community including "fighting and killing one another."

Elijah's determination to get black men and women to love themselves does not constitute hatred. Additionally, encouraging his followers — and African Americans in general — to see those who mistreated them as their enemy, is not teaching hate but common sense. Any intelligent human being who was attacked or mistreated as African Americans of that era were, would view the perpetrator of such inhumane treatment as an enemy, not as a friend. It was abuse of human rights that gave birth to the United States of America as evidenced in this excerpt from the Declaration of Independence: *"But when a long train of abuses and usurpations, pursuing invariably the same object evinces a design to reduce them under absolute despotism, it is their right, it is their duty, to throw off such government, and to provide new guards for their future security."*

ELIJAH MUHAMMAD A MAN OF NON-VIOLENCE

Elijah Muhammad's teaching blacks to love themselves above loving others, and his wonderment that African Americans insisted on showing love for people who regularly mistreated them, are two qualities often used as support by those who claim that Elijah Muhammad was teaching hate. A closer review will reveal that Elijah was not teaching hate as much as he was emphasizing the love of self to downtrodden black folks at the expense of disturbing the white status quo. Never did he teach his followers to hate any person because of their race, nor did he ever teach or promote violence.

Elijah's followers were forbidden to be the aggressors in speech or physical contact. But he did teach self-defense against those who were harmfully aggressive. He taught his followers to retaliate only to the degree of the attacker's aggression. Fard's use of African American men to build his pseudo-army — the *Fruit of Islam* — commonly referred to as the "Fruit," was his preparing of black men to mentally battle the ills black Americans suffered. Even though the "Fruit" learned judo and marched and drilled, obviously their training was not preparation for physical war because these "soldiers" were forbidden by Elijah to carry weapons, even a pen-knife.

To this day Elijah Muhammad and his Nation of Islam are antithetically compared to Dr. Martin Luther King and the Civil Rights Movement. Most historians have oversimplified the terms by always dubbing Elijah as the hater and Martin as the lover. Yet there exists important compatibilities between Elijah Muhammad and Martin Luther King that offer students of history more than the mundane passive Martin verses the aggressive Elijah.

Of course the striking difference between Elijah Muhammad and Martin Luther King is seen in their divergent approaches to obtaining equal rights, and in their public responses to the mistreatment that black people were enduring from the American white social order. But the commonalities between these two great leaders include both men turning to ideologies outside of white America for strategies and strength in their respective struggles for the advancement and improvement of the quality of life for African Americans.

Elijah turned to the foreigner Mr. W.D. Fard, a Muslim from India, or what is now present day Pakistan; Dr. King turned to the philosophy of a foreigner also from India, Mohandas Gandhi a Hindu. Both Fard and Gandhi, the authors of divergent philosophies, were concerned with eliminating the abusive colonizing by British — the progenitor of America — who were occupying India. It was an immature America that allowed African Americans to be mistreated — reduced almost to the level of field animals — that created in both Elijah and Martin their openness to seeking solutions for racial injustice; solutions that were totally outside of the control and influence of white America.

THE MAN BEHIND THE MEN

Beneath their external presentations, in some interesting ways Elijah and Martin, both Georgia-bred boys, were two peas in a pod who were expressing their efforts for justice in "good cop – bad cop" fashion. While one cop appears to be genial and understanding of the suspect's plight, the other cop presents himself to the suspect in an accusatory and aggressive manner. Regardless of their diverse styles, the ultimate goal of both cops is to arrive at justice for the victim and due punishment for the criminal. The combined strategies of both Elijah and Martin constitues the good cop-bad cop scenario. Both leaders were applying a strategy for justice, but coming from two extremes that were working for the same results — justice for the downtrodden African American.

Elijah Muhammad was a personal understudy of Wallace (W.D.) Fard. Although King never personally met Mahatma Gandhi, who passed in 1948; nonetheless, King was influenced by Dr. Howard Thurman, a classmate of Martin's father "Daddy King" while at Morehouse College. In 1935-36 Thurman led a delegation of African Americans to meet Gandhi, who challenged Thurman to rethink Christianity in ways to facilitate overcoming white racism. Upon his return to the United States Thurman shared Gandhi's message with his many students and associates, including Dr. King and James Farmer, the founder of the Congress of Racial Equality (CORE)

In February of 1959 King traveled to India to study Gandhi's principle of nonviolent persuasion called *Satyagraha*. Intriguingly, via Elijah and Martin two India-based messages, that of Gandhi and Fard, strongly influenced the thinking of the African American freedom movement. Gandhi and Fard's concepts for achieving liberation were novel yet digestible, and held in common one important factor that may have bolstered their appeal to African Americans — neither Fard's nor Gandhi's message originated with white people, nor was the objective of their messages Euro-centric.

Imam Wallace D. Mohammed probably captures a generations-old core belief that is reflected in both of these African American leaders, finding solace and guidance in messages and messengers from foreign lands. Using the Nation of Islam as a model to convey African Americans' need to have something autonomous of Caucasian influence, Wallace Mohammed in a May 08, 1999 address summarized why many African Americans made Islam their religion of choice. He explained, "We can't trust the society that reduced us to less than a human being to show us to the path to God."

Whether an African American chooses Islam, Christianity, or any other faith tradition to fulfill their life needs, as demonstrated by most African American leaders, there exists an internal apprehension in the African American soul that automatically questions the ability and sincerity of the society that used to openly oppress them, to be the same society to give them liberty.

ELIJAH MUHAMMAD A MAN OF NON-VIOLENCE

Elijah Muhammad's racially charged message, if properly distilled in search of its essence, will reveal that he was well equipped with sound strategies for alleviating the burdened African American mind and soul. If one would remove the racial language and black nationalistic rhetoric from Elijah Muhammad's message and highlight the practicalities that he taught, the remaining product is sound teachings for improving the overall condition of each and every African American. Elijah Muhammad's race consciousness does not negate the fact that the root and soul of his message was to clean up and dignify African Americans in order to place them before the world as productive human beings.

Elijah Muhammad was not a man of war, anger, hate or violence. Even when his own members were violated and killed, he did not resort to vengeance, as evidenced with the April 27, 1962 ransacking of Muhammad's Temple No. 27 by the Los Angeles Police Department. Nonetheless, he did use such incidents to reinforce his message of racial separation. But did Elijah Muhammad really want a separation of the races? If he did then one would have to question why he invited the American Indian and other non-African Americans to join his community. Some have argued that his message for separation of the races may have been another aspect of his strategy for extracting better conduct from white America. In other words, Elijah Muhammad's race-separating speech-making may have been a reverse-psychology strategy designed to embarrass white Americans into accepting African Americans as full citizens.

If there ever was an occasion for a violent reaction on the part of Elijah Muhammad, the Los Angeles police shooting and killing of Nation of Islam members provided him with that opportunity. On the heels of that situation a physical retaliation easily could have been understood and defensible in the eyes of both black and white people. Instead, Elijah bore that great loss of having seven of his members shot. That included Williams Rogers, paralyzed and Ronald Stokes dead. Malcolm X, the Nation of Islam's leading spokesman, who was ready to fight fire with fire, had to restrain his inclination to get even with the Los Angeles police. It was only after Malcolm was no longer with the Nation of Islam that he publicly spoke of physical racial confrontations between black and white America as a possible remedy to solving the problems of African Americans, as he later declared — "by any means necessary."

Elijah Muhammad forbade that type of public discourse. He was not a man given to using "any means necessary." It is quite ironic that no attention has been given by historians to the fact that Elijah Muhammad always chose nonviolent methods to redress white racism and the other wrongs committed against him and his black-oriented Islamic community.

THE MAN BEHIND THE MEN

Elijah discussed this tragic Los Angeles encounter in his book *Message to the Black Man*. Keeping true to his mantle of race consciousness Elijah Muhammad played the race card that the Los Angeles police shooting provided him. "There is no such thing as living in peace with white Americans. You and I have tried without success. Look what white Americans did to my followers in Los Angeles...They know that we, the Muslims, are a peaceful people and do not carry arms..." (204)

Elijah Muhammad forbade his followers to carry any weapons. As mentioned, even being caught possessing a pen-knife would result in Nation of Islam members being disciplined. They were taught to put their faith in God, not weapons. Nation of Islam members were taught that whenever physically attacked and forced to defend themselves they were to use their hands, not weapons.

When addressing the police shooting of the Muslim brothers and the ransacking by the police of the Los Angeles mosque, Minister Malcolm X, with signs of ambivalence, had to explain to his audiences and to news reporters why the Muslims — who many people had errantly labeled as violent — had not retaliated "eye for an eye." Over the succeeding months a restrained Malcolm, fulfilling the role of faithful student, told his audiences that the Muslims' response to the Los Angeles incident was that of waiting on God to execute justice.

In a 1972, Marvin Worth Production with Warner Brothers Inc. titled *MALCOLM X*, the shooting of Ronald Stokes is addressed by combining excerpts from two of Malcolm X's public lectures. The first excerpt states:

> In Los Angeles, CA last year the police shot Ronald Stokes through the heart. He was a Phi Beta Kappa, Korean Vet...(segue into the second excerpt)...Many of you thought that we should go right on out then and make war on the white man. You wanted to do it yourself, didn't you? Didn't you? You wanted some action then, didn't you? Cause you don't like the idea of white people shooting black people down, do you? And you're ready to do something about it, aren't you? We know you are. And the white man should be thankful that God has given the Honorable Elijah Muhammad the control over his followers that he has, so that they can play it cool..., calm..., and collected, and leave it in the hands of God.

The nonviolent Elijah Muhammad always opted to direct the attention of his followers toward having faith in Allah to handle injustices. He taught his followers not to take their situation into their own hands but instead to wait for a final solution from the heavens in the form of the Mother Plane, a spaceship that was hovering over earth equipped with 1,500 bombing planes that were ready to attack America and Britain. The Nation of Islam's Mother Plane, in addition to being a protection for its members, was prepared to apocalyptically evacuate the 144,000 faithful Muslims who followed Elijah Muhammad. Instead of leading his followers toward physical confrontations or even to public protest, as was the practice of the Civil Rights Movements, Elijah Muhammad instead directed the attention and hopes of his followers toward working to improve and develop their personal and community life until the Mother Plane delivered that "dreadful day" upon America.

Historian Dr. Lerone Bennett Jr. notes this nonviolent nature of Elijah Muhammad. Although Bennett followed the trend of most historians and glimmered over the many positive achievements of Elijah Muhammad in favor of giving more recognition to Elijah's student, Malcolm X, still, to Bennett's credit he does classify Elijah Muhammad among the nonvolatile. Bennett in his magna opus *Before the Mayflower: A History of Black America* noted:

> By the eve of the Emancipation Proclamation Centennial, nationalists like Elijah Muhammad were calling for creation of a black state in America, while other activists, with different perceptions, were pressing an increasingly volatile campaign in the streets. (383)

The Nation of Islam did promote a strong self-defense message, but it was a proclamation that was put into action primarily against black people. Even on these occasions when the need for self-defense was activated, it was against Elijah Muhammad's strictest rules to be the aggressor. Elijah told his followers to obey the law of the land. As mentioned earlier each member carried a Nation of Islam identification card that instructed law officers to arrest the "said bearer" and to mail the card to the Muslims' headquarters if the possessor of the card is caught in any illegal activity.

This non-aggressive posture produced law-abiding citizens for not only Elijah Muhammad's Muslim community, but also for America as a whole. Because of the Nation of Islam's discipline and orderliness thousands of America's hoodlums and derelicts were transformed into productive citizens contributing to the good of America's society, with many of them eventually blossoming into community leaders, educators and productive entrepreneurs.

The disciplines that Elijah Muhammad taught his followers yielded benefits for many white employers who often happily hired known members of the Nation of Islam. Laziness and tardiness were unacceptable in the Nation of Islam. Elijah Muhammad forbade his followers to give less than a full day's labor for their pay. Lying and stealing were qualities that were beneath the values of Elijah Muhammad's renewed black men and women, and frivolity was a sin. Thus, Elijah's followers in their jobs for white employers often were promoted over their co-workers due to practicing the diligent work ethics they had acquired as members of the Nation of Islam.

The Nation of Islam's antiwar stance is another example of the nonviolent character of Elijah Muhammad. Elijah and two of his sons served time in federal prisons for refusal to join the U.S. armed services. Muhammad Ali's conscientious objector status was in lockstep with Elijah Muhammad's nonviolent, antiwar stance. This nonviolent makeup of the Nation of Islam, particularly pre-1960, was further evidenced by the fact that none of Elijah Muhammad's followers who remained faithful to his teachings ever promoted violence, riots of any type, or public unrest.

Probably one of the strongest testimonies to Elijah Muhammad's constraints against violence and hate is in his response to the assassination of President John F. Kennedy. While history has focused much on Malcolm's verbal slip at the Manhattan Center in New York where he uttered the sound bite, "a case of chickens coming home to roost," much less attention has been given to Elijah Muhammad's public condolences regarding President Kennedy's untimely death. As reported in Malcolm's autobiography it was within three days of President Kennedy's assassination, that Malcolm disobeyed Elijah Muhammad, which resulted in Elijah on December 1, 1963 placing Malcolm on a 90-day suspension.

Karl Evanzz, in his typical anti-Elijah Muhammad style, begrudgingly acknowledges reports of Elijah Muhammad's condolences on behalf of the slain president. On page 271, Evanzz wrote that a Los Angeles radio station reporter had called Elijah Muhammad for his comments, and the Messenger said that members of the NOI, like their fellow Americans, were "deeply shocked by the assassination of the president, and share the nation's grief."

Elijah Muhammad, cognizant of the country's state of mourning, wisely ordered his ministers to have no comment on the passing of President Kennedy. If Elijah Muhammad was really a man of hate he could have easily pointed to the president's death as proof that God was punishing white America. Instead he chose to issue a statement of compassion.

Elijah Muhammad was not motivated by hatred or a promoter of violence. His racial statements were definitely cutting and agitating to many, but he never promoted hurting another individual unless it was in self defense. But even that self defense could not go beyond the bounds of personal safety.

Cognizant of the misclassifications that accompany most outspoken critics, Elijah Muhammad in his book *Message to the Blackman in America* carefully spelled out to his followers some of the realities they would encounter as a result of being his supporters. Yet even in this discourse Elijah Muhammad does not promote violence or hatred:

ELIJAH MUHAMMAD A MAN OF NON-VIOLENCE

> When you stand up and speak a word on behalf of your own people, you are classified as a troublemaker, you are classified as a Communist, as a race-hater, as everything but good.
> If God has revealed to me the truth of this race of people and yourself and I tell you of it and that is the truth, then don't say that I am teaching race hatred, just say I teach the truth.
> The message I bring is not for the cowards. Those of you who follow me must be ready to withstand the barbs and insults of those who come to investigate, pry, and claim that our ultimate aim is to undermine the American way of life. We have no such intentions and our critics know it. (219)

Elijah Muhammad was stern, forthright, and unapologetic in his criticism of any person or ideology that he deemed an impediment that interfered with the mental resurrection of the black man and woman in North America. But he was not a man of hate or violence. His record shows not only that he was nonviolent, but also the fact that he turned thousands of African Americans from violent lifestyles into lives of productivity. For many angry African Americans, Elijah Muhammad's Nation of Islam message served as their relief valve. It provided them an ideology that allowed them to vent and release the pressures that had built up in them as a result of enduring years of racism.

The gap between anger and hatred, as with the gap dividing love and hate, can be very thin. Without a discipline such as that taught by Elijah Muhammad, emotions left uncontrolled and unchecked by human intelligence potentially are very harmful. The nonviolent approach of Elijah Muhammad, albeit racially-based, gave many angry and confused black men and women an intelligent focus and direction in life that resulted in them being positive and productive human beings. If not for Elijah Muhammad's giving them discipline and intelligence many of these same human beings could have easily descended from a state of anger into persons full of hatred.

Elijah Muhammad saw himself as one commissioned by God, sent to save every African American who was a descendant of American slavery, regardless of the cost. His technique was bold and firm, but nonviolent. That firmness he transferred to his followers. They in turn began to display the same boldness and firmness, a human trait that American slavery had sought to destroy in Africa's children.

One of Elijah Muhammad's foremost objectives was to remove from African Americans their ingrained fear of the white man. He worked specifically on the psyche of black men and women, seeking to reach into their very souls to remove the fear that slavery and Jim Crow had manufactured and implanted in their hearts and minds.

THE MAN BEHIND THE MEN

He applied every ideology and religious scripture, regardless of whether the concept was perceived by the general society as sacred or as flawed. If it flew in the face of white supremacy or if it imbued courage in the black man and woman, Elijah Muhammad incorporated that concept into his own race-based theocracy. His primary concern was liberating black people at any reasonable cost from the clutches of fearing white people.

Elijah Muhammad placed heavy emphasis on his followers being respectful to all people, courteous to all women, and protectors of all children. His stance on self-defense is a natural quality, universal among any people who are being attacked.

The murder of Malcolm may always remain a caveat in Elijah's non-violence status. Some argue that even if Elijah Muhammad personally was not a participant in violence, still the assassination of Malcolm X is often pointed to as proof of how his teachings resulted in violence. Yes, the followers of Elijah Muhammad were ready to defend him and his honor at a moment's notice, but the violence perpetrated against the defenseless Malcolm X is not the modus operandi of the Fruit of Islam. Never before or after Malcolm's murder has Muslims in the Nation of Islam been connected to shooting people at speaking engagements or assassinating speakers.

Malcolm, after his break with the Nation of Islam, was regularly taunted in the *Muhammad Speaks* newspaper. Even if Elijah Muhammad himself did not pen the articles or condone the anti-Malcolm cartoons, their mere presence in the Muslims' publication did help create an atmosphere that led to Malcolm's death. A particular example was the article that stated that Malcolm "was worthy of death." Shortly after Malcolm's assassination Elijah Muhammad quickly distanced himself from responsibility. In partnership with CNN, a *Time Magazine* online article titled, *Races: Death and Transfiguration*, reports that on March 05, 1965, Elijah Muhammad said, "We are innocent of Malcolm's death." The Internet article further quotes Elijah Muhammad as saying, "Malcolm died of his own preaching. He preached violence, and violence took him away."

Due to his silence Elijah Muhammad carries some of the burden for Malcolm's death. Perhaps if he could have relived the closing days of Malcolm's life, Elijah Muhammad would have intervened and stopped the Nation of Islam officials' criticisms of Malcolm — and maybe Malcolm would have reciprocated by curbing his public criticisms of Elijah. Nonetheless, Elijah Muhammad's thrust towards freeing black Americans was a nonviolent approach to the major problem of white racism, bigotry and arrogance prevalent in those days.

Elijah's method was discomforting for many, yet it was not a message of hate and violence. But could his message contain the seeds of hate and violence? Not for his followers who adhered to his moral laws and his message of respecting *all* people. To a large degree Elijah Muhammad's effort worked. Whether one agreed with or accepted it partially or in totality, every African American who heard his thought-provoking message and witnessed his boldness in delivering that message, garnered a sense of pride that for the vast majority before was non-existent.

Elijah Muhammad's message was not a proposal for violence nor was hatred his goal. Following in the footsteps of men like Carter G. Woodson, W.E.B. Dubois and many other African American leaders, the goal of Elijah Muhammad was the liberation of every African American from fearing to question the white hegemony that dominated the individual and collective lives of African Americans. For Elijah Muhammad believed that Islam, as taught to him by Mr. W.D. Fard was the only solution — a nonviolent formula — for completely freeing his people.

-§- CHAPTER -§-
NINETEEN

The Possibility of Forgiving Elijah Muhammad

(Photographer and Date Unknown)

Allah will not call you to account for thoughtlessness in your oaths, but for the intention in your hearts; and He is Oft-forgiving, Most Forbearing.

— Holy Qur'an 2:225

Allah the Almighty has said: "O Son of Adam, so long as you call upon Me and ask of Me, I shall forgive you for what you have done, and I shall not mind. O son of Adam, were your sins to reach the clouds of the sky and were you then to ask forgiveness of Me, I would forgive you. O son of Adam, were you to come to Me with sins nearly as great as the earth and were then to face Me, ascribing no partners to Me, I would bring you forgiveness nearly as great as it (the earth)"

— An-Nawawi's Forty Hadith - Page 126

Elijah Muhammad was never one seeking the approval or validation of America, immigrant Muslims, or any other group or institution when it came to carrying out the mission he received from W.D. Fard. Wearing the eminent title "Messenger of Allah" assured him, in his mind, of the legitimacy he needed to move forward. Elijah Muhammad never publicly sought forgiveness, but his adjusting the emphasis in his teachings, particularly toward his later days strongly suggests that he recognized a need for fine-tuning his mission. Life adjustments, maybe even adaptations — consciously or instinctively — are methods of seeking forgiveness without loosing character and self-respect. Recalibrations that respect goodness equates to one seeking tolerance and forgiveness.

Elijah Muhammad forgave those who he thought earned his forgiveness; his family members, community members and in many ways

POSSIBILITY OF FORGIVING ELIJAH MUHAMMAD

he forgave the white man of America. And they too forgave him as he earned their forgiveness.

In this light, with the advantage o hindsight, we attempt to address a difficulty that historically has denied many people the ability to see Elijah Muhammad's greatness, which his legacy testifies to. Such denials have become a hindrance that leads to reluctance, or the inability of some people to forgive.

With the thousands of African Americans whose personal and community lives were greatly improved by the leadership of Elijah Muhammad, many may, justifiably so, argue that no human forgiveness of Elijah Muhammad is necessary. But for a man who is grossly misunderstood by the vast majority of Americans due to what appears to be intentional misrepresentations spread by historians and media outlets, surely, in their mental conclusions, Elijah Muhammad may need to be "forgiven."

Elijah Muhammad's claim that he had met "God in the person" of W.D. Fard has resulted in many Muslims accusing him of committing what they consider Islam's most unforgivable sin: Islamic shirk — the associating of a partner with God. In Islam associating anything as a partner with God — in any form, person, or ideology — is an abominable sin. But is it unforgivable?

Elijah Muhammad was a man, a human being like any other who made mistakes as he journeyed in life. The Qur'an and Bible often speak of forgiveness, even pardoning for the sin of associating partners with God. Depending upon an individual's beliefs and dogmas, differing views may be taken on this issue of forgiveness for Elijah Muhammad. But ultimately most religions and people of faith agree that divine forgiveness and mercy is determined by a power higher than that possessed by man.

Both Bible and Qur'an often speak of forgiving even the most heinous of crimes. For generations human beings too have demonstrated the capacity to forgive sins that have been committed by man upon man, whether wrongs carried out by individuals or by one religious group upon another. Since the beginning of civilization man has learned to forgive, or at least been able to offer an understanding of some of the worst sins ever committed by mankind upon humanity. Our capacity to forgive someone is strongest when we can see the totality of the situation, or the fullness of the person, who is to receive the forgiveness.

When a wrong has been done the weight of that sin must be measured by the era and within the context that gave birth to the sin. All deeds, whether good or evil, are performed based upon preexisting realities that often dictate the origin, intent, and final outcome of the deed. No wrongful deed is ever committed in a vacuum; likewise, the act of forgiving is also offered and received within a context. The continuity of the two acts, atonement and forgiveness is holistic and reciprocally connected.

THE MAN BEHIND THE MEN

The relationship between the misdeed and its forgiveness and the context in which they exist is often beyond the control of all parties involved. As environmental circumstances are determining factors in both the good and errant deeds of mankind, so too do environmental realities play a key role in the art of forgiveness. We are creatures of our respective environs with the capacity or the freedom of conscious to forgive or not to forgive.

The beliefs and dogmas that one holds, strongly impacts how a person may understand and apply forgiveness. When the topic of forgiving Elijah Muhammad is discussed a wide range of responses occur ranging from a simple "yes," to an adamant "never!" But a review of his life and mission that takes into consideration the context in which he lived may yield compelling insights that could reshape one's opinion on the subject of forgiving Elijah Muhammad. When addressing this issue it is important to remember that Elijah Muhammad, while maintaining a sincere loyalty to his "Saviour," Mr. Fard, Elijah Muhammad was still evolving as an individual and as a leader. As with the growth of any human being, Elijah Muhammad was reconciling his life and leadership with the changing conditions in society.

The Elijah Muhammad of 1933 was not the Elijah Muhammad of 1975. But the dedication that he demonstrated for 40-plus years to uplifting African Americans did not change. No matter what changes the seasons presented, in order to lift up his people, Elijah Muhammad would always adjust his emphasis and immediate focus according to his community's prevailing needs. But his dedication never wavered.

Each era of Elijah Muhammad's leadership and the circumstances surrounding him within each dispensation of time has to be considered when studying his life and the topic of forgiving him. With the exception of perhaps the final years of his life, no epoch of his leadership can take precedence over another when it comes to quantifying whether Elijah Muhammad is worthy of man's forgiveness, and more importantly of God's forgiveness. His whole life, as with any human being, must be put on the scales of justice and measured according to the conditions that influenced each season that he transitioned. Such measuring or judgment, carried out with an appreciation that acknowledges that he followed a pattern towards human excellence, may reveal a picture of an Elijah Muhammad who at the time of his death had made a peaceful reconciliation within himself, with humanity and with God.

After receiving his mission from W.D. Fard, Elijah Muhammad pursued his assignment with an unrelenting accusatory finger that was quick to point out both the racial and social wrongs that he detected in the general society, as well as the shortcomings of the African American milieu. With the exception of white Americans, the group most criticized by Elijah Muhammad was African Americans, who he dubbed "the so-Called Negro." He castigated every aspect of their life that he deemed an assimilation of white hegemony, especially their acceptance of Christianity as given to them by white Americans. He dubbed the Christianity of the United States as "the white man's religion."

When he was rebuked by Muslims from abroad Elijah Muhammad often replied in reprimanding tones. As I reported in the chapter titled *Mr. Elijah Muhammad*, his book *Message to the Blackman* states that his message and mission "to the American so-called Negroes is not in the power of any Orthodox Muslim or non-believer...that neither Jeddah nor Mecca have sent me! I am sent from Allah and not from the Secretary General of the Muslim League." (329)

Each of Elijah Muhammad's critiques was an effort to improve the lives of African Americans. Compared with the abuses endured from white racists, Elijah Muhammad's 42 years of criticizing African Americans pales significantly. The capacity of African Americans to forgive white Americans is demonstrated by the fact that many African Americans have overlooked, often with a willingness to forget, the 400 years of sins from America's past institution of slavery, as well as the evils perpetrated by the Ku Klux Klan and the other subtle forms of racism and bigotry still instituted in American society. If African Americans sincerely can forgive the four centuries of abuse received from the hands and tongues of bigoted Caucasians, then surely these same African Americans can forgive Elijah Muhammad for the discomfort he may have caused by his 42-years of reprimanding.

Many Caucasians already have forgiven Elijah while others obviously still are perplexed by their apparent misunderstandings of him. As mentioned earlier, former Chicago Mayor Richard J. Daley is one example of white Americans who demonstrated acceptance and forgiveness of Elijah Muhammad. Upon the passing of Elijah Muhammad the mayor declared February 26, 1975, "Nation of Islam Day." The May 1975 issue of *Ebony* reports Daley describing Elijah Muhammad as "an outstanding citizen who was always interested in helping young people and especially the poor." This was not the first time that Daley had praised Elijah Muhammad. The May 1975 issue of *Ebony* magazine, page 79 states that both "Daley and Illinois Governor Dan Walker, proclaimed March 29 (1974) as 'Hon. Elijah Muhammad Day.'" The Muslim leader graciously accepted the honor. The April 12, 1974 issue of *Muhammad Speak's* headline, stated in bold letters, "Thank You!" With photos of himself, Governor Walker and Mayor Daley gracing the cover, Elijah Muhammad penned his thank you letter, which included, "I pray to Allah (God), I prove worthy of such great honor...My followers and I will try with all our efforts to prove worthy of the respect and honor given to us from you as good citizens of Chicago and of Illinois."

The white Americans who may find it difficult to forgive Elijah Muhammad may consider that his message, though brusque, also was a type of moral cleanser. He provided the white racist a form of psychological therapy that helped them taste reversed-racism, thus offering them an opportunity to arrest, disassemble, and eradicate their own bigotry. Elijah Muhammad forced upon white America a conversation of black superiority and white inferiority. The advent of Elijah Muhammad suddenly gave new images to the racists among white Americans of an ethnically-reversed reflection of racism's immoral shortcomings.

Elijah Muhammad's expression of racism was rhetorical and short-lived compared to the centuries of white racism. Those who are reluctant to forgive him must remember that Elijah Muhammad's family never held white slaves or denied white Americans their human and civil rights. Nor did he raid their homes, rape their women or lynch white men.

Elijah Muhammad was a man with a wakeup message for African Americans. That message simultaneously cautioned Caucasians to inspect and improve their treatment of black people. In fact his blunt criticism of white America not only helped to save white people, he also helped to save America as a nation. How long will forgiveness be denied a man whose worst sins also have been committed by others who were forgiven a long time ago?

Inspired by Andrew Levy, author and librarian Rob Lopresti in his expose' *Which U.S. Presidents Owned Slaves?* claims that twelve U.S. presidents owned slaves, eight owning slaves while serving as president. Nonetheless — and properly so — America has forgiven them their errors and honored their achievements with national monuments, institutions, and libraries.

Many prominent individuals including sitting American presidents openly supported eugenics. The well educated Woodrow Wilson and Theodore Roosevelt promoted sterilizing the "unfit" population that mainly consisted of poor, uneducated and often mentally disabled Americans, yet these men have been forgiven and exalted. Roosevelt, in support of eugenics stated, "Society has no business to permit degenerates to reproduce." Nonetheless, today he has an island located in the Potomac River in Washington D.C. named in his honor. Woodrow Wilson has earned the honor of having institutes, such as the esteemed Woodrow Wilson International Center for Scholars and fellowships named in his honor. Is it asking too much for the largely uneducated Elijah Muhammad to be forgiven and presented his earned honor? What sin or error did Elijah Muhammad commit that justifies America not forgiving him? Should not Elijah Muhammad's name, character, and positive contributions be celebrated as other great American men and women have been honored?

Ironically still many African Americans also hold Elijah Muhammad in disdain. But what sin did Elijah Muhammad commit against his own African American race that prevents them as Christians from forgiving him? Christ Jesus, according to St. Matthew 18:22 said to forgive "seventy times seven." Literally that means, forgiveness 490 times.

Yes, he may have challenged African Americans on every moral, social, and political issue. But surely this does not constitute a sin. His open suspicions of Christianity and his taunting of African Americans for accepting Christianity at face value from white people is in line with Dr.

POSSIBILITY OF FORGIVING ELIJAH MUHAMMAD

W.E.B. DuBois and Dr. Carter G. Woodson and other African American intellectuals who, without reproach, also have criticized and questioned the African American religious experience in America. Why is it that these men of letters are held up with great respect while Elijah Muhammad is not afforded the same?

Unless Christians of any race can come up with 491 reasons not to forgive Elijah Muhammad, even acknowledging that Elijah Muhammad's disquieting challenges and criticisms of American life may be viewed by many as undue and extreme, then according to the Gospel of St. Matthew, that which Elijah said and did is not too big a wrong that it should not be forgiven — "seventy times seven."

Today's thrust among African Americans for independent thinking is a definite product of Elijah Muhammad's work in the African American community. As the Reverend Dr. Jesse Jackson said the day after Elijah Muhammad passed, "his leadership extended far beyond the membership of the Nation of Islam. For more than three decades this prophet has been the spiritual leader and a progressive force of Black identity and consciousness, self determination and economic development. He was the father of Black self-consciousness."

The works of Elijah Muhammad speak volumes regardless of one's faith tradition. A willingness to forgive serves not only as a healing for everyone involved, but also as an eye opening experience that allows possibilities for the forgiver to see the accused person anew.

Another segment of American society who could benefit from reassessing their hackneyed conclusions about Elijah Muhammad are the African American Muslims who — historically and or contemporarily — claim no connection with, or real appreciation for, Elijah Muhammad and the original Nation of Islam. It seems that many in this particular group of African American Muslims find it very difficult to forgive him. Recent efforts, beginning in the 1990s, to identify this category of African American Muslims have produced the labels "*Old Guard*" and the acronym "*HSAAM.*"

Dr. Sherman Abdul-Hakim Jackson, who regularly confers the respectful title "Honorable" upon Elijah Muhammad, is the professor of Arabic and Islamic Studies at the University of Michigan. In his book *Islam and the Blackamerican: Looking Toward the Third Resurrection*, Jackson uses the title "Old Guard" to describe non-Nation of Islam African American Muslims, many of whom fit into the group who are unforgiving of Elijah Muhammad. Dr. Ihsan Bagby, an associate professor of Islamic studies at the University of Kentucky, opted to refer to this group of Muslims by the name HSAAM, an acronym for "Historically Sunni African American Muslims."

THE MAN BEHIND THE MEN

There are some individuals among those categorized as HSAAM, or Old Guard, who are not detractors of Elijah Muhammad due to the fact that they once were diligent members of Elijah Muhammad's Nation of Islam. This minority among the HSAAM/Old Guard groups recognize, and often will acknowledge, that if not for Elijah Muhammad they may have never became Muslim or ever developed an interest in Islam. Notwithstanding, the majority of the HSAAM/Old Guard Muslims still tend to be strongly anti-Elijah Muhammad. They display very little patience with even discussing the possibility of forgiving Elijah Muhammad. In their minds and hearts even the slightest prospect that Allah may forgive Elijah for his sins and shortcomings and grant him the paradise is intolerable.

Their unrelenting charge is that Elijah Muhammad committed Islamic shirk, the supposedly unforgivable act of associating a partner with Allah. Despite the fact that the Qur'an (25:70) states that shirk is forgivable if the one who invoked the false god "repents, believes, and work righteous deeds," still these unforgiving Muslims prefer to render Elijah Muhammad to an eternal status of kafir (disbeliever).

Elijah's son and successor Wallace Mohammed defended his father declaring that Elijah Muhammad did not need to make a grand public shahadah (the Islamic testimony of faith said by initiates to become Muslim). Wallace stated in his book *Growth for a Model Community in America*:

> The Honorable Elijah Muhammad said before his passing in front of his staff: "Son, go on anywhere you want to go. Son, preach that gospel." On the tape that they brought to him to get me thrown out of the Nation, that is what he called "that gospel." So how is he a disbeliever? If someone had told the Prophet: "Oh [sic] Muhammed, go on wherever you like on the earth and preach that message." We wouldn't call him a kafir, would we? Just because the Honorable Elijah Muhammad didn't come to "the high priest" before he died and say: "I confess to you that I've been wrong, and now I make the shahadah to you," you call him a kafir. (17)

Many of the HSAAM/Old Guard African American Muslims while adamant about not forgiving Elijah Muhammad, often disregard the fact that Mr. Muhammad almost single-handedly is responsible for the popularity in America of the Islamic names Allah and Muhammad, and the Islamic terms, Islam, As-Salaam Alaikum, and Muslim. This contribution of Elijah Muhammad is particulary true in the African American community.

Dr. Sayyid M. Sayeed, the national director of the Islamic Society of North America, cited areas in which Elijah Muhammad made important contributions to the growth and development in the United States of America:

POSSIBILITY OF FORGIVING ELIJAH MUHAMMAD

Elijah Muhammad for us is the father of W. Deen Mohammed. In that sense directly he is responsible for a tremendous transformation of African Americans in America. He raised the banner of the Nation of Islam, established the Nation of Islam in the 1930s when there was very little about Islam in America.

We may not agree with the works that he promoted and he taught, but we cannot neglect, in that sense, the contribution that he made in awakening the African American community towards the potential of Islam.

We have been the recipients or the beneficiaries of his hard works in the sense that many people who he was able to clean and bring to the Nation of Islam ultimately landed in Mainstream Islam; maybe many who we would have never gotten. The Honorable Malcolm X we would not have been able to get. Muhammad Ali, the great champ, and his own sons, W. Deen Mohammed, Jabir Muhammad, and others. So in that sense he paved a way for what we see today. We really remember him as the founder, as the facilitator of the Islamic growth in America.

— *Interview Sept. 12, 2006*

Imam W. Deen Muhammad and his brother Jabir (Herbert) circa 1976
(Photographer and Date Unknown)

THE MAN BEHIND THE MEN

Another important benefit from Elijah Muhammad to the development of Islam in America is his infusing a "Do For Self," independent-thought mentality into his followers; a new mind that prevented them from adopting and mimicking the customs, dress and traditions of other races, ethnicities, and nationalities within the Islamic world.

Elijah Muhammad sincerely believed that he was introducing a "new Islam." In time Elijah Muhammad's willingness to think independently impacted not only members of the Nation of Islam but also many other African American Muslims who today want to criticize and castigate him. It was Elijah's boldness that also helped these same Muslims remove from their crippled psyche the daunting "slave ghost"; the habitual fears from slavery that continued to haunt the mind and soul of black folks.

It was Elijah Muhammad's program that equipped all African American Muslims with abilities to deal more effectively with America's pandemic racism and class system. But also incorporated in Elijah's "Do For Self" message was encouragement for African American Muslims to not become amazed and snared by Middle Eastern culture and traditions after escaping the psychological grip of Eurocentric values.

The followers of Elijah Muhammad's strict moral code, which encompassed a unique dress code, were individuals who were being cultivated and disciplined in ways that yielded unique Islamic mannerisms and etiquettes. These cultural advancements not only gave Nation of Islam members a new sense of dignity, but also reaffirmed the Islamic identity given them by the Nation of Islam. The men were renowned for their suits and bow ties, with their faces shaved and their heads cut and well trimmed. The dress of the Nation of Islam women, modest from head to toe, carried its own distinction with a taste that showed originality and cultural renewal. Elijah Muhammad's "Do For Self" program was well aware of the importance of obligating his followers to avoid assimilating the culture, dress and habits of Muslims from abroad.

Elijah Muhammad understood very well that a race that had been denied the true benefits of community life were very susceptible to unnaturally adopt another race's value system or another ethnic group's culture and dress, whether Christian based or Islamic based. He understood that a person or a group who had been denied the natural essentials of life, simply because of their skin color, hair texture or their other God-given biological traits, are persons who may not be in the best mind to properly and systematically deal with such denial, especially when factoring in the penetrating, negative effects of slavery that lingered long after physical slavery had ended for African Americans.

Elijah Muhammad knew that most African Americans despised their image as portrayed in the world, making them easy prey and subject to adopting another race's mores and customs as a means of escape from their own reality. A majority of African American Muslims who were never rooted in the Nation of Islam often adopted the dress and habits from myriad Middle Eastern and African cultures. For Elijah Muhammad acculturation of any society was not an option. For him it was more important to create and maintain a modest Islamic dress style and decorum that spoke holistically to the mental and spiritual needs of African American development.

The beginning of the 21st century witnessed the beginning of a change of heart by non-Nation of Islam African American Muslims. Indiana Prison Chaplain Ismail Abdul-Aleem of Indianapolis has been a HSAAM or an Old-Guard Muslim since 1972. "I am of the 'Old Guard', and proud of that." he said. He was personally affected by the murders of the "Hanafi" Muslims in Washington D.C. in 1973 as well as the murder of Hakim Jamal in Boston, MA a year later. For many non-Nation of Islam Muslims these two horrendous incidents, which some believe were committed by members of the Nation of Islam, created for Abdul-Aleem and others a strong disrespect for Elijah Muhammad and his followers.

Abdul-Aleem shared in November of 2005, that he had a change in opinion towards the followers of Elijah Muhammad. Abdul-Aleem noted, "My views have changed significantly over the past couple of years. Probably working with men who are in prison who are practicing Muslims, and trying to cater to their needs has given me a greater appreciation for the work of the early Muslim pioneers who dedicated their lives to the establishment of Islam in our community."

Abdul-Aleem adjusted his approach to teaching the inmates, to meet their current needs, when he recognized that many of the inmates were from challenging backgrounds and hearing Islam for the first time. "Trying to teach Muslim inmates about the exegesis of scripture and the formal logic of orthodox jurisprudence when the reason for their confinement is economic injustice, substance abuse, broken families, undisciplined sexual behavior, ignorance and a definition of self that leads to the cemetery or prison is totally absurd. Suddenly things like *How to Eat to Live* and *Message to the Blackman*, (books produced by Elijah Muhammad) makes sense to me. I must acknowledge the unorthodoxy in the Islamic doctrine of these works; however, people broken by 14 generations of servitude and 100 years of institutionalized terrorism need to address the issues confronting them."

Abdul-Aleem recognized other benefits that Muslims in general and African American Muslims in particular have received from the pioneering work and sacrifices of the early followers of the Nation of Islam, and the other proto-Islamic groups of the 1920s and 1930s led by men such as Noble Timothy Drew Ali. "Even without full access to the Qur'an or the life model of Prophet Muhammed, Elijah Muhammad and the members of the Nation sought to address the pressing needs of redefining our existence in this country." Abdul-Aleem acknowledged that the contributions and efforts of the Nation of Islam have been successful in the following ways:

> 1. Because of their efforts Islam has become an authentically legitimate African-American religion. In others words, any African-American anywhere in the United States can embrace Islam without fear of losing his identity as an authentic black man. This is something that is unheard of for white Americans, Latinos, and other ethnic groups.
>
> 2. The Nation of Islam defined Islam in a way that featured resistance to oppression, anti-black bias and addressed the reality of white supremacy and our opposition to it.
>
> 3. The Nation of Islam sought to uplift the downtrodden and those who were the victims of racial oppression.

Abdul-Aleem's reassessment of Elijah Muhammad's role in the development of Islam in America is a welcomed change. It is a sign of not only the man and his works being appreciated, but also a forgiving of Elijah Muhammad for the portions of his teachings that were not in accord with the Qur'an. Abdul-Aleem noted, "We must accept the contributions of those before us and seek to use whatever was successful in the transformation of human beings — whose souls have been broken — into God-fearing righteous men and women."

Elijah Muhammad was a man who risked his own life in order to address a multi-generational problem among African Americans that Dr. Joy DeGruy-Leary of Portland State University described as a *Post-Traumatic Slave Syndrome*. It was Abdul-Aleem's recognition of syndromes, as the one proposed by DeGruy-Leary that is allowing him and other Muslims to revisit their earlier anti-Elijah Muhammad conclusions, and to begin seeing him anew.

Dr. DeGruy-Leary's website *www.joyleary.com* states:

> While African Americans managed to emerge from chattel slavery and the oppressive decades that followed with great strength and resiliency, they did not emerge unscathed. Slavery produced centuries of physical, psychological and spiritual injury. *Post Traumatic Slave Syndrome: America's Legacy of Enduring Injury and Healing* lays the groundwork for understanding how the past has influenced the present, and opens up the discussion of how we can use the strengths we have gained to heal.

POSSIBILITY OF FORGIVING ELIJAH MUHAMMAD

Even Elijah's harshest critics cannot doubt his sincerity in wanting to see improvements in the lives of African Americans. His genuine and earnest intentions that has positively affected the lives of the four men featured in this book, and the lives of millions of American Muslims. Many Muslims have failed to see the value of Elijah Muhammad because they focused more on his shortcomings than on his sincerity and many positive achievements. The Qur'an states, "Allah will not call you to account for thoughtlessness in your oaths, but for the intention in your hearts; and He is Oft-forgiving, Most Forbearing." [Sura 2: ayat 225].

After Elijah Muhammad's passing many of his followers moved away from his racially-based interpretations of Islam to the practice of Islam as taught by Muhammed, the seventh-century Prophet. These former followers of Elijah Muhammad advanced on to a universal practice of Islam while retaining Elijah's message that assimilating the culture and habits of Muslims from abroad was not necessary for one to be a good Muslim. They kept the best of what Elijah Muhammad gave them while publicly and privately asking God to forgive him for his sins.

The Prophet Muhammed of Arabia always showed appreciation and respect for racial and ethnic distinctions of the various tribes and nations that comprised his multiplicity of followers, but he never encouraged that one group assimilate the culture or ethnicity of another. The Qur'an states:

> O mankind! We created you from a single (pair) of a male and a female, and made you into nations and tribes, that ye may know each other. Verily the most honored of you in the sight of Allah is (he who is) the most righteous of you.
> — Holy Qur'an sura 49: ayat 13

The above verse recognizes and allows tribal and nationalistic distinctions among human beings, for the express purpose that the various groups are expected to get acquainted with each other by having mutually respectful exchanges. This type of communal exchange should be comity-based where the only superiority is the advantage an individual may earn by virtue of their piety to God, not because of racial or nationalistic qualities.

The apparent inability of some African American Muslims to acknowledge that Islam allows for racial and tribal distinctions may affect how they view Elijah Muhammad. His strong stance on racial separation, consequently, may affect their willingness to consider forgiving him. To promote racial separation, especially as a basis to establish racial superiority, is un-Islamic. But what must be acknowledged is that Elijah Muhammad's aim was not solely separation, but for his followers to think universally. He repeatedly told his followers that they were brothers with all Muslims in the world. His promotion of racial separation was not a total separation from all people but a removal from the white racist of America, and a separation from the white racist's influences.

In his book *Message to the Blackman*, Elijah included a chapter titled *Clarification of Confusion Surrounding Muslims*, wherein he addressed the misconception that he taught black supremacy. In his defense against being labeled a black supremacist, ironically, Elijah Muhammad described the American black man as inferior to white people in words similar to that noted by Thomas Jefferson:

> Allah has revealed that the black is the original Man, and that's what I teach. Now, where this supremacy teaching comes in that is charged by the disbelievers — that I teach it in order to suit their particular purpose of charging us with being an aggressive movement, or intending to become such, because of the teachings of one being superior over the other.
> We say that the black man is the first man in the sun, and then they take this and just change it around — that he is teaching supremacy. And that we are not doing. We already know that we are inferior to you here in America.
> We cannot say physically or even mentally that we are equal, nor say your (sic) superior, when it comes to actual physical or educational ability. (317-318)

In order for Muslims to begin considering the subject of forgiving Elijah Muhammad for his separatist comments, they must first determine exactly which portions of his message was un-Islamic. Additionally they must remember America's dominant racial attitude at the time Elijah made his race-based statements, and the fact that his words were not made in a void. Unfavorable circumstances predicated his whole movement and in his mind obligated him to respond accordingly.

If Elijah Muhammad's contribution of providing his followers with a mind that cherished obtaining and maintaining a sense of independence was successful — and it was a success — then that contribution especially must be cherished by African American Muslims as they intermingle with their Muslim brothers and sisters from around the Islamic world. Having and maintaining one's racial distinction is not un-Islamic. However, thinking of one's race as superior to another race is un-Islamic. But the tendency to labor under the burden of self-hatred, even the deliberate or unintentional downplaying of one's own race and ethnicity in order to feign racial equality, may be just as un-Islamic as promoting the superior versus inferior racial divide.

If history showed that Elijah Muhammad simply was seeking to establish racial superiority of the black man, then his effort was un-Islamic. But studies

POSSIBILITY OF FORGIVING ELIJAH MUHAMMAD

of the later years of his life show that Elijah Muhammad, in order to keep up with the changes in America and the world, was a wis leader who repeatedly reformed and reconciled his views according to the dictates of modernity. Racism in America changed for the better and Elijah Muhammad changed accordingly. A person willing to adapt to societal improvements should easily earn forgiveness, particularly if his or her original intent was sincerely for the betterment of their people and not merely for racial pride and arrogance.

When discussing the issue of forgiving Elijah Muhammad, racial superiority may not be the most difficult barrier. When Elijah Muhammad's opponents want to deter the love and respect he is due they tend to mention three obstacles, all of which are major sins in Islam. In addition to the sin of Islamic shirk, the other charges levied against him are illicit sex and duplicity in murder.

Surely in Islam, false worship is the worst of all sins. Just the mere mention of the phrase "God in the person of W.D. Fard" enflames most Muslims. The charge of murder is revisited almost every time Malcolm's and Elijah's name is mentioned in the same breath, thus, making the assassination of Minister Malcolm X, a.k.a. Malik Shabazz, a continual sore spot for Elijah Muhammad and the Nation of Islam. And the charge of adultery for fathering children out of wedlock often finds its way to the surface whenever Elijah Muhammad is being discussed by his detractors.

The Qur'anic quote in sura 25: ayats 68-71 deals with all three of the major sins with which Elijah Muhammad's opponents usually try to accuse him of being guilty of. As mentioned earlier these verses conclude on the theme of forgiveness for those who sincerely repent, convert and amend their conduct:

> "Those who invoke not, with Allah, any other god, nor slay such life as Allah has made sacred except for just cause, nor commit fornication; — and any that does this (not only) meets punishment, (but) the Penalty on the Day of Judgment will be doubled to him, and he will dwell therein in ignominy, — Unless he repents, believes, and works righteous deeds, for Allah will change the evil of such persons into good, and Allah is Oft-Forgiving, Most Merciful, And whoever repents and does good has truly turned to Allah with an (acceptable) conversion..."
> Holy Qur'an 25:68-71

The accusation of murder and adultery; particularly since neither charge has been properly substantiated nor given due process in any judicial capacity, are too inconclusive. As discussed earlier in the section on Malcolm X, even he himself, one day before his murder, wavered on accusing Elijah and the Nation of Islam of attempting to murder him. Malcolm based his change of belief on being denied entry into France, and the fact that while traveling in Egypt, he was poisoned as well as conspicuously followed by two white men. Malcolm correctly reasoned that these events overseas were too big to have been ordered or carried out by the Nation of Islam, an Islamic community that was confined mainly to resolving the problems and needs of the black people in the ghettoes of North America.

The fornication issue, as handled by most historians on Elijah Muhammad, seems to have some interesting points and conclusions overlooked. Some of the secretaries who mothered Elijah Muhammad's babies now call themselves his widows; and many of these ladies' children are some of Elijah Muhammad's most ardent students and followers. Polygyny was not commonly practiced in the Nation of Islam, but if Elijah saw himself as fulfilling the role of the *Messenger of Allah* then having more than one wife was very plausible. Even if polygyny is ruled out, thus relegating the children as being born out of wedlock, the above Qur'anic verse still offers a provision for forgiveness for *zina* (adultery and fornication).

According to Darnell Karim of Chicago, the children born to Elijah Muhammad by women other than Clara Muhammad were all taken care of by their father. Elijah faithfully sent child support to the mothers via his son Elijah Muhammad Jr. and Supreme Captain Raymond Sharrief. Elijah Muhammad also provided each family with a home, with one family living in Mexico. Karim recalls some of Elijah Muhammad's children who were mothered by the secretaries living in his neighborhood and attending the Nation of Islam's elementary school along with his children. "I know for a fact that they were all in homes and they were well taken care of, and they were educated." Karim added, "He (Elijah Muhammad) paid for their education and they were put in homes. He took care of all of them until they all got grown. I lived around them and those kids were raised with my children." (Telephone interview)

Karim's substantiation of Elijah Muhammad taking proper care of all his children must be seriously considered. Karim was born into the Nation of Islam and a childhood friend of Elijah's son, Wallace. Karim's account represents a challenge to the typical reports on Elijah Muhammad's family life made by most commentators in the media, some historians, and movie makers who repeatedly leave the reader or the viewer with the impression that Elijah Muhammad abandoned his children as infants.

Nothing could be further removed from the truth. The 1964 filing of paternity suits against Elijah Muhammad by Evelyn Williams and Lucille Rosary, at the behest of Malcolm X, must not be taken lightly. But when the women came forward Raymond Sharrieff and John Ali were forced to admit that the Chicago mosque was already providing support for the families of both women, thus negating the charge that Elijah Muhammad was a dead-beat dad who abandoned his flesh and blood.

POSSIBILITY OF FORGIVING ELIJAH MUHAMMAD

Ismail, the son of Elijah Muhammad with Imam Darnell Karim at the 2005 (or 2006) Muslim Convention. *(Photographer Saahir Communications)*

It is understandable that Malcolm's involvement was that of a man under duress for survival, which may explain why Malcolm unwisely spread information about Elijah Muhammad's extramarital affairs. Malcolm's miscalculations resulted in an unfavorable domino-effect that forced him to up the ante. As noted by Claude Clegg, Malcolm's account of Elijah and the women — which he gave to the media and whoever would listen — "seemed to contain a different shocking element each time he retold it. (220)" Nonetheless, it is such misreporting about the babies and their mothers that, even to this day, provides Elijah Muhammad's enemies and detractors with excuses not to forgive him.

The charge against Elijah Muhammad of false worship, shirk, is a serious charge. False worship in any monotheistic religion is a major sin. But the Nation of Islam was not based upon the typical monotheistic, one God creed. Instead the Islam taught to Elijah Muhammad by W.D. Fard presented God incarnate. Fard's presentation of God was very similar to the anthropomorphic concept of the Christian god-head that promotes God coming in the person of Jesus. Fard never claimed to be the God who created the heavens and the earth; however, Fard left lessons that would allow

THE MAN BEHIND THE MEN

Elijah to conclude the un-Islamic belief that Allah had "come in the person of" Master Fard Muhammad; that Fard the "Saviour" was God incarnate.

"One of the attributes of Allah, The All-Wise God, Who is the Supreme Being, is Knowledge.

"Knowledge is the result of learning and is a force or energy that makes its bearer accomplish or overcome obstacles, barriers and resistance. In fact, God means possessor or power and force. The education my people need is that knowledge, the attribute of God, which creates power to accomplish and make progress in the good things or the righteous things. We have tried other means and ways and we have failed. Why not try Islam? It is our only salvation. It is the religion of Allah, His prophets and our forefathers."

(as drawn by E. Majied)

Taken from the December 19, 1969 issue of *Muhammad Speaks*. *(Muslim Journal file)*

POSSIBILITY OF FORGIVING ELIJAH MUHAMMAD

Ironically, Nation of Islam members have noted that both Fard and Elijah spoke of Allah in the third person, an indication that both men understood that Allah was not Fard, nor yet a human being. This conclusion is supported by another teaching of the Nation of Islam that taught "god" meant "power and force"; a concept that was based upon a belief that "the gods come in threes." Therefore, it can be concluded that when Elijah Muhammad said "the black man is God," he may have been referring to "power and force." But when Elijah prayed he was referring to Allah, the Creator.

One common Nation of Islam prayer, that Elijah Muhammad printed in *Message to the Blackman*, on page 148 clearly is not a prayer to Fard, to the "black man" or to "power and force." Without doubt it was a prayer to the same God who Fard prayed to. The prayer states: *"Surely I have turned myself to Thee being upright to Him who originated the heavens and the earth and I am not of the polythesists (sic). Surely my prayer, my sacrifices, my life and my death are all for Allah, the Lord of the Worlds. No associate has He, and this am I commanded. Oh Allah, Thou art the King, there is no God but Thee. Thou art my Lord and I am Thy servant."*

Imam Yusuf Shah while serving as the imam in Indianapolis, IN, often interpreted "the gods comes in threes" concept as a message pointing to the continuity of a leadership progression that began with Fard through Elijah on to Wallace. Using a structure for his analogy, Shah would say that the first god (power and force) was Fard who came and built the structure; and that Elijah, the second god (power and force) maintained the structure; and that Wallace, representing the third god (power and force) would come and tear down what had been built and start building all over again with the liberty to use anything from the original structure in the rebuilding process.

At a December 12, 2004 *Imam's Class* with a delegate of Muslim leaders, Imam Wallace Mohammed explained to the visiting imams how he arrived at the conclusion that his father had opened the way for him to tear down and rebuild the Muslim community that gave birth to him.

> My father said to me that if he changed what he was telling the people, the people would say that what he was saying before was not correct. He said, "Son, I am not to correct what I am saying." He was telling me it was in my hands. I had not established myself in his image. You don't know how it feels to stray from your father and undo his teachings and know that my father would be comfortable with me. My father would finish his dinner and then relax. He would just carry on the conversation. He invited me to sit with him. He said to me, "Something must be after this"! I was not confrontational with my father. "You can

have it all." He told me these things and it was a mercy not to have me feeling that my father was hating me for what I was doing. He loved what I was doing. He said, "Clara, my son has got it. My son can go anywhere he wants to preach." He said, "Preach that gospel." I had no gospel. Most of the officials were there when my father made those statements. When my father passed, the national staff was already supporting me. I was tearing down the place. I had to tear it down in order to build it up again. I knew where I was going and I knew the true believers would appreciate it.

— December 12, 2004 Imam's Class

The arcane meanings for God in the mysterious teachings that Mr. Fard left with Elijah Muhammad, resulted in multiple understandings and explanations for who and what was God. The Nation of Islam's understanding of God sometimes differed from the common and routine definitions of God as held by the general public. Elijah Muhammad's understandings of "God" as the divine being that created the heavens and earth referred to a lofty Creator, whereas the "god" in "power and force" did not carry that same loftiness and divinity. Likewise, Elijah referring to Fard as "God in the person" didn't necessarily mean that he thought the physical man Fard was actually God, the Supreme Being, but that Fard was merely a vehicle that God was working through.

Islam, as taught in the Qur'an and exemplified by Muhammed the Prophet of Islam who lived over 1,400 years ago, states clearly that God embodied in any physical form or representation constitutes shirk, which in Islam means false worship. As mentioned above, the punishment is serious for committing shirk, murder and adultery, "Unless he repents, believes, and works righteous deeds, for Allah will change the evil of such persons into good, and Allah is Oft-Forgiving, Most Merciful."

Before Elijah Muhammad died, on February 25, 1975, many believed, as explained by his son Wallace, that he had a change of heart regarding his belief in God. Elijah Muhammad's statement, "Something must be after this," is testimonial proof of a man in transition, who is at a stage in his life of accepting and believing in a concept of God, the creator of the heavens and earth, as being greater than Mr. W.D. Fard, a man who wasn't born until 1877.

Elijah Muhammad's health declined rapidly during the last year of his life, and members in the Nation of Islam sensed that future changes were in the air as indicated in the summer of 1974 when Elijah's promised helper, Wallace at the age of 40, returned. Many Nation of Islam believers proudly said, "Wallace is back!" The son that Mr. W.D. Fard promised would be a helper to his father had returned to the fold of the Nation of Islam, and was working with his father in capacities of leadership in Chicago and other cities around America.

Wallace's 1974 return to a leadership role also included teaching Islam from the rostrums of Nation of Islam temples. Unfettered from teaching according to the typical, strictly controlled Nation of Islam discourse, Minister Wallace introduced new life into his father's community as he traveled from city to city. Wallace's freedom to teach as he pleased signaled a religious conversion in the heart and mind of Elijah Muhammad towards Wallace's different understanding of Islam; further proof of a Elijah Muhammad in conversion.

Elijah Muhammad repeatedly demonstrated a change of mind and heart, and a progression in his thinking away from the narrow restrictions of the black nationalistic Islam that discounted a belief in life after death. Toward the end of his life Elijah Muhammad was moving towards universal Islam. Wallace shared that he witnessed his father openly ponder the thought of life after death. After one of the official meetings that were held in the home of Elijah Muhammad on Sundays, Wallace had a private conversation with his father.

> I recall my father and I at the table. He said, "Son, there must be something after death." I didn't ask him for that; it just came right out of the clear blue sky. That is what he said to me at the table. He said, "Son, there must be something after death." So I'm a witness that my father had begun to question things he once preached and tried to establish as reality.
> — Telephone interview

Wallace revealed other statements from Elijah Muhammad that were shared at the table in his home, that verify Elijah Muhammad having a change of mind about many of the tenets he had promoted earlier in his mission as the leader of the Nation of Islam. Wallace, elucidating upon Elijah Muhammad's comments on "Yakub's History", highlighted what appears to be a renewed perspective from Elijah Muhammad on the Yakub story. Wallace related that a few years before his father's passing, in the presence of his secretaries, a few captains along with the Supreme Captain Elijah Muhammad II, Elijah Muhammad shared a reinterpretation of "Yakub's History". Instead of seeing the Yakub report as history, Elijah Muhammad began to explain it as an allegory referring to modern times. Wallace recalled his father saying, "Brothers, I'm beginning to think that our Saviour when he was giving us that '"Yakub's History"', that he was talking about today." Wallace explained, "So that means that he didn't see it as history any more. We called it history, '"Yakub's History".' If he said it is "today" that means I don't see it as history any more." (Telephone interview)

The Islam that Elijah Muhammad taught for more than four decades was an Islam in constant transition that concludes with him giving a grand appraisal of his son's divergent message of Islam, which differed in style and content from the traditional Nation of Islam sermon. The Nation of Islam of 1975, represented a definite change from the black nationalistic version of Islam that proclaimed W.D. Fard as "God in the Person." By 1975 the Nation of Islam had been primed by Elijah Muhammad to accept the universal Islam that was being promoted by his son Wallace. In the final years of his life it is important to reiterate that Elijah Muhammad also made reconciliatory statements to white America, and discouraged his followers from using certain racially charged catechisms. In his last Saviour's Day address, Elijah Muhammad made an almost 180-degree turn in his approach to white people by showering them with the utmost respect.

Surely there are many who may never be able to forgive Elijah Muhammad. But given an appreciation for how he evolved and changed his message, with his family and staff as witnesses, then forgiving Elijah Muhammad is plausible. Further, if one considers the Qur'anic and Biblical verses that graciously open the doors to forgiveness, then one easily can conclude that God forgiving Elijah Muhammad is a very strong possibility.

Islam and most major religions teach that God is the final judge of each individual. The accusations of murder, fornication and false worship, that seem to haunt Elijah Muhammad and his many great achievements, have surely been overplayed by those who wish to portray him in only a negative light.

The good that Elijah Muhammad achieved, juxtaposed against the inconclusive serious charges against him, far outweigh his wrongs. Historians should revisit him and give more attention to accurately recording his whole life, without prematurely reaching for the hackneyed conclusions of adamant condemnation that other writers have regurgitated. Seeing this influential man in his totality is the proper foundation for discussing the possibility of forgiving the Honorable Elijah Muhammad, the man behind the men. It is a view of Elijah Muhammad that one book alone cannot adequately fulfill.

-§- CHAPTER -§-
TWENTY

The Epilogue
A composite review of Elijah Muhammad the Leader, Reformer, Educator, Businessman, Social Scientist, Social Agitator, Dietician, Family Man, Theologian, Inspirational

(Photographer and Date Unknown)

In this concluding chapter, before we fast-forward our minds towards the more mature and enjoyable America of the 21st-century, a composite review of Mr. Elijah Muhammad — while remaining cognizant of the post-Jim Crow America in which he lived — should be in order. To gain a better understanding of Elijah Muhammad it was necessary to revisit the ugly America that Elijah Muhammad knew, a racially burdened America, an old America that, as he predicted in his book, *The Fall of America*, has failed.

Comparatively, the great Rev. Dr. King heralded a visionary appeal towards hope in a more beautiful America. "I have a dream that one day

THE MAN BEHIND THE MEN

this nation will rise up and live out the true meaning of its creed: 'We hold these truths to be self-evident, that all men are created equal." Thankfully, Dr. King's *Dream* is becoming truer with every breath we take. Since the passing of these two civil rights-era leaders, we have witnessed both the fall of the ugly racially oppressive America and the rebirth of a more beautiful America. This fact was verified right before our very eyes — our physical eyes as well as our mental and spiritual eyes — with President Barack Hussein Obama's inaugural address titled "A New Birth of Freedom."

This book's return visit to the dark burdensome era that gave birth to an Elijah Muhammad was not only necessary but a long overdue journey. Still more books on Elijah Muhammad, the honorable leader of thousands — maybe millions of people — are needed if our society is to better appreciate the connection of the various components of the African American community. The journey taken by Elijah Muhammad is an expression of one man's life that resonates, even to this day, with many poor and rejected people as well as with those still laboring under glass ceilings in the workplace.

Mr. Elijah Poole, the poor southern migrant from Deepstep, GA, while residing in Detroit, MI encountered a foreigner named Fard Muhammad who went by myriad names, including Wallace, W.F. Muhammad, Wali Muhammad, and W.D. Fard. This foreigner was promoting a strange message called "Islam." Elijah adopted Fard's brand of Islam and spent 42 years struggling to lead and establish a community — a womb of sorts — for redeveloping and activating the inert minds and souls of African Americans.

Elijah Muhammad is the man who history must record as the individual who took hopeless Negroes who, after accepting Elijah as the "Messenger of Allah," were lifted up by him to become respectful and productive citizens. These Negro converts, already feeling rejected by the white population because of the mistreatment they had received due to the color of their skin, were now, after deciding to join Elijah Muhammad, also being rejected by some of the other non-Muslim "Negroes," including close family members. Consequently, those who converted to the Nation of Islam became those who were rejected by the rejected. Elijah Muhammad inherited and pursued a largely uneducated following; often morally conscious individuals who willingly opened their hearts and minds to the message he called "Islam."

While facing great odds, Elijah Muhammad raised the quality of life for not just a mere hundred followers. Over the generations he elevated the lives of hundreds of thousands of African Americans. Additionally, in many ways he has impacted the thinking of all African Americans as well as other Americans.

Elijah Muhammad produced many men and women in the Nation of Islam who deserve to have their life stories told; however, this book has focused on a select few that we have dubbed as the *four stars* because of their

EPILOGUE

international status. These are men who have been graciously welcomed and honored at palaces and state departments of nations around the world. What other person in history can claim they produced such fruits from the African American race? None. Not even his contemporary, the Rev. Dr. Martin Luther King Jr., or other past leaders such as Marcus Garvey, Charles "Sweet Daddy" Grace or Booker T. Washington. Neither they nor their organizations can claim producing disciples who became internationally renown as Elijah's men — Malcolm, Ali, Farrakhan and Wallace — are known.

The Honorable Elijah Muhammad himself was recognized internationally. He was visited by and/or received as a guest by heads of states and religious leaders around the world. As a recognized leader he was a guest of President Gamel Abdel Nasser of Egypt and his visits to other nations include Copenhagen, Denmark; Istanbul, Turkey; Lebanon; Jordan; Ethiopia; Mecca and Medina in Saudi Arabia; Karachi, Pakistan, and Mexico.

The African American journey to complete freedom continues, and Elijah Muhammad can best be understood if he is better appreciated as an important step in the many notable footsteps taken by other African American leaders on the road to freedom.

The Honorable Elijah Muhammad was a man whose leadership was in constant transition. Yet he remained faithful to his teacher Mr. W.D. Fard and to his charge to improve the conditions of African Americans. One change noted in his leadership is upon his release from prison in 1946. He began to encourage more business growth within the Nation of Islam. The influx of business life into the Nation of Islam produced an attractive showpiece of success, an image that Elijah told his ministers to "get at all cost."

This aggressive pursuit of business success delivered Elijah Muhammad an unexpected test. Imam Wallace Mohammed noted that with the business success, "...something happened. And suddenly, in the leadership there were as many "Superflies" as there were real ministers. And in time the leadership of the Nation of Islam became Superfly leadership. People showing one face to the camera, and off the camera, they were taking money from dope business, from the narcotics business. Taking money from prostitution (and) taking money from bank robbery." The Nation of Islam survived this trial and heavy burden that was placed upon their shoulders during this period, a survival made possible by the sincerity of those dedicated to the essence of Elijah Muhammad's messages of "Up you mighty people" and "Do For Self."

Another glimpse of a change in his leadership style was seen when he displayed support for Muhammad Ali when he fought George Foremen in 1974. Before this fight Elijah Muhammad constantly and consistently denounced sports, even publicly criticizing Ali's choice to pursue his boxing career.

THE MAN BEHIND THE MEN

A major advancement in the development of Elijah Muhammad's leadership is witnessed in the healing of the rift between himself and his son Wallace. After years of theological disagreement, Elijah in 1974 granted Wallace full access to the community, allowing him to speak at Nation of Islam mosques nationwide with the blessing, "Son you can go anywhere and teach that gospel."

Another striking change of emphasis in Elijah Muhammad's leadership was his theme for his final Saviour's Day address on February 26, 1974. There was no tirade against the evils of white devilry. Quite to the contrary he openly praised the achievements of white people, exonerating them of being the cause of the dismal state of African Americans. In turn he charged his own followers and African Americans in general to be more responsible for the quality and progress of their own community life.

The Honorable Elijah Muhammad's striving to improve the quality of life for himself and his followers did not go unnoticed, as shown in the praises he received during the last few years of his life. Upon his death in 1975 numerous citations and condolences poured in from religous and political leaders around America. The March 13, 1975 issue of *Jet* magazine carried the following accolades made in honor of Mr. Elijah Muhammad:

> *Elijah Muhammad has presented to Black people in this country a model of thrift, of hard work, of devotion to self, and of cleanliness of mind and body that we don't get in many other places.*
> — Julian Bond, Chairman, NAACP

> *His teachings of dignity, self-respect, discipline and a sense of responsibility are the great works he leaves behind. And this we admire no matter what our religion.*
> — Fr. George Clements
> Pastor Chicago's Holy Angels Roman Catholic Church

> *He was an outstanding citizen who was always interested in helping young people and especially the poor. He always exalted the basic family unit, which is something we should all admire, and he developed an educational system which preaches dignity, self-respect and accomplishment.*
> — Richard Daley, former Chicago Mayor

> *He emphasized the elements of self-help, self-respect, and economic independence...He made a distinct contribution, not only to his own organization but to the people of this country in that he showed what can be done with a little sacrifice and a little effort. In these participants, we would do well to emulate his philosophies and positions.*
> — Rev. J. H. Jackson
> Former President, National Baptist Convention U.S.A.

EPILOGUE

The Messenger made the message very clear. He turned alienation into emancipation. He concentrated on taking the slums out of the people and then the people out of the slums...He was the father of Black consciousness. His leadership exceeded far beyond the membership of the Black Muslims. For more than three decades, the Honorable Elijah Muhammad has been the spiritual leader of the Nation of Islam and a progressive force for Black identity and consciousness, self determination and economic development.
— Reverend Jesse L. Jackson

Muhammad was a man "of unquestioned talents and leadership ability who has left an indelible mark on his times.
— Vernon E. Jordan
Former executive director of the
National Urban League

Elijah Muhammad gave Blacks new confidence in their potential to become creative and self-sufficient people. In addition, he taught his followers the efficacy and rewards of hard work, fair play, and abstinence. It has been shown beyond a shadow of a doubt that the Muslims who have followed his economic teachings have been comparatively prosperous and have in many cases moved substantially ahead in their economic pursuits...He gave also his people a successful formula for home and family life. The rate of delinquency among Muslim children is extremely low. The rate of divorce is quite low. The stability of the Muslim home is ideal for which the rest of America might strive.
— Dr. C. Eric Lincoln
Author Black Muslims In America
Professor, Duke Univ.

Mr. Muhammad's life was one of peace, harmony and great integrity. He made the Nation of Islam a pillar of strength in Black communities throughout the country."
— Ralph Metcalfe, former Chicago Congressman

This man and his work were a new frontier for Blacks in the United States and for Black people throughout the world. I admired him and I still admire his effort.
— Rev. Leon Sullivan
Founder Opportunities Industrialization
Centers of America

THE MAN BEHIND THE MEN

It has been well over 30 years since Elijah Muhammad passed and still his Nation of Islam, notwithstanding its racial stances, remains the best model for independent African American achievement. If not for the Nation of Islam's stinging racial language and separation stances, America would have, a long time ago, crowned Elijah Muhammad's community as the top role model for African American achievement. However, it also can be argued that it was the loud racial stance and separation from white hegemony that enabled the Nation of Islam to achieve their success.

A sense of pride in "blackness," as well as much of the blackening of African American Christianity can be traced back to Elijah Muhammad. David J. Bosch, in Gayraud Wilmore's and James Cone's book *Black Theology: a Documentary History, 1966-1979, Vol 1*, on page 221 acknowledges Elijah Muhammad's indirect but effect shaping of America's black Christian theology. Bosch's defense of Christianity as a viable faith option for African Americans obligated him to acknowledge that, over the course of one decade that spanned the 1960s, the Nation of Islam's public criticism of Christianity as the "white man's religion" necessitated African American theologians to advance a blacken version of Christianity. Bosch wrote:

> To some extent American Black Theology can be described as the Negro Christians' response to the challenge posed by the Black Muslims in the U.S.A. In the early sixties the Black Muslims declared openly: "The Christian religion is incompatible with the Negroes' aspirations for dignity and equality in the U.S.A. Christian love has proved to be the white man's love for himself and his race. For the black man Islam offers the only hope for justice and equality in the world we must build for tomorrow." In contrast to this challenge the Black Theology of the late sixties has proclaimed that the Christian gospel, if preached correctly, truly aims at the dignity and salvation of the black man.

Elijah Muhammad's influence extended into many spiritual and social aspects of African American life. His influence upon them choosing Islamic and African names is undeniable. Other African American daily regimens such as pork-free diets and modest dress often reflect the teachings of Mr. Elijah Muhammad.

How well American historians adhere to the sanctity of the *Standards of Professional Conduct*, the ethics that govern historians, is crucial to how the real Elijah Muhammad will be recorded in the future. America having the proper regard for Elijah Muhammad may serve as a litmus test of America's ability to accurately and fully report, in respectful ways, difficult events and challenging individuals who have in untraditional, seemingly awkward methods, helped to shape America as a nation.

EPILOGUE

Another impact Elijah Muhammad had on the overall American scene was demonstrated with his importation of fish from abroad. Not only did he create hundreds of jobs for his followers, he also helped secure employment for the dock workers in America. From coast to coast in every major and midsize city, the Fruit of Islam men sold Elijah Muhammad's Whiting H&G fish. Imam Abdul-Karim Hasan declared that the Nation of Islam's Los Angeles Mosque No. 27 Whiting H&G fish crew of over 200 men sold over 250,000 pounds of fish monthly. "We had refrigerated trucks on the streets. We even had a tractor trailer that we bought just to do our delivering of the fish to other cities."

Hasan highlighted the fact that Elijah Muhammad was a master at getting people to get things done. "The Honorable Elijah Muhammad didn't have much education, but the man was a master psychologist. He knew how to get people to do things. He knew how to get them to feel good about doing it and knew how to get them to do it." Hasan summarized a historical fact that many writers on Elijah Muhammad often overlook when speaking of his legacy. "Regardless to how he did it, at least he did it when all the other intellectuals couldn't do it. I get kind of angry when people kind of negate the things that he did. And when you look at it, he did that with a third grade education and most of these people with PhD degrees couldn't do it."

(Muslim Journal file)

THE MAN BEHIND THE MEN

Songs were written in recognition of Elijah Muhammad's Whiting H&G fish program. In addition to the 1974 tune appropriately named "Whiting H&G" produced by musicians Kool and the Gang, members of the Los Angeles Muslim fish crew also recorded and released a tune titled "The Fish Song."

The Fish Song
By The New Creation
(Wali Ali, Rasheed Shakoor, & Hammid Abdul-Wadud)

At Last we've got it
We've got what?
Good fish of our own
At last we've got it
Good fish of our own
And we thank Allah for our leader and teacher
And we're so proud
Of Mr. Muhammad
And we're in your neighborhood with that fish today
Yeah! Yeah! Yeah!
We're in your neighborhood with that fish today
And now we got Shabazz Good Foods
Down in the ghetto
And we've got a price
That you can afford
So come on and get your fish
We will make you a wholesome dish
And we're so proud
We're so proud of Mr. Muhammad
Of Mr. Muhammad!
Of Mr. Muhammad!
And we're in your neighborhood with that fish today
Yeah! Yeah! Yeah!
Muhammad is on time
Brought it all the way from Peru
From Elijah to you
And it's imported from Peru
It's the freshest fish in town
Why don't you pick up five or ten pounds?
It's the best fish for you and me
That Whiting H&G
It's the purest fish in town
Why don't you pick up five or ten pounds?
Yes, we're in your neighborhood with that fish today
Yeah! Yeah! Yeah!

EPILOGUE

Imam Ayman Abdul-Mujeeb, the former Donald 30X, was one of the leading Whiting H&G fish salesmen in the Los Angeles area. Before going out to sell the fish door to door, the Fruit of Islam members would inspire themselves by singing their tune "The Fish Song." Abdul-Mujeeb stated, "We played it and got fired up and went out there and sold fish." He recalls, "It was intended to put this song on all of the fish trucks, but we never got a chance to do it."

The Nation of Islam's Whiting H&G fish program is one of Elijah Muhammad's many nationwide success stories that, just as his coast-to-coast school system and nationwide mosques, positively affected the lives of millions.

Elijah Muhammad's leadership in the spread of Islam in America was a notable success, including within departments of corrections. The teaching of universal Islam in prisons is common today but the impetus of Islam being recognized and respected throughout America's penal systems is due to Elijah Muhammad and his earlier followers.

Imam Abdul-Raoof Nasir, a staff chaplain for the California Department of Corrections since 1974, has concluded that Elijah Muhammad's May 8, 1942 imprisonment that landed him in the Federal Correction Institution at Milan, MI was a very significant event. Elijah Muhammad's five-year sentence for draft evasion and encouraging others to resist the draft was the initiation of the wide-spread distribution of Islam throughout America's prisons.

Nasir's research on the growth of Islam in America's penal system notes that shortly after Elijah Muhammad was incarcerated, "Within the following months over a hundred of his most loyal followers, trusted followers, were also incarcerated along with him. As far as our research has been able to discover, this is the first and the largest presence of Muslims in the U.S. penal system. I mean a concentrated presence of Muslims in the U.S. penal system." This influx of Nation of Islam followers led to many other inmates being converted while in prison due to their "contact with this large body of dedicated people to the teachings that the Honorable Elijah Muhammad was the leader of."

Elijah Muhammad was released from prison on August 24, 1946. Ironically, in February of the same year, another individual who would later become a well known Muslim, entered a state prison in Massachusetts. His name was Malcolm Little, who later became known as Malcolm X. But Nasir explained that it was due to the incarceration of Elijah Muhammad that "the reputation and the presence of Al-Islam in the US penal system is set. The seed was planted, the die was cast."

In June of 1964, eighteen years after his release from prison Elijah Muhammad's name was forever established as the pioneer of prison reform, not just for Muslims but for all inmates. The U.S. Supreme Court in ((Cooper v. Pate, 378 U.S. 546 (1964)) reversed a lower court's ruling that denied Illinois State Penitentiary inmates, who were members of the Nation of Islam, the right to practice their faith or to receive Islamic periodicals. As a result of this judicial victory for Muslim inmates the doors for prison reform for all inmates of every faith, nationwide, were sprung wide open which soon led to inmate's civil rights reforms.

The contribution of Elijah Muhammad to American culture is significant. He is a key figure in the shaping of African American diets, music, and education. Even with his constant barrage of disparaging remarks against Elijah Muhammad, Karl Evanzz admits that Elijah is responsible for contributing many positive factors that improved the life of African Americans and America as a whole. Evanzz acknowledges that Elijah Muhammad's book *How To Eat To Live*, greatly influenced the diet of African Americans who desired better eating habits.

"How to Eat to Live." *Muhammad Speaks* - May 11, 1973.
(Muslim Journal file)

Elijah Muhammad's impact upon the music industry is evidenced in James Brown's song *Say it Loud (I'm Black and I'm Proud)*, and Motown's Temptations song *Message from a Black Man*, a rephrase of Elijah Muhammad's book *Message to the Blackman in America*. Musicians influenced directly by Elijah Muhammad include Kool and the Gang, The Last Poets, Joe Tex (Yusuf Hazziez) and many other entertainers.

Elijah's educating of disenfranchised African Americans cannot be overlooked. Not only did he provide learning, he also provided — although heavily penalized by public officials — models of independent African American schools in a spirit similar to that expressed by Dr. Carter G.

EPILOGUE

Woodson, who stated in the preface of his book *The Mis-Education of the Negro*, "If the white man wants to hold on to it (European styled education), let him do so; but the Negro, so far as he is able, should develop and carry out a program of his own." (xii)

On numerous occasions beginning in the 1940s through the 1960s police stormed the schools and mosques of Elijah Muhammad. Yet he refused to give in even after the police incursions resulted in members losing their lives. Elijah Muhammad's refusal to fold under the constant harassment from police officials and truant officers who were trying to close his schools, demonstrated to other African Americans that they too could have their independent schools. The benefits of Elijah establishing an independent school system continues even today. This achievement is evidenced in the number of Islamic schools that operate in America under a variety of names, including the many Clara Muhammad Schools that are named after his wife.

Another sacrifice made by numerous Nation of Islam men and women members is time served in jail for no other reason than seeking to observe their religious duties in accord with the laws of the United States of America. Current American history only reports the Civil Rights Movement marchers who spent time in jail for standing up for their human and civil rights. However, the followers of Elijah Muhammad also suffered this same mistreatment. Although every sacrifice of spending time in jail is important, it can be argued that proportionally the sacrifices of Nation of Islam members going to jail is greatly multiplied over the losses endured by those in the Civil Rights Movement, especially considering the fact that the Nation of Islam membership was substantially smaller than the number of civil rights workers.

Yusuf Abdullah, the former Clinton X, today is the resident imam of the Nashville Masjid of Al-Islam. In the 1970s he was a member of Muhammad's Mosque No. 60 under the leadership of Minister Earl X, the now Imam Ilyas Muhammad, also of Nashville, TN. Abdullah recaptured the spirit he and the Nation of Islam newspaper salesmen had when selling the *Muhammad Speaks* publication. Often these brothers had to deal with the local police who wanted to deny them their religious rights and stop them from vending on public streets. These confrontations often resulted in them going to jail.

Abdullah explained, "We were determined with all of our strength to do whatever it takes to get the word of the Honorable Elijah Muhammad to the African American people at all cost." Abdullah admits that the salesmen's methods of selling were very "intense" and "aggressive" which may have increased the tension between Nation of Islam newspaper salesmen and the police. The Muslims were dedicated to selling their newspaper and the Nashville police were dedicated to stopping the sale of *Muhammad Speaks*. Abdullah said, "The authorities with their determination to stop it they started putting us in jail." He added, "I must have went to jail about 40 times."

Still not to be denied his civil rights to sell *Muhammad Speaks*, Abdullah explained, "As soon as I got out (of jail) I would go right back to selling papers because I believed that the paper carried the words of the Honorable Elijah Muhammad and I believed carried the words of God; and I was determined that I would give my life to see to it that that word reach as many people as I could make it reach." Abdullah acknowledges that Minister Earl X repeatedly came to the aid of the Muslim newspaper salesmen. The harrassment became so intense until Minister Earl ordered Abdullah to "stop getting arrested." He noted that all of the men in the Nation of Islam were committed to standing up for their rights.

The *Muhammad Speaks* newspaper salesmen often traveled in groups of two, three, or four brothers, still it was not uncommon to see a salesman standing alone. Abdullah noted that their small groups distinguished the followers of Elijah Muhammad from the Civil Rights marchers because in the Civil Rights Movement there tended to be a large crowd. "We didn't always have a large crowd, and we would go out and do our job of seeing to it that the words of the Honorable Elijah Muhammad reached the African American people." This determined spirit of the followers of Elijah Muhammad and their willingness to sacrifice life and limb in order to sell *Muhammad Speaks* was common throughout the ghettoes of America.

Yet there are some common traits shared by jailed Nation of Islam members and the jailed followers of the Civil Rights Movement. Abdullah noted, "The similarities are that we had a call, and I think all of us would say that the call was similar even though they were articulated differently. I think all of it was for social justice and equality for the African American people. We were all after the same thing." Abdullah concluded, "We just couldn't see another generation of living under the same conditions that were existing before the movement started."

Both Elijah Muhammad's Nation of Islam and the Civil Rights Movement that featured Dr. Martin Luther King were after the same goal, the complete freedom of Negroes. As mentioned earlier these two leaders offered white America a choice similar to what the "good cop - bad cop" scenario offers to the criminal suspect: either you can cooperate willingly, or corporate unwillingly, but sooner or later you must cooperate.

One event that evidences how the Nation of Islam and the Civil Rights Movement represent two sides of the same coin occurred on February 5, 1965 when Malcolm X met with Coretta Scott King to offer support for Dr. King who was jailed in Selma, AL. Although at this time he was no longer a member of the Nation of Islam, still Malcolm recognized the strong effect that his mere presence would have on all people, particularly on those white people who felt the need to differentiate between, and dichotomize the two African American movements. Cognizant that Dr. King had avoided his

EPILOGUE

earlier offers to help, Malcolm related to Coretta that he had not come to Selma to increase any difficulties for her husband. Malcolm's rationalization was that, "If white people realize what the alternative is, perhaps they will be more willing to hear Dr. King."

Martin Luther King and Malcom X Shabazz
(Photographer and Date Unknown)

In closing this comparison of the Nation of Islam and the Civil Rights Movement it is sufficient to conclude that Elijah Muhammad was a definite factor for social change. On the surface his direct role in the Civil Rights Movement appears to be quite diminished, yet privately there are many accounts of Elijah Muhammad anonymously posting bond for jailed, non-Muslim Civil Rights Movement workers and his giving support to their causes as shown in his giving financial assistance to Julian Bond in 1968.

The life of Elijah Muhammad is too magnificent and his contributions are too numerous to cover in this book. It was his tenacious willpower that attracted the love and support of thousands of followers. It was his courage, rare amongst African Americans of his day that influenced the four stars highlighted in this book.

THE MAN BEHIND THE MEN

The Honorable Elijah Muhammad: The Man Behind the Men is not an attempt to water down the divisive racial message that for decades was an integral part of Elijah Muhammad's teachings. This book is a review of many of his overlooked achievements and the international successes of four of his students; Malcolm, Muhammad, Louis, and Wallace.

Without taking time to properly know this man, society and many historians have prejudicially categorized, labeled and defined Elijah Muhammad. This dereliction was followed up by presenting these biased conclusions to the general public without certification from those whom he affected the most, namely his former followers.

Elijah Muhammad was sincerely dedicated to the improvement of the lives of African Americans. His devotion to his teacher, Mr. W.D. Fard, and his dedication to the message that Fard left in his trust, is a clear demonstration that Elijah Muhammad believed that the version of Islam he was teaching was 100 percent "the truth."

Elijah Muhammad was honored as the Nation of Islam's sole leader by his followers who crowned him with a jeweled fez. He wore this crown with humility as was indicated in the words he uttered to his followers at the 1974 Saviour's Day, "I hope you don't chop my head off for this mighty crown I have on."

Yes, he was controversial, challenging and tenacious. For some who were outside of the Nation of Islam he carried an air of mystique. For some he was enigmatic and just plain old racist. Nonetheless, the leadership of Elijah Muhammad was very medicinal for the contemporary problems and needs of African Americans during his lifetime. His message also provided white America an opportunity to revisit their own racial transgressions as they watched him promoting a black version of racial supremacy.

His teachings and thinking and values have melded deep into the consciousness and subconscious of African Americans. Not only is Elijah Muhammad the man behind the four internationally renowned men highlighted in this book. He also is the man behind the shaping of hundreds of thousands of other men and women who were members of his Nation of Islam, and the other subsequent groups that emerged after his death that also use the moniker *Nation of Islam*. Due to the good fruit that his tree produced and the numerous rewards that many people today enjoy because of his works, I conclude that the Honorable Elijah Muhammad — as with other great men and women in our American history — is not only "the man behind the men." He is also the man behind, and the influence behind, many of our American thoughts, feelings, and attitudes toward life.

Thank you for reading **The Honorable Elijah Muhammad: The Man Behind the Men**.

100-PLUS QUOTES OF THE HONORABLE ELIJAH MUHAMMAD

The following selected 100 quotes of Elijah Muhammad maintain the purpose of this book, which is to show him in a light different than that used by most historians. The public is well acquainted with Elijah's calling the white man the "devil" and his other separatist statements. Due to other media outlets the image of Elijah Muhammad as a stern disciplinarian who seemed to never smile is well ingrain in our minds. The Man Behind the Men is an endeavor to show other aspects of this African American personality; therefore, we have selected specific quotes that also show an unknown side of Elijah Muhammad. Whenever possible we have categorized and identified the source.

1. We are just entering into a day and time that we should have had 100 years ago.
2. We stay out of the way and let Allah fight for us.
3. The duty of the civilized man is to teach and train the uncivilized.
4. Mere belief accounts for nothing unless carried into practice.
5. A coward Muslim is not a Muslim.
6. Dissatisfaction brings change.
7. Where you find no decent women, you will find no decent men.
8. A nation can rise no higher than its woman.
9. Protect And Elevate Your Woman.
10. You and I may go to Harvard, we may go to York of England, or go to Al Ahzar in Cairo and get degrees from all of these great seats of learning. But we will never be recognized until we recognize our women.
11. My beloved brothers in America, you have lost the respect for your woman and therefore you have lost the respect for yourself.
12. She is your first nurse. She is your teacher. Your first lesson comes from your mother. If you don't protect your mother, how do you think you look in the eyes of other fellow human beings?
13. When a man puts weapons in his pockets, or a gun, I will make it clear, it takes his mind off God's protection and puts it on the gun to protect him.
14. QUESTION: How would you describe your mission? ANSWER: My mission is to give life to the dead. What I teach brings them out of death and into life.
15. Mr. Muhammad, would you make some statements about Dr. Martin Luther King and the Civil Rights Movement? ANSWER: Yes, I think Rev. King has been doing a good job, according to his knowledge.
16. The Constitution is looked upon as the legal guide, but is has never been enforced, insofar as we are concerned.

100-PLUS QUOTES OF
THE HONORABLE ELIJAH MUHAMMAD

17. If the master gave up his position as master, the slave would soon become his equal and the slave would probably vote for equal justice, go to the White House or become ruler of the country, if the equal justice was obtained the way through as it should.

18. As we have white Muslims in America, and lots of them; we have them all over the world. And they recognize and respect you. You must recognize and respect them.

19. Now remember that their flag is still flying over America. Honor and respect the man because he still has his flag.

20. There is much that can be interchanged between them and us in that way of respect.

21. Don't think that you are so great now just because God promised you the Kingdom. Wait until you get in it.

22. We must show the world that we are a Righteous people trying to set up the characteristics in our people of righteousness.

23. Since you say, now that you are righteous, then prove it. And if you say he's not righteous, he will say, he was not his maker. And that will stop your mouth. He did not make himself. It was our kind that made him.

24. Clearing a man of his past and putting him on the right road, this is a wonderful thing!

25. We are trying to do something with whatever the white folks will let us have.

26. When you have been given a chance to go for self, go for self!

27. I say that the Black man of North America, have nobody to blame but himself.

28. I don't believe in us, now in this modern time, laying down on the white man, looking for him to give us something to go for. He gave you something when he gave you freedom.

29. The earth is large! And that there is enough of it for you to have some and for them to have some. If God wants to continue to help them to live on this earth, you get that part that He gives you. And don't be worried over his.

30. Look at self before ever you start charging others, of your own faults.

31. We glorify in making fun and charging the slavemaster with keeping us a slave. He can't hold you no slave now. You're holding yourself a slave.

32. But that didn't stop him from opening up a great country that you and I are sitting here in today, glorifying our freedom.

33. I want you to remember, that if you put on a white dress, clean and spotless, and then in that dress is unclean, you can not be respected like that.

34. We can not go out and tell the public, "I'm a Muslim" unless you practice the principles of it. You have got to respect and practice the principles of Islam. I have visited the Muslim world. I have made pilgrimage to Mecca and Medina

and I have seen and I have heard. These people don't believe in foolishness. So I'm trying to clothe you, not only with the garments of salvation, but clothe you with the principles of our religion.

35. The knowledge and practice of these prayers (5 daily salats) will earn you great reward with Allah and bring about great spiritual advancement for you.

36. At present it is sufficient that you learn these prayers as we have printed them here. Some day in the near future, however, you will learn them in your own language and that of your Righteous foreparents — Arabic.

37. If a man does not treat you right, how is he going to teach you right?

38. The white man and the black man must learn to live together and to respect each other if America is to survive.

39. And Leon, (Durham — editor of *Muhammad Speaks*) I've been thinking lately, what with things in the Nation taking a turn over the years, let's not talk no more about any blue-eyed devils.

40. We get our color from the sun.

41. If little fish (people) come together, they can do big things.

42. Keep in Mind — jealousy destroys from within.

43. A true Muslim recognizes the law of Islam.

44. If one brother has a bowl of soup, you have half of that soup.

45. On Mecca: "It is the only city on or planet that is divinely protected and made sacred and inviolatable *[sic]*."

46. I'm not up here to go over the laws of the Islamic world with you if you read these things, you read them. So I'm not up here to condemn nor take away anything, only to teach you that which Allah has given to me to teach you.

47. I do not know exactly my birthday. I just know the month it came in (October). So when October passes, I say I am so and so old.

48. Now, I must tell you the truth. There will be no such thing as elimination of all white people from the earth, at the present time or at the break out of the Holy War.

49. There are some white people today who have faith in Allah and Islam though they are white, and their faith is given credit.

50. It is only through Islam that white people can be saved.

51. When two people are together at peace, they are in heaven.

52. If you choose a man to be your husband, you should live together in perfect happiness especially if you chose him.

53. Islam goes as far back as the root of Mathematics. The root of Mathematics goes as far back as Islam.

54. The greatest heaven that you enter into on believing is a peace of mind and contentment.
55. Heaven is under our feet — let's dig it out.
56. Islam is the circle of peace and the diameter of happiness.
57. Above all man's habits peace is the most satisfying of his life.
58. By nature the woman has a big job. She is the one who increases the nation.
59. A man should love his family regardless to whom or what because it is part of himself.
60. The teachings of Islam does not force the woman in no way to go out and work. It is her job to stay at home and rear her children.
61. The Muslim woman goes natural. When you see her, you are looking at natural beauty.
62. Rear your children up in the word of Allah. Allah says, 'Teach them of Me.' Burn it into their hearts.
63. By the water rising up under the foot of Hagar's child, this represents us rising up from the foot of civilization.
64. Everything written in the Bible is written to give us a picture of what is happening today.
65. The Savior gave me 104 books in the Congressional Library to study on Islam and the history of Muhammad.
66. Blessed are those who forge first to bring the way for others.
67. The sands and stars Abraham was told to count. This means Allah would raise up a nation that would be so fast in multiplying that the nations of the earth could not keep up with them.
68. The Light of God is the light of the Hereafter which will guide the people like the light of the sun.
69. When Allah bless you with His spirit you are a blessed person.
70. He (Allah) has placed a fountain in the House of Israel; drink.
71. Envy and jealousy will not make you successful.
72. There will be no end to your wisdom in the Hereafter.
73. A fool can always insult a civilized person, but a civilized person can't insult a fool because it is not his nature.
74. Proudness is sickness. This is why we are divided. We will all be one or nothing.
75. The devil has made us a slave to falsehood.
76. To go into the Hereafter and join the heavenly society you have to give up this world.

100-PLUS QUOTES OF THE HONORABLE ELIJAH MUHAMMAD

77. If you want to talk to Allah, read the Qur'an.
78. If you are guilty inside, Allah brings the guilt out in your color. He makes your color to bear witness. The guilty person turns dark because his deeds are dark. Allah makes you to reflect your deeds. Why does God make our color to bear witness to what is in us? Because the blood is the life of us.
79. If you claim to carry a clean religion, you should be clean internally and externally.
80. The property of a Muslim is sacred. This is in the Law of Islam. This means all Muslims will do their best to protect your property.
81. The more you learn, the less you seek of self advantage.
82. Just be what you are and don't try to pull one over; then you will cheap.
83. The truth separates. Allah sends a sun to separate the darkness from the day.
84. Don't be careful that you agree on right but, be careful that you don't agree on wrong.
85. Don't withhold your good just because another withholds his good. You do your part.
86. Greeting the Muslim is binding upon you, if you do not your mind is not right.
87. Your children have to be prepared for a future they have not lived. You must shape your child. Lazy parents cannot make a child successful.
88. What we long for will finally appear.
89. The right medicine for the disease in our hearts is the Spirit of Allah.
90. Whenever we would rather sin and disobey Allah's truth and guidance to make self clear then you are destroying self.
91. If you are dealing with truth, you are dealing with Allah.
92. Get in earnest with Allah.
93. Since Allah is The Master, Thee do we serve and to Thee do we beseech for help. I don't have no other one to help me but You. If I need help I have to look to You. I don't serve anyone but You. I am in my proper place as a servant. You are well able to help me. That is why I am your servant. Guide me on the right path. Now you have told Allah what path. Which is the right path? The one that Allah Blesses. The path of the righteous before me. Every word of the prayer means good.
94. Oh Allah, please let me continue to be a believer. And let no man deceive me and take away my reward.
95. Everything comes from water.
96. A well-educated, cultured and courteous people make a beautiful society when it is spiritual. The right spiritual education is Islam.

97. Speak the truth, no matter whom nor what.

98. A Muslim wants for his brother, what he wants for himself.

99. Education is a must.

100. Pay your debts!

101. I do not and the Holy Qur-an and God Do Not Approve any Muslim as being a good Muslim, that goes and makes debts (whether it is with the Believers or Infidels) and then does not pay them. This is against the Law of Truth and Righteousness of Islam! Pay your debts or do not make them!!

102. We're not a race, we're a Nation.

103. Referring to Islam after his mission the Honorable Elijah Muhammad said, "It will be a New Islam from what the old Orthodox Islam is, today. It will be altogether a New One.

104. When the new man comes, he might use what we have, and then he might not use anything that we have.

105. Not one of us will have to raise a sword. Not one gun would we need to fire. The great cannon that will be fired is our unity.

106. You are a free Black Slave 100 years up from slavery and you have not done anything constructive...for yourself.

NOTE: The preceding quotes came from the following sources:

A. *MUHAMMAD SPEAKS* newspaper September 10, 1971

B. *http://blacktown.net/ELIJAH_MUHAMMAD.html*

C. *As the Light Shineth From the East* – by Imam Warith Deen (W.D.) Muhammad

D. *Message to the Black Man in America* by Elijah Muhammad

E. January 14, 1972, Press Conference

F. From the *Final Sermon of the Honorable Elijah Muhammad*

G. From the Honorable Elijah Muhammad's book *Muslim Daily Prayer* (Feb. 1957)

H. "The Rise and Fall of Elijah Muhammad" by Karl Evanzz

I. *Salaam Magazine* July 1960

J. *100 Answers to the Most Uncommon 100 Questions* (Pub. by Secretarius Memps)

K. *Sayings of the Honorable Elijah Muhammad 'Messenger of Allah'* Compiled from the writings and conversations of the Hon. Elijah Muhammad by Sisters Anna Karriem and Captain Portia Pasha

L. The LP album *The Judgment of the World*, by Elijah Muhammad.

GLOSSARY

ARPANET – Predecessor to the internet.

As-Salaam Alaikum – The Arabic greeting, "May the Peace that only God can give be with you." The reply is, "Alaikum As-Salaam."

Ayat – Literally, "sign". Arabic for a verse of scripture.

Bilal – An Ethiopian slave living in Mecca who became the first muezzin (one who calls the faithful to prayer).

Bilalian – A word coined by Imam Wallace D. Mohammed to identify African Americans racially and ethnically.

CRAID – The Committee to Remove All Images that attempt to portray the Divine.

El-Hajj (Al-Hajj) – Title for one who has completed the hajj (pilgrimage) to Mecca. Spelled Hajjah for females.

FOI – Fruit of Islam. Male members of the Nation of Islam.

Hajj – The major pilgrimage to Mecca that includes all the rituals.

HSAAM – Acronym coined by Dr. Ihsan Bagby. Historically Sunni African American Muslims. Similar to Old Guard.

Imam – Literally, one who stands out front. An Islamic prayer leader.

Jihad – To struggle. Often misinterpreted as "holy war."

Lost-Found – African Americans who are not members of Nation of Islam.

MGT – Muslim Girl Training. Female members of the Nation of Islam.

Mother Plane (Mother Ship) – A mythological plane believed to be hovering over America that one day will rescue the 144,000 Nation of Islam members.

Old Guard – Name coined by Dr. Sherman H. Jackson to denote Non-Nation of Islam African American Muslims. Similar to HSAAM.

Salat – The five daily Islamic prayers

Shirk – An Arabic work meaning false worship. The associating of a partner with God.

Shurah – A democratic system of Islamic consultation for reaching decisions.

Sura – Arabic for a chapter of scripture.

Umrah – The minor pilgrimage to Mecca, with limited rituals.

Yakub's History – Myth of the Nation of Islam about the origin of racial differences which resulted in the creation of the white, blond hair, blue-eyed devil.

Zina – Arabic for fornication and adultery.

Zurq – Arabic for the color blue; a grayish-blue. Glaucoma.

BIBLIOGRAPHY

AalMuhammed, Jefri and Jack Baxter. Brother Minister: The Assassination of Malcolm X (1995) Format: VHS.

Al-Hadid, Dr. Amiri YaSin and Lewis V. Baldwin. Between Cross and Crescent: Christian and Muslim Perspectives on Malcolm and Martin. Gainesville, Florida: University Press of Florida, 2002.

Ali, Muhammad with Hana Yasmeen Ali. The Soul of a Butterfly: Reflections on Life's Journey. New York: Simon and Schuster, 2004.

American Historical Association. Statement on Standards of Professional Conduct. Published May 2003. Last uodated August 10, 2007. Accessed May 31, 2010. *http://www.historians.org/perspectives/issues/1989/8903/8903AHA2.cfm*

Barboza, Steven. American Jihad: Islam After Malcolm X. New York: Doubleday, 1994.

Banneker, Benjamin. Banneker's Letter to Jefferson. *http://www.pbs.org/wgbh/aia/part2/2h71t.html* ©2008 About.com, a part of The New York Times Company. Site visited May 31, 2010.

Bennett Jr., Lerone. Before the Mayflower: a History of Black America Chicago: Johnson Publishing Co., Inc., 1982 (1st Edition 1962).

Bingham, Howard. "Ali." Reader's Digest Dec 2001: 95.

--- and Max Wallace. Muhammad Ali's Greatest Fight: Cassius Clay vs. United States of America. New York: M. Evans & Company, Inc, 2000.

Brown, James with Bruce Tucker. James Brown the Godfather of Soul. New York: MacMillan, 1986.

Burton, Rev. H. Edward. Atlantic City pastor offers support for CRAID A.M. Journal (Muslim Journal) February 04, 1983. Volume 8 No. 14. Page 8.

Cheney, Charise. "Representin' God: Rap, Religion and the Politics of a Culture" ISSN:1094-902X *Volume 3, Number 1* (Fall 1999) The North Star: "A Journal of African American Religious History." Accessed Summer 2006. *http://northstar.as.uky.edu/volume3/cheney.html#back1*

Clegg, Claude Andrew. An Original Man: The Life and Times of Elijah Muhammad. New York: St. Martin Press, 1997.

Curtis, Edward E. Islam in Black America: Identity, Liberation, and Difference in African-American Islamic Thought. Albany: State University of New York Press, 2002.

CRAID Committee American Muslim Mission. Racism in Religion Evanston, Illinois. Ramadan (July) 1982.

Daley, Richard J. Sr., Ebony Magazine, "The Nation of Islam Mourns Elijah Muhammad". Vol. XXX No. 6, page 79.

BIBLIOGRAPHY

DeGruy-Leary, Dr. Joy. Post Traumatic Slave Syndrome: America's Legacy of Enduring Injury and Healing *www.joyleary.com*

Douglass, Frederick. My Bondage and My Freedom. New York: Barnes & Signet Classic, 1997.

--. Narrative of the Life of Frederick Douglass: An American Slave. Cambridge, Massachusetts: Harvard University Press, 2009

DuBois, W.E.B. The Souls of Black Folk New York: Avon, 1965.

Duffy, Kathleen. Boxing Champion Muhammad Ali Visits Ireland: Ali Visits Ennis in County Clare to Meet Irish Relatives. suite101.net. *http://boxers.suite101.com/article.cfm/boxing_champion_muhammad_ali_visits_ireland* Visited October 26, 2009.

El Muhajir, Marvin X. Teacher and Spirituality Chicken Bones: A Journal. Posted July 05, 2006. Visited October 2006 *http://www.nathanielturner.com/teacherandspiritualitymarvinx.htm*

Evanzz, Karl. The Messenger: The Rise and Fall of Elijah Muhammad New York: Pantheon Books, 1999.

Essien-Udom, E. U. Black Nationalism: A Search for an Identity in America Chicago & London: The University of Chicago Press, 1962.

File:105-24822, Elijah Muhammad, Freedom of Information Act. *http://foia.fbi.gov/muhammad/muhammad1.pdf* Visited February 20, 2007.

Fardan, Dorothy Blake, Message to the White Man and Woman in America: Yakub and the Origins of White Supremacy. Chicago: Lushena Books, Inc. - Sept 2001

Farrakhan, Louis. Farrakhan: Back Where We Belong:Speeches by Minister Louis Farrakhan. Joseph D. Eure and Richard M. Jerome (Editors), Philadelphia: PC International Press, 1989.

--. Bio-sketch of the Honorable Louis Farrakhan. The official site for the Nation of Islam *http://www.noi.org/mlf-bio.html 2006*, Visited December 18, 2006.

--. "Minister Farrakhan challenges black men" Cable News Network Online 1995. December 2002 *http://www3.cnn.com/US/9510/megamarch/1016/transcript/index.html*

--. "Fruit of Islam Meeting" Audio tape. Harlem, New York. 18 January 1975.

--. A Word of Gratitude Final Call. Special Edition March 14, 2000 Pg. 20-21.

Fauset, Arthur Huff. Black Gods of the Metropolis. University of Pennsylvania Press, - 2002 (3rd Edition).

BIBLIOGRAPHY

Franklin, John Hope. with Alfred A. Moss, Jr. <u>From Slavery to Freedom: A History of African Americans</u>. McGraw-Hill, Inc. – Feb. 2000 (8th Ed.)

Final Call. <u>Minister Farrakhan's Saviours' Day Gift</u> by A. Akbar Muhammad. http://www.finalcall.com/artman/publish/Perspectives_1/Minister_Farrakhan_s_Saviours_Day_Gift_1832.shtml. 2005. Visited September 11, 2010.

Garvey, Marcus. <u>Halt America</u>. *http://www.boomshaka.com/garvey/halt.html.* 1934.

Gilbert, Olive. <u>Narrative of Sojourner Truth; a Bondswoman of Olden Time, With a History of Her Labors and Correspondence, Drawn from Her "Book of Life"</u>. New York: Oxford University Press, 1991.

Goffe, Leslie. <u>Islam on the Rise Among African Americans</u>. *http://www.hartford-hwp.com/archives/45a/602.html* 1999, Visited October 6, 2008.

Gordon, Ed. <u>When Ali Declined to Be Drafted: News & Notes with Ed Gordon</u>. *http://www.npr.org/templates/story/story*.php?storyId=4622948 Politics & Society, April 28, 2005, Visited June 21, 2006.

Griffin, John H. <u>Black Like Me</u>. San Antonio, TX: Second Wings Press Edition, with Index, 2006.

Hanchett, Tom. <u>Saving the South's Rosenwald Schools</u>. *http://www.rosenwaldplans.org/history.html* 2004, Visited April 20, 2006.

Harris, Shanette M. <u>Black Male Masculinity and Same-Sex Friendships</u>, published in The Western Journal of Black Studies, v16 n2 p74-81 Sum 1992

Hauser, Thomas. <u>Muhammad Ali: His Life and Times</u>. New York: Simon & Schuster, 1991.

"The Healing of the Split in the African-American Muslim Community" Pluralism Project of Harvard University. February 24 - 27, 2000. December 2002 *http://www.uga.edu/islam/farrakhan.html*

Higginbotham, Aloyisus Leon. <u>Shades of Freedom</u>. New York: Oxford University Press, 1996.

"Interview with Muhammad Ali." <u>Playboy Enterprises</u> 1998. Playboy November 1975. December 2002 *http://ww3.sportsline.com/b/member/playboy/7511_b11.html.*

Islamicity.com. Hadith on the oppressed. *http://www.islamicity.com/hadith/action.lasso.asp?PageCurrent=2&PageCurrent=3&PageCurrent=2&-db=services&-lay=hadith&-format=sreply.htm&error=error.htm&-op=cn&hadith_textS=oppressed&-max=7&-find* Hadiths accessed on June 9, 2004.

BIBLIOGRAPHY

Jackson, Sherman A. Islam and the Blackamerican: Looking Toward the Third Resurrection. New York: Oxford University Press, 2005.

Jacobs, Harriet Ann. Incidents in the Life of a Slave Girl. Mineola, NY: Dover Publication, Inc., 2001 (Dover Thrift Ed.)

Jefferson, Thomas. Query XIV: The Administration of Justice and Description of the Laws? Notes on the State of Virginia, 1787. *http://mac110.assumption.edu/aas/notesonstate.html.* Site created 2006. Accessed May 31, 2010.

Kennedy, John F. Jr. "One in a Million" Truth Establishment Institute 1999. George 1996. Site visited December 2002 *http://www.truthinstitute.org/Interview.htm*

King, Dr. Martin Luther Jr. Edited by Clayborne Carson The Autobiography of Martin Luther King, Jr. New York, NY: Warner Books, Inc. - 1998.

Klinkner, Philip A. with Rogers M. Smith. The Unsteady March: The Rise and Fall of Racial Equality in America. The University of Chicago Press – 1999.

Kondo, Baba Zak A. ConspiracyS: Unravelling the Assassination of Malcolm X. Nubia Press. Washington D.C. – 1993.

Lateef, Khalid S. Look at "Self" Before Charging others...The Honorable Elijah Muhammad's Last Public Comments on Islam, Race Relations and "Black" Empowerment. Wheatley Heights, NY, 1993.

Larson, Kate Clifford. Bound for the Promised Land: Harriet Tubman – Portrait of an American Hero. United States of America, Random House, 2004.

Lester, Julius. To Be A Slave. New York: Scholastic Inc. 1968.

Lopresti, Rob. Which U.S. Presidents Owned Slaves? *http://www.nas.com/~lopresti/ps.htm.* Accessed May 30, 2010.

McElroy, Dr. Susan Williams and Kruti Dholakia. Between Plessy and Brown: Georgia School Finance in 1910. November 18, 2005. Site visited on January 11, 2008. *http://www.utdallas.edu/~kruti/georgia.pdf*

Mohammed, Abdulmalik. A Look at W. Deen Mohammed. Calumet City, IL: Ministry of W. Deen Mohammed, 1993.

Mohammed, Imam W. Deen. The Champion We Have in Common: The Dynamic African American Soul. Hazel Crest, IL: W.D.M. Ministry Publications, 2001. Pg. 6.

---. "Emam Wallace D. Muhammad's appeal to Minister Farrakhan" Bilalian News, the former Muhammad Speaks Publication April 28, 1978.

---. Growth for a Model Community in America. Chicago: W.D.M. Ministry Publications, 1995.

BIBLIOGRAPHY

---. Interview. "First Official Interview with the Supreme Minister of the Nation of Islam". By Herbert "Jabir" Muhammad. Chicago: Muhammad Speaks March 21, 1975.

---. Islam's Climate for Business Success. Chicago: The Sense Maker, 1995.

---. Muslim Journal. Life: The Final Battlefield. May 02, 2008 , Vol. 33 No. 31.

---. Prayer and Al-Islam. Chicago: Muhammad Islamic Foundation, 1982.

---. Return to Innocence: The transition of the Nation of Islam. Homewood, IL, The Sense Maker, c/o Muslim Journal, 2007.

---. Telephone Interview. 15 December 2002.

---. Public address Whittenmore House at Washington University in St. Louis, MO. October 9, 1996.

---. Public Address. "Race & Religion: How to Live Together" Muslim Student Association Forest Park Community College, St. Louis, 4 February 2000.

Muhammad, Elijah. "Clarification of Action Taken by Messenger Muhammad Against Muhammad Ali's Action" (No online date). Muhammad Speaks April 11, 1969. December 2002 *http://www.croe.org/ali2.html*

Elijah Muhammad Meets the Press. Atlanta, GA, Secretarius MEMPS Pub. (January 14, 1972 interview with no publication date or edition number).

---. Message to the Blackman in America. Philadelphia: Hakim Pub., 1965.

---. Muslim Daily Prayers. Chicago, IL: Published by University of Islam, February 26, 1957.

---. Our Saviour Has Arrived. Chicago: Muhammad's Temple of Islam, 1974.

---. Pledge to the National Flag of Islam *http://www.muhammadspeaks.com/Pledge.html*. Site visited June 1, 2010.

---. The Supreme Wisdom. Newport News, Virginia: The National Newport News and Commentator. 1957.

---. The Theology of Time: (The secret of the time). Atlanta, GA, Secretarius M.E.M.P.S., 1997.

Muhammad, Jabril "Minister Jabril Muhammad's Interview with Minister Farrakhan Part 2" April 4, 2002. Final Call April 2002. December 2002 *http://www.blackelectorate.com/articles.asp?ID=583.*

Muhammad Speaks, Vol. 12 No.14 December 15, 1972. Published by Muhammad's Temple No. 2. Chicago, IL.

Muslim Journal, Vol. 33 No. 31 May 02, 2008. Published by Muslim Journal Enterprises. Homewood, IL.

BIBLIOGRAPHY

National Flag of Islam *http://www.muhammadspeaks.com/Pledge.html* site visited January 13, 2008.

Noble, Gil "Like It Is" with Guest Wallace Mohammed/Muhammad (January 6, 1980).

Nordholt, J.W. Schulte. The People that Walk in Darkness. London, E.C. 1: Burke Publishing Co. Ltd. 1960.

Nu'Man, Muhammad Armiya. Who is Imam W. Deen Mohammed?. Jersey City, NJ: New Mind Productions, Inc., 1999.

Owens, Keith A. "The Nation of Islam: Made in Detroit" Michigan Chronicle February 22-26, 2006: 1. (Vol. 69 No. 22).

Pawelek, John M., A service in honor of the birthday of the Rev. Dr. Martin Luther King, Jr. St. Bartholomew's United Church, Hanover, PA. *http://www.hmc.psu.edu/pathology/residency/experimental/cheng%20pdf%20files/MLK%20SERMON.ST%20B'S.1.22.pdf* Presented by John M. Pawelek, January 22, 2006. Retrieved October 5, 2008.

Perry, Bruce. Malcolm: The Life of a Man Who Changed Black America. Barrytown, New York: Station Hill Press, 1991.

Pluralism Project, The Healing of the Split in the African-American Muslim Community. *http://www.uga.edu/islam/farrakhan.html* Retrieved December 19, 2006.

Raboteau, Albert J. Slave Religion: The "Invisible Institution" in the Antebellum South. New York: Oxford University Press paperback, 1980.

Rhoden, William C. Forty Million Dollar Slaves. Crown Publishers, New York: Random House, Inc. 2006.

Robinson, B.A. of the Ontario Consultants on Religious Tolerance, Human slavery – Christian support of slavery: 5th to 17th century CE. *http://www.religioustolerance.org/chr_slav4.htm* Latest update: 2007-AUG-24 (site accessed October 5, 2008).

Rock, Chris. "Bigger and Blacker" New York night club stand up. 1999 at the Apollo in New York *www.colostate.edu/Depts/Speech/rccs/theory74.htm*

Rowan, Cart T. Breaking Barriers: A Memoir. United States of America and Canada: Little, Brown and Company, 1991.

Roosevelt, Theodore. The Fertility Race: Part IV: Race Suicide *http://news.minnesota.publicradio.org/features/199711/20_smiths_fertility/part1/f4.shtml.* Site visited May 31, 2010.

Savage, Kirk. Standing Soldiers, Kneeling Slaves: Race, War, and Monument in Nineteenth-Century America. Princeton, New Jersey: Princeton University Press, 1997.

BIBLIOGRAPHY

Saviour's Day, 1975. Audio VHS tape.

Sayeed, Dr. Sayyid M. Interview. 13 September 2006.

Shabazz, Seifullah Ali, born Kevin Burke. Telephone interview. March 18, 2005.

Shah, Minister Yusuf. Audio interview. April 25, 1992.

Siddeeq, Muhammad. Telephone Interview. 4 December 2002.

Skerry, Peter. "America's Other Muslims" Wilson Quarterly Autumn 2005: 16. (Vol. 29 No. 4).

Smith, Robert C. We Have No Leaders: African Americans in the Post-Civil Rights Era. Albany, New York: State University of New York Press, 1996.

Spellman, A. B. "Interview with Malcolm X." Monthly Review Online 2001. Monthly Review March 19, 1964. December 2002. *http://www.monthlyreview.org/564mx.htm*.

Staples, Robert. The Black Family: Essays and Studies. Belmont, CA: Wadsworth Publishing Company, 1998 (6th Edition).

---. Introduction to Black Sociology. New York: McGraw-Hill, 1976.

Strathmore, William. Muhammad Ali: The Unseen Archives. United Kingdom: Parragon Publishing, 2001.

Stormfront:*www.stormfront.org/forum/showthread.php?t=152961&page=11* visited site on October 22, 2006. Last edited by Dave Cooper: 08-22-2005 at 10:06 PM.

Thurman, Howard. Jesus and the Disinherited. Boston: Beacon Press, 1996.

Time Magazine in Partnership with CNN. Races: Death and Transfiguration *http://www.time.com/time/magazine/article/0,9171,839291-5,00.html* Printed in Time Magazine; Friday, Mar. 05, 1965, Retrieved March 24, 2007.

Time-Life Books, The Editors. The American Indians: The Mighty Chieftains. Alexandria, Virginia: Time-Life Books, 1993.

Wallace, Mike with Gary Paul Gates. Between You and Me: A Memoir – Mike Wallace. New York: Hyperion books, 2005.

Wehr, Hans edited by J. M. Cowan. Arabic-English Dictionary: The Hans Wehr Dictionary of Modern Written Arabic. Ithaca, New York: Spoken Language Services, Inc. February 1976.

Wideman, John Edgar. My Soul has Grown Deep: Classics of Early African-American Literature. Philadelphia, PA: Running Press, 2001.

Wilmore, Gayraud and Cone, James H. (Eds.). Black Theology: A Documentary History, 1966-1979, Maryknoll, New York: Orbis Books, 1979.

BIBLIOGRAPHY

Woodson, Dr. Carter G. The Mis-Education of the Negro. Trenton, NJ: Africa World Press, Inc. 1993. (6th Edition).

Universal Negro Improvement Association. (No original posting date). January 25, 2005 *http://www.uaia.org/uaia/history/malcolmx.htm.*

X, Malcolm. The Autobiography of Malcolm X. New York: Ballantine Books, 1965.

---. The Best of Malcolm X. Charisma Records, All Platinum Record Co. 1973. LP.

---. and George Breitman. Malcolm X Speaks: Selected Speeches and Statements New York : Grove Press, 1990.

---. Malcolm X Talking to Reporters on Steps of Queens County Civil Court [Video]. Retrieved May 31, 2010, from *http://www.youtube.com/watch?v=i16OMrwxsm8&NR=1*

INDEX

A

AalMuhammed, Jefri, 180
Abdul-Aleem, Ismail, 285-286
    see Old Guard
Abdul Haqq, Luqman, (Kenny Gamble), 219
Abdul-Mujeeb, Ayman (Donald 30X), 305
Abdullah, Musa, 229
Abdullah, Imam Yusuf (Clinton X of Nashville, TN), 307-308
Abraham (The Prophet), 61, 139, 197, 257, 314
Abu Dhabi, 107
African Methodist Episcopal Church, 133-134, 161, 251
Ahmadiyya Muslim Community, 246
Al-Hadid, Dr. Amiri YaSin, 37-38
Aleem, Marvis, 227
Ali, Hana (Daughter of Muhammad Ali), 99, 106
Ali, John, 179, 290
Ali, Muhammad aka Cassius Marcellus Clay, 39, 40, 131, 185-186, 204, 212-213, 214, 272, 283, 299
    Ennis, Ireland, 122
    Ernie Terrell, 122-123
    George Foreman (*Rumble in the Jungle*), 114, 128-129, 299
    Golden Gloves, 104
    Joe Martin, 104
    John Grady (Ali's Caucasian great-grand father), 122
    Malcolm X, 105-107
    Muhammad Speaks (Camp of the Champ), 108, 113
    Naming of, 105-107, 113, 123
    on meaning of devil, 99-100
    Selective Service (U.S. Army), 110, 112-113, 117
    U.S. Supreme Court Ruling, 113
Ali, Noble Timothy Drew, 32, 97, 161, 285
    see Moorish Science Temples of Islam
Ali, Rahaman, (Rudolph "Rudy" Clay), 104
Ali, Wazirudin, 133
    see CRAID
Allen, Rev. Richard, 161, 251
    see African Methodist Episcopal Church
Almanza, Henry, 232-234
Almanza, Osman Sharieff, 232-234
Alps of Northern Italy, 210
A.M. Journal (American Muslim) Journal, 132, 133
    see Bilalan News; Muslim Journal
Ambrose, Nancy, 211-212
American Academy of Religion, 210
American Historical Association, 34-35
Amini, Hussien, 77-78
Angola, 249
Anglo-Saxonism, 21, 95-97, 164
    Kirk Savage, 97
    Theodore Roosevelt, 96-97
    Thomas Jefferson, 95-96

INDEX

ARPANET (Internet), 206
Asia, 83, 86, 98, 113, 121, 125, 129, 196, 251
Atlanta, GA, 63, 144-145, 147, 149, 165, 197, 216
Atlantic City, NJ, 133
    see CRAID

B

Baby Gee (Baby G; W.D. Fard's mother), 101
Bagby, Dr. Ihsan, 281
    see HSAAM
Baghdadi, Ali, 226-227
Baldwin, Lewis V., 37
Baltimore, Maryland, 141, 200, 231
Banneker, Benjamin, 96
Baraka, Amiri, (Leroi Jones), 144, 147
Barboza, Steven, 143, 169, 175
Baumfree, Isabella, 124, 161
    see Sojourner Truth
Baxter, Jack, 180
Bayyan, Muhammad (Robert Bell), 218
    see Kool and the Gang
Bayyan, Khalis (Ronald Bell), 218-219
    see Kool and the Gang
Belgium Congo, 125, 128
    see Zaire
Benin, 249
Bennett Jr., Lerone, 271
BET (Black Entertainment Network), 136
Bilalian (African American), 132
Bilalan News, 149
    see A.M. Journal; Muslim Journal
Bingham, Howard, 105, 106, 109, 112, 116
Bishop Charles J. Mason Temple, 244
Black Panthers, 58, 136
Blue-eyed devils, 51, 83, 94, 97, 101, 102, 242, 313
    as defined in Qur'an, 102
Bond, Julian, 63-64, 65, 300, 309
Bosch, David J., 302
Boston, MA, 69, 142, 285
    Mosque (Temple) No. 11, 142
    Louis X (Farrakhan), 142
Brand Nubian, 218
Brents, Linda (Harriet Jacobs), 97, 98-99
British East Africa, 125
    see Kenya
Bronx, NY, 141

INDEX

Brown, James, 42-43, 48, 91, 220, 306
Brown, Jim, 48
Buckley Jr., William F. (Firing Line), 109-110
Burke Kevin, (Shabazz, Seifullah Ali), 229-232
Burton, Rev. H. Edward, 133-134
    see CRAID
Butler, Jerry, 145
Butler, Norman 3X (Muhammad Abdul-Aziz), 85

C

Cairo, Egypt, 86-87, 107, 311
California Department of Corrections (CDC), 305
Carson, Clayborne, 244
Carter, Dr. Lawrence Edward, 209-210
Channel–11 Magazine, 199
Cheney, Charise, 218
Chicago American, 60-61
Chicago Daily News, 39
Chicago Sun-Times, 199
China, 107, 121, 151, 187, 208
Christ, Jesus, 31, 115, 132-133, 160, 169, 197, 244, 257, 259, 260, 280, 291
    Joseph and Mary, 257
Christianity:
    Frederick Douglass on, 98, 163
    "Good Ship Jesus", 259
    "White man's religion", 162, 163, 212, 247, 279, 280, 302
Cincinnati, OH, 229
Civil Rights Movement, 26, 28, 31, 35, 64, 129, 135, 223, 253, 257, 267, 271, 307, 308-309, 311
Clay, Cassius Sr., 104
Clay, Odessa, 104, 122
Clay, Rudolph "Rudy" (Rahaman Ali), 104
Clegg, Claude Andrew, 33, 40, 89, 120, 291
Clements, Fr. George, 300
COINTELPRO, *see* Federal Bureau of Investigations
Cone, James, 302
Congress of African People (COAP or Atlanata Congress), 144-147
Copenhagen, Denmark, 299
Congress for Racial Equality (CORE), 268
    see James Farmer
CRAID (The Committee to Remove All Images that attempted to portray Divine), 131-134
    Atlantic City, NJ, 133
    H. Edward Burton, Rev., 133-134
    James Sharif, 133
    Mikal A. Rasheed, Imam, 133
    St. James A.M.E. Church, 133-134
    Wazirudin Ali, 133
    see Wallace D. Mohammed

Cuffee, Paul, 255-256
Curtis, Edward Dr., 33, 164

D

Daddy Grace, 299
Dalai Lama (Tenzin Gyatso), 200, 210
Daley Sr., Mayor Richard, 27, 64, 279, 300
Deepstep, GA, 24, 54, 298
The Delfonics, 219-220
DeGruy-Leary, Dr. Joy, 286
    see Post-Traumatic Slave Syndrome
DePauw University (Greencastle, IN), 55-56
Detroit, MI, 23, 40-41, 56-57, 76, 92, 149, 159, 165, 168, 227, 232, 234, 247, 248, 256, 298
Devils, 216, 218, 225, 228, 232, 243, 264, 266, 314
    Ali's explanation of, 99-100
    blue-eyed, 51, 94, 97, 101-102, 242
    blacks as devils, 92, 102
    Elijah exempts white devils, 51, 66, 91, 101, 245, 300
    Farrakhan on white devils, 148
    Malcolm X's explanation, 100
    others who called whites devil, 93, 97-99, 248
    Wallace's explanation of, 100-101, 179
    see Yakub's History
Dholakia, Kruti, 55
Diab, Jamil, 60, 223-225, 226, 233
Digable Planets, 218
Dittmer, Dr. John, 55-56
Douglass, Frederick, 20, 95, 161
    on Christianity, 163
    on whites as "devils", 97-98
DuBois, W. E. B., 20, 95, 252, 253, 255, 275, 281
    bi-culturation, 135
Duffy, Kathleen, 122
Duffy, Ryan (Judge), 111

E

Egypt, 65, 74, 86-87, 107, 125, 187, 226, 248, 257, 290, 299, 311
    as a symbol, 125
El-Amin, Hameed, 227
El-Baz, Farouk, 150
El Muhajir, Marvin X, 34
Essien-Udom, Dr. E. U., 33, 81-82
Ethiopia, 299
Evanzz, Karl, 38-39, 51, 179, 220, 222, 226, 272, 306
Evers, Medgar, 109

INDEX

F

Fard, W.D., 66, 101, 102
    Baby Gee (his mother), 101
    founder of the Nation of Islam, 58, 79, 148, 168
    meaning of the "W" in Fard's name, 57, 171
    Wali Muhammad, 298
    W.F. Muhammad, 57, 168
    myriad of names, 298
Fardan, Dorothy Blake, 227, 228-229
Farmer, James, 268
    see Congress for Racial Equality
Farrakhan, Louis, 34, 41, 130, 165, 199, 205-208, 213, 215, 226
    50-Nation Friendship Tour, 151, 153
    Abdul-Haleem Farrakhan, 148
    Congress of African People (COAP), 144-147
    Gene the Charmer, 114, 141, 143, 157
    John F. Kennedy Jr., 150-151
    Malcolm X, 141, 142-143
    Meaning of "Farrakhan", 143
    on Prophet Muhammed, 157
    rebuilding of Mosque No. 7, 143
    rebuilding of Nation of Islam (post 1978), 148-150, 154, 205
    Sarah Mae Manning, 141
    spelling of *Saviour's* versus *Saviours'*, 153-154
    St. Cyprian's Episcopal Church, 141
    W.D. Fard as "god", 153-154
    and Wallace D. Muhammad, 147-149, 152, 186
    Winston-Salem Teachers College, 141
    see Louis Walcott "Gene the Charmer", Million Man March
Fauset, Arthur Huff, 127
Federal Bureau of Investigations, 26, 27, 31, 33, 226, 231-232
    CointelPro, 38-39, 40, 46, 47, 86
    see J. Edgar Hoover
Federal Correctional Institute (FCI), 305
    Milan (Michigan), 69, 172, 305
    Sandstone (Minnesota), 181
Final Call:
    Fard's original version, 226
    Farrakhan's version, 147, 150, 153, 154, 155, 226
Firing Line (William F. Buckley), 109-110
Fish Program, 20, 218, 303-305
    Fish Song (Whiting H&G), 304-305
Focolare Movement, 210
    see Chiara Lubich,
Foreman, George, 114, 299
    Rumble in the Jungle, 128-129
Forest Park Community College (St. Louis, MO), 167, 198-199

INDEX

France, 89, 289
Franklin, John Hope, 225, 247-248, 249-250
Fruit of Islam, 20, 61-62, 220, 229, 232, 235, 274, 303, 305
    January 1975 Fruit of Islam meeting in NYC, 152
    Louis Farrakhan, 150
    Muhammad Ali, 103
    purpose of, 267
    Wallace Mohammed, 175

G

Garnet, Henry Highland, 97-98, 99, 162
Gamble, Kenny, (Luqman Abdul Haqq), 219
Garvey, Marcus "Mosiah", 26, 32, 86, 161, 163, 195, 252-253, 299
    African Communities League (ACL), 252
    Halt America (poem), 162-163
    Universal Negro Improvement Association (UNIA), 68, 246, 252
Ghana, 74, 78, 106, 125, 249, 250
Gandhi-King-Ikeda Award, 197-198, 209-210
Gandhi, Mahatma, 267-268
Gilbert, Olive, 124-125
Goffe, Leslie, 134
Goldwater, Barry, 207
Goodman, Amy, 84
Gordon, Ed, 112
Grace, Charles M. "Sweet Daddy", 299
Grady, John (Muhammad Ali's white great-grandfather), 122
Griffin, John Howard, 95
Guadalajara, Jalisco, Mexico, 235
Guinea, 249, 250
Gulick, Kasem, 77-78

H

Hagan, Thomas, 84
    see Hayer, Talmadge
Hajj (pilgrimage to Mecca), 77-78, 82-83, 237, 261
Haley, Alex, 88, 100, 124
Ham and Canaan, 93, 94
Hamtramck, (Detroit) MI, 168
Harris, Shanette, 61-63
Hasan, Abdul-Karim, 303
Hassan, Dr. Razi (Robert C29X), 36-37
Hauser, Thomas, 104-105, 106, 112, 114, 115-116
Hawkins, Captain John, 259, 264
Hayer, Talmadge, (Thomas Hagan or Hagen), 84

INDEX

Hazziez, Yusuf, (Joe Tex or Joseph Arrington), 113-114, 219, 306
Higginbotham, Aloyisus Leon, 249
History (Standards of Conduct), 34, 302
Holly, James Theodore, 164
Hoover, J. Edgar, 38-39, 40, 86
HSAAM, 281-282, 285
    see Old Guard or Ihsan Bagby
Huff, Leon, 219

I

Indiana University-Purdue University Indianapolis (IUPUI), 33
Indiana Pacers, 215
Indonesia, 107, 226
Ikeda, Daisaku, 210
Iran, 107, 151, 226
Islam, Khalil, (Thomas 15X Johnson), 85
Israel, 125, 151
    Children of Israel, 259
    as a symbol, 314
    name of an individual, 139
Istanbul, 65, 299

J

Jackson, Dr. Sherman H., 281
    see Old Guard
Jackson, Rev. J.H., 300
Jackson, Rev. Jesse, 27, 34, 138, 281, 301
    condolences for Elijah Muhammad, 48-49, 65, 186
    recognition of Wallace Muhammad (Mohammed), 186
Jackson State University, 190-193
Jacobs, Harriet (Linda Brents), 97, 98-99
Jamaica, West Indies, 141
Jamal, Hakim, 285
Jeddah, Saudi Arabia, 61, 279
Jefferson, Thomas, 95-96, 288
Jim Crow, 19, 43, 56, 99, 123, 135, 158, 251, 273, 297
Johnson, Arthur John (Jack), 97, 204
Johnson, Larry, 214-215
Johnson, Lyndon Baines, 206
Johnson, Thomas 15X, (Khalil Islam), 85
Johnston, Betty, 105
Jones, LeRoi, (Amiri Baraka), 144, 147
Jordan, 65, 125, 299
Jordan, Vernon, 65, 301

K

Karachi, 65, 299
Karim, Darnell, 224-225, 290-291
Karriem, Elijah, 57
    see Elijah Muhammad; Elijah Poole
Keeler, Cardinal William Henry, 200
Kennedy Jr., John F., 150-151
Kennedy Sr., John F., 39, 40, 51, 75, 150, 176, 272
Kennedy, Robert, 39-40
Kenya, 125
    see British East Africa
King, Dr. Martin Luther, 34, 35, 39, 40, 44, 95, 109, 125-126, 151, 161, 164, 166, 210, 218, 268, 297-298
    Civil Rights Movement, 26, 208, 223
    Coretta Scott, 308-309
    Daddy King (MLK's father), 268
    Elijah Muhammad, 35, 38, 267, 308, 311
    FBI, 39
    Last Sermon at Bishop Charles J. Mason Temple, 244-245
    Memphis, TN, 244
Klinkner, Philip A., 110
    see Rogers M. Smith
Kondo, Baba Zak A., 38-40
Kool and the Gang, 218-219, 304, 306
    see Muhammad Bayyan (Robert Bell) and Khalis Bayyan (Ronald Bell)
KRS-One, 218
Ku Klux Klan, 94-95, 96, 223, 279

L

Larson, Kate Clifford, 161
Last Poets, 306
Lateef, Imam Khalid S., 50-51
Lazarus (as a symbol), 259
Lebanon, 107, 125, 299
Lee, Spike, 40, 130
Lerner Family (white Jewish family), 222
Lester, Julius, 248
Levy, Andrew, 280
    see Rob Lopresti
Libya, 107, 151
Lincoln, Dr. C. Eric, 31, 33, 65, 187, 301
Liston, Charles "Sonny", 105
Lopresti, Rob, 280
    see Andrew Levy
"Lost-Found" (non-Nation of Islam members), 52, 79, 139, 225, 235
Louisville, KY, 104-105, 118, 122
Lubich, Chiara, 210
    see Focolare Movement

INDEX

M

Mahomah (Muhammad), Benjamin Perez, 235-237
Mali, 250
Mann, Michael, 40
Manning, Sarah Mae, 141
Marable, Dr. Manning, 84, 179
March on Washington (1963), 129-130, 208
Martin, Joe (Police officer), 104
Mayfield, Curtis, 130
McElroy, Dr. Susan Williams, 55-56
McNair, Dale X, (Eaustria Sabir), 216-217
Mecca, Saudi Arabia, 22, 57, 61, 65, 68, 77, 82, 83, 177, 237, 257, 260, 261, 279, 299, 312, 313
Medina, 257, 299, 312, 313
Memphis, TN, 244
Metcalfe, Congressman Ralph, 301
Mexico, 65, 184, 232, 234, 235, 290, 299
Michigan Chronicle, 40-41
Milan, Michigan, 69, 172, 305
Million Man March, 129-130, 150-151, 155, 207-208, 213
Minister George of Philadelphia, 141
Minister Karriem of Baltimore, 141
Minister Lucius of Washington D. C., 141
Mohammed, Earl Abdul-Malik, 187
Mohammed, Elijah (Name on cover of Qur'an), 18
Mohammed, Wallace (*aka* Warith Ud-Din and W. Deen Muhammad), 37, 59, 72-73, 77, 79-80, 89, 100-101, 107, 115, 134, 147, 148-150, 151-154, 155-156, 206, 208-209, 213, 223, 224, 228, 242, 268, 282, 293, 299, 300
    Alps of Northern Italy, 210
    American Academy of Religion, 210
    appeal to Minister Farrakhan, 149
    Bilalian (African American), 132
    Chiara Lubich, 210
    CRAID, 131-134
    Eve of the New Millennium, 200
    Focolare, 210
    Forest Park Community College (St. Louis), 167, 198-199
    Gandhi-King-Ikeda (Award), 197-198, 209-210
    Morehouse (Atlanta), 197-198, 209-210
    NOI Minister in Temple No. 12 (Philadelphia, PA), 175-176
    on Louis Farrakhan, 149, 155
    on W.D. Fard, 169-170, 173, 176, 190-196, 197
    promised helper to Elijah Muhammad, 168, 170, 171, 177, 294
    Rome (Vatican City), 200
    Selective Service (U.S. Army draft), 181

INDEX

Wallace Mohammed *(continued)*
    Society of Biblical Literature (New Orleans), 210
    Sura Luqman, 172-173, 176
    Whittenmore Univ. (St. Louis), 174
Moorish Science Temples of America, 246
    see Noble Timothy Drew Ali
Morehouse College, 197-198, 209-210, 268
Moses (Prophet), 64, 257, 260, 264
Mother Plane, (Mother Ship), 80, 193, 195, 270-271
Motown, 220, 306
Mt. Arafat, 77
Muhammad Speaks, 37, 45, 48, 51, 61, 104, 108-109, 111, 113, 121, 125, 137, 144, 145, 146, 168, 219-220, 222, 223, 225, 226, 230-231, 238, 254, 274, 292, 306, 307-308, 309
    Champ's Corner (Muhammad Ali), 108, 113
    Wallace Muhammad (Supreme Minister), 171-172
    see Bilalian News and *Muslim Journal*
Muhammad, Akbar (son of Elijah Muhammad), 48, 174-175, 224
Muhammad, Akbar, (Minister Larry 4X Prescott), 143, 144, 149
Muhammad, Clara (Evans), 56, 168, 180-181, 182, 290, 294
    mother of Wallace Mohammed, 172, 175
    school system, 307
Muhammad, Elijah:
    adultery, 289, 290, 294
    Asia, 113, 121, 125, 129, 196, 251
    Channel-11 Magazine (Chicago), 199
    condolences, 48-49, 65, 300-301
    conscientious objector, 172
    "Elijah Muhammad Day," 279
    FBI (CointelPro), 38-39, 40, 46, 47
    Islamic shirk (false worship), 277, 282, 289, 291, 294
    Individuals influenced by Elijah Muhammad:
        Amiri Baraka, 144, 147
        James Brown, 48, 91, 220, 306
        Jesse Jackson, 48-49, 138, 186, 281, 301
        Jim Brown, 48
        Joe "Tex" Arrington (Yusef Hazziez), 113, 306
        Kool and the Gang, 218-219, 304, 306
        Larry Johnson, 214-215
        Last Poets, 306
        O'Jays, 219
        Rap Music, 217-218
        Sherman Adbul Hakim Jackson, 281
        The Temptations, 220, 306
    Kennedy, John F. Sr., 39, 40, 51, 75, 150, 176, 272
    Message to the Blackman, 52, 54, 57, 60, 91, 111, 114, 121, 159, 160, 166, 222, 254, 266, 272, 279, 285, 288, 293, 306
    "Messenger" not "Prophet", 160

Elijah Muhammad *(Continued)*
    murder, 46, 84-85, 86, 89-90, 266, 274, 289, 294, 296
    Muslim Daily Prayers, 261-263
    prison reform, 305-306
    secretaries, 75, 180, 290
    Selective Services (U.S. military), 172, 305
    Table Talk, 63, 152, 183, 295
    The Fall of America, 207, 297
    The Supreme Wisdom, 58, 60, 174, 196, 225-226, 258, 261
    The Theology of Time, 91, 172, 207
    umrah (lesser hajj/pilgrimage), 65
    U.S. Supreme Court rulings: with Ali, 113, Muslim prisoners, 305
    see Elijah Karriem, Elijah Mohammed, Elijah Poole
Muhammad, Herbert (Jabir), 114, 168, 171-172, 186, 283
Muhammad, Ilyas (Minister Earl X), 307
Muhammad, Jabril, 140-142
Muhammad, John (Brother of Elijah Muhammad), 149, 165
Muhammad, Silas, 149, 165
Muhammed ibn Abdullah (the Prophet), 30, 60, 77, 101, 119, 134, 157, 160, 166, 174, 196, 201, 208, 212, 224, 243, 257, 260, 261, 282, 286, 287, 294
Muslim Journal, 133, 215, 228
    see A.M. Journal; Bilalian News
Muslim League, 61

N

Naeem, Abdul Basit, 60, 61, 225-227
Names:
    African names, 119
    Biblical name changes, 139
    Booker T. Washington on names, 124-138
    Islamic (holy) and African names, 105-106, 113, 118, 120, 121, 136, 138-139
Names *(Continued)*
    meaning of "X" as a surname, 120
    Nation of Islam guidelines, 122-123
    Sojourner Truth on names, 124-125
Nashville, TN, 307-308
Nasir, Imam Abdul-Raoof, 305
Nasser, Gamal Abdel, 107, 299
Nation of Islam:
    membership harrassed, 269-270, 307
    John Muhammad's version, 149, 165
    Silas Muhammad's version, 149, 165
    Louis Farrakhan's version, 149, 165
    White Members, 45, 101, 148, 222, 223, 227, 228-232
    see World Community of Islam in the West
"Nation of Islam Day", 64, 279

INDEX

National Basketball Association, 214-215
New Orleans, Louisiana, 210
New York Knickerbockers, 215
Nigeria, 74, 81, 249
Nkrumah, Kwame, 125
Noble, Gil, 181
Northern Rhodesia (Zambia), 125
Nu'Man, Muhammad Armiya, 194

O

Oakland, CA, 34, 237, 239-240
O'Jay's, 219
Old Guard, 281-282, 285
    see Ismail Abdul-Aleem; HSAAM; Sherman Jackson
Omaha, Nebraska, 68
One hundred, forty-four thousand (144,000), 259, 271
Ontario Consultants on Religious Tolerance, 248
Owens, Keith A., 40-41

P

Pakistan, 65, 107, 125, 225, 226, 248, 267, 299
Parks, Gordon, 88
Pawelek, John M., 250
Perry, Bruce, 38, 106
Pharaoh (as a sign), 98, 258, 260, 264
Philadelphia, PA, 141, 175-176, 219-220, 256
Philadelphia International (Sound of Philadelphia), 219
Pickett, C. Barry, 39
Poole, Elijah, 23-24, 41-42, 54-57, 59, 99, 162, 165, 264, 265, 298
    see Elijah Karriem; Elijah Muhammad
Poor Righteous Teachers, 218
Pope John Paul II, 200, 210
Post-Traumatic Slave Syndrome, 286
    see Dr. Joy DeGruy-Leary
Powell, Adam Clayton, 109
Prescott, Larry 4X (Akbar Muhammad), 143, 144, 149
Prodigal Son, 259
Public Enemy, 218
Puddin, (Clarence 13X Smith), 80
Pueblo, Mexico, 232

R

Rahman, Clyde, 102, 228
Rap Music,
    Gangsta', 217
    "Golden Era", 217-218

INDEX

Randolph, A. Phillip, 208
Rasheed, Imam Mikal A., 133
   see CRAID
Reader's Digest, 103, 116, 204
Robeson, Paul, 26, 32, 214
Robinson, Jackie, 214
Robinson, Sugar Ray, 116
Rock, Chris, 43, 62, 135
Rockwell, George Lincoln, 178-179, 227
Rhoden, William C., 214-215
Rome, Italy, 98, 200
Roosevelt, Franklin D., 172
Roosevelt, Theodore, 96-97, 280
Rosary, Lucille, 290
Rowan, Carl T., 39
Rowe, Nicholas, 25
Roxbury, MA, 141

S

Sabir, Eaustria (Dale McNair), 216-217
San Francisco, 235
Sandersville, GA, 54
Sandstone Federal Correction Institute, 181
Savage, Kirk, 97
   see Anglo Saxon
Saviour's Day (Saviours' Day or Saviors' Day), 105, 112, 179, 207, 261
   1974 Last Saviour's Day for Elijah Muhammad, 49, 50, 78, 222, 240, 241, 242-243, 245, 296, 300, 310
   Saviour's 1975, 48-49, 107, 147-148, 185-186
   Saviours' Day 2000, 153-157
   Saviours' Day 2003, 154
Sayeed, Dr. Sayyid M., 282-283
Senegal, 249
Shabazz, Betty, 153
Shabazz, Malcolm, *see* Malcolm X
Shabazz, Quibilah, 153
Shabazz, Seifullah Ali (Kevin Burke), 229-232
   see white members in Nation of Islam Muslims
Shah, Yusuf (Chicago Minister), 171, 176, 182-184, 242, 293
Sharif, Amatullah (Georgetta X. Stokes), 138-139
Sharif, Jalal Najjar, 227-228
Sharif, James, 133
   see CRAID
Sharrieff, Hassan, 89
Sharrieff, Raymond, 224, 290
Shawnee Indians, 93-94
Shuaibe, Yolanda, 239

INDEX

Siddeeq, Muhammad (Clark Moore; Clark X; Director Clark), 63-64, 84, 144-146
Sierra Leone, 249
Sierra Mojada, Mexico, 235
Skerry, Peter, 188, 209
Slave names, 120, 136, 138
    see Booker T. Washington, Names,
Slavery,
    countries enslaved Africans came from, 250
    "Good Ship Jesus", 259
Smith, Clarence 13X (Puddin), 80
Smith, Robert C., 30, 253
Smith, Rogers M., 110
    see Phillip Klinkner
Society of Biblical Literature (New Orleans), 210
Songhay, 250
Spellman, A.B., 77
St. Cyprian's Episcopal Church, 141
St. James A.M.E. Church, 133-134
    see CRAID
St. Kitts, Eastern Caribbean, 141
St. Matthew, 280-281
St. Peter's Basilica, 200
Staples, Dr. Robert, 135
Steed, Robert (Dream Horse), 241
Steward, Theophilus Gould, 164
Stewart, Lusia Harris, 214
Strathmore, William, 129
Sudan, 74, 187, 225, 250
Sullivan, Dr. Leon, 65, 301
Syria, 107, 125, 151

T

Taha, Abdul Wahid (Clayton X), 219-220
Temple (Mosque) No. 2 (Chicago, IL), 183
Temple (Mosque) No. 5 (Cincinnati, OH), 229
Temple (Mosque) No. 7 (New York City), 36, 73, 110, 143
Temple (Mosque) No. 11 (Boston, MA), 142
Temple (Mosque) No. 12 (Philadelphia, PA), 175-176, 220
Temple (Mosque) No. 27 (Los Angeles), 269, 303
Temple (Mosque) No. 60 (Nashville, TN), 307
Temptations, *Message from a Black Man,* 220, 306
Terrell, Ernie, 122
Tex, Joe (Joseph Arrington), 113-114, 219, 306
    see Yusuf Hazziez
The Ted Mack Original Amateur Hour, 141

INDEX

Till, Emmett, 103
Thurman, Howard, 211-212, 258, 268
Togo, 249
Truth, Sojourner (Isabella Baumfree), 124-125, 161, 163-164, 166
Tubman, Harriet, 161, 166
Tucker, Bruce, 42
Turkey, 49, 65, 78, 107, 299
Turner, Henry Neal (Bishop), 164
Turner, Nat, 98
Turner, West, 248

U

U. S. Civil War, 55, 97, 255, 256
Umrah (the lesser pilgrimage to Mecca, 65
United States Army:
    Muhammad Ali, 110, 112, 214
    Selective Training and Service Act, 172
    Wallace Muhammad (Mohammed), 181
Universal Ethiopian Anthem, 252
Universal Negro Improvement Association (UNIA), *see* Marcus Garvey
University of Islam, 63, 84, 143, 145, 168, 223-224
Urban League, 145, 301

V

Vatican City, 200
Viet Nam War, 204, 213
Visosky, Joan, 216-217

W

Walcott, Louis "Gene the Charmer," *see* Farrakhan
Walker, Dan (Illinois Governor), 279
Walker, David, 97-98, 99, 162, 166
Wallace, Mike:
    Between Me and You (Memoirs), 22, 36
    The Hate That Hate Produced (Documentary on NOI), 22-23, 44
Washington, Booker T., 20, 95, 136, 252, 299
    on names of slaves, 124, 138
    White hegemony, 127
Washington, D.C., 129-130, 141, 150, 157, 179, 227, 285
Washington Post, 155
Webb, Sarah, 218
White Nation of Islam Muslims:
    Brother Sam, 227
    Brother Wali, 227
    Pauline X Williams, 229
    Seifullah Ali Shabazz, 229-232

Williams, Asbury X., 229
Williams, Diane, 237-241
Williams, Evelyn, 290
Williams, Larry, 238-239
Williams, Pauline X., 229
Wilmore, Gayraud, 302
Wilson, Woodrow, 280
Winston-Salem Teachers College, 141
Wisdom University (Tulsa, OK), 133
Whittenmore University (St. Louis, MO), 174
Woodson, Carter G., 275
    on Christianity, 211, 281
    on Europeanized education, 32-33
    on state of African American education, 306-307
World Community of Al-Islam in the West (W.C.I.W.), 148, 188
    see Nation of Islam
World Friendship Tour, 151, 153
Worrill, Conrad W., 34

X

X-Clan, 218
X, Malcolm, (*aka* Detroit Red; Malcolm Shabazz; Malik Shabazz), 22, 35-39, 41, 53, 124, 147, 179, 205, 213, 261-262, 269-270, 271, 274, 290-291, 305, 308-309
    Boston, MA, 69
    on white man as "devil," 83, 100
    President Kennedy "Chickens coming home to roost," 75, 176, 272
    and Farrakhan, 141, 142-143, 152-153
    Malcolm's murder, 30, 36-37, 53, 84, 85-86, 88-90, 107, 143, 274, 289-290
    and Muhammad Ali, 105, 106-107, 118
    and Wallace Mohammed (Muhammad), 176-181
X, Norman 3 (Muhammad Abdul Aziz), 85

Y

"Yakub's History," 80, 91, 93-94, 116, 188, 193, 242, 295
Young, Andrew, 34, 309
Young Jr., Whitney, 145

Z

Zaire, Africa, (Belgium Congo), 125, 128-129
Zambia, (Northern Rhodesia), 125

THANK YOU MUSLIM JOURNAL

Throughout my preparation of this book *Muslim Journal* newpaper, the successor of *Muhammad Speaks*, provided me access to an invaluable archive on the Honorable Elijah Muhammad and the Four Stars featured in this book.

Thank You
Michael "Mikal" Saahir

Greetings of As Salaam Alaikum / Peace be unto you!
And Welcome to the Muslim Journal!

In 1975, Muslim Journal evolved out of the era of the Nation of Islam along with the new leadership of Imam W. Deen Mohammed, son of the Hon. Elijah Muhammad and mentor to Malcolm X Shabazz.

It began with the long legacy of newspapers, the first African American newspaper, Freedom's Journal, published by Editors John B. Russwurm and Samuel E. Cornish in 1827, and builds from the decisive newspaper published by the ex-slave, abolitionist and first U.S. Ambassador to Haiti, the Hon. Frederick Douglass. And it picked up the mantle passed on from the Muhammad Speaks, an independent voice for Muslims in America.

Muslim Journal's masthead carries the phrase: "Bringing humanity together with Truth and Understanding." Its working mantra is to "Fill the Void," so its readers can "See The Full Picture!" It is a member of the National Newspaper Publishers Association, the network of over 200 African American owned newspapers in the United States.

To subscribe online, please visit www.MuslimJournal.net. Or call the Muslim Journal office to purchase subscription with credit/debit cards at 708-647-9600. Write to Muslim Journal's Editorial Department: Muslim Journal, c/o Editor Ayesha K. Mustafaa, 1141 W. 175th St., Homewood, IL 60430; fax 708-647-0754 or email to muslimjrnl@comcast.net